CW01500994

A Bit of a Writer

Brendan Behan's

**collected
short prose**

A Bit of a Writer

Brendan Behan's

collected short prose

**Edited by
John Brannigan**

THE LILLIPUT PRESS
DUBLIN

First published 2023 by
THE LILLIPUT PRESS

62–63 Sitric Road, Arbour Hill
Dublin 7, Ireland
www.lilliputpress.ie

This edition published 2024

Copyright © 2023 The estate of Brendan Behan
Introduction © John Brannigan

ISBN 978 184351 900 3

All rights reserved. No part of this publication
may be reproduced in any form or by any means
without the prior permission of the publisher.

A CIP record for this title is available from
The British Library.

10 9 8 7 6 5 4 3 2 1

The Lilliput Press gratefully acknowledges the financial
support of the Arts Council/An Chomhairle Ealaíon.

Set in Caslon by iota (www.iota-books.ie)
Printed in Sweden by Scandbook

MIX
Paper | Supporting
responsible forestry
FSC® C021394

Contents

ACKNOWLEDGMENTS

I have been promising this collection of Brendan Behan's articles to fellow Behan scholars and fans for some time now, and I have benefited along the way from much encouragement, support and advice. Andrew McNeillie showed me how to do it when he edited Behan's Aran articles for the *Irish University Review* in 2014, and has been a generous and passionate advocate for this volume ever since. Antony Farrell has been the most patient editor and guide, and I am deeply grateful for his immediate and unwavering support for the volume.

My main reason for collecting these articles in one volume is to show Behan's devotion to writing and his passion for people. It has been a pleasure to share this admiration of Behan's literary talents with many other scholars and fans. I have been fortunate to learn much from the work of Deirdre McMahon, whose doctoral thesis on Behan's work in relation to European modernism, and particularly on his time in Paris, is meticulous and inspiring. I am grateful to Trevor White and Simon O'Connor for their generous invitations to speak at the Little Museum in Dublin, and it has been a pleasure to continue to work with Simon now at the Museum of Literature Ireland (MoLI). John McCourt generously gathered a joyous coterie of Behan scholars in Rome in 2014 and then shared our work in a landmark volume, *Reading Brendan Behan* (Cork University Press, 2019).

I have been greatly encouraged by the support of the Behan family. I am very grateful to Blanaid Walker for her kind words of support and enthusiasm. It has been a pleasure to meet Janet Behan and many other Behans, along with their Kearney and Furlong relations, at book launches and readings over the years, and to hear their stories of this amazing family.

The annotations were enormously enhanced by the translations from the Irish by Ceithleann Ní Dhuibhir Ní Dhúlacháin. Thanks to Ceithleann for her diligent and sensitive translations of Behan's frequent passages of Irish proverbs, phrases and songs.

The love and support of my wife, Moyra, and our three children, Conor, Owen and Laura, is central to everything, of course. They have listened to many Brendan Behan stories over the years, and will now be able to read those stories for themselves.

INTRODUCTION

Before Brendan Behan became famous internationally as a playwright and bohemian reveller, he wrote a weekly newspaper column in Dublin for *The Irish Press*. Between 1953 and 1956 he produced over one hundred articles. Some were recollections of his childhood in Northside Dublin, some were inventive comic fictions, some told the stories of his travels and musings around Ireland and Europe. He had begun to write these articles on an occasional basis in 1951, but they became a regular feature in late 1953 when the new editor, Jim McGuinness, commissioned him to write a weekly column. McGuinness had known Behan in the 1940s – both men were interned in the Curragh military camp as IRA activists during the Second World War. When he became editor of *The Irish Press*, McGuinness set out to bring more writers to the newspaper for feature articles and columns. It is evidence of the impact that Behan had already had as a young writer that McGuinness chose to ask him alongside more established writers such as Lennox Robinson and Francis MacManus. By this time, Behan had published a handful of short stories in English, and some poems in Irish, as well as a serialized novel, *The Scarperer*, which was published under a pseudonym, 'Emmet Street', in *The Irish Times*. He had also written radio plays and presented radio broadcasts for Raidió Éireann. In 1954 his first major play, *The Quare Fellow*, had its premiere in Dublin's Pike Theatre; by 1956 the play had made him an international star. The columns published in *The Irish Press* were written in the period in which Behan achieved his first success, and in which he was at his most confident and conscientious as a writer.

'Brendan wrote his newspaper articles with ease,' wrote his wife, Beatrice, 'rarely missing a deadline.' He was paid five pounds a week and given free rein to write about whatever he chose. He rose early, and would write until it was time to bring Beatrice breakfast in bed. It was a routine not completely without interruptions, for he would occasionally go off on drinking binges, but he usually found ways of making the deadline. Donal Foley, who worked in the London office of *The Irish Press*, recalled how Behan turned up at the office one day to ask for an advance of twenty pounds. The editor allowed Foley to give Behan the money on condition that he first received four articles. Four hours later Behan returned with four articles amounting to seven thousand words, and was paid the money. Behan's column, Foley writes, was 'the best of its kind to appear anywhere at that time', and the four articles, hastily written as they were, lived up to expectations.

In later years, wracked with illness, Behan seemed to resent the fact that Dubliners were slow to recognize his talents. His most significant achievements in literature found success and recognition elsewhere. *The Quare Fellow* was rejected by the Abbey Theatre and performed only in the Pike, a small experimental theatre, before it became an international success after its West End production in London in 1956. *The Hostage* first found expression in an Irish-language version, *An Giall*, performed in the modest setting of Damer Hall in Dublin, but then likewise became a West End and Broadway success in 1958. *Borstal Boy*, his autobiographical novel, was banned in Ireland as soon it was published in the same year. Lionized by theatre audiences in England, America and Europe, and courted by journalists and broadcasters wherever he went, Behan felt shunned by his peers in Ireland. In an interview with Eamonn Andrews, broadcast on RTÉ in 1960, Behan's resentment was palpable: 'The Irish are not my audience; they are my raw material,' he professed. When Andrews asked if he would like the Irish to be his audience, Behan replied, 'No, I don't care. I don't care.'

Behan did care. In the articles gathered here, it is clear that he cared deeply about Dublin and Dubliners. He cherished the stories, songs and sayings of the people who surrounded him in his childhood and youth. There is a prevailing sense of nostalgia for the receding generations and communities of the early twentieth century – the rebels of 1916, the veterans of the Boer War and the First World War, and the oul' ones whose sharp wit and quick tongues deflated the pomposity of both the rebels and the veterans. There is also a lively sense of community with contemporary Dubliners – Behan has much to say about changes in the city, and responds to his correspondents in his column. Behan attempted to produce in his column a sense of Dublin as a 'knowable community', a place that abounded with jovial rivalries between distinct areas ('Monto' and the 'Coombe'; the Northside and the Southside), but ultimately a city in which it was impossible to get lost. In his comic sketches, and the characters he invented for them – Mrs Brennan, Maria Concepta, Crippen – he conjured up the distinctive dialectal style and conversational rhythms of Dublin speech, and a strong sense of identity and outlook. 'The Dubliner is the victim of his own prejudices,' writes Behan, but in these articles he satirizes those prejudices tirelessly, writing that he had been 'conditioned all the days of my life to the belief that people from the three other provinces, Cork, the North and the Country, could build nests in your ear, mind mice at a crossroads, and generally stand where thousands fell'.

It is, then, as a 'jackeen', a Dubliner seen as if from outside, that Behan also takes his readers on a tour around Ireland – to Wicklow and Wexford, to Kerry, Connemara and the Aran Islands, to Belfast and Donaghadee. These outings are no mere travelogues or tour guides. He is rarely interested in the 'sights'; instead, Behan displays the same warm curiosity and interest in people and their stories wherever he goes. The same is true of his adventures across the sea to France, and particularly to Paris, a place dear to his heart since the late 1940s. 'Everyone admires Paris for the artists,' he wrote, 'but I equally loved Paris for the barricades.' In truth, literature and politics are intertwined and inseparable sources of interest for Behan. The pieces abound in allusions to writers and artists, and perhaps even more so to the architects and activists of Irish republicanism. We find in them stories of Brendan Behan passing himself off as George Orwell, and stories about Yeats, Joyce and O'Casey. The pantheon of Irish heroes, from Brian Boru to Patrick Pearse, is never far from his thoughts. Yet perhaps Behan's greatest gift is to give no more significance or weight to the stories of these famous figures than to the stories of his family and neighbours. Behan was a folk writer, in the best tradition of folk tales and folk songs, a collector and teller of stories.

LIFE AND WORK

Brendan Behan was born on 9 February 1923, just six months after his parents, Stephen Behan and Kathleen Kearney, had got married. Stephen was a house-painter by trade, a passionate reader of literature, and a republican and trade union activist. At the time of Behan's birth, his father was imprisoned in Kilmainham Jail for opposing the treaty with Britain signed by the new Irish Free State. Brendan Behan would follow his father's literary and political interests closely, and for a time also followed his father into the house-painting trade. Kathleen had been married previously to Jack Furlong, a Belfast republican who died of influenza in 1918, with whom she had two sons. A committed republican herself, Kathleen had worked in domestic service for Maud Gonne MacBride, and knew many of the most significant political and cultural figures of the Irish revolutionary period, including W.B. Yeats and Michael Collins. She had a deep knowledge and wide repertoire of Irish folk songs, with which she entertained her children. Her brother Peadar Kearney wrote the Irish national anthem, among many other songs. Her brother-in-law was the actor and theatre manager P.J. Bourke. The Behan family, which included Brendan's two half-brothers, Rory and Seán Furlong, and later three brothers, Seamus, Brian and Dominic, and a sister, Carmel, lived in tenement rooms in 14 Russell Street in Dublin.

Russell Street, in the shadow of the national Gaelic sports stadium, Croke Park, beside the Royal Canal and adjoining the North Circular Road, is the scene of many pieces here. The street contained a row of Georgian houses, once the home of middle-class families, which had long become tenement houses with rooms rented out, and whole families living in one room. Behan describes these houses often, with families living cheek by jowl, doors always open, children running errands for bed-bound elders, with nowhere and no time for peace and quiet. The characters, the stories and the songs from this upbringing were the sources of his art. Almost all the men that Behan knew as a child had been to war, to prison, or both. The women learned how to survive and endure. Behan attended St Vincent's Boys' School on North William Street just a few streets from his home, run by Catholic nuns, the French Sisters of Charity of Saint

Vincent de Paul. He also joined the Fianna, the youth wing of the IRA, at the age of eight, and his first publication – at the age of thirteen – was in the organization's newspaper, *Fianna Éireann*. As a child he was deeply aware of the deeds of Irish nationalists but even more of their words. He recalled being able to recite the famous speech from the dock by Robert Emmet from the age of six.

Behan's education continued at the Christian Brothers' school, St Canice's, on the North Circular Road, from 1934 to 1937. When he left the school, aged fourteen, he followed his father into the painting trade, and took day courses in sign-writing and decorating at Bolton Street Technical School. Political activities took precedence over work and in 1937 he tried to enlist with other Irish republicans in the International Brigades going off to fight against fascists in the Spanish Civil War. He was refused because of his age, and with his brothers resorted to organizing support for the Spanish republican cause in Dublin. In the same year the Behan family was moved out of Russell Street. In response to worsening slum conditions in inner-city Dublin, the Irish government had issued decrees to clear the slums and relocate people to new council-owned houses in the suburbs. The Behans were moved to 70 Kildare Road in Crumlin. It was a house of their own, a step up from tenement living, but the family struggled to warm to their new surroundings. Brendan, in particular, was lost without the sense of close community he had clearly so enjoyed in Russell Street. He became more and more committed to IRA activities, including training as a bomb-maker.

With a suitcase full of bomb-making equipment, Brendan Behan departed from Kildare Road on 30 November 1939, and took the boat to Liverpool. The IRA, under the new militant leadership of veteran Seán Russell, had embarked on a callous and ham-fisted campaign to bomb targets in Britain, supposedly to compel the British government to cede Northern Ireland to Irish rule. Behan claimed later that his target was a battleship in Liverpool docks, although most targets of the campaign were either intentionally or accidentally civilian. Behan's mission was foiled almost immediately – he was arrested within hours of getting off the boat. As a juvenile, Behan could only be sentenced to borstal detention by the court, and so began Behan's long familiarity with incarceration. His experience of English jails and borstals became the subject of perhaps his most famous work, the autobiographical novel, *Borstal Boy*, published in 1958. Borstal detention was a relatively positive experience for Behan. He enjoyed the company of other working-class boys and found that, despite his political convictions, he had many things in common with them. He also benefited from a relatively liberal system in which he was encouraged to read, write, perform in plays and enter writing competitions.

Behan was released from borstal and deported from Britain in December 1941, but he was barely a few months back in Dublin when he found himself in prison again. At a republican commemoration ceremony in April 1942 he fired a revolver at two detectives. When he was captured, under legislation introduced to crack down on IRA activities in neutral Ireland at a time when the rest of Europe was at war, he could have been sentenced to death for his actions. Instead, possibly because his father had once shared a prison cell with the man who was now the Minister for Finance, Seán T. O'Kelly, and intervened for his son's life, Brendan was tried and sentenced to fourteen years in prison. He spent time in Mountjoy, Arbour Hill and the Curragh military prison, during which time he came to know and benefit from friendships with several writers. Seán Ó Faoláin, one of Ireland's leading writers at the time, took an interest in Behan and published his first serious piece of literary writing, 'I Become a Borstal Boy', in the most significant Irish literary magazine of the day, *The Bell*. During this time Behan also began writing early versions of both *Borstal Boy* and *The Quare Fellow*, as well as other works that have subsequently been lost.

In 1946 IRA prisoners held in Irish jails were released on general amnesty. Behan would go back to prison on several subsequent occasions for disorder and breaking deportation orders. However, while he returned to employment as a house-painter, albeit fitfully, he was now dedicated to becoming an established writer. He spent much of the late 1940s in Paris, a city where he got to know Albert Camus, James Baldwin and many others. For much of this time he lived in poverty, but began to publish some of his most daring work in *Points* magazine, edited by Sindbad Vail, the son of Peggy Guggenheim. On his return to Dublin in 1951 Behan began to publish articles in *The Irish Press*. This was the beginning of his most sustained period of development as a writer.

Over the next few years, he experimented with writing for theatre, magazines, radio and newspapers, and across a wide range of styles and genres. He became well established in Dublin's literary and artistic scene, principally based in the city's pubs. Here he socialized with Flann O'Brien, Anthony Cronin, John Ryan, and J.P. Donleavy, although others, notably Patrick Kavanagh, steered clear of his company. In 1955 he married the artist Beatrice Ffrench Salkeld, and their relationship was key to the brief period in which Behan worked most diligently as a writer. His first major success came in 1956, when Joan Littlewood's Theatre Workshop in London agreed to produce *The Quare Fellow*. Behan's play evolved through a number of iterations in the Irish language, and had been sent to the Abbey Theatre and rejected before being performed first in Dublin in the Pike Theatre in November 1954. The play was a critical success in Dublin, but its London performance catapulted Behan to fame. He became the subject of television interviews, feature articles and newspaper headlines. *The Quare Fellow* was quickly followed by the even greater success of *The Hostage*. Behan first wrote *The Hostage* as an Irish-language play, *An Giall*, for the organization that promoted the language, Gael Linn. Revised into English for Littlewood's Theatre Workshop, *The Hostage* performed to rave reviews in October 1958, the same month in which Behan published *Borstal Boy*, and in June 1959 transferred to the West End. Behan was lauded by the British press, but this was nothing compared to his reception in New York when the play was performed there in 1960.

The story of Behan's rise and fall is well known – celebrity killed him. His newfound wealth became increasingly based on appearances, interviews and publicity. The performances were followed by parties, and Behan's addiction to alcohol had a detrimental effect on his health and on his ability to write. In the early 1960s he spent months at a time in New York, Los Angeles and San Francisco. He befriended some of the most famous writers and artists of the time, including Tennessee Williams, Arthur Miller, Allen Ginsberg, Groucho Marx, Norman Mailer, Jackie Gleason and others. He was offered no end of commissions to write screenplays and books. By 1962, however, alcoholism had quelled his ability to write. His remaining publications – *Confessions of an Irish Rebel*, *Brendan Behan's Island* and *Brendan Behan's New York* – were dictated to a tape recorder and edited and transcribed for publication by Rae Jeffs. He suffered diabetic seizures, and was warned that excessive drinking could be fatal. A return to Ireland and the birth of his daughter, Blanaid, seemed to offer a glimpse of hope, but he died in a coma in hospital on 20 March 1964 from liver failure. A number of works were unfinished at the time of his death. He had been working on a novel called *The Catacombs* since the late fifties and started a new play, *Richard's Cork Leg*, eventually completed by Alan Simpson and performed in 1972. Both contain something of the exuberance and ingenuity of Brendan Behan, but neither lives up to what he wrote in the early 1950s.

BEHAN IN HIS OWN TIME

Brendan Behan's life (1923–64) coincided with the foundation and consolidation of the new Irish state. When he was born, the country was divided as to whether the independence won from Britain in 1922 was acceptable without the six counties of the North that remained under British rule. His father was committed to the anti-treaty position, and was jailed for his rebellion against the new state. From an early age, Brendan Behan was an active member of republican organizations dedicated to fighting for a united Ireland. His commitment to Irish republicanism was based on political dissent from the acceptance of partition, and from the conservatism of the Irish Free State. It was also marked, however, by a profound sense of belatedness. The IRA to which he committed himself was a shadow of the body that had fought the 1916 Rising and the War of Independence, even though veterans of both campaigns led the organization in the 1930s and 1940s. Behan's writings abound with nostalgia for events that occurred before his birth:

> When I was nine years old I could have given you a complete account of what happened from Mount Street Bridge out to the Battle of Ashbourne, where I was giving Tom Ashe and Dick Mulcahy a hand. I could tell you how Seán Russell and I stopped them at Fairview, and could have given you a fuller description of Easter, 1916 than many an older man. You see, they were mostly confined to one garrison – I had fought at them all.

The events and personalities of the war against Britain loom large in Behan's writings, and extend well beyond those of the twentieth century to the Fenians and the United Irishmen. For Irish republicans of Behan's generation, the new state did not represent the liberation for which they had fought. Behan felt that the Irish state simply took over the reins of government, but for working-class Irish people nothing changed.

For much of the 1930s the IRA leadership was influenced by socialist ideas. Behan supported socialist and communist organizations throughout his life. In the late thirties the departure of many left-wing IRA volunteers to fight in the Spanish Civil War resulted in a shift in the political orientation of the IRA towards a more orthodox and militant position. The new leadership embarked on a deadly campaign of bombing targets in Britain at exactly the time when Britain was becoming the bulwark of opposition to fascism in Europe. By the time Behan got involved in the IRA campaign in late 1939, its new leader, Seán Russell, whom Behan admired for his role in the 1916 Rising, was seeking support from Nazi Germany. While in jail in England, Behan became conscious of the growing gap between his own political beliefs and the organization of which he was a member and increasingly saw writing rather than politics as his calling. By the mid-1950s, writing the column for *The Irish Press*, he was the subject of British intelligence files for his communist sympathies and his literary connections with left-wing writers and artists rather than his IRA connections.

Ireland was neutral during the Second World War, and Behan spent most of it incarcerated first in England and then in Ireland. The Dublin he rediscovered in the late 1940s was still marked by the same poverty and insularity that had defined his childhood years. Yet there were signs of change. Culturally, writers and artists were tilted towards continental Europe. *Envoy* magazine, edited by his friend John Ryan, and in which Behan was published, was a key cultural expression of this affinity with European literature. As Behan recounts in some of the articles in this volume, he spent much of the late forties and early fifties in Paris and travelling around Europe. Paris, in particular, was a city of great attraction. It was linked, obviously, to the great modernist writers of the previous generation – Joyce, Hemingway, Proust and Stein – but it was also a city of writers exploring what art meant in a new post-war world. Behan came to know Albert Camus well; he was regarded affectionately, if rather tolerantly, by Samuel Beckett; and he was amused to share the same café as Jean-Paul Sartre and Simone de Beauvoir. His plays, perhaps particularly *The Quare Fellow*, share some of the key preoccupations of these writers with the meaning and value of human existence and the problem of ethical action in a world seemingly devoid of beliefs or principles. Paris also afforded Behan the opportunity to express himself in ways not possible in Ireland – it was in the Paris-based literary magazine, *Points*, that Behan wrote about homosexuality in 'After the Wake', and in an early version of *Borstal Boy* called 'Bridewell Revisited'.

In *The Irish Press*, of course, Behan could not risk writing about subjects that were likely to result in censure or dismissal. He was well aware of the bounds of acceptability in mid-century Ireland. He knew them since childhood – he once wrote in a letter of how he had received 'a kick in the neck' from a teacher for answering in the affirmative to the question 'Could Ireland become communist?' In *Borstal Boy* he did not include those passages in which he was most explicit about homosexuality and permitted the publisher to replace expletives, yet still the book was banned. He chafed against the stifling strictures of conservative Ireland. 'Sometime I will explain to you the feeling of isolation one suffers writing in a Corporation housing scheme,' he wrote to Sindbad Vail in 1951. 'Cultural activity in present day Dublin is largely agricultural. They write mostly about their hungry bogs and the great scarcity of crumpet.' In response, Behan wrote these articles as an unashamed 'city rat', determined to celebrate the culture of working-class Dublin.

Things were changing for the Dublin that Behan knew. It could be argued that Behan's depiction of Dublin life in these articles was already belated, describing a city and a culture that was in the process of disappearing. The tenement flats had been cleared to make way for corporation houses. The songs about Kevin Barry and Spion Kop were being replaced by rock and roll and Teddy Boys. Behan is clear-eyed about such changes, and did not approve of preserving the 'old' Dublin for the sake of tourists from Foxrock or Chicago: 'God knows life is short enough,' he wrote, 'without people wearing themselves out hauling prams round lobbies, so that we can know what Hardwicke St. looked like in 1790.'

The new houses in Crumlin may not have been to his liking, but he recognized that they were attempts to improve the conditions of working-class Dubliners. That the old Dublin produced a culture he depicts as one of vibrancy, wit and song was not an argument for keeping people in the same slum conditions they had endured for decades. By the time Behan died in 1964, a process of economic liberalization had begun that prepared the way for Ireland to join the European Economic Community in 1972 and, some have argued, to become a modern, prosperous state. We will never know how an older Behan, in his fifties and sixties, might have responded to the war in Northern Ireland; nor, if he had lived to his eighties, what he would have made of the so-called 'Celtic Tiger'. The articles collected here, however, allow us to enjoy Behan in his own time.

FURTHER READING

BRENDAN BEHAN'S WRITINGS

The Complete Plays (London: Methuen, 1978)
Borstal Boy (London: Hutchinson, 1958)
Poems and a Play in Irish (Oldcastle, Ireland: The Gallery Press, 1981)
Poems and Stories, ed. Dennis Cotter (Dublin: Liffey Press, 1978)
An Giall/The Hostage, ed. Richard Wall (Washington, D.C.: The Catholic
    University of America Press, 1987)
Confessions of an Irish Rebel (London: Arena, 1985)
Hold Your Hour and Have Another (London: Corgi, 1965)
The Dubbalin Man (Dublin: A. & A. Farmar, 1997)
After the Wake, ed. Peter Fallon (Dublin: O'Brien Press, 1981)
The Scarperer (New York: Doubleday, 1964)
Brendan Behan's Island (London: Corgi, 1965)
Brendan Behan's New York (London: Hutchinson, 1964)

BIOGRAPHIES

Behan, Beatrice, *My Life with Brendan* (London: Leslie Frewin, 1973)
Behan, Brian, *With Breast Expanded* (London: MacGibbon & Kee, 1964)
— and Behan, Kathleen, *Mother of All the Behans: The Autobiography of
    Kathleen Behan as Told to Brendan Behan* (Dublin: Poolbeg, 1994)
— and Dillon-Malone, Aubrey, *The Brothers Behan* (Dublin: Ashfield
    Press, 1998)
Behan, Dominic, *Teems of Times and Happy Returns* (London: Four
    Square, 1963)
— *My Brother Brendan* (London: Four Square, 1966)
de Búrca, Séamus, *Brendan Behan: A Memoir* (Dublin: P.J. Bourke, 1993)

Jeffs, Rae, *Brendan Behan: Man and Showman* (London: Corgi, 1968)
McCann, Seán (ed.), *The World of Brendan Behan* (London: Four Square, 1965)
Mikhail, E.H. (ed.), *Brendan Behan: Interviews and Recollections* (London: Macmillan, 1982)
— (ed.), *The Letters of Brendan Behan* (Basingstoke: Macmillan, 1992)
O'Connor, Ulick, *Brendan Behan* (London: Abacus, 1993 [1970])
O'Sullivan, Michael, *Brendan Behan: A Life* (Dublin: Blackwater Press, 1997)
Ryan, John, *Remembering How We Stood: Bohemian Dublin at the Mid-Century* (Dublin: Gill & Macmillan, 1975; The Lilliput Press, 2008)
Simpson, Alan, *Beckett and Behan and a Theatre in Dublin* (London: Routledge and Kegan Paul, 1962)
Uíbh Eachach, Vivian and Ó Faoláin, Dónal (eds.), *Féile Zozimus: Volume 2 – Brendan Behan: The Man, the Myth, the Genius* (Dublin: Gael Linn, 1993)

CRITICISM

Boyle, Ted E., *Brendan Behan* (New York: Twayne, 1969)
Brannigan, John, *Brendan Behan: Cultural Nationalism and the Revisionist Writer* (Dublin: Four Courts Press, 2002)
— (ed.), *Brendan Behan* (Special Issue), *Irish University Review*, vol. 44, no. 1 (Spring 2014)
Gerdes, Peter René, *The Major Works of Brendan Behan* (Frankfurt: Peter Lang, 1973)
Kaestner, Jan, *Brendan Behan: Das dramatische Werk* (Frankfurt: Peter Lang, 1978)
Kearney, Colbert, *The Writings of Brendan Behan* (New York: St Martin's Press, 1977)
McCourt, John (ed.), *Reading Brendan Behan* (Cork: Cork University Press, 2019)
Mikhail, E.H. (ed.), *The Art of Brendan Behan* (New York: Barnes and Noble, 1979)
— *Brendan Behan: An Annotated Bibliography of Criticism* (New York: Barnes & Noble, 1980)
Porter, Raymond J., *Brendan Behan* (New York: Columbia University Press, 1973)

CHRONOLOGY

1923 Brendan Behan born 9 February to Kathleen (*née* Kearney) and Stephen Behan. The Behan family live in a tenement flat in 14 Russell Street, Dublin.

1928–34 Attends St Vincent's School, North William Street, Dublin.

1931 Joins Fianna Éireann (IRA Youth Movement).

1934–7 Attends St Canice's Christian Brothers' School, North Circular Road, Dublin.

1936 Behan publishes his first piece of writing, 'A Tantalising Tale', in *Fianna: The Voice of Young Ireland* (June).

1937 Attends Bolton Street Technical School to learn the trade of house-painting. The Behan family are rehoused by the Dublin Corporation in 70 Kildare Road, Crumlin, in a new housing estate.

1939 Brendan Behan joins the IRA. He is arrested in Liverpool, 1 December, on charges of possession of explosives and held in custody in Walton Jail.

1940 Behan sentenced to three years' borstal detention, 8 February, and moved initially to Feltham Boys' Prison, then to Hollesley Bay Borstal, where he is imprisoned until his release and expulsion to Ireland on 1 November 1941.

1942 Behan arrested for shooting at Dublin detectives, 10 April, and sentenced to fourteen years' penal servitude. He is imprisoned in Mountjoy Prison, then Arbour Hill Prison from July 1943 and the Curragh Camp from June 1944, until his release under general amnesty in September 1946. 'I Become a Borstal Boy' published in *The Bell* (June).

1947 Behan visits the Blasket Islands, Kerry (January). He is arrested and imprisoned in Strangeways Prison for three months for breaking his expulsion order (March–July). On his return to Dublin Behan begins to frequent 'The Catacombs' in 13 Fitzwilliam Place.

1948 Behan serves one month in Mountjoy Prison, Dublin, for assaulting a policeman. He goes to live in Paris in August and stays there until 1950, with only brief visits to Dublin and Belfast. In Paris, he lived on rue des Feuillantines, initially staying with Samuel Beckett's cousin John at the Grand Hôtel des Principautés Unies, and frequented the Left Bank and Les Halles.

1950 'A Woman of No Standing' published in *Envoy*, the Dublin magazine edited by John Ryan. 'After the Wake' published in Paris in *Points* (December), an avant-garde literary magazine edited by Sindbad Vail.

1951 'Bridewell Revisited', an early draft of the opening of *Borstal Boy*, published in *Points* (Winter). From around this time, Behan abandons house-painting as his trade and devotes himself to writing, and his income mainly comes from *The Irish Press*, *The Irish Times* and Raidió Éireann until his rise to fame in 1956.

1952 Behan recounts his Parisian experiences in a radio talk for Raidió Éireann on 29 March. In the summer Behan lives in an IRA safe house in Wicklow while writing parts of *Borstal Boy*. He serves one month in Lewes Prison, Sussex, for breaking an expulsion order (October). On release in November he goes to Paris to visit Samuel Beckett.

1953 *The Scarperer* is published serially in *The Irish Times*, beginning on 19 October. Behan writes the serial parts on the Aran islands.

1954   Behan writes a weekly column for *The Irish Press*, April 1954 to April 1956. The expulsion order against him in Britain is revoked. *The Quare Fellow* opens at the Pike Theatre, Dublin, on 19 November.

1955   Behan marries Beatrice Ffrench-Salkeld, 16 February.

1956   *The Quare Fellow* opens at the Theatre Royal, Stratford East, London, 24 May. *Borstal Boy* published serially in the Irish edition of the *Sunday Dispatch*.

1958   Brendan and Beatrice go to Ibiza for three months. *An Giall* opens at the Damer Hall, Dublin, 16 June. Goes to Sweden in August to translate *An Giall* into *The Hostage*. *The Hostage* opens at the Theatre Royal, Stratford East, London, 14 October. *Borstal Boy* is published by Hutchinson (London) on 20 October. *The Quare Fellow* produced off-Broadway.

1959   *The Quare Fellow* produced in Berlin, which Behan attends. Behan goes to Paris (April) for the performance of *The Hostage* at the Théâtre des Nations Festival. Behan suffers epileptiform seizures (July).

1960   *The Hostage* is performed in the Cort Theatre, New York. Behan makes his first visit to America, where he spends much time over his last few years.

1961   'The Big House' published in *Evergreen Review* (October).

1962   *Brendan Behan's Island* published (October).

1963   *Hold Your Hour and Have Another* published (September). Behan's daughter, Blanaid, is born, 24 November.

1964   Brendan Behan dies at the Meath Hospital, 20 March. *The Scarperer* published (June). *Brendan Behan's New York* published (September).

1965   *Confessions of an Irish Rebel* published (September).

1972   *Richard's Cork Leg* opens at the Peacock Theatre, Dublin, 14 March.

A NOTE ON THE TEXT

Most of the articles published in this edition were first published in *The Irish Press* newspaper between 1954 and 1956, when Behan was commissioned to write a weekly column for the newspaper. The column appeared every Saturday, almost without fail, for two years. The articles are arranged in chronological order. This is to preserve the ways in which Behan followed the same theme, story or journey over successive weeks.

There have been three selected editions of Behan's writings: *Hold Your Hour and Have Another* (Hutchinson, 1963), *After the Wake*, edited by Peter Fallon (O'Brien Press, 1981) and *The Dubbalin Man* (A. & A. Farmar, 1997). This volume provides the first complete edition of Behan's weekly pieces for *The Irish Press* and a small number of articles published in other newspapers. Errors have been corrected but in all other respects the texts have been maintained as they first appeared. Behan's spelling of Irish language words and phrases sometimes differ from modern usage, but original spellings have been preserved here.

Collected Articles

I

TO THE MOUNTAINS BOUND

*Brendan Behan heads from Dublin to Wicklow
on the first steps of the road round Ireland.*

The boss on the painting job says to me one morning: 'Behan, I believe you are a bit of a writer.'

Remembering: 'Mr Behan handles a delicate subject with sensitivity and taste, permitting but a negligible excess towards the end; he has the rare gift of knowing when to restrain his narrative and when to let it go forward so that his tensions are always controlled and his irony never heavy-handed; but above all he has inherited the virtue of his race of writing as he talks and talking as he sings in word arrangements, sensuous, syntactical.' (*The Hudson Review*,[1] New York, Summer, 1951.) I modestly assent.

'Well, write this.' And he hands me a time-sheet.

I fill it in. Syntactically. 'Assisting generally inside. Twelve hours.' Sensuously. 'Plus two hours travelling time.'

'And take these.' He hands me my three cards. Unemployment Insurance, Wet-Time[2] and National Health. One to go away, the second to stay away, and the third not to come back.

I depart from the job and am no longer a force in contemporary painting. Like a stricken deer I wander to the shelter of Grafton Street.

Having passed a good many places on the way down town, my fourteen hours was sadly reduced to minutes by the time I reached the corner of South King Street.

Paddy, behind the bar, looked up from his polishing and said: 'I thought you were down the country.' He is the only Dubliner in the business.

'Well, I'm back.'

'Glad to see you safe home any way, Brendan.'

'Thanks, Paddy, I know you mean that.' I had been in Maynooth for one day.

'Where are you going now?'

'I am going for a walk in the sun.'

'The Lambs? The Dead Man's?'

'No. Further than that. Out of reach of this city altogether.'

'You're not thinking of the turf, are you. Though I hear there's clerical students and all at it these times.'

'I'm going to travel Ireland, all Ireland.'

'Belfast?'

'Yes.'

'And Cork?'

'Yes.'

'God bless us and save us.'

'Here's a lift for you now, anyway, Brendan and Jemmy. The other Brendan, the Wicklow one.'

'Me sound man,' says the Wicklow one. 'We were just looking for you. I'm delighted I got you, Brendan, before I left town. Any man that died for Ireland, like yourself, it's a bare-faced pleasure to treat you.'

'I don't see how he could have died for Ireland,' said a scorpy-looking individual with a hungry old face with a lot of character in it. 'He's not old enough.'

'Ah, God help him,' says Jemmy, indicating the other Brendan, 'Sure you needn't be minding him. He backed Sugar Ray against Turpin.'

'Well,' says Head of Character, reasonably enough, 'the best in the world can make a mistake.'

'Brendan,' says Paddy the bar, 'is fed up in the city. He's away. Miles and miles like Kitty the Hare. All over Ireland, Belfast and Cork and all.'

'A good start is half the work,' says Jemmy, 'to the Garden of Ireland[3] and the finest tulip in it.'

On the way down we entertained the people, whether they liked it or not, with songs, recitations and Brendan the Wicklow one did a hornpipe with as much function and capernosity as the exigencies of the situation and the passengers' feet in the way allowed. A man over from New Zealand said he never saw the likes of it. Not even in his own country. I had to tell him, of course, that we were not always as good as this.

In a Roundwood pub we spent a few hours and in the morning I was not in such good shape for my walk.

'What hurry is on you,' said Brendan the Wicklow one, 'can't you stop on a bit.'

'Sure couldn't you give a hand with the hay?' says Jemmy.

'And give an ould stave of a song in the evenings,' said Charlie the Guard, more reasonably.

But I knew the best of my play was to get out of that pub that morning or I'd be there for the rest of time. So I walked three miles and, feeling the heat and burden of the day, went up to the house of a man, of the same Anglo-Irish stamp as Frank Taaffe,[4] that fed poets and washed poets in the best of malt until Raftery destroyed his best hunting-horse and ruined the transaction. No one, so far, has killed a horse on this man, so he's there to the good *go maith go fóill*.[5]

I left there the next morning and took myself to Avoca. In the bar beside Tom Moore's tree a famous Belfast boxer and myself and some bookies and so forth, looked out at the Meeting of the Waters.[6] The boxer was travelling Ireland also. But in a motor-car. It was costing him and the others a lot of money for the car and the driver, who was getting compensation, besides his wages, for not being allowed at the counter until night time. Despite this, they reckoned they were saving money by coming down, the price of drink in the North being what it is.

On the way through Rathdrum the next day a guard stopped me.

'Hello, and how are you?'

'Have we met before?'

'Well, I saw you in Cork one time. In Patrick Street. You were in good form that night.'

It was possible.

'Just out for a stroll?'

'Hiking.'

He laughed.

'You are not in uniform.'

I wear a fawn overcoat, a blue jacket and bawneen trousers. The latter the gift of a young Irish composer. A white shirt from Simpsons of Piccadilly kindly presented by a BBC critic late of this town, but formerly and for long enough at this caper himself.

'What's this the name is again?'

To save wear and tear on his politeness, I produced my labour cards, mostly innocent of stamps, North of Ireland food cards and British Mercantile Marine card, and an invitation from the French Press attaché to attend a party in celebration of the two-thousandth anniversary of Paris.

'Good luck, old son,' said the guard. 'But you are going in the wrong direction.'

On the way out of town I passed the open door of the National Health agent. In the hallway hung a picture of the Irish Brigade in the Boer War[7] charging the British. It was called: 'A New Fontenoy'.

The Irish Press, 2 August 1951

2

WICKLOW SAILORS AND BOYS OF WEXFORD

Brendan Behan follows the road from Roundwood to Enniscorthy,
and a poem of his own in Irish on the radio.

I got a lift from Roundwood to Arklow. In Arklow there was plenty of money stirring, judging by the pubs. But there is something very wistful about seamen, even when they are ashore enjoying themselves.

Johnson[8] said of them that no man would go aboard ship who had sufficient contrivance to get himself into a jail, for to be a sailor was to be prisoner with the added risk of drowning.

I was at a hooley in Dieppe not many months ago, with Clogher Head men and Faythe men and Donal from Cork City and little Johnny from Schull, not to mention Big Mick the bo'sun and Gurrier the cook. 'North, South, East or West, Gurrier's coddle it is the best.' And indeed I was head man at hooleys nearer the Point of the Wall than the Café Normandie where the drink, in quantity and variety, would have done a few hunt balls if the people that attend such things knew as much as seamen about Mumm at ten shillings and Pernod out of bond at five shillings a bottle.

Although there was one fearful Irish maritime mixture, an amalgam of every conceivable sort of spirit from Marc to Mirabelle that I wouldn't give my worst enemy.

I walked out of Arklow and had a good bit of Wexford road over me when a man pulled up and told me to hop in. On the road to Inch we talked about one thing and another but it was only in the pub there that I discovered that I was being entertained by a former county footballer.

I knew by the tone of reverence with which the bar greeted him that he was someone a step above buttermilk. We had a discussion about the weather with the postman and a lorry driver. The postman said the heat suited him but the lorryman didn't like it. Not when he was working anyway.

Going on to Gorey the footballer told me that the postman was well-known in his own right as a champion dancer and the finest and lightest man that ever beat timber for Irish or jazz, in the county of Wexford, where I was now and for the first time, and not a bad class of people, either, if they were all as civil as the footballer.

Gorey is a fine English-looking sort of country town. I mean that as a compliment, for most of our country towns are not very beautiful. They look like cow-towns, shoved up as trading posts for the country round. And what else were they all during our history but places where one was liable to meet landlords' agents, rent collectors and bailiffs, and peelers standing outside a courthouse with a big crown over it just to let you know who the boss was, in case you'd forgotten since your last visit.

English villages have had more natural origins and have a more settled look about them.

There were Dublin people on holiday in it. One of them, a lad from Drumcondra, asked me if I had been buying cattle at the fair.

'Is it codding me, you are?'

'Oh, I didn't hear you speak. I am sorry.'

'I am sorry, too, that I am not buying cattle.'

'He writes,' says the footballer, 'books and all.'

This was a lie. But what you do well, do it often.

'With hard covers and all,' says the footballer; 'and, better still, he is going to have me in the paper.'

A tall English chap was called into the company to get very excited about this. He himself, it appeared, did a bit in that line.

'You don't happen to have anything of your own with you just now, do you?'

'Only this.' I all unassuming produce from my overcoat pocket a copy of *Down and Out in Paris and London*.[9]

"'George Orwell." That's not a terribly Irish name, is it?'

'It's not my real one. But it suited the English market. "George." The King and that, you know, and "Orwell", the River Orwell.[10] I was educated in England and that river had associations for me. The "bosky glades" and so forth.'

As a matter of fact, the River Orwell flows quite near a school I was in in England.

In Enniscorthy I asked the man behind the counter if he would turn on the wireless at nine twenty. He looked at the programme in the paper.

'It's Irish.'

'I know. It's verses I wrote myself.'

While I was listening to the broadcast a man came in and stood behind me. He looked at me and said:

'*An dtuigeann tu sin?*'

'*Tuige na dtiuginn, mar is mise do cheap?*'

'*Maithiu, begor, is fiu deoch e is fada o bhios ag chaint le file.*'[11]

I said I didn't mind if I did and if all was equal to him I'd chance a half.

The Irish Press, 24 August 1951

3

TWO MEN FROM THE NORTH

Brendan Behan, on the Road Round Ireland, comes to New Ross.

Down from Enniscorthy the road is through rich, comfortable-looking land. It has the appearance of having been lived in. There are stone barns and the houses lie snug behind big trees and old hedges. Except for the smaller fields I could have imagined myself in north-west France. But I would prefer the poorer, less efficient-looking places over Wexford way.

The houses there are honestly facing the road, and you can see them at the table and be called in off the road maybe, if they thought you needed a bit. But yet these people of the Norman farmhouses were not behind the door, as the saying has it, in Ninety-Eight.[12]

At a lovely little Protestant church I sat down under a big tree and had a read. Some Dublin kids with whom I exchanged Jackeenisms[13] any time we passed on the road cycled by.

'Will yous look at him,' shouts one Kimmage Commando to another, 'with his hair in his eyes and his book in his hand, like a bloomin' poet.'

Walking down the road came a man carrying a good raincoat, I could see the lining of it. He was from Belfast and told me that he had walked from Enniscorthy. I commented on the difficulty of getting lifts in these parts. He asked where I was going and said he would give me a lift to New Ross in his car. This was parked with a trailer attached a hundred yards up the road. Something had gone wrong and he walked into Enniscorthy for a coil. When he reached the car he discovered that it wasn't the coil was at fault and he had had his walk for nothing. Furthermore, or better still, as they say in the North, he had paid two pounds for something he did not need. He was in the motor trade himself and had any amount of coils at home.

We were debating whether or not he should go back to Enniscorthy, return the coil and look for his money back, when a car pulled up and a plump little man that obviously knew the value of himself got out and came over to us.

He asked in a Belfast accent if he could do anything to help. In the tones of Stanley to Livingstone he said: 'I saw the Northern number plate and thought I might help.'

My friend thanked him and introduced me as a Dublin chap he was giving a lift to. His fatness looked me up and down very coolly and said nothing. He took out cigarettes and offered one to his fellow-Lagonian, ignoring me completely. My friend declined and the fat one went off. The man of the good raincoat was very upset.

'Did you see where he never offered you a cigarette? I would never have done that.'

I never encountered that sort of thing in the North itself. Except with a shipping clerk from Scotland. But then I was mostly amongst decent people in the Bluebell on Sandy Row[14] and was seldom exposed to the extraordinary manners of solid men, North or South. In Anderson's of Donaghadee the Nelsons or Fosters or any of the fishermen, Orangemen all, would die if they thought they had insulted you, even unintentionally.

'No,' said my friend thoughtfully, 'he never offered you a cigarette.' Then he shook his head and laughed. 'Ah, well, I suppose it's better to be mean than at a loss. And, by the same token, I think it wouldn't be a bad idea if we went into Enniscorthy and got that two quid.'

In we went and he wasn't long before he got his money back. The Enniscorthy man even seemed pleased to have a further opportunity for a discussion of trans-Border motor business.

For some reason we drove off to Wexford and the very first place we stopped the girl behind the counter was from Cushendun in the Glens of Antrim.

They had no draught stout, but fat, squat bottles of a sort that my granny, God be good to her, used to call 'dumpers'. After a few of them I sang 'My Lagan Love' and by the time we were leaving was working round to the 'Sash'.

I parted from my Northern friend in New Ross on the steepest hill I've ever seen in a town. New Ross is a beautiful town like Chalon-sur-Saône or one of the towns around Lyon. Down at the Boat Club there is a diving board. I asked if I might use it and was given the use of a dressing room and all. I amused a little crowd on the bridge doing gammy dives off the top board. The club secretary told me the long boats cost five hundred nicker apiece. I could well believe the New Ross people have more where that came from. It seems prosperous and tidy.

In the pub I remarked on this to the man of the house, and also said it was a pity the river wasn't used more. That they didn't ship in their own coal, for instance.

'Before you came up, I came in here with coal for Robinson of Glasgow,' said a voice beside me in an accent as unlike south Wexford as my own. A little Dublin man on leave from a tanker and not long returned from Abadan, where he said the drink was dear and bad. His only comment on Persia. When he discovered I was a neighbour's child, we talked about the hard chaws that we both knew on the North Wall and opposite. A doctor chap that came over from the Boat Club said it sounded ten times as bad as the Vieux Port in Marseilles.

'Ah, not nowadays,' said the little sailorman, 'sure the young crowd coming up is no use for a decent heave. God be with the days you'd see the DMP[15] being bet from one end of the quay to the other. With their own batons of a Saturday night. But now it's like a graveyard. The young crowd is no good for anything except dancing and the pictures.'

'Deed and it's true for you,' said a big man in a fine Cork accent, 'they are not the great rackers their fathers were.'

The Irish Press, 28 September 1951

4

JOURNEY IN THE RAIN
TO WATERFORD

A bakery van stopped in the wet night between New Ross and Waterford. I sat beside the man, and we began a conversation about the cost of living. Always a safe subject anywhere, any time.

He had eight children. Although my own economic problems are not nearly so numerous, I don't like being bested. Like Lanna Machree's dog, I'll go a step of the road with anyone, and soon I was away ahead of him, describing the even greater difficulties of rearing a family in the capital. So great were my own troubles that she and I had parted. I just read my income tax assessment one morning, got up from the breakfast table, and walked out of the house. My only lodging since then, I said, with feeling, had been fields and haystacks.

'And isn't it a wonder a big able-bodied fellow like you would leave a poor woman high and dry with a houseful of little children?'

Afraid that he might, on behalf of my wholly mythical wife and children, give me in charge at the next Garda barracks, I told him a touching story of reconciliation and forgiveness, quoting a letter I had received from her the day before in answer to which I was now going home on the first train from Waterford in the morning.

Slowing up at a bend he looked round at me in the darkness.

'And where, might I ask, did she address the letter to? To the haystack? And how did she know which one you'd be staying at?' He spoke as if they were a chain of hotels.

'I collect her letters in post offices on the way. Haven't you ever heard of poste restante?'

He hadn't. Not in my pronunciation, anyway. I said it more nosy than Jean Cocteau.

'Oh, I see,' he said, adding, to be on the safe side no doubt, 'I was in the LSF[16] during the war, and we learned ju-jitsu.'

At Waterford bridge we parted. To the decent man's great relief.

It was my first time in Waterford. The river was bigger, or seemed wider, than the Shannon. The waterfront spangled like cold lights in the drizzle. It was like a scene from *Winterset*. Bigger ports, Glasgow or Belfast, have the advantages of industry. Just down from the Broomielaw and right on the river is Singer's factory. Belfast has her mills. Dublin, as a port, is but a city with a river. But Waterford, I felt, like Dunkirk or Antwerp, has never existed for a thousand years but on the sea and for the sea.

There can be no more beautiful sight, in its own way comparable to Killarney or the Glens of Antrim, than Waterford dockside by night. Especially on a wet night.

'*Feac soillsi na duganna thar abhann uainn, gear, geal, fuar.*
Eist, gairm na long, i bhad in uaigneas uainn, ar bheal an chuain
'*S dorchadas oidhche go doimhin i dtost na sleibhte,*
Go mbeannuighhidh 's Dia 's Muire dhuit,
A Phuirt Lairge, 'righean na nDeisigh.'[17]

Over the big bridge and up towards Barrack Street. I was to meet friends of mine. On the way up a voice hailed me.

'Hello, Brendan. Isn't that Brendan Behan?'

There was a lad with a very pretty girl, whose hair, as far as I could make out in the dark, was as coppery as the first penny with a hen on it.

I said it *was* Brendan Behan. The first man to give a blood transfusion to a jeep or to write his name on an ass and cart in Irish and several other things besides.

My friend was a plasterer chap I knew. He remembered me from our last job together. My appearances as painter and decorator, of short duration, are yet something in the nature of commando raids on the building industry and, though, perhaps, little in the line of a contribution to the reconstruction of our country, are yet a source of entertainment to nippers, apprentices and younger journeymen and turn them from thoughts of excitement in other trades and other lands.

Many a young plumber with his fare to Buenos Aires saved up and his mind full of gauchos chasing toros across pampas has had his thoughts turned homewards by the superior attractions as a spectacle of Brendan Behan and a foreman carpenter having an argument over the ten o'clock break, and has been permanently kept at home in Ireland as a result.

Paddy was the plasterer's name and copper-head was Kathleen. We went in the same direction for we were going to the same place. Paddy reminded me of the last party we were at together. It was above in Mount Brown opposite Cromwell's Quarters and just beside the Union, which, as the woman of the house remarked, might be a convenience before the hooley finished.

Kathleen was interested in the drama. She mentioned the Abbey fire[18] and I prepared, on behalf of the Metropolis, to accept her condolences and, perhaps, murmur consolingly.

'Never mind, little girl. We'll build a bigger and better,' and 'We never died in winter and the divil wouldn't kill us in summer,' and so on and so forth. But I was amazed and horrified to discover that my fair friend considered it as little a tragedy as the burning of the Customs House. I thought she must have a little helicopter for running up and down the country. But she mentioned some Dublin monthly magazine and then, as Wolfe Tone would say, I had her smoked.

I assured her that the Abbey had not fallen all that distance.

'Sure the chaps writing those things have to be saying something. And anyone writing for a few bob, sure they can't be saying the one thing all the time.'

'I suppose they can't,' said Kathleen.

The Irish Press, 31 October 1951

5
JOURNEY TO THE JEWEL
OF WICKLOW

'You get a bus every three minutes,' said the girl at the other end of the telephone.

'Listen with some more ears,' said I, 'when you have a three-minute service to Valleymount,[19] I'll not be needing it. I'll be using my own private helicopter.'

'Where did you say?'

'Valleymount.'

'Oh, sorry. I thought you said Dollymount. Valleymount is morning and evening. Tuesdays, Thursdays and Saturdays.'

'What does morning and evening mean?'

'You can go there in the morning and come back in the evening.'

'Of the same day?'

'Yes.'

'Wonderful. Things *are* looking up since our own took over.'

'What?'

'What's what?'

'Since who took over what?'

Finally, or as the man said, between the jigs and the reels, I got a bus going to Naas, which seemed to be the right direction. The man sitting beside me was friendly and asked me if I would take a look at a high-class paper about horses. I had a look at it, and am as wise now, as before I read it, as to what it was about. My friend had a hat with a fishhook of some feathery sort stuck in the band and a suit of material that I always associate with members of the Kildare Street Club[20] or organisers for the Gaelic League.[21] It had heather and stuff growing out of it, and I made so bold as to compliment him on the colour of it.

'Last a lifetime, this stuff,' said he.

That's what I'd be nervous of, said I, in my own mind.

'Grandfather bought a bolt of that, pre-war. I mean, of course, the first war.'

'Oh, damn the thing else. Sure anyone could have a bolt from the last one.'

'Follow the hunt?'

Into a pub. No, that would hardly be the answer.

'Hunt anything?'

Porter. 'Er, I have er—'

'Fish?'

'Bit of ray, if it's all one to you.'

'I mean what are you going to do up there?'

Six months. D Wing. 'Eh where?'

'There,' and he pointed towards the far-off hills, 'up in Valleymount.'

'Well, as a matter of fact,' don't tell anyone, like, 'I'm going to write.'

'You're going to what?'

'I'm going to – er – write.' Thanks be to God I didn't say read.

'Write what? Do you mean you will write today? Tomorrow?'

Oh, any day, now. 'Tomorrow, probably.'

'What sort of thing will you write?'

'An article for a magazine in Paris.'

'Paris, hey?'

'Oh, and a Ballad Maker's Saturday Night.'[22]

His face improved. 'Really.' But then suspicious. 'You mean the radio programme. Are you sure?'

'Oh, honest, sir. I have a contract form here in my pocket. I do it often, sir. Really. I do, sir.' I was going to add 'Honest injun,' but I couldn't remember it in time. I preferred the contract form.

'So, you do, by gad. I never miss it. Do you know the one that goes "La the la the la fine girl you are?"'

'I do indeed, it's a song from Cobh (Queenstown) called *The Holy Ground*.' He seemed to know a bit of each of them. Of the songs done by Bryan MacMahon[23] and Sigerson Clifford,[24] I shone in their reflected glory, and hadn't the guts to mention any of my own songs.

I got off at a crossroads and he went on to Naas. He waved from the window and growled some last greeting (probably Hindustani), from under his white moustache and his fierce eye fixed on me. I bowed low in the road and tried to think of some farewell.

'Death to death duties,' I said, and he nodded affably, and went off towards Naas, humming to himself. Probably an aria from a Killorglin goat opera.[25]

It was a long climb, but well worth it. My breath came back and went off again, when I was on top of the hill, looking down on Valleymount. A thin sliver of village. Church, shop, school, post office and pub. The silver-grey water all round, lapping the feet of the ring of mountains all the way round from Ballyknocken.

This width of water is our own. We, the sovereign people, directed its course to where it was most convenient to our engineers to rein and harness it.

'The history of Ireland,' said Father Tom Burke, 'is written in her ruins.' At a time when the whole world seemed set on nothing but ruins, when it was counted a crime past forgiveness amongst nations to do anything but kill and destroy, this work was begun. And while the world seems set towards another and final round of destruction, in faith, it goes forward.

Some of the people were sad, of course, for the old homes left at the bottom of the Electricity Supply Board's new lake, but their new houses are trim, and the whole area has a look of fresh prosperity. Many a time the tar barrels blazed on the mountain tops in freshened confidence of eventual victory. Now the electric lights shine out over the hills, and star the land with hope.

It is a beautiful land round here, and would be better known if the natives were as vocal as the Killarney people. Maybe they want to keep it to themselves.

The priest and teacher are Northside men like myself, and conscripted me for service at a concert in aid of the new schools. I played the mouth organ, but the real interest of the more juvenile element lay in the puffing and blowing that accompanied the attempts of your man (of girth) here to get enough of wind to take him through Ravel's 'Bolero'.

The kids themselves sang like angels *'Cad a dheanamaid feasta gan adhmaid?'*, 'Loch Lein' and *'A shaighdiurin a chroi*, will you marry marry me?'[26] They were trained to a T, although a certain young gentleman from the village shoved his sister from beside him in the front row. Four other ladies, between the ages of eight and fourteen, came down from Granamore, and said it was well worth the walk. There was a play, and the blacksmith, as a cute old farmer, put up with some terrible abuse from his son and daughter-in-law.

I had a drink and gave news of the literary battlefront to the master, who does a bit in that line himself.

Then home, and over the mountain, through the quiet night and the electric lights gleaming far away over the waters, and the roar of the great dam of Poulaphouca faint across the lakes.

> *'Eirighidh, a huisce, nigh na tire,*
> *Báthtar an bhochtanais, id' dhoimhneacht,*
> *Tonntaibh I gcomhacht, fé shrian I gcomhar,*
> *Neart Éireann id rás, a haibhne.'*[27]

The Irish Press, 25 October 1952

6

OVER THE NORTHSIDE I WAS
A CHISLER

Over the Northside, and I a kid, there were three classes of houses: private houses, set houses, and houses. A house was a private house if it had a shut hall door and the tenants had each a key of his own. Visitors gave a certain number of knocks to be let in. And God look down on you if you have any ra-ta-ta that came into your head and brought down an oul' one from the top back to let you in to visit another oul' one in the back kitchen that she wasn't speaking to anyway.

A set house had a hall door, but it was shut only at night to keep out lobby-watchers (poor men who slept on the stairs or any dry place they could find). Houses might have no hall door or, if they had, it was never shut. Most times it had no lock. Nobody ever washed the stairs, and if they had it would have been small addition to them. The hall was used as a public thoroughfare. Fellows played cards there. Couples courted. The kids had concerts of a wet night with a mouth organ and a paper comb, and on winter nights ran through it chased by a rozzer (Civic Guard) or playing Relieve-ee-o.

The young mots in the street got a bit upset over this when they went into the factories and started using lipstick and looking for fellows. Most of them wouldn't let on to live in our street at all. Walking home from work with other girls, they'd go up the North Circular Road and miles out of their way and only come back when they'd left the other ones home so as to let on they lived in Drumcondra or some such fancy quarter.

I remember three girls and they lived in Number Sixteen, which was a diabolical enough class of a grip if you weren't used to it.

Besides these three mots there was living in it an oul' one who was what we called a picarooney. She went to the Sloblands in Fairview and rooted round for jam jars, old porter bottles, cinders, rags or any old thing she'd get a few makes for. God help her, when she got enough in her old pram to buy it, she used have a go at the spunk and jungle juice, a noted cocktail of methylated spirits and fine old Invalid Port.

These three girls, as I was saying, didn't like the other mots in the factory to know that they were living in our street and certainly not in Number Sixteen. So they ran on ahead up the Circular Road, reached the street in safety and ran up the steps to heave over the hall door, when who comes round the corner only the ones they were avoiding. They could not get in quick enough and there they were left, swinging by the whiskers, so to speak. The others walked down and stood at the steps, looked up and said: 'Oh, we always thought yous lived in Clonliffe Road.'

Our poor neighbour's children were a bit knocked out by this, but not for long. 'We do, but there's an oul' one here does a day's work for our mammy.'

And she starts to bang away on the knocker as if it was a real proper hall door, not liking to admit that even her mammy's charwoman would have a hall door that you had to hold up in case it would fall on you, and hoping at the same time that the others would go away and let them go in for their dinner. But there wasn't a stir out of them.

'Well, we'll wait here till you come out, and then we'll walk home together the same as we do every day.'

'Well, all right. And if we're too long yous can go on and we'll go down Jones's Road after yous.'

And she kept up the hammering on the door. Bang, bang.

The drawing-room window opens and the picarooney woman nearly throws herself through it, in a froth of mad rage and the old tawny port glaring out of her eyes.

'The curse of this, that, and the other may meet and melt yiz. It's not bad enough to be lying up here in the high jigs, but yiz have to go playing your tricks on that oul' knocker, and yous knowing that it hasn't been used in this house since yiz were born in it. It'd answer yiz better to go and ask your oul' ma to pay me for the four-pence-worth of cinders she got off me two weeks ago.'

In the back kitchen of Number Sixteen there was the oul' one with her son and daughter. The daughter hadn't spoken to anyone for twenty years and communicated with her mother by a series of notes.

Whenever the oul' one would sneak over to the corner for a gill, the daughter would chase after her and slip notes through the door of the snug: 'Agnes Mary Assumpta Doran is over in Fanning's mopping up porter and not a crust in the house. Signed, your affect. daughter, La-La.'

When the mother had a sup in her, she'd sing the song of the Invincibles:

> '*I am a bold undauntitude,*[28] *and Joe Brady is my name,*
> *From the chapel of North Anne Street boys,*
> *One Sunday as I came,*
> *To my surprise who should I spy but Moreno and Cockade:*
> *Says one unto the other: "Boys, here comes our Fenian blade."*'

Round our way they thought a lot of the Invincibles, surgeon's knives or no surgeon's knives. The old people would tell how Tim Kelly's mother shouted to him after he was sentenced, 'Good on you, son. You'll not see twenty, but you're no informer.'

Mostly in our street there were big young families. People came round now and again to look at the ceilings and fireplaces. A couple of toffs came once to look at some shelves in the wine cellar of our house. They had been used in the time of the gentry for stacking casks on. The Lestranges were living there, the father and mother and seven children, in the wine cellar.

The father was a pensioner out of the Big War. He was gassed and used to lie in bed coughing. One of the kids, Shaybo, was the same age as I. He told me that when his da coughed you could see the gas coming out of his mouth in little puffs. Anyway, these two gents looking at the shelves fancied them so much that they offered five pounds for them.

'They're yours,' says Shaybo's father, jumped out of bed, gas and all, and tore down the shelves.

'They're Adam's,' said the old toff, giving him a cheque.

'They're yours now,' says Shaybo's father, 'and you can have the rest of the house for another ten quid.'

In the summer we swam in the canal or in the sea at the Middle Arches. In the winter's night we played games in the street: Relieve-ee-o, Hock-hock arooshy, Billy oxtail.

If the night was fine we'd stand round the lamp till after twelve singing songs or telling stories we'd hear our fathers tell about the Big War or about the Black and Tans.

It was down our street the British went to attack Croke Park on Bloody Sunday. The country fellows at the match ran into the houses and the people hid them under beds or anywhere they could. The Tans and the British Tommies slaughtered all round them, but a couple of them got lackeried round our way.

One Tan got that excited he ran down a back stairs and into a card school. Some of the fellows were playing a game of 'Fat', and this Tan ran right in among them. They jumped him and gave him a desperate kicking. The other British didn't miss him till they got back to barracks, and though they came back the next day they never got him.

At an All-Ireland Final we made a bit, minding bikes for the country-men. Small kids didn't get a bike pitch, but we'd go up to a countryman in a car and say to him: 'Mister, give us a few makes and I'll mind the valves of your tyres.'

Sometimes they were decent enough but sometimes they'd say: 'Go on outa that. Me valves can look after themselves.'

He'd know all about that after the match when he wanted to drive home to Mayo or wherever he came from.

We went most to Tolka Park or Dalymount. Sometimes we went to Croker, to the hurling to see O'Tooles. We got broken hurleys during the matches; we played on the street with them, or with a cricket bat or anything we could get. After an All-Ireland we'd nearly all have half a stick anyway. I played with a stick that had been thrown away by Lowry Meagher.

We never played Gaelic football and knew nothing about it. But we followed our own soccer team, 'NCR, AFC,' all over the place – to the Thatch (where the Ellenfield housing scheme is now), to Windy Arbour or the Fifteen Acres, to cheer them against Mervill or Bendigo of Waterford Celtic. Waterford Celtic had nothing to do with Waterford, except that they were from Waterford Street.

We knew all about Matthews of Rovers, and Larry Cervi and Kronge Dunne and Jimmy, his brother, and Harry Cannon and Paddy Moore, the Lord have mercy on them and even the stars of English soccer, Alec James, Hugh Fallon from Derby County, Hapgood and Bastin; but the only Gaelic footballer I ever heard discussed at our corner – except for Ned McCann of Parnell's, whom we all knew – was John Joe Sheehy.

During the late twenties and the great matches of Kildare and Kerry we cheered, strangely enough, for Kerry. Kildare being next door to us, we neither realised nor considered. The country was the country to us, and it started where the tram tracks ended.

There were a few English people and country people in the street. They were popular enough, but in a row someone might tell them to go back to where they came from. Religion didn't enter into it. Indeed, when my father came out of jail after the Troubles, a Protestant man got him his first job and said: 'Come down in the morning with me. This place is overrun with bogmen and English, and we have to look after our own.'

But if we wanted to imitate a policeman, it was always a country accent we used. We had never met a civic guard or a teacher or a doctor in the hospital that spoke like ourselves. We accepted that as the natural law.

'If you want to stop there, you better move on.'

'*Sin amach do lamh.*'

'Why didn't you wash that foot before you came up to the hospital?'

When we talked about the rest of Ireland, we never divided it North or South. It was all the country, outside and around. In ways the bog was an enchanted land. When we weren't jeering it, we were very respectful about it.

The whole Northside ablaze with railways sleepers and every street corner running hot with asphalt after an election victory, we sang the sacred songs of Zion around the bonfires: 'He Was a Bold Tipperary Lad', 'Tipperary So Far Away', 'God Bless My Home in Tipperary' – Tipperary being the heart of the ends of the tram tracks. Then a kid, Pigeon Brennan, that later played for Brighton and Hove, or myself, would put up one of the songs we learned at school:

'*Is oth liam feinig buaileadh an lae crainn do dhul ar Ghaedil bocht is na ceadtai slad.*'

And nobody knowing a word of it, they'd cry for the sound of the holy language till they recovered and we went back to the songs we all knew:

> '*Get me down me petticoat,*
> *Get me down me shawl,*
> *Get me down me petticoat*
> *For I'm off to the Linen Hall.*'

Kerry Champion, 16 August 1952 (published anonymously; originally broadcast for radio on Raidió Éireann, December 1951)

7

THE LONG JUMP TO ARAN

Brendan Behan likes the islandmen so well that he thanks God
Aran lasted up to his time.

In Galway, I was told that the *Dun Aengus*[29] was not running. I went down
the docks to look for a jump to Aran. I was reared in sight of cranes and
sound of foghorns, and knew, that whether you drank or not, the best dart,
as the man said, was the pubs round the quays. Overcoming whatever prejudices I might have in the matter, I went into one of these places.

The customers were big men with mahogany faces, and navy-blue
sweaters, talking Irish. All along the docks it is the speech of the tavern, and
none of these places a bit more stylish than places I remember in Glasgow
or Rouen. Which is a pity for the Metropolitan Gael-hunters, fugitives
from Justice, Finance, Industry and Commerce.

For in snug darkness abideth the outlawed Milesian, and if in Galway
it's for him you're looking, it's in the pubs on the Quay you'll find him, and
nowhere else.

A man said to me: '*An* Dun Aengus? *Taid a' ra go bhuil rud eicinnt con-*
tralta lei. Engine trouble, *silim*.'[30]

I should not be surprised if the people of Aran, now so used to the
advances and retirements of the good boat, began to think that the terms
are synonymous. A psychiatrist will shortly be able to make a pass at any

of them: 'Engine trouble,' in the certainty of getting the drowsy response, '*Dun Aengus.*'

She has been running to Aran since 1910. It is widely believed that they are trying to preserve her for as long a span as her patron fort on the cliffs over Inis Mór, which has of course, a good head start of three thousand years. Still against that the boat is seldom exposed to the elements, while the fort has to stick it out all the year round.

WHO HAD FIRST CALL?

I was directed to a party in the back: three fishermen and a bigger, older man, in tweeds and a leather jacket, as if he had come from far parts. I asked if they knew of a boat going to Aran and they replied civilly that they were going there themselves at half past eleven that morning. They looked up at the big man in the tweed suit and he nodded that I might come.

They invited myself and a friend of mine I walked into in Eyre Square that morning to join them. Which we did. My friend was a Dublin painter on a job in Renmore and he insisted that he had first call, and every one swore rightly or otherwise that he had first call, but eventually the business was settled without calling in the police and we set to.

The big man talked as one who knew a good many places between his native Aran and the far ends of the earth. He was the only one that wouldn't drink, but talked with a kindly cynicism of people, from fishermen to film directors, till at last in deference to the well-known ways of tides, we went down to the boat and with a parting gift of a half-dozen and a wave of the hand, we swung out to the West.

FROM CARNA THEY CAME

Our boat was called the *Columbia* and the men were a family group, Seán and Padruig, and their brother-in-law, Peadar. From Carna they came, and were to Carna bound, but the big man was going to Aran, so they went out of their way, forty miles, to take him there, and glad to do it. That's the sort of man he seemed to be. He had as much sway over the hearts of men on Aran and the coast opposite as any monarch left in Europe.

Once out in open water, he curtly informed me that he had been out of the country some time and wished to speak to the men. He took his place on a bale of rope and the two young sailors sat at his feet, and when he was into his stride, laughed delightedly, as with steady gaze, with waving hands, he spun yarns of magic in hard, bright Irish.

Dismissed, I went aft and talked to the skipper, and for a while took the helm from him. The sea was like glass and I steered with my legs, at first for a high point on Inis Mór and afterwards for the sheds on Kilronan Pier, when they came in sight. What they used for a wheel and a binnacle in other weather, I don't know.

They were a casual, happy crew, and put the helm under a chain when we went below to eat about a pound of steak a man, and a lump of butter that would choke a bull and potatoes boiled in sea water.

We drank the half-dozen and had a few drains from a five-naggin bottle. Like that, and not much the matter with us, we reached Kilronan.

THEY LAUGH A DEAL IN ARAN

There was a regal welcome for the big man, and he at last decided to take a drop, as he treated his people to a rossiner.

They laugh a deal in Aran, and are not much given to telling their troubles. They don't look to anyone to do anything for them.

They would like to go out a few miles and catch the fish that lie off their shores, without having to go such a long way round about it.

They would like to have boats, trawlers.

They like that sort of work. They go as far as Milford Haven and Fleetwood to get on a trawler. They have a good chance of a visit home, for the Lancashire and Welsh trawlers come up, with the Norwegians and the Spaniards, round Aran, and the Aran man has a chance of going ashore in Kilronan with the others. Without the fish of course. That goes back to Milford Haven or Fleetwood and will only come back to Erin in a box.

The Aranman wishes it was less complicated a business, his getting on a trawler. So do I, and plenty of his countrymen, as far from Aran as Sundrive Road and Cabra West. Apart from the Irish language, I like fish.

I was called on for a song, and after singing 'Casadh an tSugáin',[31] settled down, glass in hand to enjoy the company, and the laughter and the beautiful speech and thank God that Aran had lasted up to my time, anyway. That I hadn't died without seeing it.

The Irish Press, 20 May 1953

8

THESE FISHERMEN PUBLICISE
GAELIC AT ITS BEST

Dubliner makes himself at home on Aran.

On a hazy day in June, I walked out from Kilmurvey[32] and down to the tip of Inis Mór, at Bungowla. I walked along the edge of the land, and the sea dancing in the sun, and the blue of the Connemara mountains, majestic, vaguely indolent, stretching themselves in a veil of filmy gauze, over across in the other world.

On one side of the road lay the seashore, and in the potato fields on the other, which began at the roadside and went up the mountain for three-quarters of the way, there were men working.

At what particular stage of potato production they were, I don't know. I suffer from the national disease, agrophobia or fear of agriculture, and didn't dare find out. It might not be lucky. You could be left like that.

CULT OF GROWTH

Many's the one is running round Crumlin, with a shovel and a fork and a barrowload of muck, through the same curiosity. I've heard them in the Floating Ballroom, of an evening.

'How's the spuds, Lar?'

'Coming on nicely. I put used garbage from the knackers[33] on them. Got it through fellow who goes with mot's[34] youngest sister. He's a cook in it.'

'A cook?'

'A glue cook. Like his father before him. Took first prize, the year of the exhibition, for rendering down a carcase. Before the crowned heads of Europe.'

'Good enough for them. I'm using sawdust and soot on mine. Got the tip from a chap out in Newtownmountkennedy when I was on me holidays. No time for this artificial stuff.'

'Nothing artificial about my manure. Did you ever smell it? And only two quid a load ex-works.'

SAXON SONG

But the Aran people and myself were never short of conversation.

'*Bail o Dhia ar an obair*,'[35] I shouted, and Michil Tom and Stiofán threw down their spades and came down the field.

Michil is the proprietor of Michil Og, a person of about five. He has brothers and sisters, but I remember him under the title of Michil an Smig, because he had a fall on his chin the day I met him.

Michil Tom, himself, worked as a painter in England, in the early days of the war, and leant over the ditch to tell me how the Connemara man described to his newly arrived friend the sort of song the English sang.

HOME'S THE WRITER

Bhuil 's a't an sórt amrháin, tá ag na Sasanaigh annseo?[36] 'Run rabbit, run, down Mexico way.'

Stiofán is his nephew, a capable man of seventeen, who came back from college on the mainland to help run his parents' business. Stiofán's young eyes regarded myself with pleasant indulgence, as something in the nature of a good joke.

'*Dhein tú mortán olbre ar maidin?*'[37] he asked.

I said I had done a good bit of work this morning, and he nodded and, pointing to the rows of potatoes, said he and Michil hadn't done too badly, either.

In Aran, writing is taken as seriously as any other sort of work. They are used to writers and painters coming over in the summer, but apart from that the storyteller and the poet are held in high regard.

The Aran people are a good advertisement for Gaelic civilisation. Like the Algerians, their architecture and painting are in the spoken word. Nowhere else have I found it so easy to sit down at the typewriter, and work away, without feeling that I was in any way regarded as a criminal lunatic of idle tendencies.

OLD MARE DIES

I left Michil Tom and Stiofán to it, and went on a bit. I met Brian with a new mare. My acquaintance with horses is limited to the odd one I used to meet in a traffic jam, when I was a painter's apprentice balancing a six-foot double ladder and a couple of gallons of colour on my sports bike, and trying to balance at the corner of Nassau Street, between a Number Six tram and a Guinness's dray.

Brian's mare was a massive upstanding beast, with the sun shining on her flanks. I praised her, and Brian accepted my praise, but we also thought of the old horse of his we buried a couple of Sundays before.

The burial was largely attended by people from near and far – the boys of Kilronan and the men from Seacht d'Teampuill – and we dug his grave on Kilmurvey strand.

The Irish Press, 22 December 1953

9

TRAVELLING FOLK MEET A
LANGUAGE PROBLEM IN THE WEST

and Brendan Behan helps to solve it.

I was coming back through the village of Eoghanacht,[38] and the dust and heat of the day had me choked. I was thinking of the good dive I'd have off the pier after I'd eaten – if I survived the mile walk back to Kilmurvey, without a drink. There was a man leaning at the door of a cottage, and I asked him would he give me a drink of water.

'Come in,' he said, in Irish, 'and sit down a minute. Be not like the bird, that you'd be hearing the sound of his wings, and be long gone past you.'

'I won't so,' I replied, going in.

'You won't what?' said a voice from the cool dark of the kitchen. It was an old woman in the corner.

I didn't want to go through all that again, so I just said, 'I hope you're well, ma'am.'

'I'm not,' she said, putting her hand to the side of the head, 'no more than reasonable. Are you from Connemara, son?'

'I'm not, ma'am; I'm from Dublin.'

'I was never there. I was never anywhere, but in Boston, and in Woburn, Massachusetts. There was great work in the leather place. Myself and his father were ten years there.'

'I'd suppose you have plenty of English, then.'

'Himself had a share of it, but where would I get it? In Woburn, it was all the Middle Island crowd. They say "*a dhreabhairin*", and "*a dhrairin*", that's the way they say it, when they're talking to you, and when I went to Woburn first, I thought it queer American Irish, for I had never been on the Middle Island,[39] and I didn't know that that was the way they spoke.'

'You'd see them all, leaning over the gate smoking their pipes or doing their bit of knitting of a Sunday afternoon, and they were calling over to one another: "*Seadh a dhreabhairin*", "*Ni headh, a drairin*" ("Yes, little sister", "No, little brother").'

She put her hand to her head.

'The boy is thirsty, Peadar, get him a drink of milk.'

I got the milk in a great mug that would wash ten mile of road out of your throat.

'I'm crucified from pains in the head,' said the old woman, 'but I suppose I can expect no more till I go under the sod. I'm four score years.'

NEAR THE HUNDRED

'Sure, that's nothing,' said I, lowering the mug. 'They're walking round the city of Dublin at ninety (I was nearly going to say 'at twice that') and not a bother on them. It's when they start dragging the two or three near the hundred, they're a bit worried.'

'And some will tell you,' said the old woman, 'that you should be glad to be getting so close to the next world.'

'Bedamnbut, I see no great hurry on them, going there,' said Peadar, 'for all they praise it for other people.'

'I saw a dancer in Paris,' said I to the old woman, 'and she dancing before everyone, and she was five year older than you are now.'

'I would not believe that,' said the old woman.

'Well, you can, then,' said I, 'for it's as true as I'm sitting here, and that the next drink of milk I take out of this mug may choke me if I'm telling a lie.'

A GREAT HEART

'The angel of God against your prayer,' said the old woman, 'but she must have been the shameless old hag. All the same,' as if impressed, in spite of herself, 'she must have a great old heart.'

'It wasn't the heart made the money for her at all,' said I, 'but the legs.'

The old woman chuckled, and waved her hand, 'Oh, God forgive you, you're a wonderful son. What's her name, and I'll say a prayer for her?'

'Her name is Mistinguette.'[40]

'Oh, sure I'll never remember that. I'll remember her, though, as the old woman of the legs.'

On the way down the road I met some tinkers.

Tinkers,[41] with respects to MacDonagh and MacMahon, do not speak Irish, and some of the houses they were visiting looking for business had no English-speakers.

ABOUT THE POTS

Anyway, again with the height of respect to the two Macs, their Elizabethan prose is not easy to follow. One fellow told me he'd axed the woman of the house, and I thought he'd gone for her with a hatchet, and it turned out he'd only asked her about leaks, in pots.

I'd met them in the pub at Kilronan, and one spider recognising another, we went down like a dinner with one another.

'Will you axe the wamman ah the house, Brindan, haws shay fixed for lakes?'

I was more in humour of the beautiful meal I knew was awaiting me at Kilmurvey, but went up to the house the decent man pointed to.

'*Dia dhibh istigh,*' said I to Siobhán and Bartle, sitting either side of the fire, '*Tá tinnceir annseo, sé ag lorg oibre, is gain focail Ghaeilge aige.*'

TINKER TALK

'*Muise, go raibh maith agat, a Bhreandáin,*'[42] said Bartle, 'but I can English the man myself,' nodded importantly to Siobhán and rose from the fire.

'Fair enough,' said I, 'go to it, Bartle, he's all yours.'

He went to the tinker at the gate, and having greeted him with goodbye, they set to business.

Bartle looked down at the tinker's raw materials. 'I see you've plenty leather.'

'Tass so,' said the tinker, 'you wants a pat?'

Bartle said he did not want a pot.

The tinker held one up. 'This wan?'

Bartle shook his head. 'Too big. I want a young one.'

The Irish Press, 29 December 1953

10

SAVED FROM CERTAIN DEATH BY THE ISLANDERS

Brendan Behan fancies a swim.

In Pateen's there was a framed certificate in the bar, attesting to Pateen's military services in the US. 'Patrick Munnelly has served with Corcoran's Irish Legion, Meagher's Irish Horse, the 169th NYNG, the 69th NY Regiment ...'

A lighthouseman from Dún Laoghaire, having his last drink with me before going out on the rock, looked up at it and remarked, 'Bedad, and Pateen had his hands full. The only thing he wasn't in, be the looks of that, was Slattery's Mounted Foot, and the Mud Island Fusiliers.'

Old John the Lifeboat laughed into himself. He liked a bit of a laugh, in either language, and could rise one – though the man that could take a rise out of him would keep a bakery going eating loaves.

The doctor found that out one day.

John was with the crowd at Kilronan Pier watching the unloading of *Dun Aengus*.

A large box, the property of a visiting savant, was being put ashore, and on its side was written the scholar's name and the letters 'L.L.D.'

'*Cad is brí leis na letriecha siúd*, John?' asked the doctor.

'*Muise, Leig Leat "Dhoctuir"*,'[43] said John.

He was a noted referee at handball matches.

ON EUROPE'S EDGE

In their white sweaters and the pants of homespun and the Aran beret, the *bobailín*, on their heads, they moved in lithe magic over the alley, sliding like oil in the hide shoes. The word 'pampootie'[44] does not exist in the Irish language.

Once, they brought me fishing along the stark Atlantic side of Aran. Here Europe presents its battered edge to the Western Ocean, in a gaunt height of rock and weather.

WRONG GUESS

We passed a rectangular pool and I wondered at the thoughtfulness of the tourist people in leaving such a perfect swimming place for the visitor.

It was very warm and, like Winston Churchill, I'm not particular about togs when I fancy a swim.

Off with my clothes, and I'm poised over the edge of the pool, to show the fruit of early training in the Royal Canal, and at the Sloblands.

This is Poll na bPeist,[45] the hole of the worms, so called from worm-like markings on the rock.

It is fed by an underground tunnel, and the last person that dived into it never came out. The water comes in with terrific force and comes out just as quick, so that Brendan Behan would have been the leavings of atomic battering before he even emerged from the ocean side of the pool.

'Only for you, Stíofán, and I was gone for the ha'porth of milk in the milk can,' said I, or words to that effect, in Irish, reaching for my clothes.

'I know,' said Stíofán, 'and you promised me the words to "*O Ro, Thaighg, a gradh*".[46] If you had dived in there, I'd not have got them.'

MISUNDERSTOOD

I went back to the pub in Kilronan, and damn glad to be safe in it again. It was full of visitors. I like visitors. I meet other ones. That's not saying I don't like myself, too.

I was cured of the conventional attitude towards trippers at an early age when a teacher in North William Street was giving the pay one Monday morning about the carrying-on of trippers out in Killiney.

A bit of an old wiseacre hastened to agree with her about the vulgarity of the masses.

'Sure, that's nothing, Miss,' said I, 'you'd want to see them out in Dollymount.' Which is the Riviera of Russell Street, North Circular Road.

She looked at me impatiently.

'But Dollymount – that's *for trippers!*' she said.

One man with a higher executive's head on him (wherever he got it) gave measured judgement on life and letters in the capital.

The Irish Press, 30 December 1953

II

BELFAST WAS FIRST RIGHT ...
AND THEN JUST STRAIGHT AHEAD

remembers Brendan Behan.

If you went up the North Circular as far as the Big Tree, Belfast was on the first turn to the right. Straight ahead. I knew that when I was seven. The country lay out there. I visited it with my grandmother, one day she and Lizzie MacKay went out for a breath of air.

After dinner, on a Sunday, she put on her black coat and hat, and a veil with little black diamonds on it, and off we went. We went up the canal from Jones Road Bridge, to Binns Bridge (and that was nearly in the country already) and into Leeches.

There we sat, having a couple, till it was shutting and time to get the tram into the real country.

Lizzie and she got a dozen of large bottles and the loan of a basket, and we got a currant pan and a half-pound of cooked ham in the shop next door, and got on the tram for Whitehall.

END OF THE LINE

'I see yous are well-healed,' says the conductor, looking at the basket.

'Well, the country, sir,' says my grandmother. 'You'd eat the side wall of a house after it.'

'You're going all the way?'

'To the very end,' says Lizzie MacKay. 'All the way to Whitehall.'

'And I don't suppose that'll be the country much longer,' says the conductor. 'There's houses everywhere now. Out beyond Phibsboro church.

'They're nearly out to where Lord Norbury disappeared on the way home, and the coachman only felt the coach getting lighter on the journey and when he got to the house your man was disappeared and the devil was after claiming him, and good enough for him after the abuse he gave poor Emmet in the dock.'

My grandmother and Lizzie MacKay bowed their heads and muttered 'Amen.'

TRESPASSER

'They're nearly out to there,' said the conductor, 'and it won't be long before they're at Whitehall,' giving the bell a bang to hurry the driver up, before the builders got there.

We found a fine ditch, only a few yards from the end of the tram tracks, and nice and handy for getting home, and there was grass, and trees over it.

I ran into a field and across a big park till an old fellow, with a straw-bainer hat, started chasing me, and cursing, till I got out again, and ran to my granny and Lizzie.

They sat up in their ditch and took the bottles from their mouths and looked over at the old fellow who was shouting with his red face, from the gate.

'Go 'long, you low scruff,' said Lizzie, 'myself and this lady here, with the right of being buried in Kilbarrack, and was here before you were let out of wherever you were let out of. Talking about your park. Anyone'd think you owned it.'

The old fellow danced a bit more with temper and his red face, but they waved their bottles at him and he went off.

SHY AND TIMID

'Me poor child, you'd want something after that old fellow frightening the little heart out of you. Open another bottle, Lizzie, and give him a bit of ham, to take with it.'

We sat on in the setting sun, eating and drinking, and my grandmother and Lizzie MacKay making remarks about the way the fellows going past were either walking in front of, or behind their girls.

'Look at that fellow, Lizzie, swinging his stick; a mile behind the poor one.'

The young man looked over at them, and hurried on, to get out of earshot.

'You'd think the poor girl had a contagious disease.'

The man and the girl took one fearful look over at them and fled up the road.

When we got home that night from the country, the people asked us where we'd spent the day, and my grandmother said we'd been on the Belfast road.

HEROES' LAND

All I had ever heard of Ireland and her green fields, and rakes up in rafters and women of three cows, a *grá*, was for me situated in north County Dublin and the Belfast road was the golden way to Samarkand.

I learned early on that it was a bit up the road from us that Setanta beat a hurling ball into a dog's mouth and became Cúchulainn.

Out on that road lay Gormanston where my father was locked up and where he saw me for the first time when I was six months old. Seán T. was in with him and I thought that made Seán T. a fairly important man too.

My cousin, who learned more about cattle on the North Circular Road than many a one reared in the Argentine, had charge of a big house for some time out Swords direction.

It was a big mansion with an estate and hay barns and cow barns and statues in the gardens. There were about fifty rooms in the main building and a lodge, as Chuckles Malone said, the size of the Bridewell.

YOUTHS' HIGHWAY

People round our way couldn't see anyone lost for a bit of company in a big place like that.

I was brought out for the air and was followed by my father's aunt who wasn't too well. Some of the neighbours brought out a couple more invalids and our team, NCR AFC were in the final of the Conway Cup that year, and they thought it would be a good place to get a bit of training, and with the sick people looking out the windows at the footballers and screaming advice and abuse to young Coughlin to be not so mangy with the ball, and telling Johnny Foy that he got his head for something else besides keeping his hat on, my cousin said the place was a cross between the Pigeon House Sanatorium and the Fifteen Acres. There was the best of gas and the life of Reilly to be had by one and all.

And in the summer nights I'd lie in bed and over the noise of the fellows and girls down in the big hall dancing round the coats of armour to the gramophone playing 'On Mother Kelly's Doorstep' I'd hear the cars going past and sometimes sneak to the window and follow the noise and the red tail light till it grew faint and dim going on to the end of the Belfast road through green fields and dusky magic.

The Irish Press, 8 February 1954

12
WE CROSSED THE BORDER

After 1916 the family found refuge in Belfast ... decent Orange folk warned us of police inquiries ... the memories are pleasant ... but there was something very close to a shindy[47] that other day...

My mother had two husbands, not at the one time, of course. She married the first a little time before Easter Week 1916, and spent her honeymoon carrying messages, for her husband, brother, brothers-in-law, and generally running round with my aunts and her sisters in misfortune, shifting one another's dumps and minding one another's babies for a long time afterwards.

The peaceful Quaker man that founded the business would be very surprised that, with the Post Office, where Uncle Joe was, and Marrowbone Lane, where Uncle Mick was, his biscuit factory was to my childhood a blazing defiance of Mausers, uncles and my step-brothers' father, against—

> '... *odds of ten to one,*
> *And through our lines they could not pass,*
> *For all their heavy guns,*
> *They'd cannon and they'd cavalry,*
> *Machine-guns in galore,*
> *Still, it wasn't our fault that e'er a one,*
> *Got back to England's shore ...*'

Give over, before I hit a polisman!

Belfast figures as the refuge in cosy remoteness, and peace, after the battle had ended and the hunt left behind, because it was there my mother had her first home, and her husband had his first job, after the Rising.

It was there that she began her married life and, after the guns and the bombs, and the executions, began a stock of more homely domestic anecdotes, like the time she tried him with a curried stew, and he ran to the tap after tasting it, wondering why she was trying to poison him.

YOUNGEST IRB MAN

They weren't the only refugees either. A former Captain of the Guard at Leinster House is remembered with indignation, for coming in amongst the twenty or thirty people assembled in close formation from the Sunday night *scolriocht*,[48] and remarking through the haze of Irish tobacco smoke that the place was like an oven.

And after Rory was christened 'Roger Casement' in the church, my uncle Peadar, a sort of walking battery of Fenianism, held him in his arms on Cave Hill and, with the baby's father acting as sponsor, swore him into the IRB.[49]

The little house in the Mount became a clearing house for the Dublin crowd to and from Liverpool and Glasgow.

And to this day, my mother remembers the kindness of the neighbours. Their great interest was the baby Fenian though, being respectable and polite, they never referred to his politics, nor to the comings and goings and up-country accents of the young men visiting the house, at all hours of the day and night.

ORANGE WARNING

There might be a satisfied remark about the larruping[50] the Germans were getting on the Somme, but when the peelers came nosing around the quarter, it was the widow of a Worshipful Master[51] came up with the wind of the word.

'There was polis round here this morning, ma'am, enquiring about some people might be hiding from the military in Dublin. Rebels, if you please. Round here.'

'Sure as we all said it's an insult to a loyal street to think the like. Rebels, Sinn Féiners, hiding round here. And how's our wee man the day? Did you do what I said about the—'

PATRIOTIC WATCH

My first visit to the North, or for the matter of that to any part of Ireland outside Dublin, took me to Newry, with a trainload of soccer players, accordionists, corkscrew operatives, the entire production under the masterly direction of my Uncle Richie.

He was a non-military uncle, and, indeed, had been accused of only remembering the significance of Easter Monday, 1916, by reference to the gold watch, his possession of which dated from that time.

Another souvenir of the six days was a pair of fur-lined boots, which were worn out by my time, though they still hung in their old age under the picture of Robert Emmet and 'Greetings for Christmas and a Prosperous 1912' card from 'Dan Lehan, the Patriotic Sand Dancer and Irish National Coon. Performed Soft Shoe before the Crowned Heads of Europe, also Annual Concerts, Mountjoy and the Deaf and Dumb Institution.'[52]

When Uncle Richie had a sup up, he'd fondle the old fur boots and looking from Robert Emmet to the Irish National Coon, remark, 'By God, there was men in Ireland them times.'

STROKE PREPARED

When the other Jacobs and GPO uncles were hard at it, remembering the sudden death of a comrade, Uncle Richie shook his head with the rest.

'When you think of what they did to poor Brian. Poor pig. Cut the two legs of the man. Them Danes.'

Gritting his teeth and controlling his temper, looking round the room, and a good job for the Danes there weren't any of them knocking around our way.

He wasn't really my uncle at all, but a far-out relative of another branch of our family, or one of our family from around north and east Dublin.

Mostly he didn't bother much about the cause or old Ireland, or any of that carrying-on.

When he was bent in thought, it wasn't the declining Gaeltacht was knotting his brow, nor the lost green field, but we respected it just the same.

He sat in a corner and looked the same way as our uncles remembering the time they met John Devoy,[53] or killed one another during the Civil War. But we knew that this deep cogitation meant that Uncle Richie was thinking up a stroke.

BIG BALL GAME

His final stroke brought me to Newry. He hired an excursion train for a deposit of thirty shillings, and our team went up to play a team representing the Ancient Order of Hibernians.[54]

In consideration of his putting up a set of solid silver medals for the contest, Uncle Richie's nominee was allowed to take half the gate, and he collected the ticket money from the people, on the understanding that he would bring it to the GNR on Monday morning and receive a small percentage for his trouble.

The whole street saved up for a while and the train was packed, with old ones, young ones, singers and dancers, on the way up.

Uncle Richie got the team in a corner and swore that by this and that they had to win those medals, and seemed very serious about it.

Someone asked who were the Ancient Order of Hibernians and was told they were a crowd that carried pikes, and someone else said they'd lodge an objection, that you wouldn't see the like of that with Merville and Bendigo in the Fifteen Acres.[55]

The Ancient Order of Hibernians had no pikes but, before half-time, they could have done with them. They were all over our crowd in everything except dirt.

The double tap, the hack, the trip, the one-two and every manner of lowness, but to no avail. The AOH won 2–nil.

Uncle Richie had to hand over that set of medals, and though he wasn't a mean man, you could see he felt it.

He muttered to Chuckles Malone, to get us down to the station quickly, and lock the doors. He wouldn't be long after us.

UNCLE MAKES IT

Neither he wasn't, as the man said. But came running down towards us with half the town after him, and they shouting and cursing about the medals.

Someone said they weren't bad medals considering they were made out of the tops of milk bottles.

The crowd were in full cry after Uncle Richie, but gaining little.

We shouted encouragement to him. 'Come on, Uncle Richie, come on, ye boy, ye,' till at last he fell against the gate of the Residency, and we hauled him in the nick of time, from the berserk natives.

Carrie Swaine, a Plymouth Sister from Ballybough, called out in triumph, 'Go 'long, yous Orange –s,' which for some reason, drove the Ancient Order of Hibernians AFC to a very dervish dance of fury.

Past Clontarf Station Carrie smelt the Sloblands and, from an excess of emotion, shouting 'Law-villy Dublin,' put her head through the window without taking the trouble to lower it and nearly decapitated herself.

Uncle Richie gave a big night in the club and was seen off by the whole street to the Liverpool boat.

He expressed no bitterness against the town of Newry or its inhabitants except to remark that the medals were waterproof.

I don't know what he told the railway company.

The Irish Press, 20 March 1954

13
TORONTO SPINSTER FROWNED

Brendan Behan remembers a visit to fair Donaghadee.

Myself and Winston Churchill were once upon a time in the same organisation: he, as an Elder Brother of Trinity House[56] and I as a painter for the Irish Lights. His position is more decorative than functional. I painted striped lighthouses, banded lighthouses and spotted lighthouses.

On the way down from Laganbank Road to Donaghadee, a schoolboy sitting beside me in the bus pointed out Stormont, on one side of the road, and remarked that Purdysburn Mental Hospital was further down on the opposite side.

I laughed, in my rich southern brogue, low but musical, and an acid-faced lady in the seat in front called the schoolboy to order. When the seat beside her was vacant, she called your man over to it and glaring at me, breathed fiercely in his ear, and he answered, 'Yes, auntie,' and 'No, auntie,' and sat staring straight in front of him for the rest of the journey.

It appeared that she didn't like 'southerners'. I had not encountered this kind of carry-on before, and it made me feel important and tragic, like the dust-jacket of a Peadar O'Donnell novel in the big block letter of the thirties.

THE LOST EAST

By the same token, I wondered how Ireland lost one of the cardinal points of the compass. We have songs, sneers, jeers and cheers for the Men of the West, the gallant South, the North Began, and the North Held On, God Bless the Northern Land, and all to that effect, but damn the ha'porth about the East, except where Micheál Og Ó Longáin gives us old Orientals, a leg-up in a song about Ninety-Eight:

> *'Mo ghreidhn iad, na Laighnigh,*
> *A d'adhain an teine beo*[57] *…'*

Maire MacEntee has a blood-rising translation of it, but even at that it's in praise of the province – not a mention of our geographical direction, nor a line for the Men of the East.

When someone calls me a 'southerner', I feel like Old Black Joe.[58]

'What part of the South do you come from, Rastus?'

'Ah sho' don' know, massah.[59] It was dark when ah left.'

LIGHT REMINDER

When I heard her speak to the boy at the end of the journey, I was surprised to notice that she had an American accent.

In the bar that night, I remarked on this to the fishermen I was with.

'Och, aye,' says Old Andy, 'that'll be Miss Mackenzie. She's from Toronto, and she's in some Ulster Society over there to save us from yous.

'She can't bear the sight of a southern man and it's very dacent of her, seein' as she was never in the country before in her life.'

And to cheer me up: 'Of course yous have a crowd in America, too, that goes round blackguarding us?'

In the morning, I had to rewrite the notice on the lighthouse: 'Permission to view this lighthouse must be obtained from the Secretary, Commissioners for Irish Lights, Westmoreland Street, Dublin.'

Only a portion of the old sign showed through the fresh paint, but enough to let Miss Mackenzie know that an Ulster lighthouse had some connection with the rebels.

PATRIOTIC LEGEND

She was amongst a crowd of holiday-makers out for an after-breakfast stroll, and breathed fury as I rewrote the sign on a surface previously coated with raw linseed oil: 'Permission to view this lighthouse must be obtained from Éamon de Valera, Leinster House, Dublin.'

I thought Miss Mackenzie would explode. She fulminated in the crowd, but the people that go to Donaghadee in the summer have a deal to bother them, fishing young Sammy out of the harbour and trying to save Wee Bella from death by ice-creamitis. They gazed with mild interest after her, as she dashed up to the Harbour Office.

By the time she got back, of course, I had the board rubbed dry, and the official legend rewritten. She put her hand to her head and searched, distracted, for the offending words.

The harbour official looked at her, and muttered something about the heat and ould ones going round in their bare head. With innocent diligence I went on with my work.

DIPLOMATIC SONG

The Fosters and the Nelsons were the names of the fishermen. A quiet, decent crowd, and names of magic to the Belfast children, generations of them, who know that the sea is blue and misty soft, where it's nearing the smudge of Scotland, and the Lough a drowsy blue, all the way to Bangor. That it's always summer at Donaghadee.

On the eleventh of July, I was tactfully requested to refrain from servile toil the following day. I put up with this check on my industry as best I could, and so well did my morale stand up to the enforced idleness that I was in singing order amongst a pubful of Orangemen that night.

I was let out of school.

When called upon for a song, I chose *sli ordha na measardhacta*,[60] the golden way of moderation, and sang 'The Dear Little Town in the Old County Down'[61] which, though it's me says it that shouldn't, went down like a dinner.

Later, in the evening, I was one third of the ghetto in the hotel bar. Myself and our French chef stood chatting with Anna the barmaid.

Myself and our French chef weren't usually that gone on each other.

CONSCRIPTED

Anna was nineteen and I was twenty-five and our French chef went mad when I pointed out he was born the same year as I. He said I was born at the beginning of twenty-three and he at the end of it. Three more days and he'd have been born in twenty-four.

I have never felt very favourable towards any age older than thirteen and a half, when, with a bit of remission for my behaviour, I was let out of school.

Neither could I be responsible for our French chef being born on the twenty-ninth of December. The arrangements were none of mine.

Our French chef and I were being conscripted for Mass in morning. I thought it might be a Latin defiance of the Nordic doings of the day before but it turned out to be some private devotion of Anna's. I wasn't so favourable to it when I'd to get out of bed in the morning.

JULY PUNISHMENT

On the way home from the little back-street chapel, I virtuously sniffed the morning air, the salt and the sun, and Anna stepped it out between us.

There were some that had not gone to bed at all. A few devoted revellers had made a night of it. They stood wearily on the corner, and old Andy asked me what time it was. I told him.

'Thanks be, it's all over for another wee while,' said he. 'I'm beat out.'

'And there's another feast tomorrow,' said I to him.

'Le Quatorze Juillet,' said our French chef.

'Is it a Fenian do?' asked old Andy.

'It's the greatest republican feast of the year,' said I, 'the Fourteenth of July, and you better come down the hotel with me and our French chef.'

'It'll kill me,' pleaded old Andy.

'Well, we celebrated yours,' said I.

'Deed yous did,' said old Andy, resignedly, 'and fair is fair.'

The Irish Press, 27 March 1954

14
TURNIP BOAT

*Diplomacy – that's what did it – we're dab hands at diplomacy, at
sailing a ship, at making the skipper, poor man, feel at home ...*

For some reason, a friend of mine wanted to ship turnips from a Six-County
port. He wanted to ship anything from a Six-County port because he
wanted to sail into a British port with a British customs manifest, or whatever Mac Lir[62] would call it.

Our little ship was about the size of the Terenure bus. It was eighty-six
tons in weight or capacity, gross or net. Again I leave it to the experts.

We sailed with a mixed crew. Some had been on a boat before, and more
hadn't. I was betwixt and between. I did many's the trip on the *Larssen* and
the *Royal Iris*,[63] as a bona fide traveller, but had never actually rounded the
Horn, or stifled me main brace or anything of that nature.

The real sailors were the skipper, the mate and the fireman. The rest of
the company were merchant adventurers along with the owner, and I was a
merchant adventurer's labourer, so to speak.

The real sailors slept forrard, and we had accommodation aft, where, as
Sammy Nixon said, villainy could be plotted in peace.

GETTING READY

Sammy came aboard wearing rather tasty pin-striped kid gloves, and a Windsor knot of some dimensions. His hat he wore on the Kildare side, even in bed, for he had not a rib between him and heaven.

He had come straight from a pub in Belgravia, flown to Collinstown.[64] And after a stop for refreshments in Grafton Street, or thereabouts, had come down by taxi to the North Wall, where he had her tied up.

Sammy had never been on a boat of any description before and till he had heard from Eddie thought they'd been done away with, like the trams.

'Muscles' Morgan, his china,[65] was due on a later plane, and what old Muscles would say, when he saw this lot, Sammy did not know.

Muscles, when he arrived, dressed in the same uniform as Sammy, all eight stone of him, said 'Corsalawk e'n it? Lookah er namber one, cock,' which he repeated many times during our subsequent voyages, and Eddie, Sammy, Muscles and I, retired aft to drink rum, like sailors.

The sailors we left forrard, brewing their tea, darning their socks, winding the dock watch and, with infinite skill putting little ships into bottles. There would be no shortage of bottles. Before we thought of calling the skipper, we had a couple of empties ready for the little ships to be put into them already.

MEET THE SKIPPER

The skipper was an Anglo-Irishman, connected with a wealthy family of brewers. His mother was a Frenchwoman, when she was in it, and I like the French.

He had been educated in English public schools and on the continent, spoke French, Spanish, Italian, German and Flemish, was a technician with the BBC and a first-class sailor.

He fell to our level, through drinking, gambling and sniffing. Just common sniffing. I am not unacquainted with the national catarrh, but he was a most hangdog-looking man, with a sad puppy's face pleading for friendship or at least tolerance, and his shape and make was that of a Charles Atlas in reverse. And the whole world of ineffectual weakness was in that sniff.

Eddie picked him up in the West End, and brought him over with the boat.

SENTIMENTAL JOURNEY

He sniffed nervously to me that he had never been in Ireland before, though his family had a house in Mount Street, and if I possibly thought, if it would not, sniff, be too much, sniff, trouble could I, would I not, presuming on our short acquaintance, tell him how to get there? His father was born in it.

Better than that, I would bring him to it. And did, after a couple of stops at other points of interest on the way. And he cried and sniffed, and when I stood him with his back to Holles Street hospital, he looked up along Fitzwilliam Square and Fitzwilliam Place, lit by the sun on the mountains behind, the long range of golden Georgian brick, and wept again, and said there was not the like of it anywhere else.

OFF TO FRANCE

So I got Eddie to call him down, and he sat in a corner and apologetically lowered an imperial pint of rum and hot orange. I think he took a subsidiary couple of rossiners, to make up for the orange.

For if it's a thing I go in for in a human being, it's weakness. I'm a divil for it. I thought of the Katherine Mansfield short story, where the 'Daughters of the Late Colonel' are afraid of the old chap, two days after his funeral, leaping out of the linen press, on top of them, and one of them cries: 'Let's be weak, oh, please, let us be weak.'

He even sniffed an apology to Muscles and Sammy for their seasickness the first two days out, while they lay in their death agonies, and shuddered from the cup of rum he would minister unto them.

He lowered it himself and weakly took himself up on deck to look for the Saltees.[66] We had a reason for going to France, before the Six-Counties manifest would be of use to us.

PEACE POPPIES

When we came back for our turnips, the final arrangements had to made with what I will call the Turnip Board, and we marched up the main street of a northern port, on Armistice Day.

Eddie went into a shop and came out with two big poppies. I shook my head.

'No bottle,' said I, in his native language.

'None of this old malarkey,' said he, 'there's a reason why I must get a cargo of turnips off these geezers.'

'That's not what I mean. They won't fancy poppies.'

'This is "Northern Ireland", 'n't it? They're for the King and Queen and all that lark 'n't they?'

'Not here. This is "Southern Northern" Ireland.'

Eddie sighed, 'Only a nicker wasted,' and dropped his two ten-shilling poppies in the gutter. 'I get on – mostly RCs[67] here, eh?'

UNITED COLOURS

We met the chairman of the Turnip Board in a hotel and Eddie shook him by the hand.

'I think it's an 'orrible shame the way, the way these Protestants treat you 'ere, Mr MacConvery.'

Mr MacConvery's plum face turned blue, and his stomach went in and out at a hell of a lick.

'The cheek of you,' he croaked, 'my old friend' – he indicated a little man like an undertaker's clerk sitting nearby.

'Mr Macanaspie, respected member of the Presbyterian community, vice chairman of the Turnip Board, we have it one year, they the next, chair and vice, turn and turn about ... I ...'

His indignation collapsed for the want of breath, and I got a chance to explain that it was a joke, and it gave Eddie a chance to tell how he'd taken a prize in the Band of Hope,[68] himself.

And in the heel of the hunt we got the turnips and some months later, in the bar of the Latin Quarter us old sea dogs hove into, Eddie remarked that Partition was strategically useful.

The Irish Press, 3 April 1954

15
TOO OLD TO SOLVE THE POSITION

in the last half-province once you're over the thirties' waterline,
says Brendan Behan.

In his three years at sea, Billy John voyaged but ten yards, any direction, in Belfast Lough, aboard the prison ship *Al Rawdah*.[69] 'Well, at least,' said I, 'you'd have found your sea legs. You'd never get seasick.'

'Crossing to Scotland, not long after we came out, I thought I'd die from seasickness. It's different with the engines running,' he said.

In the centre of the crowd a boy in his teens was singing, lemonade clutched firmly in his hand and his eyes raised to the ceiling.

We ordered a couple more pints, in orderly whispers, and the song went on:

> *'May you and I be faithful, to her underlying cause,*
> *Till we have reaped the seeds the boys have sown,*
> *Then we'll settle down in Ireland, only ruled by Irish laws,*
> *In the cottage down the old Dungannon Road ...'*

TOO OLD AT THIRTY-FIVE
As serious as first love, he lowered his eyes to the tumbler, while they clapped.

'Good man yourself,' said Billy John, and muttered to me: 'The cell's already whitewashed for him. God be with the youth of us. You're too old at thirty-five for freeing Ireland, round these parts.'

He twisted his mouth in a tuneless parody of 'The West's Awake':[70]

> '... *But, oh, boys, oh, we must not crack,*
> *We must keep Cathleen on our back ...*'

But the young fellow was off again, on a relentless tramp:

> '... *An Ulsterman I'm proud to be,*
> *From Antrim's glens I come,*
> *And though I live far from the sea,*
> *I have followed flag and drum,*
> *I have seen the tramp of marching men,*
> *I've watched them fight and die,*
> *For youth was strong, in the battle throng that followed Henry Joy ...*'

Other youngsters watched him, stern-eyed and grim-lipped. I noticed that most of them were drinking minerals.

'They're drunk enough, on the memory of the dead,' said Billy John, 'and the dawning of the day. They're looking forward to it.'

'I know. You've only to look at them.'

WHERE PUBS COMPETE

I was never reared to believe that Orange and Green should compete for the hypothetical favours of the British Raj by running after 'fair-minded English opinion', or arguments of the 'you can carry the tricolour through Piccadilly' variety.

In Belfast, it's sad to see the pubs in different areas competing in the ghosts of liberal and conservative politicians.

There is the Beaconsfield Bar, and the Salisbury, and on the Falls a pub named for Gladstone.

ROMAN BOGEYMAN

Right down in Sandy Row are the Boyne Tavern and the Boyne Bridge. And, of course, the Bluebell, run by a cheerful hard deal of an Orangeman that, by his dark hair, big shoulders, springy gait and lively smile, you'd take for a Kerryman, from round Glencar direction.

He gave me his card, which read in ecclesiastical type: 'Good friends and good wine are the solace of life' and having enquired whether I minded a story, 'again your side', didn't wait to see whether I did or not, but went on with it. It was short and sweet, like Moll's dance.

An Orange lady (if I say Orangewoman, it sounds like someone from Moore Street)[71] was calling her child out of the parlour, before he'd break something. She shouts from the kitchen: 'Wully, come out of thon. Wully, I tell ye come out of thon. Come out when I bid you. Wully.' Pause. 'There's wee popes in thon.'

WRESTLERS AND LIONS

They told stories of Buck Alec, in his wrestling days when, like other sporting notabilities, he possessed a pair of young black lions, which he kept in the back yard.

Battling Siki and all had them, and you might as well be out of the world as out of the fashion.

The Buck's menagerie was quite famous, so that a juvenile delinquent, returning from business in the small hours of the morning, when stopped by the polis, who wished to enquire into the contents of his sack, replied hopefully: 'It's only dead cats for Buck Alec's layins.'

OFF TO PORTRUSH

I was going to Portrush on the evening train, and my friends in Sandy Row had as much idea of the way to get there as my father would have of getting to Newtownborris.

That didn't prevent wild argument, and struggles for the telephone.

'Hey, miss, do you want the mon to miss his train?' and 'Hey, boy, give me thon a minute.'

'Ah bet ye a sauce tae a wing, it's from the LMS[72] you go to Portrush.'

He won his wing. It was the LMS and the taximan only made it, and I left behind me a life of George Douglas, author of *The House with the Green Shutters*, I'd bought for sixpence earlier in the day.

Still, I got the train, and had for company a railway engineer who talked Irish with me about Joe Tomelty's[73] new book, till we reached Coleraine, where I left him to get on a bus for the last stage of the journey to Portrush.

ONE PEOPLE

There was a well-fortified crowd of farmers bearing in their midst a neighbour returned from Australia after many years.

He sat, a big North Antrim man from the very top of Ireland, twisting his gloves in an ecstasy of embarrassed delight.

They talked about crops and bastes,[74] and the big night prepared at home for the returning exile.

There was lashings and lavings left in, though the minister had to visit someone that was sick, and could not call till the morning.

I couldn't have joined in their talk of the land, but I doubt if they'd have long been strangers on Aran.

And when I saw their rocks and fields in the damp spring light, I knew they fitted them, moulded in the history John Hewitt[75] remembers for them all:

> '*So, I because of all the buried men,*
> *in Ulster clay, because of rock and glen*
> *and mist and cloud and quality of air,*
> *as native in my thought, as any here ...*'

The Irish Press, 21 April 1954

16
BIGOTRY

Here's a thought should you be tempted by its sinful lunacy.

Books, plays and pictures, on the radio and television, in regional characteristics, are handed out like snuff at a wake. 'Hot southern blood', 'stubborn
Saxons', 'methodical Germans' and 'gay Frenchmen' write about one another
and, though the business may decline in the face of cheaper air travel, and
increased knowledge of one another's little vagaries, in Ireland it still thrives.

North and South, among Protestant or Catholic, from the cottage in
Connemara to the literary hooley in Pembrokery or Baggotland,[76] the cheeky
Corkman and the reliable northerner compliment each other on their quali-
ties (each one taking the one he fancies most), and we are all stout believers
in the theory that people vary from county to county, like the colours of
the atlas.

INVASION
A football team travelled from a village in south Monaghan to a point ten
miles distant, where the Gaelic football championship of the area was to
be decided.

One of the non-playing supporters, a vociferous and hot-eyed youth of
some sixty summers which, counting the winters, would leave him a sen-
sible age, was a small and hardy Celt of withered countenance, attired in the

high fashion of the place; a blue suit with double-breasted waistcoat, and an indignant mouth that could be better described by Carleton,[77] if it was a thing that he was alive and in the humour.

He took charge of the second line of defence on the sideline and, to get them all ready for the fray, he led the procession through the enemy town, till they came to a public house, where they would remain till the match began.

Having glared at the assembled locals, he called angrily for fifteen pints and ten bottles of stout, and a bottle of minerals for a young lad standing beside him, who was not, as yet, promoted to porter.

HATE US

'Will you come on there with the few drinks?' shouts Danny Mann and, as the barman pulls and pours away, his angry eyes glare defiance at the counter.

'The match'll be starting in an hour, and we with nothing in us after the journey. Scurse you,' he mutters in the direction of the barman, and looking up at the face of the boy beside him, as much as to tell him that it's no good hiding the hard facts of life from him any longer, with a thumb indicating the barman and the locals, admits with ferocious sadness and savage shakings of his head: 'They hate us, because we're Irish.'

Mr St John Ervine,[78] in his life of the Dublin-Italian Carson, hates us because we're Éireanns. Every damned one of us: Oscar Wilde, the Bird Flanagan, Father O'Flynn, Bishop Berkeley, the Colleen Bawn, Mat the Thrasher, Burke and Hare, the Rakes of Mallow, the Boys of Wexford and Bernard Shaw, who gets off with a caution for having been born in Dolphin's Barn.

My uncle worked under Mr Ervine, in the Abbey, and said he was as decent a man as ever stood up in trousers, and very much more popular with his staff than other inhabitants of the National Valhalla.

Joyce,[79] who wrote more, couldn't do with less than All-Ireland, and everyone in it: Bloom, the Dublin Jew; Crofton, 'the decent Orangeman'; Skin-the-Goat, the retired Fenian; the Quaker National Librarian, and the founder of the GAA. He got down to the business of Belfast half-joking, all in earnest, in *Finnegans Wake*:

> 'And, when you'll hear the gould hammer of my heart, my floxy lass, bing-banging against the ribs of your resistance, and the tenderbolts of my rivets working to your distraction ye'll be shivering w' all your dinful sobs …'

See now, what I brought you.

And in a letter to Forrest Reid,[80] he seems to take it for granted that such Éireann carry-on as a performance of *Riders to the Sea*, in Zurich, will be of interest to the general public of Belfast, for he asks Reid to pass on to any newspaper in Belfast the enclosed: 'A photograph of my wife, who took a part in Synge's play. As she was born within sight of Aran, I think Synge's lines were spoken with the genuine brogue.'[81] (Taken from a letter published in the Joyce edition of *Envoy*, April 1951.)

REID'S VIEW

And Reid himself never learned to distinguish the Éireanns from the Ulstermen.

Not that he wore his youth out thinking about it, but enjoyed Cambridge, and was greatly interested by Ronald Firbank, the delicious novelist, as he sat ... 'on the hearthrug and smoked drugged cigarettes ... To me, it was a strange evening, and I shouldn't have been surprised if Dorian Gray had dropped in ...'

That's a long way from the Lisburn Road, but the visit of the Abbey Players to Cambridge awakened in me a kind of nostalgia for my own country. While I was living in Ireland, I had taken Ireland very much for granted. Now, in an alien land, Yeats's Cathleen Ni Houlihan aroused in me an eager spirit of patriotism, the very existence of which I had not suspected.[82]

'It was strange, because it was not in the least mixed up with politics. It was more like a family feeling – the feeling one has for brothers and sisters which lies dormant and unrealised until an outsider perhaps says something in disparagement of them.'

BROAD ASPECT

All his life he loved the city and its inhabitants, without hating the rest of us.

'There was the beauty of an autumn afternoon in the Ormeau Park at dusk, when, with the dead leaves thick on the deserted path, I had sat listening to a German band, playing somewhere out of sight, through the railings. Through the twilight, with its yellow twinkling of street lamps ...'

In Antrim 'had I not, even in this land, blessed by St Patrick, caught a glimpse of that ill-mannered boy who, mocking the great Demeter while she drunk, was straightaway transformed into a lizard?'

Forrest Reid was born in a big house at Mount Charles and died at Warrenpoint, which is nearer Tara than Banna Strand is, in 1947.

His memorial was unveiled by his friend E.M. Forster, who was also a friend of the late Muiris O Súileabháin, author of *Fiche Blian ag Fás*.

When tempted to the sinful lunacy of prejudice, we should remember Reid against all sorts and sizes of bigotry.

One of Auden's[83] verses to E.M. Forster[84] says:

'As we run down the slope with hate, with gladness,
You trip us up, like an unnoticed stone, and just as we are closeted with madness,
You interrupt us like the telephone …'

That's what Forrest Reid could do for the Dungiven Committee – and maybe for more of us than that.

The Irish Press, 1 May 1954

17
SPRING

It brings back memories of Dublin, London and Paris
in the hopeful days of May.

How am I? If I was any better I couldn't stick it. Farewell to foul winter, spring has come at last, nothing I have gained, but my true love I have lost. As regards that part of the transaction, it's a question of who was losing who. As Joyce says, one story is good till you hear another. But honest, that bit of sun the last few weeks was the making of us.

Seán Ó Faoláin[85] tells us that Señor de Madariaga[86] tells him that we are a Mediterranean people gone astray and lost up here in the damp cold of the far north. As they say on the waterfront of this newspaper, *Quién Sabe?*[87]

Brian Merriman[88] had it weighed up, in that front bit of *The Midnight Court* we learned at school:

> *Ba ghná mé ag siúl, le chiumais na habhann,*
> *ar mháinseach úr is an drúcht go trom …*

Consider my nationality (I am one of the compulsory Irish),[89] I am quite fluent and almost comprehensible in the second official language.

GLADDEN THE HEART

(Proceeds to demonstrate this modest accomplishment):

> 'Twas my joy to walk the morning stream,
> The meadows fresh with the dew's wet gleam,
> Beside the woods, in the high hill's shade ...[90]

In this city, in the old Georgian heart of the Northside, now recondi-
tioned flats for the use of the people whose ancestors built it, and in the
new breathing spaces of the Dublin people – Cabra, Crumlin, Kimmage
and Ballyfermot – are young men of twenty-one and going on twenty-two,
enjoying the May weather, and rejoicing, if that's what they call it, in the
Christian name of 'Lauri'.

If they want to know, it's my mother's fault. Their mothers weren't strong-
minded enough for her, the year of the Congress, when her edict went up
and down the lower depth of the North Circular Road, that all male children,
1932 model, were to receive in baptism the name of the Papal Legate.[91]

A decade or so earlier, in spite of some people she didn't like by the
name of Murphy, and local publican by the name of Byrne, they got 'Larkin'
for a moniker.

Both lots hide under the diminutive of 'Larry' like any of the thousands
named after the great O'Toole,[92] but they'll be found out when they go
looking for their voting papers.

BOULD AS TAY

If they want to make anything of it, they'll have to wait till she gets back
from London, where she and my father have been assisting at the inaugu-
ration of my new niece.

This niece's mother was born the year of the Congress, is married a
few years now and lives happily with her Scots husband and a previous
daughter in Kensington, near, according to her direction or his, the Oval or
the gasworks.

It makes me feel as bould as tay to think that I took part in the election weeks before she was born, and sang and danced at the bonfire in the
middle of NCR[93] the night of the final result.

All over our side the whole night through, the flames leapt high, and the
tricolour topping the lamppost, while we rent the winter air and the ears of

the very respectable class of people lying sleepless, with songs and cheers for the Republic.

SUPER BONFIRE

The fire brigade called to the bonfire in Gloucester Diamond, under the impression that the Custom House had moved up town and gone ablaze again.

And our own bonfire, construction supervised by 'Chuckles' Malone, head buck-cat round our corner, occupied, like the Bastille in the Place de la Nation, the space at the junction of Emmet Street, Fitzgibbon Street, Russell Street and the North Circular Road, and could be seen from Summerhill to the Park Gate.

My mother was welcomed in London by a genial landlord, to whose hostelry she had been brought before, by her connections, a redoubtable clique, drawn from the best society of Yorkshire, Glasgow and Dublin north-east.

STRINGS ARE FALSE

To mark the occasion, this versatile man delivered his greetings in a jovially affected Irish accent.

'An' Mrs Bey Hann, and sure, and begorra, and how's the ould sod?'

'He'll be here in a minute,' said my mother, 'he came over with me, this time.'

'And how do you like London, this trip?'

'I always like it.'

'Brendan wouldn't stay five minutes in it,' said Jock, my brother-in-law.

'He wouldn't be let,' said my mother. 'They've too much sense. I like London, and I'd like to see Paris, too, before I die.'

'Not much chance of seeing it afterwards,' growled my other respected parent, who had arrived and was watching with stern eye the man filling the local equivalent of a half. 'I hope you can spare all that.'

'Oh, certainly,' smiled mine host, politely.

'Wouldn't like to deprive sick people. Useful in an emergency.' Looking down into his glass. 'Is your thermometer broke or anything?'

GLENCREE OR PAREE

And if my mother wants to see Paris, it had better be before she dies; it's only good Americans go there afterwards.

Myself and Jack Brennan sat outside the Mabillon,[94] one fine May day with some of them.

'That's right,' said Brennan, who has lived in Paris, by various ways and means, since he was about twenty, as he says in charming candour about himself.

'It was either Paree or Glencree – we're Irish.'

'Say, I'm Irish too,' said this American, 'and so's my buddy, Herman, here.'

'Well,' said Herman, modestly, 'I'm really only half Irish.'

'I see,' said Brennan, looking at him, as if to see which half.

'I'm from Boston,' said Herman's buddy. 'What part of the States are you from? New York, Philly, Chi?'

'We're not from the States, we're Irish we said,' said Brennan. 'We're from Dublin.'

'You're from Dublin, Ireland.'

'That's it. See, look at our passports.'

CLOSE THING

'Well, whaddyouknow. These guys, Herman, they're Irishmen, from Ireland. I wondered why they spoke so funny. Not like real Irishmen back home. And look here, this thing's got de Valera's autograph on it. Gee, how much do you want for this, buddy? I'll give you ten bucks. That's nearly four thousand francs.'

No man in the quarter knew the value of such an article better than Brennan. He let a scream of fright, and dived to its rescue, and caught it to his bosom muttering incoherently: '*Votre papiers, m'sieu? Liberté, égalité, carte d'identité.*'

'Well, I only thought you might,' said Herman's buddy, sulkily. 'It looked real cute, with harp and green cover and all. Where would I get one? Can you get them in Paris?'

'Certainly,' said Brennan, '37 rue Paul Valéry, off the avenue Victor Hugo. Where it says *Ambassade d'Irlande*. You'll see one of these harps over the gate. You just go right in and ask.'

He smiled, cynical and heartless: 'Say Brendan Behan sent you.'

The Irish Press, 8 May 1954

18
PARIS

Visit it only in the spring.

'*Some day maybe, I'll go back to Paris,*
And welcome in the dawn at Châtelet,
With onion soup and rum to keep us nourished,
Till the sun comes up on Saint-Germain-des-Prés …'

And, as the man said, it wouldn't be the first time. This is the time of year for it. In the winter, Paris is habitable by brass monkeys and, in the summer, you'd die for a breath of the sea. That's when people from here learn to appreciate our situation. A shilling will take you to the Bull Wall or the Forty Foot[95] but, in the heat of the Paris summer, it'll cost you two shillings to go into the Piscine,[96] which is a sort of floating swimming pool, on the Seine.

For one hour, only. They control the length of time by a system of coloured tickets, and when they shout out that it's time up for the yellow tickets or the blue tickets, it's no good gaming on that you don't know what *jaune* or *bleu* means.

TIME, GENTLEMEN

You can't stop there till it shuts, and they'll charge you the difference afterwards – like travelling first class on a third-class Metro ticket. The inspector, if he catches you, will waste no time bemoaning the dishonesty of any part of the human race, yours or his. He'll hold out his hand for a ten-shilling fine.

And once, at a party held on a little island, under the auspices of some students from Trinity College, Dublin, I dived in from the Pont Notre-Dame. The *pompiers*, or river fire brigade, shone searchlights from their boats.

I hardly had my clothes on when the *flics* were down, wanting to know what I thought I was making of the place altogether, and where I was from, and had I my papers?

I showed them my papers, and they saw the cover of the passport and bothered no more. One nodded to the other not to mind me, that I was an Irishman, and tapped the side of his cap, to indicate that I was one of the Gormans of Grange,[97] and a foreman in the puzzle factory.

He saluted and wished me a civil goodnight and they went off, much gratified, to the strains of the 'Marseillaise', sung by the Trinity scholars, in the version attributed to its distinguished alumnus, known as the 'Pope':

'Oh, the Board takes grave excep-chi-o-on, … yours sincerely, Matty Fry …'[98]

As the Paris police are mentioned, let me say this much about them. Some people from the island across the way, and Irish visitors from that strata of society that would eat cooked Kenyan, if they thought the quality over the way were doing likewise, adversely criticise them as armed state police, as compared to the dear old village constable in Dry-raching-under-the-water.

My grandmother's favourite toast was: 'Here's to the harp of old Ireland, and may it never want for a string as long as there's a gut in a peeler,' and I am not that mad about police of any sort myself, but my experience of the Paris police has been a pleasant one.

In a spirit, quite in keeping with the democratic tradition of their country, they will reprimand the wealthy *rentier* in his Delage,[99] and the workman, carrying his child on the back wheel, and as freely assist them.

French or foreign, rich or poor, they are at everyone's disposal, and, if your papers are right, they don't care how little else you have in your pocket; you can go on home, and the sleep will do you good.

BEST PERCH

The best spot from which to view the chestnuts, and beautiful Paris in the spring, is the top of the Arc de Triomphe.

I was up there, like any other tourist, and worse is to come, a true-born Dubliner. *I have been on top of the Pillar.*[100]

I first noticed the Pillar, one day, not long ago, when I met a man, a pal of my cradle days.

We graduated together to the more serious considerations of 'The Make In', 'Fat', Pontoon, and the ha'penny Rummy, before emigration parted us.

He went to the Navan end of Cabra, and Paw and Maw and us broke virgin soil in the highlands of Kimmage.

I came out of Henry Street, and who should I see but my old school mate, staring up at the top of the Pillar before.

'Me tearing man, Jowls, I didn't know you were out.'

'Aw, hello, the hard. Yes, this three weeks. Wasn't bad; I was in the laundry during the winter.'

He was still examining your man on the Pillar as closely as he could from a distance of a hundred feet.

'Very interesting that. Up there.'

'Nothing got to do with us.'

He looked at me angrily.

'Why hasn't he got something to do with us?'

I had never suspected such loyalty in the bosom of the Jowls, who sat with me, a boy, under the watchful eye of the French Sisters of Charity, in the North William Gaeltacht.

'Did you ever go up and looked at him?'

WE GO UP

I started off the usual long spiel about being a Dublin man. But Jowls cut me short.

'Come on up, and I'll show you. It'll give us an appetite for a couple.'

We started in, to cut a long story short, and I died seven deaths on the way up, all from shortness of breath.

Jowls was in better condition, being just back to this sinful world from his place of retirement.

We got up to the top and I crawled out after him to the platform, or whatever you call it, and knelt before Nelson. I hadn't the strength to stand.

Jowls looked up at the Hero of Trafalgar, sighed deeply, and reached up to pat the sword, the victorious shield of England, home and beauty.

I looked up at Jowls and said humbly: 'Napoleon wasn't a bad one, either.'

He came out of his reverie: 'Wha'? Do you see that?' He tapped the point of the sword.

I nodded up to him.

'D'you know what I'm going to tell you, there's about a fiver's worth of scrap in that. It's not much, but not much trouble, either, of a dark evening, and bring it down wrapped up in brown paper; they'd never miss it till morning.'

The Irish Press, 15 May 1954

19
LET'S GO TO TOWN

and hear what they have to say about us.

If you don't get up and get down town, you'd hear nothing, nor find out what they're saying about you. And God send they're saying something. Good or bad, it's better to be criticised than ignored.

And it was such a fine fresh mild morning, that even I was tempted out in the air. From the highlands of Kimmage, you could see the mists rising off the city, and the sky rosy and pink, out over the head of Howth. The time was seven o'clock and, if Roger Bannister[101] could manage the mile in four minutes, I could get from Sundrive Road to a stationer's in Dame Street in two and a half hours.

I could and did and had time over for a word with a friend outside the Irish House, at the bottom of Michael's Hill or Winetavern Street. Have it your own way.

KNIVES ARE OUT

Dressed in his sober black, and carrying a small black box, he rubbed his white moustache in greeting.

'You must have had a bad way of lying. It's not eight o'clock yet.'

'I rambled down from the house. I thought the walk would do me good. It's what you'd call close, though I'm sweating.'

'I'm going to wash off a ceiling for an old one in Foxrock.[102] "Lot of dirt in this room, painter," she says to me yesterday. "I didn't bring any of it with me, ma'am," says I. I've a second stock out with me. I don't suppose you'd care to come out and give us a hand?'

I shuddered. I'm allergic to stock brushes and afraid of knives. Putty knives, hacking knives and glazing knives.

'Well, I only asked. And you're sweating.'

WIGS IN KETTLE

I wiped my brow.

'You should save that, Brendan. There'd be a cure in that.'

'It's a bit early to be getting the Foxrock people out of bed. What about moseying over as far as the market and see how the fish and fruit and all to that effect are going on?'

'I suppose we might do worse. I could do with a rossiner, myself.'

We went over the bridge.

'Do you see the Four Courts there?' he said. It was not the sort of thing you'd miss.

'The Free Staters missed the bit of it I was occupying in 'twenty-two. But that's not what I wanted to tell you.

'Before they started shelling it at all, I was standing in the centre of it under the dome, and I a kind of naggin-bottle brass-bat.

'A section commander I was, and had to do me bit towards keeping up Volunteer discipline, and what do I see but a young fellow, one of our crowd from a country unit, going out of the robing room, with a thing like a tent, nearly the size of himself.

'"What's that you have there?" says I, real stern.

'"Ah, sure," says he, "'tis the Lord Chancellor's wig, and I only wants it a minute, to take the kittle off the fire."'

MATRIARCH

In Michael's they were listening to the radio, and only took their attention from it to greet us.

There was Mrs Brennan, and she and I know all belonging to one another from the time of the Invincibles,[103] though her way of talking is infectious and I keep calling her 'Mrs Brenning'.

She comes down to deal, and get her stuff out and on the road, as she's done this sixty years; though nowadays she directs operations from a seat in the corner, and children and grandchildren keep running in and out to get her directions, on the price of this and who's to take what go-car of fish, fruit or vegetables where.

LITERARY FOLK

And Crippen, who has resigned from active participation in the great world of commerce and industry, and is by way of being a literary man, to the extent of writing three-cross-doubles for the female clientele of the bookies up the street. He also had a connection with a well-known literary journal, as a broker in International Reply Coupons, which he changed in the bookies.

'So your man is in London, eh?'

'A shocking lot in Londing,' says Mrs Brennan to her friend beside her in the corner.

'Ah,' says Crippen, casually, 'it's an editor we used to know.'

'An editor,' murmurs Mrs Brennan to her friend impressively. 'Mind that now. If Mr Cripping and Mr Being didn't go to school, they met the scholars coming back. It's all the educayshing.'

SECOND PRIZE

'Well,' smiled Crippen, modestly, 'I dare swear I could make out the odds to a hundred to eight shot as good as the next. 'Course this man was a 'varsity man. National and Trinity, and all to that effect.'

'Look at that now, Maria. In the National Trimity College.'

'He's on the Third Programme,[104] now,' said I.

'And the same fellow,' said Crippen. 'He could be on the First if he only minded himself.'

'And where do you leave Brending Being, there, beside you? Took second prize of ten shillings or six pound of fresh beef at the Carnival in Mountjoy Square. Saw him myself. Not today nor yesterday. Playing the mouth orging.'

She looked at my friend the painter.

'It was in aid of the new hall in Phibsboro, Near Dalymoungt.'

'I know it up there,' said the painter. 'I worked in a presbytery not far from it. Grained and varnished the priests' desks.'

RADIO FUN

'Look at that now, Maria, what the man did. Vanished the priests' destes. You'll have luck with it, sir.'

'And I should be on my way out to a bit, this morning.'

'Ah, hold your hour and have another. You should take Brending with you and get his weight down. I heard he gets his clothes made in the Hammongd Laying Foungdry, these times.'

'Just wait till you hear a bit of this on the wireless. It's shocking funny.'

'That's right,' said Crippen, 'turn it up there, Michael, till we get another bit. It's better nor horse opera.'

'He talks massive,' said Mrs Brennan, 'you have to give him that.'

'... *and I'm glad to see they are all well muffled up, as they walk towards the quayside. This cold morning air can be quite sharp ...*'

'I'd have sent over the loan of me shawl if I'd a known,' muttered Maria.

'*And they are, yes, they are, I'm sure they are shivering, though ever so slightly; this morning air from the sea, and a swell is rocking the vessel ever so slightly ...*'

'The cheek of it.'

'... *and I really think that they are, in actual fact, I'm sure they have, or are going to, if they have not already, but I must really now, pass you on to my friend Redmond ...*'

'... *thank YOU, Cedric Hall-Ball, and now, briefly to recapitulate the journey out, some months ago, was the first they had flown in an aeroplane ...*'

WE SPLIT FORCES

'They usually flew in a wheelbarrow,' said Crippen.

'All the same,' said Mrs Brennan, 'it's a bit of gas, and I like to start the day with a bit of a laugh. Good morning all. We've to go up as far as Camden Street.'

'We'll be out with you,' said the painter. 'I've to start out for this old one's ceiling in Foxrock.'

'And I've to buy a new ribbon for the old Remington.'

'Mark that, judiciously, Maria,' said Mrs Brennan, 'he's to buy a new ribbon for his Renningtom.'

The Irish Press, 22 May 1954

20
TO DIE WITHOUT SEEING DUBLIN!

It worries some.

One of the Michael Dwyer crowd,[105] whose breed still flourishes round New Street and thereabouts, was back on a visit from the Coombe to the Glen of Imaal, where his grandmother's sister lay dying.

After she was washed and made right for the road, the priest sat taking a cup of tea, and chatting with her. 'Well, now, and how do you feel, Nan?'

'I feel right enough, now that you've been and settled me, what would be the matter with me? I've known that I was going to die this eighty year past. It happened all belonging to me. Though them that does have all the talk about how nice it is, in the next world, I don't see any great hurry on them getting on there.'

'I suppose you don't, Nan. But you've no regrets for this one. You reared fine men and women, and saw their rearing up here on the mountain.'

'I have no regret, Father, only the one. I was never in Dublin.'

SAMMY WATT

Sammy Watt in Portrush has the same regret. In his youth there were no paid holidays and now, in ampler times, he's nervous that the republicans would recognise him and have him shot, maybe lynch him, as he walked along O'Connell Street, or tie him to the Bowl of Light place and, as a special Tóstal attraction,[106] have him beaten to death with bound volumes of the *Ulster Protestant*.

For Sammy was on the other side in the Tan time.

I have never met anyone who boasted of having fought against the rebels, except the commissionaire of a Liverpool cinema who told me he was in the Black and Tans and took part in a military operation. This included a raid on a clerical outfitters in Dame Street.

Suitably garbed, he and his comrades, who had raided a pub or two earlier on, stood in the lorries and blessed the passers-by, with upheld Mills grenades.

But the commissionaire only joined up because his girlfriend wouldn't leave her work in a tripe factory. And wanting to forget, he had not got the fare to the Foreign Legion and had to make do with the Black and Tans.

Besides he thought it was more dangerous, the money was better, and he could help his widowed mother, who was an invalid and could do nothing but sit all day in a bath chair embroidering moral notices, suitable for framing, reading: *Beware!*

'Just the one word,' said I, 'and the same one on all the notices.'

WEAK ON SPELLING

'Ah. She weren't much of a speller, my old woman. Nor much of an embroiderer, neither. She weren't bad though, considering the only training she'd ever 'ad was sewing mailbags, when she'd be doing a couple of months up in Walton.

'She sent her embroidery all over the world with the missions. You could read *Beware!* in my old woman's sewing all over the British Empire. Some places, they didn't know enough English, and 'ad to 'ave it explained to them what it was about.

'When I was in your country, forgetting this Judy[107] what gave me a job in a tripe factory, my old woman, she sent me an embroidering, and it 'ung over the canteen counter – *Beware!* – in black and red wool, till the shinners let off a land mine.

'It blew the roof in on top of the sergeant major where 'e got over 'is nerves and got up and dusted 'imself, 'e said to take that so-and-so notice off the wall, or 'e'd go over to Norris Green and slit my old woman's gizzard, at 'is own expense.'

KING AND EMPIRE

My commissionaire didn't count, because he wasn't much interested in the rights or wrongs of the war, so long as it kept his mind off his troubles.

Sammy spoke with the ardour of the pure souled and dedicated patriot about his services to King and Empire, in those strenuous days.

All my life, I've known the opposite convention, where anyone old enough would mutter darkly about their doings, and if they weren't in the GPO in 1916,[108] it was because they were doing something more important, and to which the element of secrecy was so vital that it hasn't been made public nearly forty years after.

A change is as good as a rest.

'I'm a man that knows what I'm talking about. I was through the whole lot, so ah was.'

'And what, pray, were you through? asked his wife, from the far side of the table, 'Barrin' it'd be a lock of porter barrels?'

'Och, hould your wheesht, you, Hanna, you knew nawthin' about it, nor was let know. A right thing, if every gabbing ould woman in the County Derry could be knowing the secrets of the organisation.'

'Och, what organisation? Filling the wee boy's head up wi' your lies and rubbish.'

DAVE O'LEARY

I signalled hastily to the barman.

'Port, please, for Mrs Watt. No, not the Empire, the Portuguese port.'

It's not every day in these weeks I get called a 'wee boy'. It might never happen again.

'And a couple of scoops for myself and Sammy.'

We got settled down to his military reminiscences.

'Ah was an intelligence man.'

'The dear God protect us from the Father of Lies,' muttered Hanna to herself, putting down her glass.

Sammy did not condescend to hear her. 'Yes, ah was an undercover man like—'

'Dick Barton,'[109] said Hanna.

'Ah was a spy, to tell you straight, though you were on the other side; good men on every side and you're a Fenian; you mind Dave O'Leary?'

All in the one breath, and I had to sort it out as best I could. Fenian Dave O'Leary?

'Would it be John O'Leary, Sammy? He was a Fenian, but he was in the one grave with romantic Ireland, a long time before I was born.'

'Och, don't talk daft. This man was in the grave with no one. He stayed out in Portstewart five miles out of the town, only last summer. Isn't he the head one in the Free State? Damn it, sure everyone knows Dave O'Leary.'

'De Valera?'

'Damn it, isn't that who I said. Deyve Ah Leery.'

'CAME TO PRACHE'

'Fair enough. What about him?'

'You mind the time he come to Columb's Hall in Derry? Well, Ah goes in, carrying me life in me hands, among all these Fenians, that's packin' the hall out, to give him a big cheer, when he comes out on the stage to prache.'

'To?'

'To prache the meeting. Ah'm sitting in the sate minding no one, and hoping no one will mind me, but I'm in disguise.'

'What was that,' asked Hanna, 'a temperance pin?'

'I took me hat off, and no one in the place had ever seen the top of me head from the time I got bald, so they didn't know me.

'Till, when Dave O'Leary comes out on the stage there's a big cheer, and a roar, and the next thing is, the peelers is trying to get in the doors and the crowd is bating them, and Dave O'Leary is away there, up on the stage, and he says that he comes to prache, and begor, he's going to prache, and damn the one will stop him, and in the middle of it, I've got down under the seat, and Head Constable Simpson says 'Got you,' and he doesn't know me with me bald head, till he turns me round, and recognises me, from me face, and near drops, from surprise.'

IN HIS DISGUISE

'And what and under the dear good God are you doing here, Sammy Watt. D'you think we hadn't enough trouble, with the Fenians?'

'Ah'm an intelligence man,' said I. 'A spy.'

'"Take yourself to hell out of thon, or I'll spy you, with a kick where it won't blind you." There was me thanks.'

'Ah sure wasn't it always the way. Look at Parnell.'

'Ah wonder would they hould it again me in Dublin, if I snaked down for a wee trip on the Enterprise?'

'Couldn't you disguise yourself? Take off your hat until you got back on the train?'

The Irish Press, 29 May 1954

21

FLOWERS ARE SAFE AT
DOLPHIN'S BARN

Put them on a pedestal.

If I got my hands on whoever made it up, I'd give him 'Bimbo'. It's bad enough having to do the work before you get the money, without having 'Roley-Poley-Oley-Oh' bawled at you from every house in the block. It penetrated the oak panelling of my spacious library and drove me out to vote.

In the hot sun Corporation painters were burning off sashes and hall doors at the rate of a mile a minute. If anything could cheer up that mysterious body, the rate-payers, their heart may rise with the information that the squad decorating municipal property this year are as fast and efficient a gang of painters as ever I've seen.

The painters themselves, like everyone else that lives in a house, are rate-payers. With a small 'r' because they don't, as Cyril Connolly[110] would say, 'make a thing' about it.

Newspaper columns sometimes carry a sarcastic note on the navvy straightening his back and taking ten full seconds over it, all unconscious of the scribe taking notes, from the snug window opposite; and the cleanest, jolliest fun round the suburban breakfast table is excited by Papa's reading out from the morning paper a bit about a hole at the corner of Grafton Street, and some good-humoured chaff at the expense of the chaps at the bottom of it.

FLOWERED PLEDGE

Coming out of the voting, I passed over the canal on the way into town. The grass roundabout on the corner was a vivid green and, to tell the truth, I don't know what else to call it.

The important thing was the blaze of scarlet flowers in the centre. There was neither guard nor railing on them and the children playing round and about them, while their mothers and big sisters knitted and chatted on the edge of the roundabout. And the flowers as safe, as are the orchids above in the Botanic Gardens.

Now, roundabouts and grass plots at the edge of Greater Dublin pavements have been put down before, and walked over, before the grass got a chance of shoving itself up, much less flowers, and I think I know the reason this one at Dolphin's Barn bridge survived, when others didn't.

It is raised on a stone base three feet high.

Now, few of us can take a leap like that in our stride, whereas it requires a conscious effort of will to walk round, rather than over, a space on a low cement coping almost level with the ground.

Like the apple trees that greet you on the roadsides of north Wexford, the unguarded scarlet glory at the Barn bridge is a pledge to the dead that our slanderers were liars.

LA POLITESSE

The coy carry-on of the women voters was worth listening to on Election Day.

Two elderly women, who have voted for opposing parties since women got the vote, walk over together to the schools.

'Ah, sure Julia, it's like what poor Dan O'Connell[111] said—'

'The Lord have mercy on him,' said Julia, politely.

'—to the man he met on the road. This man was breaking stones, and he asked Dan who was going to get in. "Whoever gets in," said Dan, "you'll still be breaking stones."'

'Ah, sure, isn't it the truth for you, Maria?' said Julia, 'I have to go over here, at the other door. I'll see you when we come out.'

LA REALITÉ

'I'm glad to see you so united in your politics,' said I.

'Is it me be united with that one? Sure, she's gone over to give her one, two and three to the other crowd. Pity she wouldn't break her neck and

God forgive me for saying it before she got to the ballot box, but I'd never blame her for being always the one way, and her ould one a scrubber in the Vice Regal.'

And when they came out, 'Ah, there you are, Mrs Jewel, I was just waiting on you. I was just saying to this chap here isn't the day very changeable. You wouldn't know what to pawn.'

The Irish Press, 5 June 1954

22

UISCE, AN EADH?[112]

It's important how you say it.

This is not my first appearance before the Irish public. By no manner of means. Tripping over my musty trusket, or whatever you call it, I made a stand for Ireland at the Mansion House in 1935, in a play by the name of *Tóirneach Luimnighe*,[113] and had a speaking part of three words, and they may be the best-rehearsed three words in the duration of Feis Atha Cliath,[114] on that or any other stage.

For weeks before, in school and out of it, I tried them with every possible shade of intonation. Just the plain: 'Listen, give over the malarkey, and a straight answer to a straight question: *Uisce, an eadh?*'

Then the sinister: How do you know, so you think you double-cross the greatest bandit in all Mexico, Leo Carrillo,[115] the Ceesco Keed: 'Eeescha, huh, *an eadh?*'

Or the hurried, efficient violence of Cagney, or Edward G. Robinson: C'mon, fish face, 'n come across, accompanied by a slap in the puss with one hand, while the left gripped the forelock, and the victim whimpered, Boss, boss, I didn't did it. Don't gimme me that, mugsy, but before your dawgs goes into this bucket of nice fresh cee-ment, uh, uh, or huh, huh, '*Uisce, an eadh?*'

NATURAL LOYALTIES

It depended what was on at the Plaza, the Drumcondra Grand, the Bohemian or the Phibsboro[116] for the three months of rehearsal how my style of acting varied, as one form of diction seemed good, till you got another fourpence for the pictures, and encountered the next.

On my way across Mountjoy Square to the bakery in Parnell Street for fourteen outside-split loaves for my mother, I'd pass Mrs Schweppes on the corner, where O'Casey[117] wrote *Shadow of a Gunman*, and more local loyalties would assert themselves, and I'd return to my naturalistic interpretation of the part: Poor little Mollster, me dollser, and Tommy Owens and Fluther and Captain Boyle, and me bould Jack Clitheroe, yous are toilin' and moilin', and gunnin' and runnin' and fightin', and yous wouldn't help a body out of a hobble and she wriggled in her corporal form be the frightful exertion of an upturned landmine that she sat down on to rest her poor bones to use towards the holy heights of heaven be the force of the explosion unexpected, listen to me, yous, '*Uisce, ui-is-ce, an eadh?*'

DECISION

At the bakery, I tried them over, and was cursed in the queue for delaying the man.

'Eh, go-be-the-wall, what's that you said you wanted?'

'*Uisce, an eadh?*'

'I'm after saying fifteen times there's no turnovers till five o'clock.'

When I'd completed my errand and left the shop, with my bag over my shoulder, the crowd looked after me strangely as I muttered my way up Middle Gardiner Street: '*Uisce, an eadh?*'

But the day before the show, my mind was made up for me, at the cheek and impudence counter of Hugh MacCallion's shop in Dorset Street. It was said that you paid for the pig's cheek and the impudence was thrown in for choice.

Still, Hugh was a decent old skin in his own way, and maybe it was only the uncouth Derry accent that made his utterance so harsh on our refined metropolitan ears. No matter what way you looked at it, he was a match for his customers.

TWISTED GLANCE

This old one asked him for a shilling pig's cheek, and while he muttered about himself paying more than that for them, and all to that effect, the usual old shop man's cant, he was rooting in the barrel for something that he could sell for a shilling and still add something to the Hug Fund out of it.

At last he emerged from the blood-red depths of the briny barrel, bearing aloft the three-quarter profile of a pig, very much battered. It seemed that this cheek had been squeezed up against the side of the barrel by the others, and his appearance was certainly very odd.

'There's a grand cheek now for the money,' said Hugh.

The old one looked at it, very doubtfully, and in its twisted way, it returned her glance.

'The Lord between us and all harm, Mr Hug Mac Scallion ...'

'Hugh, Hugh, and ma neems Mac Callion.'

'Whatever it is, and Hew here, or Hew there, that's a very peculiar-looking cheek.'

Hug swelled up bigger than the barrel, looking from her to the cheek, as much as to say that if it went to looks, there wasn't much between them, and roared: 'An' what do you axpact for a shillin' – Mícheál Mac Lallimore?'

CASTILIAN BROGUE

I'd seen the noblest youth of the Fianna and heard Mac Liammóir's[118] high Castilian brogue: '*Eist, a chuid de'n tsaol. Siad na tonntracha chanfhas abhrán ár bpósta dhúinn anocht ...*'[119]

I regretfully decided there would be no excuse accepted for gagging this bit into the Primary Schools Cup competition, but I could model my interpretation of my part in *Toirneach Luimnighe*, on Diarmuid's last words: '*Uisge, a Fhinn, tabhair deoch uisge chugam ...*'[120]

Well, they are not quite the last words. He says at the finish: '*Breathnuigh isteach sna súile orm, a Ghráinne.*'[121]

But I didn't think Feis Atha Cliath would wear an interpolation of this nature, either, but I'd do the best I could with my head turned sideways, till the great moment came.

SAIGHDIUR EILE[122]

I was nearly deformed for life, waiting for it. I had to wait, head to one side, like I'd seen your man at the Gate, till the *saighdiúr eile Éireannach*, crouched the far side of me, wondered whether there was something offensive about himself or his accoutrements, my head turned away from him for half the play.

A fellow called 'Pa Bla', from that good day to this, though he has since held commissioned rank in the armed forces of this State, comes out in his French uniform, shouting like a Gallic-Gaelic bull: *'Par bleu, cad is fiú botúins, thall's a bhfhus.'*[123]

The significance of which message is forever lost to me, owing to overdue concentration on my twisted neck, so that I might have presented the starboard side of my face when the time came.

MAKE SURE

A boy from Summerhill called Pigeon is hit by a cannon ball, and falls off Limerick's walls, or whichever of them he was on, before being bombarded by the other crowd, and moans, *'Uisce … uisce.'*

Up I leaped, in my profile. Into bed or out of barracks …

'Uisce, an eadh?'

'Seadh,' mutters poor Pigeon.

I see. Nothing like making sure. I'll repeat it. *'Uisce, an eadh?'*

'Seadh, seadh.'

I think I was just a little, er, underdone, that time. Besides you can't get too much of a good thing. *'Uisce, an eadh?'*

'Seadh, seadh, SEADH.'

VETERAN RECOVERED

All right. No need to take the needle over it. Just answer a civil question. I walked over, head twisted sideways, to get the water, tripped, and nearly broke my neck over a Dutch cavalryman in the wings, and the play went on, in my absence.

Pigeon recovered from his cannonball wound, and played professional soccer for Brighton and Hove, in England, long after the Siege of Limerick.

TAILPIECE

FEAR AGUS SAR-FHEAR:[124]

'"Does Bernard Shaw[125] write in English as well as Irish?"

"So far as I know he only writes in English," I said.

"Yes?" His voice sounded scornful and patronising. "It says here that he is Irish, so I think it more likely that he writes in his native language. You have no doubt read translations."

I knew that it would be useless to argue with him. I got up and went out to the sinister tennis court.'

— *Maiden Voyage* (1943) by Denton Welch[126]

The Irish Press, 12 June 1954

23

SWINE BEFORE THE PEARLS

I read the middle page of the Irish edition of the *Sunday Express*, which was given over to the Beaverbrook[127] prophet resident in this city. It was an article about Éamon de Valera and so full of 'smoke and stars', 'the dour black porter of the Celt', 'a Machiavellian mind for statesmanship', 'myth, mystery and legend' and ... Chinese laundry-keepers and even loyal sons of St Patrick, as to make one wonder whether its author is not in grave danger of meeting himself coming back.

There is more gas with the locals on the rest of the paper. Get on this, for instance, a letter to the editor:

> *I read in the SUNDAY EXPRESS last week, that a woman fell into the Victoria Memorial fountain when the Queen was on the Palace balcony. I was that very wet person – or rather, one of the two who went in.*
>
> *But who cared? I had seen our Queen and to see her was worth getting wet and an hour's journey home to dry clothes.*
>
> *(Mrs) D.L—, N.9*
>
> *Mrs. L—, 51-year-old nurse, has been in love with royalty as long as she can remember. She has seen two Coronation processions, three lyings-in-state and most public functions attended by royalty during the last forty years.*

The hireling scribe on the same page 'has been hearing about the masque which undergraduates will stage for Princess Margaret's visit to the Oxford women's college, St Hilda's, next month':

> *The masque, Porci ante Margaritan, has been specially written for the occasion.*
> *The Princess will be greeted as 'Fairest of all pearls, the world thine oyster,' and*
>   *will hear her astrological future foretold as:*
> *Perhaps you will be meeting someone new,*
> *Romance will very likely come to you,*
> *Perhaps you will antagonise a friend,*
> *But make it up, most likely, in the end.*
> *Miss Mann, principal of the college, saw the script and sent it to the Queen*
>   *Mother. It was approved.*

Translated, the masque's title is: 'Swine before a pearl.'

OR BEFORE A PINT

'My first was the very same. Poor Gonzaga Ignatius "Hogger", I called him for a pet name,' said Mrs Brenning. 'Lost in the Boer War, and never found. Lovely fellow, wasn't he, Maria?'

'Not tall enough to pick shamrock,' muttered Maria.

'All the same he was lovely, in his little pillbox cap, and his dotey little face with the big black moustache. You could nearly lift him up by it. And he was the very same about swine. Swine before pearls, or diamonds, or anything.

'He'd get up in the middle of the night to eat swine, from the crubeen to the tip of the left ear. Swine before a pearl. Or before a pint. You couldn't beat his little hands away from this counter, till he'd sunk twenty of them, after a feed of pig's cheek.'

'God be with the days, you'd get a head for two shillings and only newly married couples got a cheek between them,' sighed Maria.

'It's well I remember it,' said Mrs Brenning. 'Why wouldn't I, and I married and a widow before I was eighteen.'

CHAMPION WIDOW

'I was the champion widow of the quarter and, if there was a widow's five furlong sprint, I'd have won it, with a length in hand, fifty years ago. For a long time I was betwixt and between, of course. Not knowing whether I was in it, or out of it.'

'So?'

'And more so, Brending Behing. The War Office had no news of him for weeks, and thought he might have been a prisoner, and still alive. Though, in the heels of the hunt, we gave up all hope.'

She sniffed into the butt end of the tumbler.

'Ah, yes. When they found six Dubling Fusiliers buttings in a lying's dem.'

'Them lions,' said Maria, 'You could never trust them.'

POET'S CORNER

'And there was boings with the buttings.'

'Buttons and bones,' said I.

'That's it,' said Mrs Brenning. 'Once they got the buttings and the boings, and God help poor little Hogger, you'd have known his boings anywhere, they fixed me up with me pension.'

'Perhaps you will be meeting someone new,' I quoted.

'Ah, don't be talking. Didn't I meet him coming out of the 1906 Exhibishing?[128] Just leaving the native village he was, after leaving two dozen of large bottles and a quarter of brawn for the chief of the Royal Izumbis, and earl of Addis Ababababababa, a chap be the name of Hogan, from Malpas Street.

'His father was a chef in O'Keefe's, the knackers. Oh, indeed and I did meet someone new. Just like the man says in the poing.'

'I wrote a poem one time,' said Crippen.

'I wouldn't doubt you,' said I.

'And indeed I'm sure and you did, Mr Cripping, and it wouldn't be your best.'

'Say a bit of it, so,' said Michael, from behind the counter.

LIKE A MISSION

Crippen glared angrily round, as poets do, and shouted, 'And sure, there yous are again, tormenting and annoying and persecuting me, because I trust a bit of me heart's core, a part of me pain, a bit of meself, a moment of me experience, pinned down in its trembling torture to the paper, like a butterfly to the board, yous meritless, jeering, sneering throng—'

'He's lovely,' sighed Mrs Brenning, 'like a mishing. Give the man a half, Michael. Go on now, Mr Cripping. Tell us the poing. As poor ould Tom Moore said, "Carry on with the coffing, the corpse'll walk."'

'All right, so,' said Crippen, watching Michael fill out the half with a sneer, 'mind your hand doesn't slip. I suppose there'll be neither peace nor ease, nor any kind of good left me, barring I reveal my soul and my hurt to yous.'

'A bit of order now,' said Mrs Brenning, 'and let the man show us his soul and his heart.'

BAD

Crippen lowered the half and projected his gaze far through Michael's window. Precisely, to the other side of Arran Street East, ten yards distant, the wall of the cabbage factory. He spoke in the agonised tones of one who had seen much, and didn't fancy any of it. That's the way he spoke:

> *'There is a sadness in my sadness when I'm sad.*
> *There is a gladness in my gladness when I'm glad.*
> *There is a madness in my madness when I'm mad.*
> *But the sadness in my sadness,*
> *And the gladness in my gladness—'*

'And the madness in your madness,' muttered Mrs Brenning, respectfully.

> *'—Are nothing to my badness when I'm bad.'*

There was a moment's silence and Mrs Brenning shook her head in the direction of the poet.

'Mr Cripping,' she sighed, 'you're rotting. Rotting with braings.'

The Irish Press, 19 June 1954

24

HERE'S HOW HISTORY IS WRITTEN

and literature, for good measure.

'He had a face like a plateful of mortal sins,' said the Bard.

'G'way,' said Crippen, 'you haven't a snap?'

'There wasn't much snaps going that time,' said the Bard, 'and our provoke sergeant, it was trying to forget him we were, after we got away from him, not to be carrying round snaps or pictorial representations of him one way or another, except if he was to swing the wrong end of a rope. But that was the British army for you, them times.'

'Well,' sighed Crippen, resignedly, 'to hear of a fellow the like of that, it'd kind of resign you to what me and me likes did to the same British army afterwards. Aye, even if I done jail over it.'

'More luck to you,' muttered an old fellow, grimly, from the corner.

'Arrested, I was, at the Curragh races of twenty-one, and charged with obtaining money by means of a trick, to wit, Find the Lady and The Sliced Woman, from a few Tommies that was only after coming over for training.'

SIX MONTHS

'I took twenty-two bar off them, but pleaded to the court that we were entitled to some of our own back after all England robbed on us, and me solicitor said it was only plaguing the Egyptians, but the old beak said they weren't the Egyptians, but the West Kents, and I got weighed off with six months. But I wasn't the only decent man in jail that time.'

'Bedad, you weren't,' said the old man, with a twisting of his gums. 'Aye, and many's the decent man was hung, and not a word about him.'

BALLAD TIME

I struck up, to the air of the 'Rising of the Moon',[129] and vehemently:

> *'They told me Francis Hinsley,*
> *They told me you were hung …'*

'Good on you,' said the old man, his hand on his ear, for fear he'd miss one word.

> *'With red protruding eyeballs …'*

'More luck to me one son,' said the old man, in tears of content.

> *'And black protruding tongue …'*

'Ah, your blood's worth bottling,' screeched the old man.

'Is that one of Yeats's?' asked Crippen.

'No, that was written by Evelyn Waugh,'[130] said I.

BELCUDDY

'And, bedad, and she wasn't a bad one, either,' said Crippen, shaking his head', "I'll dress myself in man's attire and fight for liberty," what? Eveleen was far from being the worst. Whas this crowd she was with, now? I just can't think of it for the minute.'

'Wasn't it the Belcuddy Battalion, or the First Battalion of the Third Belcuddy Brigade?' said I. 'You should know that, Crip, above anyone.'

He spat on the floor and looked seriously round the company. 'Not a man in Ireland should know it better.'

'What part of the country would that be, now?' asked the Bard, who is himself a native of the far North, Ballymoney direction.

'What part of the country would it be?' asked Crippen, incredulously. 'Is it coddin me y'are or what?'

He looked over at the old man.

'Can you believe your ears. A man here does not know where,' he paused a minute, 'er, eh …'

'Belcuddy,' said I.

'That's right,' said Crippen, 'Belcuddy it is.'

The old man looked over and waved his stick: '*Ná bac leis.*[131] Leave him to God!'

Crippen fixed the Bard with a severe look.

'Certainly. I'd a thought anyone would a known that. Nawbocklesh. It's about eight mile this side of it. Nice little town, too.' His lips softened in a reminiscent smile. 'Nawbocklesh,' says he, 'and the blue sky over it.'

Crippen sighed, and the old man gazed on the floor, thinking of old times, and ground his gums together with a noise like a sand lorry on the mountain road outside.

ENCORE

I rose my eyes to the ceiling, and opened my mouth in a patriotic fashion:

> *'Oh, down in Belcuddy they fought the glorious fight,*
> *All through the day, and through most of the night.*
> *And never knocked off, for sup, bit or bite …'*

'Ah, me good living youth,' said the old man.

'Ah, there was great men in the country, that time,' said Crippen. 'Aye, and women too, like the one that wrote the bit of a song your gills there was singing.'

'Is it Evelyn Waugh?' asked my gills.

'The very woman. Eveleen Wars. The Bardess of Belcuddy, we called her.' He looked at the Bard. 'You and her might have made a match of it. Set up in the bard line together. But I believe she was sweet on the commandant and when he got killed in the Butter Tasting and Poultry Station, she never did an hour's good. It's all in a poem she wrote, the time of the death:

> *'I leave up me Thompson, and me short Webley,*
> *Distribute me hand grenades among the foe,*
> *I'm fed up fighting for dear old Ireland,*
> *And to a convent I now will go.'*

'A lovely thing that.'

KILLED ENOUGH

'It's like what Bob said to me, the time of the Boer War. We were all out to be reviewed, thousands and thousands of us, in lines as long as the eye could see, but Bobs (Lord Roberts was his right name, but we called him that for short) rides up to where I was in the ranks, and calls out, "Fusilier R'Raw."

'"Sir," says I, taking a pace forward, and coming up to the salute.

'"Wipe your bayonet,"[132] says he off the horse, "you've killed enough." The provoke sergeant wasn't half choked, I can tell you.'

'That's the fellow with the face like a plateful of mortal sins,' said I.

'The very same,' said the Bard.

'Yes,' said Crippen, 'you were telling us about him.'

'It was this way,' the Bard began.

The Irish Press, 26 June 1954

25

THE ROAD TO CARLISLE

Besides the Bard, Crippen, myself and Mrs Brenning, there was a duffle coat in the corner containing, newly arrived off the Liverpool boat, a young Irish poet of uncertain age, for the only part of him visible was a bald patch on the top of his head.

'No,' said Crippen, in answer to Mrs Brenning, 'he's not a monk. That's a poet's get-up he has on. And he leans his head on his hands because it saves his energy for writing poems, and roaring at the people. I'll just see if he's in form yet.'

'Ask him if he knoos that one o' Burns,[133] *Hoo Crool,*' said the Bard.

Crippen went towards the recumbent form of the Young Irish Poet and shook it. He looked round at the people and said, 'This is like a poem of Burns and all, *The Wind that Shakes the Duffle Coat'.*

'God forgive you, Mr Cripping,' said Mrs Brenning, 'you're a deeming.'

'Eh,' said Crippen, in the ear of the YIP, 'do you know that one of Burns—'

WOE UNTO YOU

The duffle coat that shook itself, and the YIP shook himself and glared at us, with the fury of a newly woken squirrel.

'Do I know?' he screamed, 'do I know, woe? An ignorant, meritless crew are you—'

'I told you, Bard,' said Crippen, 'he'd leave you in the ha'penny place. Words at will he has, rhymed and ready.'

'—crew are you. That never as much as glanced at the last issue of *The Blunt Instrument*, the last of the little reviews with the fifth of my cantos in it:

> *Woe, there is a lot of it flying round,*
> *More often the sound, sniff, sniff,*
> *Of woe,*
> *Than any of your damned ha, ha, ha, or*
> *Hoe, hoe, hoe.*

He slumped back in his duffle coat and waved the back of his hand to us before submerging again.

LOST BURNS

'Massive,' said Mrs Brennan, 'especially the cursing at the end.'

'Fine fellow,' said Crippen, 'you want to read a poem he wrote one time called *Where Am I?* Took a degree in Knowledge at the National University, Trinity College, Dublin![134] Never did a day's work in his life, but a lovely dancer.'

'Burns was the very same,' said the Bard.

'Oh, the very same,' said Crippen. You know the bit where he says:

> *'You may hay the growsy or the grunk,*
> *But a mon's a mon a mon a mon a mon,*
> *And hay ye don't like it, I no care*
> *Tá me, it's all the won.'*

'I don't recall that bit,' said the Bard.

'And hard for you,' said Crippen, 'for it was never let out to the ordinary public. Case the other crowd would be made as wise as themselves. But I got it from the right quarter, chap in the gas company. That's all fine and large but I'm telling you that it's not what you know but who you know: and a shut mouth will catch no flies; better to be mean than at a loss, have you me?'

SCOTCH TERRIERS

'There's a lot in what you say,' said the Bard, 'I mind the time I was in Dumfries. When I was in the army.'

'Was in a Scotch regiment myself,' said Crippen, 'the Submarine Kilties. Deserted the time of the Economic War.[135] Wouldn't sell my own ould country. Besides, they started giving us New Zealand mutton.'

'Well, this was in the First War. I was after coming over from Larne through Portpatrick, and enlisted in a moment of foolishness in the Scotch Terriers. They were a guid enough mob, they called them the "Dogs of War", but the provoke sergeant—'

'The one with the face like a plateful of mortal sins?' asked Crippen.

'The very same,' said the Bard.

'Well,' said Crippen, 'just so as we'd know him.'

'I was left minding the canteen one night, an' what happened but I left a tap running when I'd fallen asleep. And there was nearly a hogshead short and the provoke sergeant wakes me up and says I was under close arrest and I could take my choice of being tried under military law and being shot for deserting my post by falling asleep under the barrel, or being tried under civil law and hung for sacrilege.

'To give me time to consider me position I was locked up in the guard-room, which was a wee place with a window looking down into the barrack yard thirty feet below.

'I looked around me and there was nothing in the guardroom but a water jug, table and stool and a cupboard in the wall. There was nothing in the cupboard when I looked but a lot of rifle pull-throughs, lengths of cloth, three feet long. And I had an idea of a sudden.

'There was eleven of them. That meant thirty feet and something over for the knots. I could make a rope. No sooner said than done.'

ESCAPE

'I made me rope, attached one end to the window, slid down and over the wall and was on the road to Carlisle before you could say—'

'Mull o' Galloway,' said Crippen.

'But when I got to the border between Annan in Scotland and Longtown in England, what do I see but a sentry box blocking me way to Carlisle and the London road and me with no papers. But I sneaks up beside the box and rubs me feet on the road, and the sentry shouts out, "Halt, who goes there?"

'I said it was me, and he shouts at me like he's talking to a half-fool:

'"And where do you think you're going at this hour of the night?"

'"If you please, sir, I want to get into Scotland. I live in Annan, and me mother will be worried about me."

'"You should have thought of that before twelve o'clock. Get back there, to the English side now, for your mother will have to do without you until morning. Come on now," he says, waving the rifle at me, "Get back there, and if I catch you trying to sneak into Scotland past this post, I'll put one through you, you loon, you."

'And he puts me on down the road and I'm safe and sound on the way to Carlisle.

'Till I got very tired after all the walking and sat down on an empty box on wheels, a sort of a watch box, to rest myself, and was only woken up by a low and savage growling, like a beast of prey.'

'The provoke sergeant?' said Crippen.

'No,' said the Bard, 'but what was nearly as bad. A ferocious looking watchdog.'

'An Allegation,' said Mrs Brenning.

'There was only one thing to be done. Grab a hold of his tail. I manoeuvred round as best I could till at last I got a grip on it, and he let a roar and a howl out of him like the zoo on strike, but I held on till he tried to run away from me, and the watchbox went along on its wheels on the road, and the harder he pulled to get away from me, the tighter I gripped, till he drew me on the watchbox the whole way to Carlisle.

'Then, just as dawn rose over the spires of the town, I let go of the dog and he dropped down dead.'

The Irish Press, 3 July 1954

26
VIVE LA FRANCE

Wednesday next will be Bastille Day …

'A Lonndain-doire, bolgach chugatsa,
ar nós na scáile ar ladadh le púdair,
's a liacht farairi, fada fionn lubacht,
Gan fosc on ngaoith, na chré dhá gcumhdacht,
Och! Ochon … '[136]

This choice blessing on Derry Walls for the Twelfth of July[137] was part of the lament for Patrick Sarsfield,[138] written by a poor Irish ex-soldier, as he sat on the Hill of Howth after the Battle of the Boyne, and wishing himself in France with his comrades.

As a doctrinaire republican, I seldom lost an opportunity, in the enthusiastic days of my youth, of making propaganda for the rights of man and the principles of 'eighty-nine by singing any songs about France that backed my own side.

'Is ar Bonapartaidh mar dhéin orainn feall,
Go dtiocfhaidh ar gcairde i measc ar namhad,
Go gcuirimid scrios ar chlann nan Gall … '[139]

MOTHER

Fáilte roimh na bhFranncach Bána agus céad mile acab.[140] And I particularly relished a 'ninety-eight ballad of my mother's that brought in a rather broad hint to local tyrants to be minding themselves:

> 'I met a man from Wexford, with valour in his eye,
> And he sat upon a tumbril with his head thrown back on high,
> He sang the song of freedom with his brown face all aglow,
> Singing autumn, it is coming and a-reaping we will go,
> And a-reaping we will go …'

I was not so partial to her version of Seán O Dhuibhir a Ghleanna:[141]

> 'Here's a health to your and my king,
> The sovereign of our liking
> And to Sarsfield, underneath whose flag,
> We cast once more a chance,
> For the morning's dawn will bring us,
> And the summer's wind will wing us,
> To take a stand and wield a brand
> Amongst the sons of France …'

'And the soldiers and chiefs of the Irish Brigade' weren't much better.

NO KING

I had no king, nor wanted any, and if I went looking for a chief, I'd know where to look for him – above in Arbour Hill,[142] where my old man, not long out of Gormanston himself, brought me, and held me up on his shoulder to give him three cheers with the rest of the crowd on a Sunday morning.

Máirtín Ó Cadhain,[143] in the Fianna, told me I thought that Ireland was created in 1798 by Theobald Wolfe Tone, and then tried to prove to me that it wasn't.

The fact of the matter is there is everything to fit an Irishman in France. He can find a good Irish excuse for getting into any political argument there.

ALL SIDES

If the President of the Third Republic was a MacMahon,[144] General Clusère,[145] commanding the forces of the Commune, was a personal friend of James Stephens, and invited to command the Fenian army, in the event of a rising in Ireland.

CONFESSION

I hope my taste in French politics may be indulged so far as to permit me to repeat the story of Desmond Francis Ryan, best known Irish journalist in Paris, about Marshal MacMahon.

He was being interviewed for the press shortly after his installation as president and was asked a question about his health.

'I do not feel well at all,' replied the old man. 'Anyone that ever suffered from cerebral meningitis would be as well off if they died from it. For it either kills one or leaves one a hopeless idiot.

'And I should know – I've had it three times.'

One of the avenues off the Étoile, at the top of the Champs-Élysées, is named after him. Next but one to avenue Mac-Mahon is the avenue Hoche, named for the Bantry Bay general.[146]

DIARY

The door opened and a very handsome, well-made young fellow in a brown coat and nankeen pantaloons entered and said: '*Vous êtes le citoyen Smith?*'

I thought he was a chef de bureau, and replied, '*Oui, citoyen, je m'appelle Smith.*'

He said, '*Vous vous appelez aussi, je crois, Wolfe Tone?*'

I replied, '*Oui, citoyen, c'est mon veritable nom.*'

'*Eh bien,*' replied he, '*je suis le general Hoche.*'

Bad luck to the wind at Bantry, said I to myself many a time, walking down the avenue. St Joseph's church is there, and outside you'll see the crowd gathered on a Sunday or holiday, just like any Irish church anywhere. The ambassador and embassy crowd, Aer Lingus officials, some very correct governesses, a few nurses from the American Hospital at Neuilly, an odd artist or musician on a scholarship to the Beaux-Arts or the Conservatoire, some business people, and a collection of citizens whose most prized possession, next to their Irish passport, is a hard neck.

FR O'GRADY

They are the gayest of the crowd and, though the governesses move closer to the ambassador as they moved off, they bow their hard necks in grateful homage to the embassy staff as they move on towards the Arc de Triomphe, and the diplomats smile to each other in resignation, and the stout figure of Father O'Grady, CP, appears at the door to wave a benevolent hand on all and sundry, and it would be a poor sort of an Irishman could leave Paris without a salute in his direction.

Another of the avenues off the Etoile is named for Victor Hugo who, as León Ó Broin[147] tells us in his *Parnell*, made a personal appeal to Queen Victoria to spare the life of Pat O'Donnell, who was hanged for shooting James Carey,[148] the informer.

ALLONS!

Hugo was born very far from the elegant street named after him, in the rue des Feuillantines, off the rue Jacob, and not far from the Irish College over whose walls, it is said, a student climbed in 'forty-eight[149] to join the barricade at Saint-Germain. His name was MacHale.

It is no one event in her history, no one selfish interpretation of this piece of her history, or that we remember July 14, but our affection for her place in our own history in bad times, and now, in better, it's *Rath De uirthi*[150] – *Vive la France!*

The Irish Press, 10 July 1954

27

HERO OF THE GODS

'The O'Grady is as proud a title as any of your earls or dukes, and bedamned to you. I may be an English officer, but I am also an Irish gentleman!'

And with that, he flung the scarlet coat, gold epaulettes and all, on the floor and, in a frenzy of fury, foaming at the mouth, to the cheers and shouts of 'Up the Republic' and croaks of 'Up Skin-the-Goat' from the more venerable of the multitude, leapt the high steps of a slip jig, on the cloth of scarlet and gold.

'God bless you, P.J.,'[151] screeches an ould one from the gods, 'that's me dream out. You'll turn yet.'

OUR UNCLE

Rory and Seán and I looked round the parterre in a weakness of adoration from the stage, wishing there was someone there to tell the people, pointing from us to the stage, and its centre, glorious against the lights, a strapping lad from Kildare in his lawn shirt and velvet breeches and say, 'See those three kids there and, see your man there, the O'Grady, the colonel that's after telling off the other rat of an English officer on the court martial, well, he's their uncle.'

And at the Wicklow wedding, he led the floor, and came out to face his fancy with a smart rap of his buckled shoes, and his back hand holding up the tails of his homespun coat, and his impudent, lovely head to one side, in signal to her to take the floor with him.

Shy enough she was, till the fiddler ran through the first bit of *Haste to the Wedding*,[152] when she looked up from the floor, gazed, proud and fearless at him, and away they went.

LOVELY MAN

'Isn't he the fine man. God bless him,' you'd hear an ould one mutter, as they rapped their way, she firm and light, and he easy and strong, through the hornpipe, a murmur of one fiddle, played by the old man in the corner of the kitchen, while the orchestra in the pit looked up, in unbegrudging admiration. 'A fine lovely man.'

So he was at that, and never lived to be anything less. The light of heaven to them all, for the fiddler was Alec Fryer, and we could easy recognise, under the old *caipin* and the rough frieze coat and slender grace of the amorous Latin of last week's *song scene*, with the Queen's Moonbeams, or whatever they were calling those well-ventilated lovelies of the time.

We had seen him as a bullfighter and as a Carl Brisson hussar on the peak of a ship and in a monastery garden.

GORJUSS

We were a bit puzzled to know what he was doing there, but it was Alec all right. You'd also know him by his fiddle: no matter where he was, he brought it with him. Although, now I come to think of it, it was a Persian garden, and not a monastery one at all.

Tom Dunne, too, has joined the majority. Well I remember a tough old party by the name of O'Dea,[153] pushing his Morris Cowley off the stage, and Jimmy, for some reason, begging and imploring of all and sundry to try a 'deeny bit of seedy cake,' to the delight of everyone except an elderly relative of ours, who sat in suppressed fury and fiercely judging us for laughing, and muttered about the cheek of James Augustine getting up there to make a show of himself in a pantomime, 'a beautiful Shakespearian actor, and such gorgeous elocution'.

If Maureen Potter[154] had been in existence at the time she would have got the full flavour of the velour voice: 'bewtyful', 'Shekspurree-an', 'gorjuss'.

I was four or five at the time, and had known for years that this old citizeness was mad, any way you looked at her, but Rory went to the trouble of asking her what brought her there at all.

'To hear P.J. reciting Emmett's speech from the dock, of course, and J.C. Browner singing "When I'm jog, jog, jogging along the high road." Basso profundo, the real classical.' (Pron.: 'clussical'.)

DANCERS

D.J. Giltinan remarked in *The Bell*, some years ago, that he has seen a tenor of international repute strive in vain against the charms of the squeeze-box, or piano accordion, in a Dublin theatre. That, or Irish dancers. Far removed, of course, from the frightening atmosphere of the official *feis*, with their grim faces and the snakes and ladders on their habits and blankets.

Like a poker-faced imp, the aforementioned Potter gives a performance of that nature that crippled the ribs of a Gaiety[155] audience when I saw it a year ago. Real dancers from the hard-working professional schools of the city doing what they were paid for doing, and doing it well.

TINY

The *pièce de résistance* was always a solo bit by a tiny tot, who came in front of the line when the rest of the orchestra knocked off for a minute, and danced on her own.

With all due respect to tiny tots and their fathers and mothers and teachers, and the whole world of tiny tottery, my elderly relative had scant time for that carry-on, either.

The Irish Press, 17 July 1954

28
SERMONS IN CATS, DOGS –
AND MICE

Come all ye lads and lasses and listen to my plea for fairer play for
rabbits, cats, dogs, mice – and anything that moves on four legs –
if only for the long list of services rendered …

There is a collection of essays in the Penguin series called *Music at Night*. They were written by Aldous Huxley[156] about twenty years ago. Although a Penguin-educated citizen myself, I read this book a lot of years ago, before it was in Penguin, at a time when I was leading a more contemplative life and had plenty of time to think about what I read.

One of the essays deals with the next world, and what we are likely to be doing in it, and is called 'Squeak and Gibber'.

I was thinking of the essay Huxley calls 'Sermons in Cats'.

A man wishing to be a writer wants Huxley to tell him the best way to go about it. Now, don't think I'm going to set up in an advisory capacity on this matter.

Seán Ó Faoláin, father-confessor, nursemaid and prison visitor to some of my grade, used to say that the equipment of a writer should consist of pen, paper and a time sheet. To write and see that you wrote a certain amount every day. And a ledger to note what you sent out in the way of mss, and what you got for it.

WRONG ROAD

Huxley advises your man to watch cats. They live and love, are jealous, mean, generous, and all to that effect.

He says that the man to whom he gave this advice did not seem very grateful for it.

I'd have picked up a cat and hit him a belt of it. Only I happen to like cats.

For his advice was rubbishy, and there is nothing about human beings that cannot be learned better from human beings than from any other creature that lives on earth.

FILL'S PRAM

The man who said that the more he saw of mankind the more he liked his dog was some species of informer, or hangman's labourer, that his own mother would run away from, could she but lose him in a big enough crowd.

And the dog was the leavings of a lurcher that only stopped with him because he was too weak with the hunger for his legs to carry him any more than two yards in the one day.

'I'll never forget our poor ould bowler,' said Mrs Brenning, 'poor ould Pram. Poor faithful ould K-mine.'

'What's mine?'

'K-mine. I don't like calling him a brute. I know they've no souls, but you never know what he might be in another world listening to us. Not, but what,' she added, significantly, 'but what they might be as well entitled to souls as certain individgeyoulums I know.'

'That'll do you, now,' said Crippen. 'None of your theology. This is a respectable house.'

Mrs Brenning, lost in mournful recollection, sighed: 'Ah, poor ould Pram.'

'Pram?' said I.

'That's right. We called him "Pram", after the dog that belonged to Fill Mac Coon.'

PREFER RATS?

Cats are not know-alls. They are independent enough, and nobody ever saw a cat at one end of a lead and a policeman at the other. Belloc[157] says they are of the breed of the devil, and cannot be poisoned. Too often, this has been disproved.

People for some reason, of the would-be yokel variety, like to hang their tongues, village-idiot fashion, and tell you how they cannot stick cats.

'Well,' my mother's first mother-in-law would say, 'd'you prefer rats?'

Leaving that to one side, cats have their rights as well as anyone, under the constitution of this State, and it's a punishable offence to put them into areas in the new converted Corporation flats, so that they're trapped and die of starvation and thirst after days of agony.

REMEMBER

The older people in those parts know that only for the cats we'd never have survived in those rat warrens. Children growing up in better times may not realise this.

That is the point of this sermon. And if they don't take it to heart, I know certain little devils that will be getting a kick where it won't blind them.

ESSAY

The late Sister Monica, who taught generations of boys, including Seán Russell,[158] one of the editors of the *Irish Digest*, and the present writer, at North William Street School, was encouraging a boy called Champers who, even for that district, was considered a chaw of some dimensions.

Some doubted whether he was a human being at all, and by his shaggy looks and his taste for raw vegetables and chewing tobacco, he might have escaped from a circus.

Champers, by dint of much pen-chewing, finally produced a composition: 'The Autobiography of a Mouse'.

'I was a muss. So was me mother and me father and we all et chess till the cat kem an et me da and me ma and me an all.'

REPLY

'Now, Stanislaus Kostka,' this was Champers's real name, 'that is really very good indeed, and most interesting, but,' and she looked at him earnestly from under her big linen bonnet, 'if the mouse was eaten by the cat, how could he have written his autobiography?'

Champers looked at her scornfully and asked, with great patience: 'Listen, Sister, how could a mouse write his beeyografee anyway?'

The Irish Press, 24 July 1954

29
MEET A GREAT POET

'Brending Behing.'

'Good morning, Mrs Brenning.'

'And good luck.'

'As the crow said to the duck.'

'You too, Maria, and your friends in America.'

'What I want to know is, where might you be going with the Renningtom. Not a visit to your uncle, so early in the morning?'

'There's so much value in scrap these days,' muttered Crippen, from a corner. He has literary ambitions himself, and bitterly resents any pretensions, in that direction, on the part of anyone else. The sight of my battered old typewriter is a cause of severe illness to him. If I wanted to see him jump off Butt Bridge I'd have only to walk down East Arran Street, carrying a briefcase.

TESTIMOLEUM

'Ah, I don't know now,' said Maria, with an amiable sniff.

'I know you don't,' said Crippen, 'I heard all about you. When the white gas meters came out, you were an hour trying to get into the Balladmaker's Saturday night, on your one.'

'Ah, now, Mr Cripping, Maria's not all that bad. She can count her change lovely, if whatever it is she's buying hasn't gone up from the last time she bought it. We can't all be jeemases like yourself and Brending Behing there.'

'And if you want to know,' said I, 'I'm taking this machine to be cleaned and oiled.'

'And it's not all that bad of a machine, Mr Cripping. Do you not remember the testimoleum he did for poor Henrietta on it?'

'I do not,' said Crippen.

HIS LORDSHIP

'Ah, don't you remember. He came here one morning and poor Henrietta, she used to follow painters, cleaning houses and washing up their dirt after them, before she took to the lifting, and then she wasn't able to get a job, on account of not having a testimoleum, and where would she get it, barring they'd give her one of the 'Joy, but Brending Behing here sat down in the corner, opened up the yoke, and there and then wrote her a beauty of a reverence.

'You'd have got yourself a job on the strent of it. To the effect that she was the nanny of his children till they were big enough to beat her, and he knew that she was a lifelong teetotaller, and a lovely knitter, with a soft hand under a duck, and to who it might concern, and them it didn't could go and do the other, and it had his signature and all to it. What's this it was now? Lord Williamstown and Booterstown and Monkstown, and—'

'Blanchardstown,' suggested Maria, helpfully.

CROSS DOUBLES

'And she got a lovely position with some old one from England, and took everything that wasn't nailed down, only they caught her carrying out the sundial. Very unlucky thing to be caught with.'

'I know this much,' said Crippen, 'if I was doing me writing, I couldn't do it on one of them things.'

'God knows and you're right there, Mr Crippen. I'd like to see the bookies, the day of a big race, and everyone trying to write their three cross doubles and the same back, on them things. All them machines going together, you'd think it was the Hammond Lane you were in, and how would a body hear a result or anything?'

'I wasn't talking about writing three cross doubles,' said Crippen, crossly.

'Well, accumulators, wouldn't they be worse, and …'

'I was talking about writing poetry,' said Crippen, in some exasperation. I mean, looking as if bad words would be sullying his lips any minute.

'Oh, yes, Mr Cripping. Now I have you.'

GREAT CRIPPEN

He looked sternly at me: 'Tell me any great poem was written on one of them things.'

'Well,' said I, 'I was going to say that I didn't stand over the shoulders of great poets to know what way they went about it.'

'"Well," "well",' quoted Crippen, 'that's what you look for when the beer runs out. But you can't answer me. And remember I wrote poems before you come up. *And* translations from the English language, the Irish language …'

'The deaf and dumb language,' offered Maria.

'I didn't know you wrote Irish,' said I.

'You didn't know. You didn't know because you never went to the trouble of finding out.'

'Well say one now, Mr Cripping, go on, say it up, now, and the divil thank the begrudgers.'

'I'll say it, though seeing as yous don't understand the language, yous won't be much the better of it.'

He looked round at the audience and fixed Maria with an arrogant glance: 'Like a sow looking into a swill barrel,' he muttered, elegantly.

'I know a bit of Irish,' said I.

'You do, but it's only the new stuff they have in the schools. Dots and dashes. But this is the real goat's toe.'

PILLALOO

He cleared his throat and began:

> *Pillaloo, wirrastroo,*
> *Sure, I'm kilt,*
> *May the quilt*
> *Rest light on your beautiful form,*
> *When the weather is hot, or*

(he waved a complacent hand)

Again when it's not,
I'll roll you up,
Cosy and warm.'

'That's massive,' said Mrs Brenning. 'Have you e'er another one? I could folly nearly every word of that.'

'This one is a lot harder.'

'Well, never mind, it's all for the cause. Me poor father had a lovely pone, called "Never Hit a Lady with Your Hat On", but it was only English.'

MASTERPIECE

'Hhhhm,' said Crippen, clearing his throat, and throwing out his hand in declamation:

'Come out, my shillelagh,
Come out, love to me,
On the bright Cruiskeen Lawn
We will dance the Banshee;
And while bright shines the moon,
Lady Luna above,
In the groves of Na Backlesh,
We'll lovingly rove,
And softly and sweetly I'll murmur to you,
Musha, and allanna, astore, tiggin too.'[159]

'Massive,' muttered Mrs Brenning, rubbing her eye, 'Oh, leave it to you, Mr Cripping.'

But going out, Michael called me, and said out of the side of his mouth: 'He never made them poems up.'

'No?'

'Course he didn't. They were written by Yeets. Y'often heard of him, owned the Half-Way House above in Drimnagh.'

The Irish Press, 31 July 1954

30

FROM DUBLIN TO LES CHAMPS-ÉLYSÉES

Paris, as the man said, *est toujours Paris*. Always her own sweet self. She looks much the same as usual, except for the fact that the Metro is gone up to thirty francs and the government of Mendès France gets a little less abuse than previous governments.

The talk about local politicians and other notabilities in a Paris bistro is like a breath of home to the Dubliner, far from the scurrilities of pub conversation in his native city, and just as intimately savage. So, it will be seen that the present government of France is enjoying a summer of great popularity.

Thirty francs is about eight-pence and, for a short journey, is fairly dear. But once you buy a ticket you are at liberty to go anywhere the Metro goes, and it will take you right from one end of the city to the other.

UNRETURNED

For a worker living in Belleville and working in Montrouge, say, which would be as far as from Kimmage to Dún Laoghaire, it is not much dearer than CIE.

The buses are dearer than the underground, and are much less comfortable and up to date than ours. They are all single-deckers, and when I went to

Paris after the war, I was told that there was a shortage of buses, the Germans having taken a great number of them with them on the retreat of 1944.

Judging by the length of time I waited for a Number 95, in the avenue de l'Opéra, they must not have given them back yet.

Though, looking up at the destination board on the lamp post, I felt I could forgive a lot to a vehicle that made regular journeys to places like Saint-Germain-des-Prés, the Louvre and Carrousel.

SARTRE'S HQ

Saint-Germain-des-Prés, on the Left Bank, or south side of the Seine, is to the post-war intellectual, genius or phoney, have it whatever way you like, what Montmartre was to the artist of Picasso's[160] youth, before the first war and, as a refuge of sinners, has succeeded Montparnasse, stamping ground of Hemingway[161] and Scott Fitzgerald[162] in the twenties.

It gained notoriety as the headquarters of Jean-Paul Sartre,[163] just after the Liberation. He had a flat on the corner of the rue Bonaparte, and the adjoining licensed premises, the Deux Magots and the Flore,[164] became the twin cathedrals of existentialism, of which philosophy he is the high priest.

BURGLAR POET

As regards 'existentialism', see the more learned literary page of this journal. Try MacManus, Kiely or Williams. I am doing my best for you when I pass on Cecil Ffrench Salkeld's definition of it. He said it teaches that 'man is sentinel to the null'.

And as good an excuse for robbing all round you as any other, as Monsieur Jean Genet[165] has proved, with great profit to himself.

This man was a burglar for many years, and also a poet. He was arrested many times for breaking and entering, and each time refused to recognise the court. Like Marlowe,[166] who countered all objection to his home production of coin of the realm with the remark that he was as much entitled to mint money as the Queen of England. Monsieur Genet told the court that he robbed as an existentialist, and had a conscientious objection to keeping his hands easy.

In a less civilised country, he would now be engaged in the production of mailbags, four stitches to the inch. But Sartre, and a number of other writers, demanded that they leave the boy alone. And he is now an honoured French writer, a credit to his country and the proprietor of an estate in the country.

He doesn't need to do any more work in the burglarising line, and lives on the proceeds of his books.

I had extracts of his autobiography read to me, some of which rose the hair on my head. And, as my mother once remarked, that which would shock Brendan Behan would turn thousands grey.

Oscar Wilde[167] died in a hotel down the street, in the rue d'Alsace, and tradition has it that it was a priest of Saint-Germain-des-Prés church attended him on his death bed.

DEARER

The first thing one learns on visiting Paris is that it is not what it was. I was told that some years ago, and for the first time, was able to pass that remark to some Irish students, half a generation younger than myself.

I do not really believe it, though things are a bit dearer. A hotel room is five hundred francs a night, which is ten shillings and not much, if you think in terms of Galway race week, but twice as much as six or seven years ago.

Old Raymond Duncan,[168] who ran an Akademia of Greek culture in the rue Dauphine, is either dead or in America.

Time was, when I watched him, in the midst of his disciples, elderly ladies and gentlemen dressed in blankets and sandals, a sort of kilted costume that bore as much resemblance to the clothes of the ancient Greeks as to the uniform of the Fintan Lalor Pipe Band[169] to that of Brian Boru in solemn procession, to greet the dawn at the bottom of our street on midsummer morn.

With what ecstasy I saw them trip over a wire thoughtfully provided by the boys of the Beaux-Arts[170] and stretched ankle-high across the road. God be with the youth of us, the simple pleasures of the poor.

WARRIORS

The Bonapartist, who used to march along the boulevard Saint-Germain in his long coat and cocked hat, sword ever at the ready to avenge the slightest insult to his emperor, was no longer in evidence; nor was Confucius, an old Chinaman or something, who specialised on one branch of English literature, and that a bilingual catalogue from Messrs Whiteleys of London of which he would read you a couple of hundred pages, so that you might know how 'three-piece Chesterfield suite, twenty pounds ten', or 'oak double bed, eleven pounds, ten shillings; mattress, best flock extra', sounded in Chinese.

And dare you move an inch, till the last huckaback towel was disposed of, for he was a man of wide culture and, in addition to his literary talents, was a ju-jitsu expert.

REMEMBERED

But the Pergola is still open, '*jour et nuit*', and its proprietor still large and affable, and very wide awake behind the bar, though he could hardly have got a sleep since the last time I was there.

He remembered me and shook me warmly by the hand when I went in. He asked me how I was, and how long I expected to be around this time.

I told him I was off to the Riviera in the morning, and he smiled even more cordially, and did not seem at all upset by the prospect of my departure after so short a visit. He remembered me, all right.

The Irish Press, 7 August 1954

31
THE ROAD TO LYON

The poet Yeats disliked parsnips.

On the boat from Newhaven I met three Queen's University students, who were also bound for the south of France.

The train costs about seven pounds from Paris to Cannes, and though I knew how to get a fruit lorry from Les Halles market for a couple of thousand francs, that sort of travelling does not appeal to me anymore. I would sooner leave it to the Boy Scouts and to An Óige.[171]

So when these fellows told me that they knew of a bus service that took you to Cannes for less than four pounds, food and lodging included, I gladly availed myself of the information.

At four o'clock in the morning, I decided, it was too late to bother getting a hotel, and as it was a pity to break up the company, my friends announced that they would stick it out, till it was time to get the autobus, which left the rue l'Arcade at seven o'clock.

POET'S PARSNIPS

So we had another couple, just to show no coolness, and settled down in the Pergola for another couple of hours. An American, upon being introduced, and being told I was from Dublin, asked me if I had known James Joyce. I regretted that I did not have that honour, but told him that my mother had cooked a meal for W.B. Yeats in Madame MacBride's house[172] in Stephen's Green, and that the poet turned up his nose to the parsnips.

'He did not like parsnips?' said the American, reaching for a notebook. 'You're sure this is factual?'

'It is to be hoped,' I replied, 'that you are not calling my mother a liar.'

'No, no, of course not. But she might have been mistaken. Maybe it was carrots,' he added, hastily.

'You must think I'm a right thick to have a mother that can't tell a carrot from a parsnip.'

'No, certainly not. I'm sure you wouldn't. I mean I'm sure she could. But this is very important.' He wrote in the book: *Parsnips, attitude of Yeats to.* 'And you say he didn't like Stephen's Greens, either. Now, what sort of vegetable are they?'

MY ICELAND

At this point the patron introduced a Belgian to me, who shook me warmly by the hand and said he knew my country well. In connection with an American construction company during the war, he had twice visited Reykjavik. With some relief, I got back to my vegetable man.

When we went out to get the Metro for my autobus to the sun, the dawn was as bleak as a summer's morning at home. I got my ticket, got aboard the coach and fell asleep. I did not wake up till we were going past Fontainebleau. My companions were a Belgian, whom I questioned closely about his wartime activities till I satisfied myself that they had not taken him to Reykjavik, and two young Frenchmen.

Further up the coach I heard a strong Lancashire voice, and in the course of the journey, discovered it belonged to a little man from Preston, which he told me (proudly), has the reputation of being 'poor, proud, and Papist'.

At Avignon we walked round the Pope's palace, in a proprietorial fashion, before refreshing ourselves with a couple of rosiners. Very good red wine, of course, at about two pence a glass.

LIKE VINEGAR

I was about to remark that a country with such beautiful drink and a hundred and twenty different sorts of cheese was still well worth a visit, when my companion wiped his lips and spoke.

'Desperate stuff, isn't it? Ee, it's like vinegar. And that there crawling muck they call cheese. Why, a man'd be run in, in England, for even possessing the like of that, much less selling it. A danger to public 'ealth, I'd call it.'

'It's shocking all right,' said I, wondering where I'd buy a litre of wine and a box of Camembert or a bit of Brie for the trip to Aix-en-Provence. Luckily, I'd be in the back of the car, and he would not see me devouring it. 'We might as well have another, though, seeing as we can get nothing else. *Garçon, encore du rouge, s'il vous plait.*'

I knocked it back, as best I could, and my companion looked at me suspiciously.

'You swallowed that like you liked it,' said he.

'Best to get it over, quickly,' said I, 'it's good for warts.'

MY PREJUDICES

Our bus was parked by a Roman Arch, like a miniature Arc de Triomphe, the father and mother of all arches of triumph, including the Marble Arch, and the arch at the top of Grafton Street which commemorates Ireland's victory over the Boers, or the foundation stone of Wolfe Tone's memorial, removed, as an obstruction, by police order.

But it was only when we got to Lyon that my mind began to run on the wrongs of the dead, for it was here I discovered that my ticket did not cover hotel expenses. I should have known that. Four pounds is not much for a journey twice the length of Ireland, but like many another, the Dubliner is the victim of his own prejudices.

Conditioned all the days of my life to the belief that people from the three other provinces, Cork, the North and the Country, could build nests in your ear, mind mice at a crossroads, and generally stand where thousands fell, I implicitly accepted the word of these northern fellows, who had never set foot in France before, against my better judgement, and lived riotously all the way from Dieppe to this Lyon, where we were heartlessly dislodged from our seats and put out on the road, to get hotels we had not the money for.

TO THE RIVER

Still, it was some consolation to see the three Queen's men walk abjectly towards the riverbank.

'The mon says we have to find our own hotel,' said their leader, miserably, 'and it just doesn't run it.'

'The Rhône is first turn on your right,' said I, and walked on considerably cheered. Besides, I remembered that I knew a journalist in the place.

On a visit to Dublin I had arranged for him to meet the leader of the Irish underground, a chap that worked in a basement store, and he had asked me to call in any time I was passing.

The Irish Press, 14 August 1954

32

AHEAD TO THE SUN: FROM LYON TO THE OCEAN

We left Lyon early in the morning and drove on towards the sun. It was getting warmer. We went on through the vineyards. I think 'grapefield' would be a better description, for they grew in rows and rows in huge fence-less fields, as common as cabbage in Ireland.

Beautiful as it was, we lost interest in it after a while and only wished to be woken up at a stop, to get out, quench our thirst and stretch our legs, for all the world like a Kerry All-Ireland crowd on the long road to Croke Park except that we were silent, and not so carefree. We had been the best part of two days travelling, and no matter how beautiful the destination, man is not made for so much running around. Travel is a great inducer of gloom.

MINE VIFE

The Belgian beside me agreed. 'No matter where you are, you must take yourself with you,' he said.

The lady in front of us turned around, and fixed a stern look on him.

'Mine vife,' he muttered in English.

'*C'est ça*, mine vife,' said the lady superfluously, and spoke rapidly in Flemish.

'No, my love, I said must take *myself* with me,' he said very meekly. I do not understand Flemish, but so I thought he said. They had not previously spoken to each other aboard the bus.

She looked at him, as much as to say, *I know I had the misfortune to marry the biggest eejit in Belgium, but could you not try and not demonstrate it in public before half of Europe.*

FEATHERED FRIEND

But just then the driver said we would see the Mediterranean over the hill, and she gave her husband a look as much as to say, *My fine feathered friend, when I get you to myself in the hotel, you'll know all about it*, glared at him, glared at me and turned to prepare herself for a glare or two at the Mediterranean.

It was as blue as I expected. We turned left as you go towards Italy, and just as they say about Killiney, there it was. Only like a stretch of fifty Killineys and the sun high in the heavens, stretching away to the left, and Cannes all shining white, the sea on one side, and the endless tangled growth of the mountains going away into the Alps on the other.

CAMPS AND CARS

There were camps and cars all the way in. The Parisian worker refers to the Blue Coast, the Côte d'Azur, by another name, which refers to the gang of international loafers, millionaire layabouts and royal bowseys that have made this place famous, but for a long way before we came to Cannes were camped along the road the tents of quite ordinary and no doubt respectable French families, and the long-legged sunburnt youth of many nationalities, boys and girls, richer than any of the smart ones in their ten-pound-a-day hotels, or on their luxury yachts, for they were young and healthy, and if the royalty and plutocracy had wealth at their side, these youngsters had youth.

'To hell with that for a yarn,' said the Belgian, 'what about them that has neither?'

Some people are never satisfied. I was glad when we reached Cannes.

I GLARED BACK

'Goodbye,' said the Belgian, 'I go now, vit my vife.'

'I'd sooner you nor me,' said I.

'Tank you,' said he. The wife told him to get looking after the baggage, and glared at me.

I took heart of grace and glared back.

'Very good, I say goodbye for now.'

But I was not in such good fettle myself when I asked for a bus to my destination and was told it was another twenty miles away, back up on the mountains, and that a bus went within four miles of it, but only once a week, and that was usually yesterday.

'Come here,' said a policeman, 'I'll show it to you.'

ONLY THE WOLVES

He pointed up towards two or three hundred miles of mountains, but being a stranger in the place I did not know one Alp from another.

'Your road is up the rue Carnot, turn left and keep walking. About twenty-six kilometres. You can't miss it. Nothing else up that way.'

'Only the wolves,' said I.

'No, not this time of the year.'

'Well, *merci, m'sieu l'agent. Au revoir.*'

'*Au revoir, m'sieu. Bonne courage.*'

'I'll need it.'

The Irish Press, 21 August 1954

33
TERROR IN THE ALPS OF FRANCE

I alped my way for some weary hours till the sun went down and I found myself alone in the mountains, and in the dark.

I remembered a book we had at school called *Seilg I measc na nAilp*,[173] or *A Hunt in the Alps*, and, when I saw a bright light appear and re-appear in front of me, wondered with something approaching terror, as they say in books, whether I might be the object of this one.

A hoarse barking, as if in suppressed rancour, and not all that suppressed, broke on my ears, and I started to run. But it was not much use running, for the light appeared in my path, and the grunting bark grew louder, and anyway it was too far to run to Dolphin's Barn.[174]

DAITHI REMEMBERED

Not all the sins of my past life passed in front of me, but as many as could get room in the queue. Not since I slept in a barn at a place called Rambouillet,[175] the other end of France, next to a horse that mended his own shoes in the small hours of the morning, was I so frightened.

I struggled on, in this alien wilderness, and for company's sake thought of King Daithi,[176] killed at the foot of the Alps. Why did not anyone ever warn both of us to keep out of them?

The light appeared again, and the barking kept on, and it was better than a mission. I sweated about seven pounds till a car came round the corner, and caught me in the headlights.

MIDNIGHT LIFT

It stopped, and I never heard brakes go on with greater pleasure. I mean, never with greater pleasure, did I hear brakes go on. I was in no humour for worrying about my prose style at that moment. I didn't care if it was Dracula driving that heap of scrap, only to hear a semi-human voice, and known there were other ways of communication beside this barking-grunting.

It wasn't Dracula. At least if it was, he was not in uniform, but a man on his way home from work.

'C'est le route à Montcolin?' I asked.

He said it was the road to Montcolin and, what was better, that he would give me a lift to within a couple of miles of Montcolin.

'May your shadow never grow less, oh, man of the van,' said I with fervour and got into it.

FIREFLIES

I staggered into the Irish encampment, a villa high in the mountains, in the small hours of the morning, and was fed and given drink, and related my story. I spoke of the lights and the barking.

My host laughed.

'Those lights were fireflies. And the barking you heard was the grunting of the frogs.'

'Why, of course,' said I, 'how silly of me.' But I had never experienced anything the like of that on Sundrive Road.[177]

Time heals all things, and I woke up twelve hours later, as good as ever I was.

The village of Montcolin is shortly to become famous over Raidió Éireann, and you will know more about it than many of its inhabitants, and certainly more than anyone outside it, for it is locked high up in the Alps Maritime.

COLAS

We went down to Cannes by car, and swam in the Mediterranean.

At Juan-les-Pins[178] Sugar Ray Robinson[179] was performing in the Hollywood night club, where a beer would cost you something in the region of a pound, if they sold you one, which they would if you were wealthy enough.

The usual drink is champagne but I was told of an American in a hotel who wanted a Cola with his lunch.

Colas are quite popular in France, but this hotel did not stock it, so a waiter was sent round the corner to buy one from a stall for fifty francs, and twenty on the bottle.

The Cola was duly bought and taken on a tray with ice and a napkin round the neck to the gentleman, who drank it, expressed himself pleased with the quality, and cheerfully paid eight hundred francs for it (sixteen shillings), plus two hundred service, which made it the even quid.

The man that sold it to the waiter told me, and he was told by the waiter when the waiter came back for the twenty-franc refund on the bottle.

PEDAL BOAT

We went to our beach, which was called the Rio, and there for the day you could hire a seat and a parasol to shade you when you were out of the water for a couple of shillings. You could get a quart bottle of iced beer for about one-and-ninepence, and, best of all, you had the whole shimmering sea from there to Africa for nothing.

They also had for hire a kind of paddle boat in which you sat and propelled yourself by a sort of pedal action on the same principle as a bicycle. I heard that people had tried to pedal to Corsica on them, though why they weren't satisfied with where they were is beyond me.

Myself and a gang of kids, Irish, Anglo-Irish, Dutch-Irish and Russian-Irish, got in, and it would have taken a bayonet charge by the First Battalion to get us out.

NO ICE

There is no swimming till you swim in water like that. No breaking the ice. No diving in to 'put yourself out of pain' as we used to say in Dollymount.[180] Just a matter of languidly rambling out till you are into it and alive again, after being comfortably comatose in the sun.

I cannot understand why very small children, when swimming on your back, cannot get the idea of holding on to your shoulders rather than half strangling you by the firm pressure of baby hands on your windpipe. Still, we enjoyed it.

BEST RAFT

I was more than repaid for the perils of the deep when I heard the smallest and most lethal one reply, when someone asked from the beach whether she wanted her big rubber raft: 'We don't want the wubber waft. We got Bwendan.'

So she had, in a drowning man's grip, though I lived to tell the tale.

Talking about Dollymount reminds me of when I was at school.

The teacher, one Monday morning, came in and said that she had been at Killiney the previous day, but that she had not enjoyed it, the place was crowded with trippers.

I had very little idea of what she was talking about but, like Lanna Machree's dog, I'd go a bit of the road with anyone.

TRIPPERS

'Dollymount is the very same, miss,' said I. 'Them trippers. Place is rotten with them.'

She looked at me incredulously. 'But – but Dollymount is for trippers.'

I'm a tripper here, and so is nearly everyone else. Just a tourist, though it's a word of loathing to most of the English-speaking foreigners.

There is an American cartoon that shows a man, with straw boater hat, camera, blazer and flannels, and he is saying to his wife: 'I look like a tourist. I am a tourist. So what?'

I wouldn't mind being left like that.

The Irish Press, 28 August 1954

34
THREE CELTIC PILLARS OF CHARITY

This life is full of disappointments. The band of the Beaux-Arts school is one of them. Not in noise, volume or variety of costume but, as the man said, basically. This way:

The École des Beaux-Arts, or School of Fine Arts in Paris in the popular imagination, is a sort of Tír na nÓg of young geniuses, painting and sculpting with fresh, savage efficiency during the working day, cursing the professors, damning all academies, till the light fades, the stars rise over the garret, and Mimi, the little midinette, knocks timidly on the door and comes in with a bottle of wine, the piece of veal, the garlic, the bread and cheese purchased, mayhap, with the fruits of her long day's stitching for the rude and haughty ladies of the rue du Faubourg Saint-Honoré.

And if, at festival time, he dashes madly through the streets most daring of his band, well, youth must have its fling, and the staid conventions of looking where you are going are not for such ardent spirits as these.

BAND
The present Beaux-Arts school has a band. Its instruments are not the usual instruments of brass and reed: they are composed mostly of household instruments.

During the summer nights they have a march-out, at least every Saturday night, up and round the narrow streets of the Latin Quarter, playing in close harmony, on buckets, tin cans, biscuit tins, old motor horns, auctioneers' hand bells, basins, bowls, with a male and female voice choir, in sections variously represented: the howl, the screech, the moan, the groan, the roar, the bawl, the yell, the scream, the snarl, the bay, the bark, in time to the steady and rhythmic thud of the big bass dustbin, and the more sombre tones of the tin bath.

Along the street, the foreigners smiled and nodded indulgently at each other. Dear old Paris. Dear old Latin Quarter. Has never changed since Mimi's hand was frozen; since Gene Kelly's[181] feet were hot; since the last time we were over.

GAS MEN

We wondered at the sour looks on the faces of the French, and the disgruntled voice of the big vegetable porter who cursed the noise and said people had to be up at five in the morning to go to work.

Don't bother with work, we thought: those lads outside aren't worried about work. Free spirits. Another cognac there, garçon: the noise did not upset us. This is what we came to Paris for. Outside they were advancing on Saint-Germain. Someone beat the bath on the boulevard.

I turned to Donal and, amidst the satisfied sighs of the foreigners and the curses of the French, shook my head indulgently, and remarked apropos the vegetable porter and other native grumblers: 'Woe to the begrudgers. Aren't they gas men, the art students? *Is maith an rud an óige.*'[182]

'They manage an imitation of it,' a voice beside me said.

DISCORD

I turned, and saw that a girl had come in and was standing beside us.

'What does who manage an imitation of?' I asked.

'You said in Irish that youth is a great thing. You were obviously referring to those dreary architects making a nuisance of themselves up the street.'

'What architects? Anyway, how do you know what I said in Irish?'

'I suppose I went to school as much as you did.'

'That'd be small trouble to you. But what architects are you talking about?'

'Those fellows going around the place, doing the hard chaw, keeping everybody awake. You, like all the tourist—'

I choked with indignation, and my fellow travellers, an American textile foreman, a Scots honeymoon couple and two London schoolmasters, gazed at her with disgust. The foul word that had just left her lips stamped her, in all our eyes, as a cad, or a caddess. It's not a word used in polite society along the boulevards, unless you are speaking of somebody else, of course.

WILD OATS

She went on relentlessly.

'You people think it's all very romantic, but those little architectural students, as soon as they qualify, buy a nice suit, grow a moustache, and refer to this period as the time they were sowing their wild oats.

'I wouldn't mind but I've got to get up and go over to Neuilly, and be at the church of Saint-Pierre, in the morning.'

'Tomorrow is not Sunday,' said Donal. 'Is it a holy day over here?'

'Maybe it's a wedding you're going to,' said I. 'Have another citronade on the head of it.'

MLLE MURPHY

'No, thanks. I'm for bed. It's not a wedding I'm going to. I'm going to work. Some people do, you know. I leave my tools here, on my way from the school, and Madame is just gone to collect them. Ah, here she is.'

She beamed back at the fat old patronne, whose face for the first time since I'd seen her was split in a smile as she handed over the counter what looked like a kit of tools belonging to a bricklayer.

'Merci, Madame.'

The old one smiled again. That's twice in the one twenty-four hours.

'Service, Mademoiselle Murfee.'

Mlle Murphy said good night to us, too, and went off up the rue Dauphine, a trim slip of a girl, as they say at home, but swinging her hammers and chisels with an air.

SAINT-PIERRE

The church of Saint-Pierre is the parish church of Neuilly, in south-west Paris. It is about the size of the Dublin Pro Cathedral and is nearly a hundred years old, no older than the University Church on Dublin's Green, and as beautiful, in a different style.

Like Chartres, Bruges, towering and mighty, since the age of faith, this modest and middle-aged suburban church was decorated by a group of sculptors, unpaid, and giving themselves, mind and muscle, for God's sake.

The parish priest of Saint-Pierre had about enough money to keep the church in repair and pay a couple of charwomen and a verger. He had nothing over for ornamentation, for the lovely stone that practically shouted for a chisel.

God's help, they say in Irish, is never further than the door, in this case, the door of the École des Beaux-Arts.

Someone in the school heard of all this lovely stone going unadorned, and, the next thing a squad of students are out fighting to divide the church up amongst them.

Kathleen Murphy, of Ballymore Eustace, comes away with three pillars, and, with hammers upraised, poises her slim self to strike a blow, *do chum ghloine. Dé agus onóra na hÉireann.*[183]

CELTIC WAY

These pillars represent in their tortuous Celtic way, the struggle of Christian France against the Huns, the Creation and the Deluge.

Standing there, in the quiet of the avenue du Roule, in the church of Saint-Pierre, the noise of the traffic round the Étoile, and on the Champs-Élysées, dim in the distance.

I noted, lovingly, the twisted features of each cantankerous countenance, thought of Raphoe, Cashel, Clonmacnoise,[184] and heard the waves of the Atlantic break on the Aran shore, and the praising voice of the holy Irish long since dead, soft in the gathering dusk.

The Irish Press, 4 September 1954

35

WHAT ARE THEY AT WITH
THE ROTUNDA?

I was reared a strict Dubliner. My father's people came from the cul-de-sac (not a French word, by the way, they call it 'impasse') called 'George's Pocket',[185] at the back of St George's Church in Temple Street, which is the most beautiful bit of city anywhere.

My mother was born in Capel Street, and my father's earliest memories were of his grandmother, a hardy old sort from the lock house on the Royal Canal above Mountjoy, screeching in anguish to the chiming of the bells of St George's, 'Oh, God forgive yous, there's the come-or-stays, there's the come-or-and yous wouldn't go as far as Wren's for the little message.'

'Get up, La, shake yourself, Boo, Christina, think of your poor ould ma, which a yous, wan a yous, any a yous, hurry over there before Wren's is shut and get the little message.'

The come-or-stays were the chimes that rang at seven o'clock just before evening service on Sundays and were so called because they were a hurried gathering of noise that seemed to say, 'Come to church or stay away, come to church or stay away.'

CLOSING TIME

Though we were proud of St George's, Johnson's jewel, of which St Martin-in-the-Fields is said to be an imitation, none of us had ever set foot in it, and the main significance of the chimes lay in the fact that besides calling sinners to repentance, it also meant that the time was nearly 7 pm, and the pubs would be shut, if La (Laurence O'Toole, an intimate friend of one James Fitzharris,[186] known to history as 'Skin-the-Goat',) or Boo, my grand-uncle, or my grandmother did not go with all dispatch, and a gallon can for the 'little message'.

By the same token, if a native of this city may be permitted to mention *Ulysses*, Wren's is the pub occupied by Larry O'Rourke in 1904, on the corner of Eccles Street, which the BBC Third Programme announcer calls 'Ekkles Street'.

REMOVE THEM

I have naturally some affection for the lovely Georgian Northside but I hope, when they rebuild Temple Street, they won't do, as they did with Gardiner Street, and preserve a mock Georgian facade.

Let them tear the whole lot down and build new modern flats for the people.

It's easy enough to come over in your new Chev[187] from Mount Merrion or Foxrock, and have a nostalgic glance at the Dublin of Joyce and O'Casey before taking the visiting artist to Jammet's,[188] but a bit of light and air would be more to the taste of the families to be reared in them.

The Wide Streets Commissioners built well in their day for a class that only allowed the ancestors of the later inhabitants into their beautiful homes as servants. But let Ireland, building for its own people, do the best that modern technique can do for them.

God knows life is short enough, without people wearing themselves out hauling prams round lobbies, so that we can know what Hardwicke St looked like in 1790.

IN THE LUG

Incidentally, the Hall there was the premises of the National Theatre before they moved to the Abbey, and was a drill hall for the Fianna before Easter Week and, if I may say so, for long after. Con Colbert[189] drilled in it, and it was for long the headquarters of the Academy of Christian Art.

Once, interrupting a lecture by Father Myles Ronan, just as he was about to reveal who pinched the ogham stone outside Dan Murphy's door, I was the recipient of a stout box in the lug from that tough veteran, George Noble, Count Plunkett.[190]

I was the slowest mover of a pitch and toss school being held in the yard whose proceedings deafened the ears of the Christian artists inside.

What I want to know, howsomeover, as they say in those parts, is, what are they at with the Rotunda?[191] The picture house part, I mean. Whatever it is, they shouldn't have been let. The stonework has been plastered over with some awful-looking substance that looks like granite-coloured glue.

I could see some sense in tearing it down and shoving up a new building if they wanted more room, but to leave it the same shape, covered with that stuff, does not seem such a good stroke.

If Pat MacNamara knows about it, wherever he is, God rest him, there'll be some choice blessings bestowed on the work.

Many is the time I saw him head the bill there, though I appeared on the boards of a rival house myself. Conscripted would be more like it. And a good many years ago now.

CRISIS

At that time there were three places running variety along 'Parneller'. There was the Rotunda, which also had pictures; there was the Star, opposite the Rotunda, and now a store for Aer Lingus; and there was the Torch, which was in Capel Street, the headquarters of the Dublin Trades Council.

A relative of mine, a young married man of nineteen years of age, was knocking it out for the wife and family running a revue at the Torch. I was out walking with my father one evening when we met him and they adjourned for one.

The usual how-are-ye and is your granny still in the Union and all to that effect went on, and my father asks your man what kind of houses are they getting below in the Torch.

Your man shook his head mournfully and ejaculated one word. 'Shocking, diabolical, in the language of James Clarence Mangan,[192] gapping. They're running a singing newsboy in the Roto, and a crippled singing newsboy in *The Star*.'

Even I, less than ten years old, standing in the corner supping me Vimto and glad to get it, knew what that meant in a district where everyone is a newsboy, an old newsboy, or the female relative of a newsboy. And a crippled newsboy. Sure, that'd leave them after the first verse with a lump in the throat you'd want to take to a blacksmith.

'But,' said he with a shake of his black head, 'Aughrim is never lost. We're not beat yet.'

'Be no manner of means,' says my old man. 'Have you booked Tetrissinny?'

'No, but I've the beatings of them.'

'A snake-charmer with uilleann pipes that can brush his hair with the sole of his boot, singing "You have me in a knot" at the one time.'

'I have a blind crippled singing newsboy.'

'That'd do them. If such a thing was to be had.'

'I have him here,' said the man, looking round.

I looked round, following his glance, but could see no newsboy, blind, crippled or any other sort.

'Where?' asked my old man.

'Here,' says your man, putting his hand on my shoulder.

'Damn it,' says the old man, 'you wouldn't blind and cripple him for the sake of a week's engagement? Different if you were doing the grand tour of the thirty-two counties of Ireland and Newtownmountkennedy.'

STAR

I wasn't blinded or crippled, but the next Monday night saw me on the stage of the Torch, my few poor papers clutched to my side as I leant on my crutch and gazed upon the sobbing multitude through black glasses, balanced precariously on my one leg and my other strapped up to the small of my back, singing the 'Blind Ditty':

> 'Or the flowers that are so bright,
> I can hear sweet voices calling,
> And to me they are so kind,
> Bordsandbeesen flowers …'

I sang 'Ramona, when day is done I'll hear you call,' for an encore, and 'Oro, mo bháidín ag snámh ar an gcuan.'[193]

After that I was billed as 'the blind, singing, crippled newsboy (and with gold fáinne)'.

The Irish Press, 11 September 1954

36

VOICE LIKE A CINDER
UNDER A GATE

The Paris correspondent of another Irish newspaper met me when I came back from the south, and we went into a place off the avenue de l'Opéra, and sat for a while sipping a drop of pastis.[194] And for once in a way, I listened to somebody else. And not to want to listen to Desmond, a man would want to be a savage of a different variety to me.

He went to France as a child to learn the language which, indeed, he speaks beautifully, according to the French themselves, and they have a great regard for their own tongue.

So much so, that I was corrected on a point of grammar by an old vegetable woman in one of the poorest parts of the city.

I was telling somebody I had been over to the markets in the morning. These enormous glass-roofed enclosures, built by Baron Haussmann, when he redesigned the city in the last century are known as 'The Halls', in French 'Les Halles'.

I pronounced it 'Lez All', but this old woman looked up from her glass, and looked at me earnestly.

'No, Rabelais, it is not "Lez All", but "Lay All". "Lez om" (*les hommes*, the men) would be correct, but "Les Halles" is pronounced "Lay All".'

The patron of the shop told me that this woman could neither read nor write.

RIVALS

Desmond learned his French at the right time. He was sent to live with a countess and her family in Brittany for, curiously enough, the French have the same idea about their Celts speaking the language with a good accent, as the English have about the people of Inverness and the Dublin middle class.

The family ruled an area almost half the size of County Louth, in the far west, so to speak, and consisted of the lady herself, two sons, aged about twenty-nine and twenty-seven, two girls of fifteen and seventeen, and a hunting dog of large and ferocious aspect.

Guy, the young count, had succeeded to the title on the death of his father, and was begrudged the dignities and revenues of his office by Yves, the younger brother, to such an extent that not one of them walked ahead of the other in the hunting field if there was a chance of a shotgun going off accidentally and indeed, their conversation at table was limited to an occasional demand to pass the cider or the Calvados or apple-jack distillate of same.

They usually got through a gallon or so of cider, and a couple of bottles of Calva, before falling asleep over the deed, when the countess and Desmond, who was thirteen at the time, would retire to the parlour and sit before the fire with the pair telling stories and playing games.

DISCORD

The most enjoyable of these times from the point of view of the young people was to get the old woman to render an aria or two from *Pagliacci*. For she had a voice like a cinder under a gate. The most appalling noise like a throttling of cats would proceed from her swelling bosom, and a verse from her would clear the parish.

By a dispensation of Prudence, a shortness of breath forbade her to go any further but, with the perverse taste of adolescence, Desmond and the sisters would be in a black fit from laughing long before she got past her opening stanza.

The proceedings would end when the countess was left down into her armchair, and the children disposed themselves on the mat before the fire.

They could signal away to each other all unknownst to milady up above, for an adequate diet had built her to such an extent that she found it difficult to see anything nearer than three yards away.

PENANCE

The girls would signal to Desmond to coax her to take a little drop of *frambroise*, a fruit liquor (made from what we called 'frockins' in the Dublin mountains).

She could generally be prevailed upon to indulge to the extent of a ten-glass bottle, then would begin the performance.

They would ask Madame Comtesse of her girlhood in the convent at Rennes, and of the time the girls got up an opera.

'I was beautiful, then,' the old lady would say, smacking her chops over her drink, 'and one old nun called me into the room one day. She heard me singing.'

'Must have been for a penance,' muttered Desmond from below.

'Yes, my dear boy, she loved music, and told me that for the greatest good for my voice I should only sing in the open air. She recommended the bottom of the garden.'

CELTIC HEART

Then she could be plagued into giving a few songs. Screwing up her face, and twisting her head about half a turn on her thick neck, the old strains would emerge.

'*Pauvre Pia, Pa – au – re Pi – aa – aa,*' to an accompaniment of the dog, as the mangy-looking brute rolled his huge weight by the heat of the fire, and groaned and snarled in slumber, protesting, or sympathetic.

Only once did she lean over and catch Desmond, his young face screwed against the sound of suppressed laughter.

'Ah yes,' she murmured tenderly, 'the Irish heart, Celtic like ourselves. So easily, deeply and quickly moved by beautiful music.'

The Irish Press, 18 September 1954

37

THE BEST RED WINE

I do not know how it is, but North Africa produces a *vin rouge*, much stronger than anything from metropolitan France. Because its inhabitants are mostly Mohammedan,[195] and it is well known that the Prophet laid down a strict rule, that his followers must not indulge in alcoholic liquids of any degree, whatsoever.

It is called mascara, and is very cheap, even for France. It is sold mainly in working-class areas, and costs twenty francs, about fourpence half-penny, for a little less than a pint, to drink in the café, though you can get it in a grocery for fifty francs the litre, which is one shilling a quart.

IN PORT ROYAL

I had some the other night in rue des Cordelières, away in Port Royal in South Paris. This is where the followers of the Jansenist heresy[196] had their headquarters. The monastery must have been a homely and jolly spot, with the community assembled for their call-over of gloom, and debating whether the odds on damnation were more or less than a million to one on.

This is a slum quarter, and indeed is said to be a 'tough' area, and not quite safe for tourists. Dark tales are told, in the cafés nearer the Champs-Élysées, of visiting English or Americans waking up in the gutter without passport or wallet, and any Arab quarter is regarded as unsafe.

I, however, have never in my travels met anything worse than myself, but then I don't know if they take me for a tourist. For the matter of that I don't know what they take me for. I had a friendly drink with North Africans in many a place and found them a decent, quiet-going people.

TOUGHER THAN—

I know there are some hard chaws amongst them, and I would much sooner see the tinkers fall out at the fair of Aughrim than watch an Arab row.

On the Place Maubert, not far from the Boul' Mich' and just across the river from Notre-Dame, on a Saturday night I saw two of them get stuck into it. My life has not been a sheltered one, but I hope never to see another heave like it.

It was totally unlike anything I ever saw at home. Two Arabs came out of a restaurant, one of them rose his foot and kicked the window in, and having armed themselves with pieces of glass they began slashing each other, in complete silence, which to an Irishman made it a scene of indescribable horror.

Nor did the crowd which quickly gathered make the slightest attempt to interfere. They stood, casual and quiet, till the short double moan of the siren announced the arrival of the salad wagon, as they call the Black Maria, and scattered as the police jumped out.

But it's seldom enough one hears of, much less sees, rows like that, and even Marseilles is nowadays famous for the superb quality of its municipal architecture, rather than for the ferocity of its apaches.[197] Which is a word seldom used by the people it is said to describe.

REMEMBERED

I can understand that, for I remember a line by an English poet, recalling his alleged memories of my native city, in which he described:

> 'The ancient bowseys call their aging mots
> Along the city wall ...'

And when I read this to one well qualified to hear the title, from the antiquity of his bowseyhood, his only comment was a pious wish that the poet should go and get a Mass said for himself.

Even the slums in France have a quality of light and cleanliness that you do not find in the deserts of East London or the Gorbals,[198] or Malpas Street,[199] for the matter of that.

POLITE YOUTH

And their youth are extremely well behaved to strangers.

In the rue des Cordelières, the boys of the local boule club were celebrating the winning of some cup or league or other.

The only people over twenty years of age seemed to be their trainer and his wife.

They ate dinner together, and then sat over the wine, codding the girls and codding each other over their girls, and then started a sing-song.

The songs they sang were mostly folk songs though solo performances of the modern numbers in the style of M. Jean Sablon[200] were well received, but it is a fallacy to believe that the Empire of Hollywood and Tin Pan Alley[201] extends to Paris. Most of these people had never seen a foreign picture in their lives, and could easily go through the rest of their life without doing so. What makes an Irishman envious of the French is the *completeness* of their culture.

STAGY BOYERS

And when we talk of the stage Irishman, we should remember that the world has been presented with a picture of forty million slinky-voiced Charles Boyer,[202] going around muttering about '*l'amour*', and throwing the national joyful optic at every woman younger than their granny, which is far removed from these people, hard-working all the week, but able to make a Saturday night of gaiety from the simplest ingredients.

By the way, I *don't* know what sort of a game boules is, or how it is played.

I wondered could it be the game beloved of Corkmen, which they call around Gurranabraher way 'bowels'.

The Irish Press, 25 September 1954

38
BEANNACHT LEAT A SHOMAIRLE
MHIC SHEOIN

An article, more or less, about the learned lexicographer Dr Samuel Johnson.

I had reason to go into the office of an Irish newspaper, in Fleet Street, and while waiting for the man I wanted to see, was entertained by the man who operates the telegraphic machine to Burgh Quay.

Amongst other things he told me was the story of the woman taken bad, just outside the *Daily Express* building, and all the people running round wondering where they were going to get medical attention for her.

'Oh,' said one bright young office boy, 'I know where you can get a doctor. Just up the street here. He's got his name on the door. Doctor Samuel Johnson.'

BULKY SHADE

The great man's house is still there, as ever was, and has survived war, riot and civil commotion. I passed it, and, going by, greeted the bulky shade of the old cantanker with a few words of Irish.

He might have learned a bit up there, in the one and three-quarter centuries since his death. He always had a great smack for the language, even though he didn't know much of it.

You find him writing to Charles O'Connor, of 'Ballinegare, in the county of Roscommon in Ireland', in the year, 1757:

Sir,

I have lately by the favour of Mr Faulkner, seen your account of Ireland, and cannot forbear to solicit a prosecution of your design. Sir William Temple complains that Ireland is less well known than any other country, as to its ancient state. The natives have had little leisure, and less encouragement, for enquiry; and strangers, not knowing the language, have had no ability.

I have long wished that the Irish language were cultivated. Ireland is known by tradition to have been once the seat of piety and learning; and surely it would be very acceptable to all those who are curious either in the origins of nations or the affinities of languages to be further informed of the revolution of a people so ancient, and once so illustrious.

What relation there is between the Welsh and Irish language, or between the language of Ireland and that of Biscay deserves enquiry. Of these provincial and unextended tongues it seldom happens that more than one are understood by one man [except David Greene,[203] who is not born yet – B.B.]; and, therefore seldom it happens that a fair comparison can be made. I hope you continue to cultivate this kind of learning, which has too long lain neglected, and which if it be suffered to remain in oblivion for another century may never be retrieved. As I wish well to all useful undertakings, I would not forbear to let you know how much you deserve, in my opinion, from all lovers of study and how much pleasure your work has given to, sir,

Your most obliged,
and most humble servant,
Sam. Johnson.

TEUTONIC!

I don't know whether he died better informed, but his knowledge of the language didn't gain anything from his conversation with 'E.' Twenty years later, when he was within a month or two of his seventieth birthday: 'E. said that "the Irish language is not primitive. It is Teutonic, a mixture of the northern tongues. It has much English in it ..."' Well *ta sé sin* all right.

But the old man's feeling for Ireland was no mere fascination with the time of long ago, 'when Ireland was the school of the West, the quiet habitation of sanctity and literature'.

In his old age, his 'general indignation' could break out, in massive anger for her wrongs:

> The Irish are in a most unnatural state; for we see there the minority prevailing over the majority. There is no instance, even in the worst persecutions, of such severity as that which the protestants in Ireland have exercised against the Catholics. Did we tell them we have conquered them it would be above board; but to punish them by confiscation and other penalties, as rebels, was monstrous injustice. King William was not their lawful sovereign; he had not been acknowledged by the Parliament of Ireland, when they appeared in arms against him.

SCOTTISH OSSIAN

I have never quite figured out the rights or wrong of the controversy regarding MacPherson's Ossianic poems.[204] MacPherson is alleged to have forged old Gaelic manuscripts and said they were ancient transcriptions of Ossian's poems.

If they were phoney, it's all the more credit to him surely, if the poems were so good.

I learned a poem of Ossian once, and very sad it was too. Every verse finishes up, '*Is fada anocht in Oil Finn.*'

But Johnson was in no position to judge, if he really believed that 'there are no Erse manuscripts. None of the old families had a single letter of Erse that we heard of. You say it is likely that they could write. The learned, if any there were, could.'

BOLT COURT

The dear doctor, at this point I would say, for politeness' sake, does not know what he is talking about. For not alone could they write their own language, but there was a commerce between themselves and good foreign songsters, as witness the courtly Florentine verses of Gearóid Iarla, the Great Earl of Kildare, and the similarity in form between Villon's ballad against the detractors of France, '*Qui mal vouldroit au royaume de France …*' and the Irish man's poem against the detractors of women, '*mairg adeir olcris na mnaibh …*'[205]

But, for all that, Dr Johnson had good time for us, as the County Clareman says, and going up Bolt Court, in the gathering dark of a London evening, before we pass this murky, ancient alley, across the mists of two centuries, we leave him a friendly greeting, with undiminished gratitude, 'Beannacht leat, a Shomhairle Mhic Sheoin.'

The Irish Press, 2 October 1954

39
DON'T ASK ME ABOUT THE ROUTE

It is said that the sedan chairmen of eighteenth-century London were Irishmen. It is believed that their peculiar gait, from long practice in bog-trotting, made them lithe and delicate carriers of frail and elegant *grandes dames*, to and from the ball and the rout.

Don't ask me what the rout was. For long I suspected that it described an entertainment similar to a meeting of tinkers at Ballinasloe horse fair. That sometimes finishes up in a rout, but the London aristocracy wouldn't be decent enough for that sort of sport.

Up to the middle of the last century the Irish language was used extensively in the East End, and I was myself, not many years ago, in the York Road area of Leeds, greeted with '*Kay kee will too?*' by an elderly man, who otherwise spoke the purest Yorkshire.

WITH NOSTALGIA
He told, wistfully, that this was the way all the old people in his part greeted each other and, with nostalgia, described the Saturday night scenes of his childhood, when the old crowd gathered outside the Yorkshire Hussar on the way home, while a 'fine hupstanding woman, she were, 'ad reared 'er family, after 'er man was killed in mine, upcountry, working twelve hours a

day in mill', threw back the shawl from her head, and sang up to the dark and alien sky over the upturned, toil-worn faces of the men and women listening to her, lost in memory and back on a spring morn in Connacht, the song of the Red-Haired Man's wife.

SHONEENISM

Incidentally, myself and another were conducting an argument in Irish, in an 'Irish' public house, in this town but a few days ago. Now, the blunt and simple facts of the case are that we were using Irish because we did not want people to know what we were talking about. So I do not want it to appear that I am asking sympathy for two persecuted patriots.

I have never done much for the Irish language, beyond what I wrote and was paid for, but I would like to show you the brass-faced impertinence and the pathetic shoneenism of some of the people who leave Ireland without knowing enough about it, or about anything, to have more than a coolie's[206] pride in themselves.

This London porter-seller came up to us and asked us, might we not 'give over this carry-on, and speak English like everyone else and stop making a show of yourselves'.

I'll thank you to judge for yourselves was the courteous reply, in the mellifluous tongue of Shakespeare, Milton and Johnson, he received from your correspondent.

However, these were but a few introductory remarks, about the Celt and of his tracks on the banks of the Thames.

You know that Pádraic Ó Conaire,[207] Michael Collins,[208] Sam Maguire[209] and Dr Mark Ryan[210] lived and worked here. And if I may mention one I had the honour of meeting myself, the late Seán MacGrath,[211] *go ndeanaidh Dia trocaire air.*[212] But did you know that Manannán mac Lir is commemorated in these parts?

Tradition is the most persistent of man's creations. Pedants and scholars have often been proved wrong when some archaeologist takes the old myths and traditions seriously.

Eighty years ago nobody believed that the Trojan War had ever been fought, except in Homer's imagination, until Schliemann actually dug up the flattened walls of Ilium and proved to the world that Homer's Trojan War was as real as Tolstoy's Battle of Austerlitz.

It is difficult to believe that the city of London is named after a Celtic god, Lud, whose name survives today, unchanged, in Ludgate Circus, near St Paul's, and in a public house, called The Lud's Head, hidden beneath the towering bulk of Wren's masterpiece.

KING LIR

Lud's name is identified by Celtic mythologists with Lir, the Irish sea god, who brought the secret of the calendar alphabet to Ireland. In our alphabet, each letter represents a tree which is sacred to a certain month. I can only remember a few of them: *ailm* (elm), *beith* (beech), *coll* (I don't know), *dair* (oak) but you'll see them in Dineen.[213]

Incidentally, I can't understand why they are not taught in the schools. Apart from anything else, it would give children the names of the trees.

Lir's principal home was the Isle of Man, which you probably know as well as I do, and are not waiting on this morning's *Press* to find out about. But to proceed.

ST BRIDE

Nearby is the church of St Bride, the most popular saint of all Celtic peoples, Britain, Scotland, or Ireland, her home.

How many of the thousands of Londoners, to whom these names are familiar, give thought to the common Celtic heritage of these islands from the days of antiquity.

Last week a Roman temple was discovered in a building site near Saint Paul's, in the very centre of the city. A workman uncovered a piece of stone, which turned out to be the head of Mithras, favourite god of the Roman legionaries. Shortly afterwards, they took out the head of an attendant youthful god, or saving their presence, a god's labourer.

The Irish Press, 9 October 1954

40

THOUGHTS BEFORE ALBERT MEMORIAL

I was reared in the belief that the greatest disaster that ever befell mankind was the defeat of Napoleon at the Battle of Waterloo. That it opened a century of unparalleled misery for the people of Ireland, and that the little corporal, even at his most cynical, was a more civilised figure than the licensed thug, and loud-mouthed head bailiff, whose victories on behalf of European reaction, and the privileges of landlords, are commemorated in the Phoenix Park.

Bonaparte's royalist pretensions and imperial lunacies were more worthy of a talentless, dull race of well-to-do nail and saucepan merchants, depending upon the revelations of homely native bodies about an imported royalty, to give a bit of colour to their lives. And they ruined him, but at least he is remembered by the Code Napoleon and the straight roads he built.

Wellington, the made-in-Brummagem Iron Duke, if he is remembered for any law, it is the Poor Law,[214] if for any building, it is the workhouse.

As for the obelisk in the Park, it was put there by the enemies of the people of Ireland and should be shifted, now that they are no longer powerful enough to enforce its preservation.

NO CLAIM

Neither has the Martyr of the Pillar any claim on our consideration. As Bernard Shaw said, he won victories he'd have been deservedly shot for losing, and anyway has nothing to do with us.

One occasionally hears about the attachment of the 'old Dubliner' to these objects, but in this context an 'old Dubliner' is usually some immigrant employee of the Castle or one of the banks, that came over as a trustworthy messenger or diligent hall porter about fifty years ago, and has only as much right as any other Irish citizen to debate the matter.

The oldest Dubliners, the descendants of the native Irish, that crept in and settled round Ballybough (an Baile Bocht – 'the poor town'), regarded the Wellington Monument and the Pillar as a gibe at their own helplessness in their own country.

WRONG TOWN

I remember as a very small child travelling with a grand-aunt of mine. She was born and reared at Blessington Street, near the Basin, formerly the City Reservoir, and whose waters, she claimed, were cleaner and purer and better for making tea than the 'new stuff' from Roundwood.

We sat in a tram and listened to an elderly gentleman inquire of the conductor whether the tram went to 'Kingstown'.[215]

The conductor replied in even tones that he did not know of the existence of any such place.

The old gent with some impatience replied that the place, with the chopping and changing of modern times, was now called something else, 'er-Done-Lakery or some such'.

DUNLEARY

This bit of fencing, the old gent pretending he did not know how to pronounce 'Dun Laoghaire' and the conductor pretending he had never heard of 'Kingstown', continued till at last, to cut a long story short, it was decided that he was on the right tram.

'Of course,' said the old gent, 'it was called Kingstown by the old people.'

'Excuse yourself,' said my grand-aunt, 'excuse yourself, sir. I don't know how old you are, but I'm nearly eighty, and I never called it anything but Dunleary. I don't know how long you're in the city, sir, but my mother, who stayed with friends in Glasthule, every summer, went to her grave without ever knowing it was called anything else.'

MEMORIAL

I was thinking about all this as I walked through Hyde Park. Till I stood before the Albert Memorial,[216] I never knew how much we had to be thankful for in the matter of nineteenth-century British memorials.

On a broad base surrounded by stone elephants, stone mahouts, stone Red Indians and other inhabitants of his wife's empire, there rises to a point, sixty or seventy feet above the lowest stone moccasin, a sort of shrine, the centre of which can be best described as a Gothic watch box, where your man crouches, sheltering from the rain.

His young wife stands waving to him from outside Kensington Palace,[217] in sculpture executed by her daughter, a young German princess, who'd have been better advised to stick to her own business of kissing kangaroos and dancing with the Maoris.

HYMN

It is a bit difficult to believe that the native language of this mortuary, could they but speak, would be German, and that after the Prussian victory at Sedan[218] in 1870 the royal family assembled at the chapel in Windsor to give thanks for the victory in a prayer composed by another artistic princess whose bent was for literature:

> *'Let's join our heart with cousin Bill,*
> *And praise the heavens, with a will,*
> *Ten thousand Frenchmen sent below*
> *Praise God from whom all blessings flow.'*

REPLY

I remember many years ago a preacher of Irish revolt in Hyde Park. His following seemed more personal than organisational, but he did not lack support for all that. He was very fond of demanding: 'D'you think I done fifteen years in Maryboro[219] for nothing?'

This silenced all interrupters, except on one occasion when a man with a similar accent to the speaker replied with easy familiarity: 'You did not then,

Tom, 'twas for pushing a boy into the Shannon. You were a lucky man you weren't hung.'

The Irish Press, 16 October 1954

41

WE TOOK OVER A CASTLE

You may find it hard to believe that I was ever an invited guest in a castle, but in my childhood I spent a great number of months in one, as such.

This is how it happened. My connection with the agricultural interest and with the backbone of the country was so slight that when the teacher was explaining how much we owed the farmers of Ireland and asked me where our food came from I replied: 'Summerhill' and when that strapping Christian Brother moved towards me, in a manner that behoved no good to Brendan Francis Aidan Behan, though I knew I had given the wrong answer, the only alternative that came readily to mind was 'Dorset Street.'

I had no relations on a farm, and was not personally acquainted with a single farmer. I approved of farmers, particularly from Tipperary or West Cork, because I had heard older people speaking of Breen[220] and Tom Barry.[221] Up to quite an advanced age I did not know they used real horses at the races. I thought it was all done with telephones.

As far as the landlord class are concerned, well, I've learned since that their main activities were shoving copies of *The New Statesman and Nation*[222] under the half-doors of the peasantry by night, and presenting them with Ganymede Press[223] reproductions of Gauguin.

ANGLO-IRISH

But I had never heard of the Anglo-Irish. I knew there were Protestants because I played with half a dozen of them. I knew there were Jews because I knew some, and they had a cemetery in Fairview,[224] and I thought they were a pretty daft lot because they had the date '5683' written on the stone over the door, though one of them from our way *did* write 'Did Your Mother Come from Ireland?'[225] But that was later than the time I was in the castle.

Well, who let me into the castle? It was this way. A relation of mine was a young chap in the cattle trade. He was as good a judge of a beast as you'd get from here to Mulhuddart, though he was born round N.C. Rd the same as the rest of us, and learned all he knew up in Prussia Street, working for a sales master.

INTO CASTLE

There was this castle out in County Dublin, and the people that owned it left it for a bit, because they got nervous during the Civil War.

But the place, from being left empty, was being ruined from damp and going to rack and ruin, and all to that effect, and the people that owned it wrote from Margate or Miami, or wherever they were, and asked the sales master would he get someone to go and live in it for a bit.

To cut the long story short, our Richie, the young cattle fellow, said he didn't mind and out he went.

The next thing was, of a Sunday, my granny and two of her sisters went out on a visit to see how he was getting on and my granny said the air was a very good thing out there and would do all the good in the world to her and her other poor sister, Henrietta.

Poor Henrietta caught a bad cold at Parnell's funeral, and hadn't been expected to live this forty year. She was only able to lie in bed and moan, 'Is any of yous ever going to make the drain of tea?'

When the teacup was not actually at her lips, she was bemoaning the fact that she was a 'poo-er opher-a-n'. I ran out of *The Phantom of the Opera* because Lon Chaney put me in mind of her.

TRAINING GROUND

It was decided that the bit of air would do me good too and I joined the merry house party, but damned nearly passed out because they gave me a room to myself. I was eventually brought in with my granny, for I didn't think much of this solitary-confinement act.

Our team was playing in the final of the Conway Cup in the Fifteen Acres, and the boys decided this was good for collective training. So they came out too, bringing with them a gramophone and a record with two sides to it, 'On Mother Kelly's Doorstep' and 'Oh! Gee, Oh! Gosh, Oh! Golly I'm in Love'. And a fellow called 'Thirsty' that trained greyhounds.

My Aunt Henrietta sat in the window over a field at the back to watch the team practising, and would shout dog's abuse at the players if everything wasn't going to her liking. Thirsty said they wouldn't mind him keeping the dogs in the drawing room for a while. The kennels were leaking at home and it wasn't doing them any good.

DANCE
Our Richie said the place was a cross between a sports ground, a sanitorium and a relief scheme and he was fit for the puzzle factory,[226] and they said he could go on up there, they'd look after the castle till he came out.

We had a dance on a Sunday night. There were a lot of girls working in factories at that time, and they used to bring out cigarettes and sandwiches and cake for the team, and after tea there was dancing to the record, one side after the other, turn about being fair play.

Everything went like a canal boat up a hill till this Saturday night Richie came up, all white and pale, like someone on a weekend pass out of Glasnevin.[227]

VISITATION
'You must have got a bad result,' said Thirsty.

'I'll be put up in the Joy,' moaned Richie.

'It was the Gorman yesterday,' said our outside-left. 'But a change is as good as a rest and it'll be nearer your work.'

'They're coming up the drive. Right now.'

So they were; the people that owned the place.

'Quick,' said the outside-left, 'out in the grounds the lot of yous.'

'Someone of yous wait here and give me a hand with me aunt.'

She was asleep, for once in a way, and they dumped her in a closet and left her there. The others went out with the footballers.

'I only hope them this-and-that dogs keeps easy,' muttered Richie to himself.

'I hope so and all,' said I.

'Oh, I'd forgotten you. What am I going to do with you?'

'I know,' said I, 'I can get under the dead dog in the front room.'

'That's not a dead dog, it's a dead tiger; but go on, get under it, only hurry.'

BANSHEE

I did, and only in time, for the next thing, I heard the door open, and this old one, and old fellow, speaking to Richie.

They weren't gone very far when I heard a long and deep moaning.

'Cedric,' said the old one, very shiveringly, 'did you hear that? It's the banshee.'

But it wasn't, only Thirsty's old bitch. She moaned again.

'Don't you think we'd s-s-see it better by daylight, C-Cedric?'

Cedric said nothing but the next thing my Aunt Henrietta woke in her closet and moaned out through the door, 'Is any a yous ever going to make the dr-a-in a te-a-a. Sure I'm only a p-oo-er …'

But the old one let a screech out of her and ran for the door and down the gravel path, leading Cedric by a short head.

What did I do? Just lay under the tiger, that's all. My Aunt Henrietta would scare you, even if you were used to her. You should have heard her!

The Irish Press, 23 October 1954

42

HOW SORRY THEY ARE
TO RETURN

Nobody enters, or re-enters England with greater reluctance than the intellectual native of that country. Howard and Monica went down the gangplank at Newhaven like early Christian martyrs. People have gone into Mountjoy with less reluctance.

For the matter of that, the intelligentsia of all countries is notoriously lacking in that sort of fervour that shows itself in frantic devouring of the old sod, to see if it tastes the same as it did on the way out.

Howard is a higher civil servant, and had finished a tour of British military establishments in various parts of the Continent. His wife went with him to keep him company and for the sake of the holiday.

We began a conversation on the way over from France. They asked me whether I intended to stay in England for long, and I told them I'd be there for a couple of months. Monica wished to know if I knew it well. I said I knew a few places extremely well, without specifying what places.

MAD

Monica wanted to know if I liked living in England, and watching with mounting distaste the white cliffs looming on the horizon, I did not like, for politeness' sake, to give her a straight answer. I said I thought my trip would be interesting.

But I need not have bothered. They both seemed to think that anyone, of his own free will, leaving the Continent for England, must be more than a little mad.

After that we went down like a dinner with one another, and exchanged such pieces of cultural information as the story about the last words of Gertrude Stein,[228] who sat up on her deathbed a couple of minutes before she died, and asked: 'What is the answer?' A second or two later she enquired: 'But what is the question?'

'Ah'd say she knows be this time,' said an Irish voice behind me. It was one of a band of students from Belfast I had met on the way over.

I left my Northern brother giving grim consideration to these matters, and went through the customs with my friends.

UGLY

For all they looted and robbed, the English made considerably less use of the swag than smaller imperialisms. The ugliness of most of London is unbelievable.

I was surprised to pass Piccadilly without noticing it, and Marble Arch is only about the same size as the Boer War memorial that they put up in place of Wolfe Tone's monument at Stephen's Green.

It is the second biggest suburb in the world, coming in length and breadth of built-up area considerably behind Los Angeles, which I am told extends for a hundred miles.

In the sense that I understand the word, the 'city' does not extend beyond the West End. A mile in any direction outside that, and so far as entertainment is concerned at eleven o'clock at night you might as well be in Drimnagh or Ballygomartin.

Its people are kindlier, nosier and more respectable than any I have ever met.

MYTH

The famed British reserve is as much a myth as the idea of the broth-of-a-boy-Irishman, he of the ready wit and the warm heart and the great love for a fight.

Try it on the landlord or the grocer sometime. Tell him you'll give two rounds of the shillelagh in place of whatever you owe him, and wait for the witty answer.

The landlord over here will know all about you if you remain with him for more than two days. And if it's a landlady she'll want to know more than that, in twenty-four hours.

They also have an idea that most Irishmen go out in the morning and travel long distances by Tube to dig ditches for Lord Wimpey and Earl McAlpine.[229]

I was wakened at six o'clock on two occasions 'to go to work'. Luckily my accent, which, I just discovered, is as much of a 'brogue' as Barry Fitzgerald's,[230] made unintelligible most of the flow of language with which the poor old one was greeted in the brightening morn.

CATTLE

Always I was met with the enquiry as to what I was. This was not meant in the Six Counties' sense of Fenians or Orangemen, which political or religious curiosity, I am beginning to think is not the most troublesome kind.

What the landlady wanted to know was what was I in terms of the industrial effort.

I thought of saying I was a progress-chaser or a Powers-Samas operator, both of which occupations I have seen mentioned in the newspaper advertising columns. But for both these occupations one must have false teeth and a taste for sausage rolls, so I said I was interested in cattle.

She made further enquiry as to what part of the cattle business I was interested in, and I answered: 'Oh steak, silverside, corned beef, brains, liver, heart, any part as you might say, though I never tried the nostrils. That, madam, I am bound to admit.'

MURDERS

I am writing this in Bayswater, which is quite a pleasant mid-Victorian suburb, one of the residential areas of the great manufacturing bourgeoisie and now famous for its murders.

Mr Christie had his private morgue just up the road in Notting Hill; Flying Officer Heath's strangularium was across the way in Gloucester Road. And the sink down which Haigh poured numerous of his acquaintances is in a kitchen round the corner.[231]

The day is dark and grey, though brightened by a memory of the wise and smiling south, like a flash of sun, a reminder of the summer.

LUIGI

In Westbourne Grove, outside Lawrence's Store, he stood, a stout little Italian with a figure that owed nothing to privation throwing out from the roots of him and rising over the basses of his own accordion, his splendid tenor voice: '*Ave Maria … gratia plena.*'

O craft, thy name is Luigi. The strong West of Ireland faces and the softer, smoother looks of French and Italian smiled into one another, and navvies and waitresses, barbers and busmen, Cork and Calabria, remembered their mothers' people, it being Saturday and they out on the holiday promenade, and rewarded Luigi well for reminding them of it.

The Irish Press, 30 October 1954

43
I MEET THE HYPHENATED IRISHMEN

I come from one of the few parts of Ireland with no tradition of emigration. I knew a family in our street whose widowed mother knocked it out for seven of them by selling apples and 'Half-Time Jimmies'[232] at football matches. The eldest boy assisted at All-Ireland finals[233] with the teams' colours decorated at the time with 'Come On, Kerry', and photographs of the immortal Sheehy, or the black and amber and Lory Meagher's head.

They thought as little of distance as they did of the foreign games controversy,[234] and would cross over to Liverpool for a big match with as little difficulty as they would go up to Dalymount or over to Shelbourne Park.[235]

The pram of apples and chocolates was to be found as often outside Goodison Park[236] as outside 'Croker'.[237] Half the district went over to Liverpool for the laying of the foundation stone of the new cathedral, so I shouldn't say we were totally untravelled but, until comparatively recently, I never heard of many going to work in England and no one seemed to go to America.

A man in Ballinasloe said to me one time that the reason was that we wouldn't be let in.

For some reason, however, the idea of hyphenated Irishmen never interested us very much. An Irishman to us was someone, Catholic, Protestant or

Jew, born in Ireland, and we could not very well understand why any other should claim or wish to claim the description.

ANTHEM

Neither did 'O'Donnell Abu'[238] ever strike me as the sort of song one raved over to the tune of an almost endless number of rapturously received *encores*.

These reflections are prompted by a morning's vocal exercise I've had in Danny Meehan's Irish hostelry in King's Cross where Tinny MacPhail, a Glasgow son of Scots-Irish parents, and an O'Donnell on his mother's side, made me sing the maternal clan anthem often enough for him to pick it up.

Now he is well equipped to send the war cry arising on the gale forty or fifty times over himself.

Not that the Glasgow Irish do not have their own songs. Besides the lament for Johnny Thompson,[239] Celtic goalie killed on the football field in 1934, they sing almost as a national anthem the song of the 'Smashing of the Van', about the attempt to rescue Frank Carty in the Tan time:

> *'They arrested Father Mac Rory,*
> *a Catholic clergyman,*
> *But they only showed their ignorance,*
> *At the smashing of the van.'*

TEDDIES

And these are also the local hyphenated Irish.

Like most people I have seen reports in the papers of more or less inoffensive citizens being battered unconscious by Teddy Boys, teenage boys whose uniform is an elaborate imitation of what the well-dressed man was wearing in the days of Edward the Seventh: drainpipe trousers, long jacket with velvet collar and what my father would call an All-for-Ireland-League MP's overcoat.

The other night I was standing at a coffee stall, nourishing myself with a cup of tea and a sandwich, watching half a dozen of these gentry devouring jellied eels.

By the same token I am a great believer in sampling the local delicacies anywhere I may happen to be, but I draw a very firm line at jellied eels. I understand from an article by Mr Benedict Kiely[240] in this newspaper that they come from the burns and glens of County Antrim and that numerous canty bodies make a wheen of ha'pence of the export trade, from Toomebridge to Waterloo Bridge.

I will take his word for it that jellied eels are wholesome fare for man and beast, and leave it at that.

THREAT?

Anyway, I was at this stall at about one in the morning, and these Teddy Boys seemed to be giving me searching looks. I am not notoriously a nervous type, and was not reared in such a sheltered atmosphere as to feel I was slumming it by going down the East End.

But I was a long way from barracks, and while I was not less than twice the weight of any two of these anti-Parnellites, I did not feel in the humour for taking on six of them.

Besides, the world and Garrett Reilly has learned from Sunday reading that the least offensive of the Edwardian armoury includes a bicycle chain and a blunt instrument fashioned from the strap-hanging equipment of the London Passenger Transport Board.

AHRISH

The most velvety Teddy Boy looked over at me at last, and said: 'Eye.'

'Eye,' said I, learning the language apace.

'Yew Ahrish?'

I admitted as much, and wondered which of them I could drop before the belt on the back of the head. I could see the headstone in the 'Nevin[241] if they ever gathered up the bits and sent them home: '*Breandáin O Beacháin, coshálta chun báis ar Droichead Waterloo, 1954.*[242] His memory is an example to us all' … to keep away from jellied-eel fanciers.

He turned to his friends and said: 'Vere, who eye sye?'

He smiled at me, and said: 'These geezers contradicted me. I knew you was Ahrish w'en I 'eard your browgue. We're all Ahrish 'ere.'

Proudly he pointed out his friends: 'E's Mac Carfy, en 'e's O'Leary, en 'Ealy, en 'Ogan, en Kelly, en my name is – give a guess.'

'Murphy.'

'That's it,' said he, delightedly, 'and my mum is a Flanagan.'

'Gentlemen,' said I, 'I'm really pleased to hear this,' and raised my cup in salute.

'EATHENS

A young lady employee of the Irish government here worked for a Catholic Youth organisation and told me of a dance they ran, which was visited by Cardinal Griffin.

The archiepiscopal party beamed on the young dancers who pranced round sedately till they left, and then went into the wildest and liveliest sort of jiving.

My friend commented on this to one of them, and on the rapidity with which they accelerated the pace of the light fantastic once the visitors were gone.

'Well?' asked the lad indignantly, 'what did you expect us to do? Be-pop in front of an archbishop? What do you take us for, 'Eathens?'

The Irish Press, 6 November 1954

44
TIME I MET A SHEIK

I was in the Strand the other night – I should have said the Strand, London, in case people thought I meant the North Strand and I didn't get the credit of my travels.

Irish people, who for some reason have the reputation of being insular, have great *meas*[243] on the traveller.

It's almost a competition: a man from Ballyhaunis will no doubt get great credit for his weekly run to Sligo or Athlone. But he has to shut up about the glories of both places when Micky Fitz, that's working above in Dublin, comes down in the summer holidays.

And the Dubliner, on a visit to smaller centres in the west or south, will almost certainly be introduced to some mild old man, who stands innocently at the counter and plies your man with questions about the wonders of the great metropolis, listening with wide-eyed astonishment to descriptions of traffic lights and buses, and the flashing jewels of neon signs that shine across the width of O'Connell Street to each other.

BY MEASURE
The old man greets the account of metropolitan majesty, from Store Street station to O'Keefe's the knackers, with 'oh' and 'ah' and 'glory be', and your

gills is condescendingly pleased to have brought a hint, at least, of the colour and bustling life of urban civilisation into the old man's last days, until he discovers that the old pig-minder has been getting it up for him, rich and rare. That he spent forty years in a saloon on Broadway, or drove a truck for Al Capone in Chi., and that he performs this Simple-Simon act on every visiting Dubliner for the benefit of his friends and neighbours, who are in no way averse to seeing the jackeen being made look a gilly.[244]

For some reason, the old fellow who has been to America is better thought of than the fellow who only got as far as Liverpool. I think they must sit up with maps measuring the distance, so as to know to what honours the returning exile is entitled.

SHEIK

In hotels and bars, in Youghal, Caherciveen, Donaghadee, Tallaght, Camden Town, Inisheer and Kilburn; in any place where our people have gathered, I have bested them all.

If someone said he had been to Texas and hunted cattle, I was hot on his heels with my story of a weekend spent with a sheik in East Tunis.

By the same token, I met the sheik under rather peculiar circumstances. He fancied himself as something of a huntsman, but there was very little to be hunted in his own country unless you count the sandflies.

So when he was invited by the French government to shoot deer in the Vosges[245] he was delighted, and would hardly go to bed the night before the hunt was to begin.

But in the field, he proved a very bad shot. The only deer he would have got a direct hit on would have been the one in the hall, and they wanted that for a hat rack.

WHITE DEER

The French were very anxious to keep on the right side of the old sheik, and they didn't know what to do till the next morning he sneaked out on his own, and they heard the bang and the crash of his guns, and squeals of delight in Arabic, not to mention the thud of falling bodies as his victims hit the dust.

He ran in ecstatically, and screeching in his own language: 'All of them have I killed, the woolly, white deer.'

And when they followed him out, they discovered about twenty ton of dead, prime mutton belonging to the neighbouring farmer.

He was duly fixed up with a sum of money that more than compensated him for the loss of his 'woolly white deer', and the old sheik returned home with a shipload of stuffed sheep heads, which trophies of the chase now line the walls of his castle in Beni Rah Kosi.

How did I come into the story? I tied the 56-pound weights on the legs of the sheep, the previous night, with the man who owned them, a chap from Granamore, County Wicklow, by the name of Mike Burke.

LEPROSY

I drove a man in this city nearly mad with yarns the like of that the other night.

He was standing at the counter with his friends, and smiled when he heard my accent. His own was an Irish one heavily mixed with Paddington. He paid tribute to the country of his adoption with the vowels, but the 'th's' betrayed the land of his birth.

"Ello, you're from Ahland. Just come over, Paddy?'

'That's right. Guilty on both counts.'

He smiled indulgently. 'Ah bin ere nah abaht fifteen years. D'now when Ah was ome last.'

'I got in today from Baghdad.'

'From wheah?!'

'Baghdad. I'm over here for an operation.'

'From Baghdad? For an operation? For what?'

'Leprosy. I'll tell you how I got it. There was this sheik I knew. Manbe the name of Mohammed Ali Bababa. Lived in a place be the name of Beni Rah Kosi ...'

The Irish Press, 13 November 1954

45
LANE PICTURES

So many notabilities have talked of these.

> '*Now, autumn leaves are falling,*
> *The light is growing dim,*
> *The painter wipes his pot clean down,*
> *And throws his brushes in …*'

Or, as the saying has it, 'cover me up till the first of March'. That was the kind of saying I was forced to put up with, and I a painter's apprentice in this city. Though in reply I could remark that putty and paint made the carpenter a saint.

Howsome-ever, as the man said, first carefully removing the butt from his lower lip, I was not all that good of an apprentice. Though not devoid of ambition in the graining, lettering and marbling line, it was agreed that my real talents lay in the placing of dockets, and running out for the charge-hand's curer of a Saturday morning.

POOR MATHS

My mathematics played me false the day Workman won the National for, acting on information received from a little match-makeress who got it in the factory of its owner, I switched all bets on to the winner, including alas, heavy place bets on Kilstar and St George, which paid fantastic prices, even at one-fourth the odds, so 'twas little enough I made for my trouble.

My father and grandfathers were painters, and at an exhibition of Patrick Swift's,[246] Victor Waddington[247] remarked that of all present, my father was the only painter with a union card.

My granny was forewoman gilder in Brindley's of Eustace Street, and on my mother's side the Kearneys were, and are, similarly engaged.

ALLERGIC

For all that, mayhap because of that, I am allergic to painting. Not to paint, mark you, but to putting the stuff on. (Grim chorus of assent from walking foreman and chargers, from Dublin, Cork City, Youghal, Belfast, and Donaghadee: 'You don't have to tell *us*.')

I even like looking at a job well done, and have been known, in the middle of Debussy's *Pelléas et Mélisande*,[248] to force the attentions of Messrs John Ryan[249] and Frederick May,[250] who had the good fortune to be sitting either side of me (otherwise they might have missed it) to a rather neat bit of repair filling on the Gaiety ceiling.

And in company with another literary refugee from the trade, Mr Joseph Tomelty, I commented adversely on the papering of a nightclub in Villiers Street, London. Joe and I agreed that it was 'lapped' where, in an establishment with any pretence to decency, it should have been 'butted'. Which drew, from the cynical lip of Mr Con O'Leary,[251] the comment that in a new town, the first thing a tinker looks at is his horse.

BRACQUE

Strangely, there are few house-painter painters, picture painters I mean. Few *peintres en bâtiment* become *artistes peintres*.

I can think only of one famous modern painter who began by painting houses, Georges Braque.[252] Though for that matter Monsieur Braque was also, in his day, a professional boxer.

There have been fireman artists, Grandma Moses peasant artists by the acre, priest artists, policemen artists, child artists, and there are people who would claim that the famous English artist, Sir Winston Churchill,[253] is an author.

For the matter of that, there are not wanting those who make out that his colleague, Sir Alfred Munnings,[254] is a horse. But seldom do you ever hear of a house-painter artist.

SEA CHANGE

I remember once there was a fisherman artist, and his work was hung in very august surroundings, and big ha-ha in the papers about him being an uninstructed simple man and all to that effect, and at the opening of the exhibition old ones from the cultural areas of the 6 and 7 and 9 and 10 bus routes were all gabbling round this chap, who had cleaned off the herring leavings for the day and stood, rather more stylishly dressed than the ordinary artist artists, modestly giving his opinions of life and art.

Then the door burst open and a very well-known Irish artist stood there, his massive frame adorned in the habiliments of a trawlerman. Enormous sea boots, a blue woollen jersey, sou'wester and rubbers he wore, and trailed from his shoulder was about twenty yards of tram net.

The first to recover from the apparition was the then chief among artists, an old man of ancient lineage who directed a stern and indignant inquiry towards the figure in the doorway.

'Sir, what is the meaning of appearing amongst your friends and brothers in this preposterous costume?'

From the doorway came the drawled reply: 'Oh, I thought you knew. *I—*' with a nonchalant shrug of his net-draped shoulder in the direction of the serge-suited fisherman artist, 'I am an artist fisherman.'

OURS

I could give as glib a bit of guff about 'tactile values' and the 'melodic line' as the next but it is not from any expert knowledge of painting that I write of the Lane Pictures.[255] It just happens that they are as much my property as yours, or Montgomery Hyde's[256] or any other Irishman's.

And I have *seen* them, or some of them. Besides the Corot, Renoir, Manet, Degas and Pissarro pictures, there are a couple I wouldn't sentence my worst enemy to look at more than once, and then only for a laugh.

There's one bit of Victorian anecdotage called *The Mountebank*, showing a poor showman lying on the grass in a country lane with his faithful dog and horse.

Its only interest for Lane would have been the Irish origin of the painter, John Lewis Brown. He was born, reared and died in France, and was patronised by Napoleon III. His work shows every sign of it. This one is not exhibited.

NOTABILITIES

Montgomery Hyde's name goes down in history with the very interesting list of those who fought for the return of the Lane Pictures, including the Countess Markievicz, Dr Thomas Bodkin, Oliver St John Gogarty, Lady Gregory, Jim Larkin, Major Bryan Cooper, Dermod O'Brien, Seán O'Casey, Éamon de Valera, W.B. Yeats and Sarah Purser.

On the other side may be mentioned the name, scarcely remembered in any other connection, of Lord Duveen, who gave a new wing to the Tate Gallery on condition that they held on to the Lane Pictures. The building, incidentally, was given 'to the British nation as a thanksgiving for peace'.

Most prominent of those who caused the trouble in the first place, by refusing a proper home in Dublin for the pictures, was the late Mr William Martin Murphy.[257] It seems that his concern for the welfare of the Dublin working class overcame his aesthetic inclinations.

He thought that while slum conditions were as they were, they should build no new art galleries. Furthermore, he said in a letter to his own *Irish Independent*: 'I believe the Lord Mayor is mistaken or misled if he thinks there is any burning desire on the part of the ratepayers of Dublin to contribute £25,000 towards a memorial to Sir Hugh Lane in order to house a few pictures.'

EFFECT

One of the pictures I saw is Renoir's *Les Parapluies* – some people caught in a shower of rain, with umbrellas raised over them. A holiday crowd, perhaps, enjoying Sunday afternoon in the park, and including a little girl holding a hoop.

But you might as well hope to know the blue of the sky from a wireless commentary as gauge my idea of this picture, from a description of it.

Its effect on me was like the first hearing of Beethoven's Fifth Symphony on Hector Berlioz, who said: 'Leaving the hall, after the orchestra had finished, I could not find my head to get my hat on.'

The Irish Press, 20 November 1954

46

PEADAR KEARNEY BALLAD MAKER

If Peadar Kearney[258] was not the greatest of republicans, he was, as Pearse[259] said of Rossa,[260] the most typical of them. Of Dublin working-class republicans, that is to say.

He was distinctly under the impression that there was a connection between liberty and speaking Irish, between winning a strike and winning a hurling match, between the French Revolution and the Four Masters, between Fionn MacCumhaill and Theobald Wolfe Tone.

Peadar's republicanism was the secret of the hidden Ireland nurtured over a tenement fire. It was the dawn of a new day, seen through a slum window, rising over the Dublin mountains, over all Ireland and for the matter of that, over the entire world. As his own song says:

> *'We send our hail to lands afar,*
> *Where'er our struggling brothers are,*
> *Each shattered crown, each crumbling throne,*
> *Is labour's call to claim our own.'*

PAGEANT

Croke Park was big enough for family intimacies, and at the All-Ireland hurling final of 1935 I'm quite sure Peadar left without noticing whether Kilkenny or Limerick had won. The joy of being among so many Irish people, Gaels to boot, got the better of him: 'Here I stand amid swaying thousands,' and he had, it would seem, a vision:

> *'Stalwart youths behind Cuchulainn*
> *Join the mighty hosts of Fionn,*
> *Come to share this day of glory,*
> *With their living kith and kin.'*

And so on, for a pageful of Irish boasting of all our pagan generations gaily marching o'er the plain from the dawning of creation, to the Paschal fire of Slane, Art MacMurrough,[261] Fiach MacHugh, Red Hugh, brave Hogan, Father John Murphy, Michael Dwyer, O'Neill Crowley, not to mention the 'feared O'Hanlon, gently, stately debonair, who could spit a thieving Saxon with a calm and courtly air', and we leave them 'ever hoping that some day, we'll meet all, on the playing fields of Heaven, there to puck the golden ball'.

You may have noticed that the late Dan O'Connell is not on the team, and Parnell himself would only have made first sub.

TIPP. STOCK

I took up a pamphlet of the troubled times, as other people unrelated to me call them, and was interested to discover that Peadar was of Dublin birth but, to take the harm out of it, so to speak, of Tipperary peasant stock.

In the early days of this century the countryside, Kiltartan Cross and all to that effect, was the go, and you might as well be out of the world as out of the fashion as to be born nearer the Five Lamps than Mullinahone.

But I'll say this for Peadar, there was nothing wrong with his choice, if it was his. If you must have peasant stock they'd be as well to come out of Dan Breen's country as anywhere else.

BIOGRAPHY

My cousin Séamus de Búrca,[262] who is finishing Peadar's biography, says in his introduction to the collection of Peadar's songs published by Martin

Walton that he was born at 11 Lr Drumcondra Road (now 68 Lr Dorset Street) on 12 December 1883.

He was named after his grandfather, who hailed from Funshog, Ardee. His father was John Kearney and his mother was Kate McGuinness of Rathmaiden, Slane, County Meath.

Seamus de Burca continues: 'Let me make the Nation's ballads and I care not who makes its laws.' This is the philosophic content of a famous declaration by the old Scottish writer Andrew Fletcher of Saltoun (1655–1716):

> 'Revolutions have a habit of being pioneered and consolidated by poets and song writers. Sincerity, rather than high artistic merit, gives inspiration and finds response in the hearts of the oppressed.'

The French Revolution owes much to Rouget de Lisle and his "Marseillaise". The Irish Revolution owes quite as much to Peadar Kearney and his "Soldier's Song".

BALLADMAKER

The comparison with de Lisle would have pleased Peadar. Many's the time I heard him, in my childhood on the Northside, fill the kitchen with the 'Marseillaise':

'Allons enfants de la patrie, le jour de gloire est arrivé ...' Then he'd break off in the middle, and tell us how our people on my mother's side were buried, generations of them, in the Grange cemetery near Drogheda, and the oldest burial spot in Europe, from the time of Conall Cearnach, greatest of the Kearneys.

He made the nation's ballads all right. He succeeded as none other has done in writing songs that passed effortlessly into the minds of the Irish people so that today, in his own lifespan, had he made three score and ten, they are as familiar as an old hill.

ANONYMOUS

Even before he was dead, Don MacDonagh who, as one of the clique himself, might have known better, referred in an article in *The Bell*, to 'The Three Coloured Ribbon' as an anonymous ballad.

I was away, some place, at the time, and don't know whether anyone drew Peadar's attention to it; if they did, he should have been pleased. What's a ballad for? Only to go round like a five-naggin bottle at a wake, and so far round it's forgotten who first provided it.

I wish I could sing out of this page at you, to give you some idea of a snugful of Kearneys, Behans, Bourkes, Slaters, Furlongs, Trimbles, shamelessly proud, and roaring:

> *'Our fathers oft were naughty boys,*
> *Whack fol de diddle ol the di do day,*
> *For guns and pikes are dangerous toys,*
> *Whack fol de diddle ol the di do day,*
> *From Beal an Atha Buidhe to Peter's Hill,*
> *We made poor England weep our fill,*
> *But ould Britannia loves us still,*
> *Whack fol de diddle ol de di do day.'*

ANTHEM

In 1907 he wrote, in collaboration with the late Paddy Heeney, 'The Soldier's Song', which the throaty roar of the Dublin crowd made a song to defy the Black and Tans.

Heeney was born on the Northside, at 101 Railway Street, of Dublin parents, and died in Jervis Street Hospital in 1911. He also provided the music for a song about Michael Dwyer, which, I am happy to say, I heard a choir of schoolchildren sing the other week, and with vengeance, as the late Páidin O Caoimh might say.

Phil Shanahan's,[263] at the corner of Foley Street and, incidentally, but a few doors from the residence of the late Fluther Good, was HQ for Peadar and his friends during the Tan time.

Phil was a native of Holyford, County Tipperary, and, I am really happy to recall this, became first TD for that area (I think it's the North Dock) when he won the seat for Sinn Féin against the Redmondite Alfie Byrne.

GLORY-OH

His countrymen Dan Breen and Seán Treacy[264] found refuge there. Michael Collins knew it well, and Seán Russell and Oscar Traynor.[265]

> *'Sad is the news and the theme of my story,*
> *Gone are the days of the song and its glory.*

Dark are the clouds that are hovering o'er me,
Far from the village we tarried so long.
'Heigh ho, slan to the revelry,
Shouting and drinking and singing so merrily,
Red nights we never again shall see,
Down in the village we tarried so long.'

'Down by the Glenside' has been glory-ohed from the national throat, between the Falls Road to Fenit, so often that it might be thought it grew there.

Peadar wrote it to an air he got from an old woman in the Coombe and, in *The Irish Press* for Saturday, 31 August 1935, he published his own Irish of it.

SLÁN

I can see it this minute, in the big Gaelic type they used in the days of 'Roddy the Rover' and M.J. (it's not difficult for me to see it; my mother had the cutting in her album all the time).

He died on 23 November 1942 and left after him, besides his sons and grandchildren, his loyal and great-hearted sweetheart, comrade and wife, Eva (*née* Flanagan).

Neither of them expected anything for what they did. The cause was their life and they lived it. And it's a good job for his widow that she expected nothing, for that, precisely, is what she got.

'Slán béo leis na blíanta ar a bhfuilim ag smaoineadh;
Fé sholus na ghealaighe ba mhinic do chifhinn,
Na fir óga ag ullamhughadh chun troid ar son saoirse.
Céad beannacht óm' chroidhe-se ar Oglaoich na bhFiann.
...'s na Flaithis táid suidhte ae dheas laimh ár dTighearna.
Céad beannacht óm chroidhe-se ar Oglaoich na bhFiann.'[266]

The Irish Press, 27 November 1954

47
TRAILS OF HAVOC

'Brending Being.'

  'Mrs Brennan.'

  'How's Londing?'

  'Who?'

  'Londing. Didn't you come home from the Contingnent be Londing?'

  'That's right.'

  'Well, came meal a vault yeh.'

  'What me?'

  'There's the Irishman for yous. Came meal a vault yeh – a hundred, thousand welcomes.'

  'Thank you, Mrs Brennan, that's more nor civil of you.'

  'I'd a thought anyone would have known what 'came meal a vault yeh' meant. Usen't it to be written up over the stage in the Queen's, isn't that right, Mr Cripping?'

  Crippen lifted his head from the unvarnished half of a pint tumbler and nodded, gloomily.

  'That's right. "*Céad míle fáilte*," kindly remember you're not at home and do not spit; nor pass out tickets after second interval; orange-sucking pro-hibited during cornet solo. But don't talk to me about London.'

DESTRUCTION

'Ah,' said Mrs Brennan, feelingly, 'poor ould Crip, he's like that since the other day at the Curragh, Lester Piggott[267] let him down for a three cross double and the same back, anything to come, first fav. at the other meeting.'

'Thanks be to God,' said Crippen, 'he doesn't come over more often. The short while he was here, he done more damage than Cromwell[268] or Willie Nevitt.[269] I'd *him* at the end of length of accumulators the size of a summans in the Irish Two Thousand and he let me down, for one pound one and three (less tax).'

'Ah, sure, Mr Cripping, that's months ago. It's no use keeping up a thing like that forever,' said Mrs Brennan. 'Better to forget it.'

'I can never forget it, and me with three pounds eighteen and threepence, less tax, going on to a two-to-one shot.'

'We keep the past for pride,' said I.

INCANTATION

'Oh, he's like that, this week past,' said Mrs Brennan, 'and if you had have seen him in the shop when the result came in, he was like a raging deming. Going round looking at the sheets, and muttering, Omagh, Armagh, Armagh, Omagh, like an incantating charm or smell, like what you're warned against in the Catechissing. I don't think it's lucky.'

'Still, Mr Cripping, sup up, you're in your granny's, and don't make strange. In honour of Mister Brending Being's safe return to his native vegigibble market. Concepta.'

An ancient, indestructible countenance, wrinkled and rugged enough to contain a shower of rain, but at present holding no more than the faintest traces of previous repasts of snuff, upturned itself from the inside of a shawl: 'Mrs Jewel and darling, did I hear you say something?'

'I've to go and watch me grandchild's eldest, the Lotty one, get a couple of skips of fruit over to me pitch, the butt-end of Moore Street. You know the pitch poor ould Funny Noises willed me?'

'"Deed I do, the Lord have mercy on her, a good poor soul, poor ould Funny Noises. Still, she couldn't take her bit of Moore Street with her.'

'Still and all, it was decent of her, and I looking for a bit of ground for me descendings. You might as well have a half in respect of her, not to mind Brending Being being home, Me-Hall.'

'Yes, Mrs Brennan, ma'am,' said Michael.

'Two pints of stout for the menkinds, and us ladies will have two half ones, and a bottle of Johnny-jump up.' She turned to me. 'A surjing gave me the tip. Lovely man, he was. Only for the ould drop. Too fond of it.

'Man sent up to be operated on for an ingrowing toe-nail, me poor surjing read the card wrong and thought it was a head amputating was required. Amputated the head, God love him, very severe operating, the patiengt never come out of it and the poor surjing was disgraced for life.'

'I knew one of them Swaines up in George's Packet, had his thumb amputated.'

'I remember them,' said Mrs Brennan, 'they were married into the Leadbeaters.'

APOLLO

'That's right,' said Crippen, cheering himself up with a pull on his pint. 'Well, they were in a kind of religion that was very conscientious about the last day and about getting up out of the grave, the way you were in the world. Well, Apollo Swaine.'

'Apollo?' I enquired.

'Yes, he got that name from hawking refreshments and shouting at the football matches: "Cigarettes, chocolate, toffee app-oll-oh." Well, anyway, when he came out of the hospital he brought the thumb with him and had a kind of a little wake for it, in Jimmy-the-Sports's bar up on our corner.

'Had it on the counter beside him, bringing it up to bury it. "I'm going to put it where the rest of me will be when I die," says Apollo. "A fellow would look well on the last day, running round the 'Nevin like a half-thick and asking everyone and they gathering up their ould traps themselves, *Eh, did you see e'er a sign of a thumb knocking round?*"

FAREWELL

'So we all agreed that there was a deal in what he said, and he invited us to the funeral of his thumb. We got up to the 'Nevin and buried it, and some was crying when the thumb was covered up in the ground, but Apollo mastered himself, and gave a bar of a song before saying farewell.

'I can hear him this minute, and we all joined in with him when he sang out to his poor ould thumb, "*And you will sleep in peace, until I come to thee.*"'

'Still, it wasn't like having a head amputating, having a tum amputating,' said Mrs Brennan. 'When all is said and done, a body does have two tums.'

The Irish Press, 4 December 1954

48

HE WAS ONCE CRIPPEN THE PIPER

'In the Brishish milisha, he was, my poor fellow, wasn't he, Maria Concepta? And a fine man, too,' said Mrs Brennan.

'He was all that,' said Maria Concepta, 'and I heard my own fellow saying that your fellow was as safe as houses in the war. He only had to put on his busby and march away. The Boers thought it was a hedgehog moving.'

'But, all the same, I was thrilled to bits, waiting for him to finish his month's training on the Curragh. I was faithful to him the whole four weeks and, when the dread millingterry word of command rang out, and the period of separashing was over, and the sergeant major roars: "Milisha, to your workhouses, poorhouses, dosshouses and jails, disperse!" there I was, standing behind him, waiting to pick him up as he fell out. To pick him up and carry him home.'

'Aye indeed,' said Maria Concepta. 'A tough little man he was, too, like the day he punched the countryman in the ankle for asking him whether he was a child or a midget.'

WAS I WHAT?

'Were you ever in the army, Mister Cripping, sir?'

Crippen gave a mirthless laugh.

'Was I ever what? Are you codding me or what? Are you getting it up for me, or what? Was I ever in the army? Did you ever hear of the Malpas Street ambush? Did you ever hear of the attack on O'Keefe's the knackers? Did you ever hear of the assault on the soap works in Brunswick Street? Or the raid on the Sloblands? Did yous?' He glared at me. 'Well, mouth almighty, did *you* ever hear tell of the dead who died for Ireland? Well you're looking at one of them.'

'I'm sorry for your trouble,' I muttered, for want of something to say.

'I suppose yous never heard of the pitched battle at the back of the pipes? And, I suppose, talking about pipes, yous never heard of the lone piper who played at the massacre of Mullinahack? There was a song written about it.

'I was not long learning the pipes. But now yous know it, I don't mind telling yous that my nickname in the old Seventh Bat. was the Cock of the North.

'That was really on account of me mother keeping the poultry above in Phibsboro. Ah, when I think of the old days ...' he sighed, looking into the depths of his tumbler.

'I was through the whole lot. The Tan War,[270] the Civil War,[271] the Economic War.'

'Ah, more luck to you,' said Maria Concepta, 'didn't I sing for the boys.'

'You sang?' I asked.

'She did, Brending Being. If you heard her singing "Home to Our Mountings" you'd know all about it,' said Mrs Brennan.

'I don't doubt you,' said I.

USELESS

'That woman,' said Crippen, pointing to Maria Concepta, 'was principal soprano in the Hammond Lane.'

'That's right,' said Mrs Brennan, 'in the Hammingd Laying Fouingdry Choir.'

'I suppose,' said I, with a weak grin, 'yous put on that opera, *The Rose of Castille*. Have you got me? *The Rows of Cast Steel*. It's a joke,' I pleaded, 'from a book by a man by the name of James Joyce.'

'Do you think,' said Crippen severely, 'we're all thicks and idiots here? Certainly, we heard of James Joyce, the man who wrote *Useless*. I was in the inntellimigentsia—'

CHAMPION

I'd forgotten Crippen's connection with the world of letters. He had knowledge of a bookie who took stamped addressed envelopes and international reply coupons to the odds and ran to this bookie regular errands for both members of the staff of a cultural quarterly, since deceased.

'By the way, what happened your gills?'

'The former assistant editor?'

'Of course. D'you think I was enquiring about the charwoman?'

'He's still with the BBC.'[272]

'I wonder, Mr Cripping, if you'd ever give me youngest grandchild's eldest a bit of a note to him. He's the next of me descendings to leave school and at the moment, he seems fit for nothing but to be this year's netball champying. He's mad to be an enjing driver, and if your friend in the CIE[273] could—'

'It's not the CIE,' said Crippen, 'it's the BBC.'

'I beg your parding, Mr Cripping.'

HOWL

'Give us that bit offa song you sang in the trouble,' said Crippen, in the direction of Maria Concepta.

'I might as well. Wait till I clear me throat.'

A sound as of the death rattle came from under her shawl, and then, without further warning, a most bloodcurdling moan went through the shop, as she threw back her covering and bayed at the ceiling. 'Howl, howl, howl—'

The cat glanced anxiously round and, at the third note, got down from the window and slid out the door.

'You never lost it,' said Crippen, nodding his head in appreciation.

Maria Concepta screwed up her face another bit and went on: 'Howl, how long will dear old Ireland be unfree?'

'Lovely,' muttered Mrs Brennan, rapping on the counter and humming to herself. 'Oh, never marry a soldier, an airman, or a maree-ing, if you can get a rebel in his uniform of gree-ing ...'

The Irish Press, 11 December 1954

49
THE NORTHSIDE CAN TAKE IT

But now it has need of all it can get.

Doctor Johnson said the Irish were a very honest people, that they seldom spoke well of each other; but I'm sure you're as well able to put up with a bit of the truth as the next. We're not writing or reading an English Sunday paper, with cups of tea and a saucer of milk for the cat, and Cockney kindness and Lancashire love and 'we can take it' sentiment given out ad lib.

The Northside CAN take it; HAS taken it, but the fact remains that there has been a great deal more blather than action in the matter of relief.

I am a native of this area, and before my temper gets the better of me at the miserable scale of relief being afforded these people, let me plead with you.

Subscribe to this fund.

If you are from the country, particularly from Tipperary or Cork, forget any little jackeen sneers at the bog you may associate with this area.

REMEMBER WHEN THEY WERE THERE TO HELP
Remember how, on Bloody Sunday,[274] they took you to their hearths and homes, and had their blood spilled and their ornaments smashed – and if you knew how much they thought of the same plaster horrors, you'd wonder which they felt most – and the overflow of Croke Park miraculously hidden. Lloyd George's[275] and Winston Churchill's slaughtermen could really go to town.

If you are a Protestant, remember that these are the people of St Barnabas's parish, homeland of your illustrious co-religionists, Seán O'Casey, Alex Stevenson,[276] who played for Barnabas soccer team and my friend Ernie Smith,[277] who battled in the ring for Ireland in the Olympics.

If you are a Jew, I would remind you that in this quarter lie the bones of many of your dead, in honoured peace.

Más Gael thú, biodh fhios agat go raibh cónai ar Sheán O Donnabhan, comrá-dach Petrie agus O Comhraidte i 49 Bayview Avenue, North Strand le fada an lá. Agus dála an scéal, na dein dearmad ar an rud adeir sé féin mar gheall ar an gcarranthacht suarach.

Ní hí an bhoctaineach is measa liom.
Ná bheith this go deo.
Ach an tarcuisne leanann í,
Ná leighisfhidh na leomhain ...
(as 'Sioladóiri', le Bráthair Criostamball).[278]

If you are from north-east Ulster, remember that this was the first refuge of the people found at the time of the pogroms, when the women of the Northside went down to Amiens Street and met the trainloads of tragedy with tea and comfort and anything they could give or pledge for.

FIRST THE FIREMEN HELD THE PASS

Is there anyone I will talk well about in connection with these floods?[279]

First and foremost, the men of the Dublin Fire Brigade, particularly the men in the gap, the first four, who held the pass on their own, from one in the morning till the army came round at five o'clock – firemen Carroll, Mitten, Gordon and Meyler.

At times they were so cold that, as they said themselves, they didn't know but they felt warmer in the water than out of it.

Also talked well about on the Northside are firemen Jem Dowling, Tara Street, Larry Carroll of Buckingham Street, Barney Collins, Buckingham Street, and District Officer MacDonnell, who was in charge of the fire engine that drove to the collapsed GNR bridge at East Wall.

Fireman Bill Murphy, one of a great collection of Kerry brothers, took out a poor woman whose only request was to let collect a Baby Power so that he could fortify himself against the water.

AND A GOOD WORD FOR THE GARDAI ...

And now, if there's anyone in the depot or in College Street Barracks with a weak heart, let them read no further.

Brendan Behan, aged thirty-one, described as a journalist, is about to talk well about the Garda Siochána.

Not a one round Ballybough and the Strand but has a great word for the Gardai and the great work they did during the flood.

'The young Guards were great,' was a phrase I heard constantly repeated by the old women in particular. Great they were, and we'll leave it at that.

> *'Here's a health to the men of the brave rank and file,*
> *And the lion-hearted women of Erin's green isle,*
> *Let true men salute them, with wonder and awe,*
> *For they played the best game, played the best game played,*
> *In Erin go bragh ...'*

So goes the old 'sixteen ballad.

COULDN'T FIND THE DOORSTEP

Tom Campbell, aged fifty-eight, who dislocated his arm when he couldn't find the doorstep in the water, and he rescuing his mother-in-law.

His son, Christopher, aged seventeen and unemployed (a wink being as good as a kick in the ribs, if any of you have a job for him and want a right lad; his address is 17 Tolka Road) 'left the Elec' Cinema, after seeing *The Lady in the Iron Mask*, walked home as far as Ballybough, saw a crowd at the bridge, went into the water as far as Gaffney's of Fairview, and shoved some stranded car as far as Windsor Avenue.

'And then,' he says, 'I finished the night with George Crowther – he's nineteen – taking people and goods (forty crates of eggs) out of Cadogan Road on an *Evening Press* van.'

My old friend and neighbour Mrs Mary Hogan, 120C Ballybough Flats, rescued a flock of Duffys from No. 22 on the bottom floor, under her own place. These included Eileen Duffy (10), Buster (9), Francis (7), Marie (6), Pat (5) and Noel (1).

... THEN THE TOLKA KNOCKED HER FLAT

Mrs Elizabeth Kelly, who has thirty-four grandchildren, came through 'sixteen, the Tan time, the Civil War, was in England for doodlebugs, bombs and rockets and, after all that war, riot and civil commotion, was never frightened till she saw the Tolka not come over the railings of the flats but *through* them, right into her place, to sweep past the hall door and knock her flat in the hall.

Reproachfully she said, 'I never thought the ould Tolka would do the like of that.'

The last word, from one and all around Ballybough and the North Strand and Fairview: 'God help the poor people on the Shannon.'

Amen, and let the rest of us do the best we can for them, too.

The Irish Press, 13 December 1954

50

TOUR OF NATION VIA
THE TOLKA

The Coombe crowd are hot stuff. Never mind your *Dublin Opinion* jokes about Corkmen and Northerners. The Liberty boys would give them a run for their money any day of the week. No need for them to go into the Civil Service or this *teóranta*[280] or that *teóranta*, or into newspaper offices for the matter of that, to get a crust and a sup of tay.

If you ever bought 'a sticka taffy' or 'a bara jocklit' at the Curragh[281] or Leopardstown, its money on that it emanated from Blackpitts, or thereabouts, and the 'hang sangwich' you nourished yourself with at Baldoyle more than likely had its origins in the *haute cuisine* not of France, but of Francis Street.

I'll admit that in the palmy days of our adolescence, this kind of Coombe-olatry would, in my native Monto, have been regarded as dangerously near treachery to the Northside. Spike wouldn't have liked it.

TOLKA

But since the times of the amphibian battle of Tolka Park, the day of the combined land and water operation and the Kevin Street Commandoe, a lot of water has gone down the Tolka, too much, perhaps.

And anyway, we're all that mixed up in the last twenty years of new housing that, as the woman said in the Flats: 'You never know what kind you'rs going to have beside you.'

She had just discovered that her next-door neighbour was *his* mother.

BORU'S SON

I'll get back to the Coombe in a minute but, it just occurred to me, there's no song about the Tolka.

And, as the man said, if it wasn't much of a river, it was the best we had. Brian Boru's son[282] was drowned in it, and it's not every river you could say that about.

Seán Russell littered Annesley Bridge with dead ones in Easter Week. Go on, Behan, your blood's in your knuckles.

On the other hand, it is said that a Dublin Fusilier,[283] *in extremis*, on the battlefields of Flanders, when offered a drink of water, shook his head, and told them to bring it home and give it to the Tolka, which needed it more.

The only reason I can think of as to why there should be no song about the Tolka is the impossibility of rhyming 'Tolka' with anything else but 'polka'.

Not that there are many songs about the Liffey, or the city itself, for the matter of that.

ERSATZ

There have been ersatz efforts like the following by Lady Caterwaul, or some such name, that wouldn't go away and leave the people die in peace the time of the cholera:

> *'Oh Bay of Dubling,*
> *My heart you're trubbling,*
> *Like frozen fountaings ...'*

More power to you, Mrs Brenning ma'm; your blood's worth bottling.

> *'The sunbeam's bubbling ...'*

There's nothing like the Belfast mill songs:

> *'You'll be sure to know a doffer,*
> *When she goes down the town,*

With her shawl and her clogs,
And her hair hanging down ...'

JOE LYNCH

I don't suppose they're the correct words. But it's a real song, though geographically more of the Irish school of canty bodies. And certainly nothing to equal the beautiful songs of Cork City, which do not receive their just due, any more than anything else barring Joe Lynch, from that delightful land of pig meat and porter. Probably because they never did anything on us.

'You're getting very fond of the Corkone-yeeings in your old age, Brending Being.'

'Ah, sure maybe it's only to spite the other crowd, Mrs Brenning, ma'am.'

BARRY

I do not mean 'The Banks of My Own Lovely Lee', though I know every word of it, and have, before now, reduced audiences to tears by the bucketful with my rendering of it; nor do I mean even the more genuine and stirring airs of West Cork:

'From east to west, from north to south,
They tried to hunt the column out,
Till a muster at Roscarbery's rout,
Awoke them from their dreaming.
Come, piper, play a martial air,
For the gallant boys who conquered there.
A merry tune to banish care, not mournful,
Nor solemn,
But the grandest tune that was ever played
By the fighting squad of the Third Brigade,
Whose glorious deeds, shall never fade,
The boys of Barry's column ...'

'This is like a Curse Umper Erring tour of the country, Brending Being; when are we getting back to the Coombe?'

Next week, good people, via Timahoe Bog.

The Irish Press, 18 December 1954

51
HEART TURNS WEST AT
CHRISTMAS

For some reason, deep in our past, I suppose at a festival time even so double-dyed a Dubliner as myself tends, in the sad remembering of friends departed that accompanies even the happiest of Christmases, to think towards Kerry, Connemara ... Aran.

In a snug in Fleet Street, or at the butt end of the Alps, in a Paris bistro, or sitting in a café in Cannes eating 'bweeabass' (there's them that can spell it, but can't pronounce it; and there's them that can pronounce it, but can't spell it – it's part of my stock-in-trade to gam on that I'm of the latter persuasion), or moseying round Green Street and Arran Street East, I often sighed for the magic summer nights, and the walk over the pale sand up to Joe Mháirtin's house.

CISCO'S HAT

And I think of Micheál Meachair, who was Pearse's friend, and Synge's 'native scholar', and his fine and vigorous comment on men and women and life and death. And I remember the Sundays I sang away with my other old friend Peadar O Conghaile.

Peadar wore, and I hope he's still wearing, and God leave him his health to wear out a dozen like it, the old-style black hat with the lace round his chin, which occasioned a private joke between myself and his sons and grandchildren.

He wasn't supposed to hear it, but he did, and came up to me and asked me what I meant by it.

'*Cia hé an Cisco Kid*[284] *seo?*' he asked me.

'*Cé'n Cisco Kid sin agat?*' letting on not to know what he meant, and prepared, if necessary to do my Peter Ustinov[285] act, learned from that gentleman personally, of sobbing denials of knowing anything about it.

'*Airiom gur b'shin sin an tainm a tugann tú orm-sa. Anois, cia hé an Cisco Kid í ndarire?*'

I got a copy of *The Irish Press* and showed him the strip cartoon at the back. He studied it carefully and handed it back to me.

'*Fear maith iseadh an fear sin,*' he said. '*Go raibh maith agat, a Bhreandáin.*'

In my other hostelry up on the hill was Seán, a fine presence of a man, fit to keep even Brendan Behan in order and direct the activities of a household ranging from his eldest son, just finished college, to Rita the baby, not to mention Nero his dog, as good-natured a beast as you'd meet in the width of the Atlantic.

Aran is, of course, the Shangri-La[286] of the Irish intelligentsia, and a bright coloured *crios* may sometimes be seen as far away as Bayswater and the Latin Quarter. But, when all is said and done in the line of good, it must be owned up to that it exercises a calming influence on all who go there. It damned nearly civilised me.

GAN SOLAS

More than the Flahertys and Conneelys will think in exile from Toronto to Tyneside, any Christmas night, of Aran, and Seán T's other islands, from Peadar O'Donnell's and Maire's Aranmore, down to my poor deserted Blasket, so well remembered in Pauline Maguire's article on this page a few weeks ago.

There will be no candles in the windows there, this year.

'*Beidh an fhairrge mor.
Fé luí na ghréine mar ghloine.*

Gan bád fé sheol na comhartha
Beó ó dhuine
Ach an tíolar or deireannach
Thuas ar imeall an domhain.
Thar an mBlascaod uaigneach
Loite.
'... is sóideadh na gaoithe ag
Luascadh
Go bog, leath-dhoras,
Is an teallach, fuar fliuch.
Gan teine, gan teas, gan cosaint.'[287]

FÉ MHAISE

'God knows, Brending Being, the water-bags is very near your eyes.'

So they are, Mrs Brenning, and there'll be no shortage of lights and laughter from Kilmurvey down to Forma this night. Thanks be to God, there's a few of us left, as the man said as he was crushed to death in Croke Park.

For the matter of that, Sundrive Road won't be that badly lit either. I was present at a practice Christmas Eve last night, which suffered from no lack of talent.

To you all there, therefore, the season's greetings from this 'collyum' in Aran, Cabra West, the Shankill, Granamore, Baltinglass, Grafton Street, Paris, Portarlington and Paddington. *Nollag fé shéin 's fé mhaise dhibh uilig,* and may we all be here again this time twelve months, and twice as impudent.

Brendan Behan acknowledges receipt of £5 10s. for flood victims ó Sagart Gaolach and Iarthar £5, and from (Miss) H. Fitzsimons of Delvin, Co. Westmeath (10s.) – herself a flood victim.

The Irish Press, 24 December 1954

52
THOSE DAYS OF *THE GROWLER*

'Listen,' said Michael this morning, looking at Crippen, 'all these ambushes at Malpas Street and Mullinahack and the raid on the Sloblands that you were talking about. How is it I never heard of them, nor no one else?'

'How is it you never heard of them?' asked Crippen, 'because they were done in secret, that's why.'

'I didn't live too far away from Malpas Street, and I never heard as much as a shot from it.'

'We used silencers,' said Crippen, 'silencers –' he looked ominously around the shop – 'and knives. As the poem said—'

'Oh, I love a poem,' said Mrs Brennan. 'I learned one meself, once, be Mangle.'

'Be who?'

'Be Mangle. James Claryawance Mangle. I learned it at school. 'Soloming. Where is thy Trowing? It is gone in the wie-ingd. Babyling! Where is thy might? It is gone in the wieingd, and all ...'

'This poem was talking about,' said Crippen, 'was printed in a secret paper called *The Growler*, and it was signed 'Seville Place'. We all had to use Irish place names. One fellow was 'Shanganagh', another was 'Slievenamon' and I was 'Seville Place'. Yes I might as well admit it, I was 'Seville Place', the whole time, and yous never knew, now did yous?' He looked at me.

'I hadn't an idea,' said I.

'Well, you know now,' said Crippen. 'Me secret's out. But what harm, we're all friends here. You might as well hear it, anyway.' He set his face towards the door and began:

> 'Twas next winter, last summer, the year before last,
> And a man with a hammer sat breaking his fast,
> To hell with Lloyd George, and he let out a roar,
> For Ireland beats England by six goals to four ...'

'That's a deep bit of a poem, I can tell yous. A deep meaning in every other word of it.'

'I've no doubt,' said I.

'Ah, sure the world and Garret Reilly knows, Mr Cripping, that you're putrid from educayshing.'

'Well, I can tell you what Lloyd George himself said at the time about me poem. In the British House of Commons—'

'The Brishish House of Commings,' said Mrs Brennan, 'let yous all mark that.'

'He said, "If I knew the miscreant that goes be the name of 'Seville Place' and wrote that poem in the dirty Sinn Féin rag *The Growler*, I'd give him, jeering and jibing and making little of people. I'd cut the two hands off him, and leave him, that he wouldn't be able to pick a one and one much less write poems." (Irish nat. interjections of 'Mitchelstown'. Cheers from gov. benches.) It's all in an old paper I have at home.'

'You done your bit all right,' said Maria Concepta.

'Oh, sure Wolve Towing was only in the ha'penny place to Mr Cripping. And he never feared debt.'

'Death?' said Crippen, with a scornful laugh, 'I was used to that a long time ago. Like the time I lost the coffin.'

'Lost a coffing, Mr Cripping?'

'That's right, ma'am. I was living out be Cloghran at the time, taking the country air for meself, on account of some lead disappearing off a roof, and bad-minded people ...'

'Bad luck to them,' said Maria Concepta, don't mind them, sir.'

'No, just tell us about the coffing.'

'I was coming from Cloghran into Dorset Street for a few messages and a man be the name of Jowls Hanratty come up and told me his old father was dead, and would I bring out a coffin on the back of the pony and cart.

'I said I would, and he said just to get stock size and brass handles, and off I went.

'On the way back it started to snow, and I'd been into a few places to warm meself up, and was nearly home when I looked around and the coffin was gone.

'I walked back and searched the road as best I could, when a peeler comes up. "What are you doing round here this hour of the night?" said he. "I'm after losing a coffin," said I. "I'll give you coffin," said he, "if you don't move on out of that." So I had to take an hour explaining to him that I really had lost it.

'Oh, it's genuine all right, constable,' said I. 'I'm after losing a coffin, and I wouldn't mind, constable, but it's not my own.'

'You'd feel awful, right enough, and maybe it's what people would think you were after doing away with it, the same as you did with the lead off the roof,' said Maria Concepta, finishing in some confusion, when she felt Mrs Brennan's indignant eye on her.

'I hope you're not instiganayshing that Mr Cripping is a teef?'

To cause a diversion, I asked them what they were having.

The Irish Press, 1 January 1955

53
A PICTURE OF DUBLIN'S OLD
VOLTA CINEMA

'Ná dean gáire, a leanbh
Níl aon aoibneas ann,
Ná h-éist leis na scéalta sidhe.
Níl aon sidheógai ann
Ná tóg do chúile I n-áirde,
Ní thuas atá na flaithis,
As gach scamall screada___
An bhás ... [288]

(Séamus O Néill)

I was going in the general direction of the markets, and in the antique shop, or one of them, near the Four Courts I saw something which interested me. It was not the *Memoirs of a Land Agent* by A. Hussey.[289] The only wonder I had about this was Mr Hussey being left to live long enough to have memoirs.

Nor, for the matter of that, was it *The Life and Speeches of Daniel O'Connell* by his son for, in the estimation of the people I was reared with, he and the son rated with Queen Victoria and the well-known Dublin-Italian, Edward Carson!

And neither was it the history of the Royal Academy – *The Varnishing Irish?* – oh, ha, ha, that's what comes of reading Myles na Gopaleen; many's the one was left like that. And I had little enough interest in the housewife's manual, how to treat your servants with firmness but courtesy.

JAMES JOYCE

All right, I'll tell you what it was. It was a picture of the proprietors and staff of the Volta Cinema, Mary Street, taken on the opening night, and included in the company is James Joyce.

As soon as I get paid for this article, I'm going back down to buy it.

The dealer had the good sense to ask me three shillings for it, though I only said I wanted it because my Aunt Ace (Summerhill for Esther) was the lady on the left, with what looks like a parcel of fried fish under her oxter.

By the time this article is in print, the deal will be done, and the antique dealer will be fit to be tied as the thoughts of what he'd have got off Harvard University for the picture.

They could hang it up in the Joyce thesis factory. It is to be taken for granted that so cultured a man as the antique dealer reads this column.

As the lady on the 81 bus would say, 'Folly's me up, every Saturday.'

I came away from the bookshop and, drawing the mantle of Lear[290] more tightly round me, wended my way up to Michael's.

PATRIOTIC BURGLAR

Old Andy was there, and we fell to talking of old times and all to that effect, and Billy the Burglar and patriotic robber, who tranced the Gresham jewels forty years ago.

Billy used to play the church organ in the Old House on the North Circular Road, and on St Patrick's Day 1905, was reported to the governor for thundering out, all stops out, or in, or whatever way makes roar like the Bull Wall, as the prisoners were going out after Mass, the strains of 'A Nation Once Again', to which the holy cry lannavs, banner merchants, ballmen, murderers, rogues and robbers, felt they had as much right as the honestest men living.

Incidentally, the governor was named Munro, the father of H. Munro, 'Saki',[291] the short-story writer, who spent part of his childhood up at the 'Joy.

So myself and O'Casey are not the only two writers from NCR.

'I'm sure that's a very edifying class of a conversation,' says this big vegetable man.

'Thanks,' said Andy, 'we aim to please.'

SUB JUDAS

'I'll have you know,' said this fellow, beside the vegetable man, 'that me friend here is the Peas Commissioner.'

'The less said about peas in this town, the better,' said Andy, 'especially when the issue is sub Judas.'

'I didn't mean peas, I meant peace. He's a peace commissioner,' said the PC's friend, 'A great man for oats.'

'Oats? And peas?' asked Andy.

'Oaths, oaths, oaths,' said the PC's friend.

Michael had just come in and looked sternly at the PC.

'You'll have to control your tongue in this shop, my man. I don't stand for anything the like of that. It's not lucky. Keep your oaths to yourself as long as you're here.'

'That softened your cough,' said Andy.

The Irish Press, 8 January 1955

54

UP CORK — FOR WIT, AND SONG

A few weeks ago I started to tell you why I thought the Coombe crowd beat the country, Cork and the North included, for being quick off their mark, getting their heads to the ball and minding mice at the crossroads.

I heard an old woman in Pimlico say that if a fiver (actually, as we say in West Kensington, she called it a 'flim') fell from a man's hand in Belcuddy, the paw of a Liberty boy would be under it before it touched the floor.

I got involved in apologising for talking so well about South Dublin, and made reference to the fact that there were no songs about the River Tolka and, indeed, no songs of any sort about the city as such, and if you'll permit me to say this about ballads while I think of it, I'll get back to my original thesis: 'The Coombe crowd would do anything for money, or the Liberty boys is fit for bottle or draught.'

CORKONEENS

There are no better singers in this or any other country than the Corkmen. Nor is there better company than that of Cork City people. Nor, for the matter of that, is there a more citified people, in the walls of the world, than is to be found between Christy Horgan's and Dan MacCarthy's, which is the length of Blarney Street.

Joyce, whose father was a native of it, once said that there were few Parisians, no cockneys, but that Cork City was full of Corkoneens.

Samuel Beckett,[292] Joyce's friend and for years his secretary, once told me that there was a recognisable Cork lilt in his accent, and, sure enough, a couple of days after I heard Sam say this, an American played me a record of the master's voice: 'Hithering dithering waters of … Anna Livia.'

You could hear the leaves above Chapelizod rustling in the dark, and the accent was mostly Cork; not the Coal Quay, I'll admit, but the sharper, cultivated but still vibrant high Castilian brogue of Mac Liammóir and Seán Ó Faoláin.

ULSTER

To get into the company of Ulster-born people is to be bored within an inch of your life with dialect stories of Northern wit.

Usually the Protestants tell stories of pawky Papists and funny Fenians, and his Catholic confederate returns the compliment with the desperately amusing remarks of larky Lutherans and witty Wesleyans.

The unfortunate Dubliner, usually terrified out of his wits, for they are tough kiddies from up there, has to grin and bear it and swallow it with their other guff about some 'dacent man' giving another 'dacent man' a glass of water after he was taken from under a two-ton truck, the dacent men being of different religion.

And it all goes to show you have Protestant dacent men and Catholic dacent men living between the Clogher Valley (wherever that is) and the Lagan.

FAIR HILL

God leave me my health to go back down again and sit in Dan Mac's at the top of Blarney Street and hear Jim Mac's brother-in-law sing 'The Boys of Fair Hill', and hear again the cut and thrust between city man and Macroom, as I heard once in a casual conversation over a pint and a pig's foot.

To hear again the full-throated chorus of the devil's own people's anthem, at the devil's own hour of the morning:

> *'The boys they won't harm you,*
> *The girls they will charm you,*
> *Here's to them all, said the boys of fair hill.'*

'I heard it said for a positive fact that six months before a Macroom child was born, the mother walks along Patrick Street picking out a shop for him.'

'Did you now? I heard there's someone dead belonging to you. It's not yourself by any chance?'

The Irish Press, 15 January 1955

55

ON ROAD TO RECOVERY

It's after taking as many weeks as there are since the New Year for me to recover from the festive celebrations of my friends and my friends' friends in the County Kildare. They ebbed and flowed (ebbing in the morning and flowing at night) at various points between Kilcock and the North Wall and from Naas to Grafton Street, with occasional incursions into counties Wicklow, Meath and Wexford.

There is an idea that the flatlands of East Leinster are somehow lacking in the native characteristics of eating and drinking, and singing and arguing, and that they breed a race of quiet bullock drivers.

It should also be remembered that they are also bullock-eaters, and show every sign of their diet, as you'll agree if you remember the Lilywhites in the famous Kildare–Kerry All-Irelands of the late twenties, or saw the Meathmen stamping around Croke Park.

HEBER

And if you're talking of 'Boiler' McGuinness, my own great-grandfather was a McGuinness from Slane, from a place called Rathmaiden and, as a correspondent was good enough to point out in a letter to this newspaper, the homeland of Francis Ledwidge[293] and F.R. Higgins.[294]

My great grandmother came there from her own place in Duleek, where the Hickeys lived from the time of Heber and Heremon. Incidentally, Heber is still a common enough Christian name in those parts.

She spoke good Irish, but not to me, for she's been lying above in Newgrange this fifty years. There was good Irish in the County Meath up to the time of Father O'Growney's[295] childhood, and it was from the old men of Meath he got his first knowledge of it that set him writing the little books.

O'GROWNEY

I found old copies of them at home at odd intervals during my childhood but not a word could I make out of them, no more than if they were high Dutch.

As a matter of fact, I'd have made a better shot at high Dutch for a friend of mine, Mimi Sinclair, that's married to a Dublin fellow in Geneva, speaks that language, and I've heard their children, Frankie-schoen and Anne-shoen at it.

But anyone that ever learned Irish from Father O'Growney's books, it is not a fainne[296] they should have got but a wig, to make up for the hair they lost studying.

I was discussing these matters with Billy in Kilcock, with a picture of Domhnall Ó Buachalla[297] looking down from the walls at us, and smiling through his beard that, of all people, makes him resemble the late George V whose representative he was supposed to be at the culminating point of his revolutionary career, until, with his last work for Ireland complete, Domhnall was free to retire and remember the times when the job was more dangerous and less entertaining, marching the Kildaremen.

Along the banks of the canal they went, from quiet Maynooth to the game old city, bombed, battered, punched and pounded, the heart burning out of them, but still able to manage a defiant screech from a Howth Mauser.

TOLKA

From the north County Dublin out, the broadlands produced good men and hearty ones and, by the same token my remarks about the Tolka not being mentioned in verse (except for a mention in Ríobeárd O Faracháin's *First Exile*, where he's writing about Columcille, and says you wouldn't get enough water in the Tolka to drown a pinkeen) have provoked the following from a correspondent whose chosen nom de plume is 'Brian':

'That none other sings of the famed old Tolka, this I draw,
Familiar with thy every bank,
Rise or fall on either flank,
Here within the city's maze,
Where brave Brian, great his praise,
Smote the Ostman's power to dust,
Neath thy wave, their weapons rust.
Brave Dalcassians' axes too,
Fell within the bloody brew,
Thy tide upon that April day ...'

MICK McGEE

'They swept their foes into the Bay
And later by nine hundred years,
Closely by Drumcondra's weirs
In ambush lay another Brien.
With Mick McGee, schoolmate of mine
Another and more murderous foe,
To wait beside thy even flow,
Alas, before the time was meet,
A traitor sent his message fleet.
Before the plans were fully laid,
One hero's heart in death was stayed,
My old schoolmate, Mick McGee,
The other Brien, on the gallows' tree,
With five others shed his blood,
Whelan, Moran, Doyle, Ryan and Flood.'

SHORT ANSWER

And after a verse for the late Brigadier Dick McKee, our bold Brien goes
back to the time King James got the short answer from Lady Tyrconnell:

'... e'er long the royal intruder speaks,
For Stuart James himself 'tis seeks
Shelter in cowardly flight from the Boyne,
The Tolka saw him, heard his whine,

Your countrymen they ran away,
And heard you, too, the prompt reply,
Swift as a rapier thrust it flashed
On James's ears like thunder crashed.
The gentle lady says with grace,
'Twould seem your Highness won the race.
Was Stuart pride e'er humbled more
Than here on dear old Tolka's shore?'

Epilogue: by B.B., who decrees:

'A photo finish in this race,
Because we have got no more space.'

The Irish Press, 22 January 1955

56

I HELP WITH THE SHEEP

A woman came to Pádraic Pearse complaining about her son's progress, or lack of it, at school. 'He doesn't seem to want to do anything,' she said. 'I don't see any future for him, except playing the tin whistle. What am I to do with him?'

'Buy him a tin whistle,' said Pearse.

In my capacity as shepherd on Timahoe Bog, of which, I warned you, I was going to tell as soon as we got 1954 over us, I stood in the town of Kilcock, 'the famous town of Kilcock' as its inhabitants call it, and listened to the music of some half a school-load of Christian Brothers' boys playing 'The Wearing of the Green' and '*Fáinne Gheal an Lae*' on their tin whistles.

CONSCRIPT

I hope the young Byrnes and O'Connors will excuse me so describing them. I know that in the school they are described as flageolets, but, to us older shams who write and read *The Irish Press* they'd be more readily described as tin whistles.

Anyway, they made very good music with them, whatever you'd want to call them, and I listening next door.

Snug enough I was, too, before they dug me out and we went up to the sheep.

Accursed and vicious breed. Nest of vipers. Coy and humorous, if you can call it humour making a man of fourteen stone charge over barbed wire and land to his armpits in the mud of centuries.

You never saw me chasing sheep? You've never lived. I was left in such a state after them that my nearest relative would have felt sorry for me.

The object was to get up to Timahoe Bog, get them marshalled into some sort of order and get a hundred of them carted into Prussia Street.

SPELLING

We left Billy's after interrupting a discussion I was having with the man of the house about the practice which, we agreed, was a disgusting one, of spelling such old words as Dún Laoghaire 'Dún Laoire' and céilidhe 'céilí'.

I was telling Billy that everyone that had occasion to go there, whether from England or Ireland, knew the port as Dún Laoghaire, and that the only one I had ever heard to get himself mixed up with the word 'céilidh' was my friend Eddie Chapman,[298] who, on leaving a boat with me at Clyde Quay in Glasgow, told me that he would see me at the 'Celluloid Bar' in an hour's time.

But he, despite the uncompromising Scottish spelling of 'Céilidh Bar' on the fascia, found the place all right.

It was cold for that bog, and it was nice and warm and jovially scholarly inside with meat and drink of the best.

But I was between the devil and the deep sea – a Liberty boy and a Kerryman.

'When you're sure you're finished with the Tishel Genewhack[299] there, we'll have a run up to the sheep.'

So off we went. The bog itself was lovely in warm blues and browns that stretched as far as the horizon, and the sky bright with a Christmas glitter.

The sheep, when we got near enough to them, were munching away, not minding anyone, and I felt kind of sorry for them going off to be assassinated. But I consoled myself by thinking that they weren't going to be croaked just yet. They would all live to see their progeny next spring.

I thought of Tolstoy's[300] remark in *War and Peace* to the effect that when a sheep is taken from the common fold to be specially fattened, the other sheep, watching his more rapid growth in the neighbouring and specially favoured pasture, must consider him almost in the light of a god, so much fatter than themselves does he become. And when he leaves for the slaughter house and they see him no more, they must come to the conclusion that he has been divinely translated to fresh fields and pastures new, by supernatural intervention.

RECOGNITION

By the time I had chased after a few of them, I'd more than Tolstoy to worry me.

It is said that the commander of a Japanese submarine that came to Cork was asked what he thought of it, and he replied that the only difficulty he and the crew had was in distinguishing one Corkman from another.

I had thought the same of sheep. But it wasn't long after I had dug myself out of the muck of County Kildare for the first time that I began to recognise one sheep from the next.

There was one vicious female criminal that persisted in waiting until they were all nearly at wherever they were supposed to be going. Then she'd take a sly run round in the opposite direction, leading half the gang after her.

I'd know her, and I'd know the sixth generation of her if I caught her looking up at me from a slab in Moore Street ten years from now, if God leaves either one of us our health.

COMPLAINTS

However, we got them off to Dublin and we went back into Billy's, where I heard the complaints of one man to another.

'You did. You called me out in the pouring rain to walk home with you, and then you got into the car and walked off.'

The muck drying on me, and a tumbler in my hand, I settled down to listen to a bit of human argument and rest myself from sheep.

The Irish Press, 29 January 1955

57

THEY DIDN'T MAKE THE FAMINE

On my last Sunday evening in Paris we sat, Desmond and Mary and I, outside the café and talked after dinner far into the soft evening and past midnight, in the cooling darkness, on the rim of the right from the café window.

Desmond has lived almost everywhere – in Ireland, the States, England, France, Bermuda and Italy. In Italy he lived in Capri; and in Ireland, it was Carlow he knew best.

Perhaps Carlow has been unjustly neglected in literature, for I cannot remember having heard it mentioned in travellers' tales before, but Desmond said its inhabitants were as hospitable and entertaining as any people he had met anywhere.

So, in the soft Paris night, we raised a glass to the scallion aters.[301]

NUMEROUS

After all, it's one of the few places where people of my own name are quite common.

'I should say the Behans would be common anywhere,' said Desmond, 'the nature of the beast. You can't help it. But what you mean is "numerous".'

He knew Norman Douglas,[302] the author of *South Wind*, and Axel Münthe,[303] who wrote a more famous book about Capri, *The Story of San Michele*.

I cannot help it if your literary prejudices favour the other side, but I was delighted to hear that Douglas detested Münthe and remarked in this connection that he never knew a Swede who was not either a freak or a fraud.

My prejudice is not so generally directed against the Swedish people, for, as my granny was prone to remark about peoples of whom she had little knowledge, 'Twasn't them that made the Famine.'

Nor am I like the cook of an Irish boat who refused to drink Danish lager 'on account of what they done to poor Brian'.

I think Douglas was the better writer, that's all.

And from Carlow we got by easy stages to Tipperary, with which county Desmond has family connections. In the latest Irish papers was a report of some celebrations in honour of Dan Breen, and we decided he was worth a toast to himself, there being no reason why mere distance should separate us in feeling from other right-thinking people.

Incidentally, his book *My Fight for Irish Freedom* is on sale, in translation, in the Breton bookshop off the boulevard Saint-Germain.

COUNTESS

Desmond told me more of the countess in Brittany with whom he had stayed, *en famille*, when he was thirteen, and learning French.

The old lady came to him one day not long after he arrived and said she was very worried about his five-o'clock tea.

It seemed that she was under the impression that no English speaking person can survive twenty-four hours without a pot of tea, which must be administered at five o'clock.

Though a supply of the raw material could be procured from Paris, or maybe even from as near as Rennes, there was nobody amongst the servants that could prepare the infusion, and to tell the truth, she didn't know much about the stuff herself.

PORT

Did he think he would be kind enough to accept as substitute a bottle of port, a drink of which she knew some English milords were quite fond, together with a plate of sweet biscuits? The wine had not been touched from the days of her late husband, but in his time several of his friends had spoken quite tolerantly of it.

. So every day at five o'clock this plucky youth of thirteen summers was sate in state in the library and served with his pint of Cockburn's Crusted and his biscuits.

As he said himself, at first it was the sweet biscuits appealed to him, but by degrees he was able to put up with the wine too.

I had to go home to be up early for the boat train in the morning, and walked in sweet melancholy from the avenue de l'Opéra towards the Behan HQ situated in the rue de Charenton, and – not inappropriately, some may think – near the Place de la Bastille.

DIFFERENCE

My way lay through the edge of the Market districts, where I spent many a happy sunrise, and I was having a cup of coffee there when some porters I knew came in. They were having some refreshment to hearten themselves for the night's work and invited me to join them, but I had to refuse.

Time and the British Railways wait on no man.

The journey, though, is one altogether to the advantage of that organisation, the profits and responsibility of the traffic being equally divided with the French railway.

This may account for the difference in comfort on the route Victoria – Newhaven – Dieppe – Paris, and the horrors of travelling between Dublin and London.

On the sea journey the French ships *Londres* and *Arromanches* take it, turn and turn about with the English ships.

I cannot see why CIE doesn't demand a similar arrangement on the run between Ireland and England, and enforce better treatment for the passengers, most of whom are Irish people anyway.

Mac Lir referred to this point in his article some months ago and, as part of an excuse to not doing it, said that Dieppe was much bigger than Dún Laoghaire.

Well, I don't know what that has to do with it, but I have been having another look at Dieppe and, though I don't know the population figures for either place, it does not look any bigger than Dún Laoghaire to me.

PLAYBOY

At Saint-Lazare station, I need hardly say, I very nearly missed the train. I had lost the ticket of my luggage. You wouldn't get much for the lot on Cole's Lane,[304] but my typewriter was amongst the scrap.

I was arguing as best as I could to get it back before the train left when a young clerk of the kind that would kill his own mother for a spare ticket to a Raidió Éireann symphony concert came up and asked me where I was from.

I said Ireland, and his face lit up as he bustled about.

'Syracusecque,' he muttered, 'Syracusecque,' and came back with the luggage and ten minutes to spare.

'Syracusecque,' he said, in triumph, and shook my hand.

'The same to you,' said I and was on the train, and half way to Rouen, when I figured out that this incantation referred to Cyril Cusack,[305] latest hero of the theatre-going population of the city behind us.

'Twas the Playboy himself procured my release, mister honey.

The Irish Press, 5 February 1955

58
YES, QUARE TIMES

At Naas races I wondered why the chalk fell from the bookies' paralysed paws when they came to the name of Quare Times.

Being an eager seeker after information about anything except picks and shovels, I decided to ask a bookie why this was. I looked round and, though I have been acquainted with some of them since childhood, there was a forbidding look of foreboding about them all that did not invite enquiries as to the cause of their worries. Except Billie Carran, whose bland and pleasant smile swept round the multitude like a beam of a lighthouse on a dark and troubled sea. I went over, stood under and looked up at him.

'Liam, *a chara*.'

'Just a moment, Brendan, till I'm done with this gentleman.'

He muttered something about four score and ten to his clerk, though whether it referred to your gills's age or not I do not know, though they threw the old man's tenners in the bag as if they were sure they were to stay there, and asked of me: 'How's the form?'

EXERCISE

'Very good,' said I, 'as a matter of fact if I was better I couldn't stick it.'

'More of that to you. Are you having a small punt?'

'It would not be right for me to bet you sixty pound to forty pound that this horse will be first past the post. I'm not the bookmaker.'

'And maybe you haven't got the sixty pound,' said the clerk.

'Oh, he'd have it about him all right,' said Billy.

'I suppose you could be right,' said the clerk, measuring the front of my overcoat and muttering something about taking more exercise.

An aged turf accountant who, whenever I pass, usually takes care to flash the far side of his bag where it reads *Minimum Bet 2/-* looked at me with a new interest. I may say the near side of the bag reads *Louis MacNeice, Baa, Tonafarraga*, which I believe is in the County Belcuddy or some such place.

WHEELS

Anyway, the punters would have a right time trying to catch up to *him* in his native warren. And even if you did, there's no knowing whether they come under Seán T.'s dominion at all or not.

A small, red-faced man with the figure of a ferret nodded knowingly, as he has a habit of doing. This person, like the character in Dostoyevsky's *The Idiot*,[306] was a man who brought the art of knowing other people's business to the level of a science, and I heard him telling the true story of the Tóstal, the behindhand work that went on about the Shannon Scheme,[307] and who worked the oracle in the case of the nine million sods of turf at County Meath – wheels within wheels and it's not who you know but who you know – have you me?

TELEPHONES

In answer to my query re the bookies' reaction to Quare Times, which was worse than the panic aboard the Liverpool boat, one trip they ran out of porter and wanted the people to drink milk stout, Billy told me to go round and have a look at the animal going round the parade ring.

Which I did, and I might as well have been a sow looking into a swill barrel, for all the good it did me.

Quare Times looked a magnificent beast, but I suppose it's because long years of running with dockets from building jobs in the light and *aerach*[308] days of my youth have conditioned me to thinking that racing is all an affair of telephones and duplicated sheets, and old ones with string bags saying that they got it off a man off a boat or a train, or latterly an Aer Lingus[309] plane, so that if you wanted to make sure of the Spring Double, by considerations of distance, you'd want to get hold of a man from Mars.

OLD LARD

But my walk was not entirely wasted, because I heard two old ladies talking about a hunt to an old fellow with a bowler hat, drainpipe trousers, nap coat with a velvet collar.

One of the ladies put her teeth up in an elegant snarl and said to this old Teddy Boy: 'Well, m'lard he's paffectly impossible as an Emeffaitch. Only wants the Cambridge Drag.'

The old lard was got up for the creep, but he only said, 'Emahdone-noe, but he might finish up as the most popular Emmeffaitch they've ever had, better than the last and most frightful creature, pots of money, no breeding, shout – instead of "Tally-ho," "Come on, after the—."'

I got back and described these happenings to Billy just before the off.

Ferret-face nodded, though no one had asked him, and told us who m'lard was.

PERSONAL

I was going off when I heard him make reference to myself. 'He's a professional unionist, writes funny bits for *The Irish Press*. Very cultured class of a chap, too, writes a rubber cheque in Irish.'

I turned round and said, 'Only on St Patrick's Day,' and fled up the stand before I'd hear my true history.

The Irish Press, 12 February 1955

59
REMEMBER DUCK-THE-BULLET?

'Press,' said Mrs Brennan. We looked at her with a note of interrogation on each countenance, my own, Crippin's and Maria Concepta's. That is to say if you could describe the last mentioned as a countenance.

'Press,' said Mrs Brennan, 'and dresser, and chester drawers, and wardrobe, he'd leave them all in smithereens, and small-sized ones at that, when the fit came on him. Poor ould Duck-the-Bullet. It was really a kind of homesickness made him do it. Homesickness for the Somme[310] in 1915.'

CALLED ACE

'But by the time he'd finished with the furniture you wouldn't know the difference between the North Lotts[311] and Flanders.[312] And the drilling was the worst. His poor wife, Esther Judas, Ace we called her for short, though she preferred Judy herself, and the daughter, Nono, that was named in honour of *No, No, Nanette*, that was on in the Roto next door to the hospital when she was born, would have to get up in the middle of the night and stand there while he charged them up and down the room with the sweeping brush, and showed them how to point and parry.'

'Well, I always say,' said Maria Concepta, saying it, 'that you can't beat a millingterry man for a husband. Always a bit of gas of some description.

Me own poor fellow carried me three times around Mountjoy Square on a Sunday night in the summer of nought three, to show me how he rescued Lady Smith in the Boer War. You remember him, Mrs Brennan, ma'am?'

BIGGEST DWARF

'Indeed and I do, Maria Concepta, and a fine presings of a man he was too. Wasn't he, Mister Cripping?'

'He was all that,' said Crippen. 'I heard said they were hard set to make out whether he was the biggest dwarf or the smallest giant in the whole of the Dublin Fusiliers.'

'Ah, me,' moaned Maria Concepta, 'me dead hero. But, go on, Mrs Brennan, ma'am, and tell us about poor ould Duck-the-Bullet. Him and my poor fellow joined up together, having been let out of the 'Joy the one morning.'

'When he was half sobered up, then, he'd tell poor Ace, the wife, to cut off his head. "Here," he'd say, taking up the hatchet that he was chopping up the furniture with, "take that in your hand and say the words after me, and chop me head off. I must have got a bad half off of Dewlaps, last night, and I'm too sick to wait for the market. Go on, Ace, cut me head off when I tell you."

RENDING

'"Duck-the" – that's what she called him for short, a kind of pet name – "but I couldn't do the like of that. You'd be going around like Hanna Bow Lane with your head tucked under your arm."'

'Poor ould Duck-the-Bullet, I used to love the way he'd rend the marching song,' said Maria Concepta. 'I heard the day meself and me own fellow got married.

'I'll never forget in the sacristy, me a bride, and the groom so fine and fierce-looking in his red tunic and blue trousers and waxed moustache, and the priest lifting him up to kiss me and his pals of the regiment outside and they singing the marching song, led by poor ould Duck-the-Bullet.'

A frightening noise, like the cry of an out-of-work banshee, came from the lips of Maria Concepta:

'Oh, with your left right, right about turn, this is the way we go,
Charging with fixed bayonets, the terror of every foe,

The glory of ould Ireland, and a thousand buccaneers,
And a terror to creation were – The Dublin Fusiliers ...'

BETTER OFF

She finished on a sigh: 'Ah, if only he was here to hear me.'
    'Ah, sure, he's better off,' said Mrs Brennan.
    'You could say that again,' muttered Crippen.

The Irish Press, 19 February 1955

60

EXCUSE MY MISTAKE

I was on the boat from France to Merrie England. And to crown me, didn't I get a half-idiot of a fellow from some built-up bog of London called Tooting Bec or Balham's Ass or some such in the carriage with me, giving out the pay about the hardness of the French.

This means they took money off him for whatever they sold him, just the same as if he were not a Briton at all, but a Wog, or a Chink,[313] or a Mau Mau.[314] He talked about the nastiness of the wine, and how all that messed up stuff they give you to eat couldn't be 'ealthy; and 'ow glad 'e'd be to get 'ome for a good cup of char, wouldn't you?

I replied frigidly that I was not going home. I was going to England, which was not my home.

'Well, excuse my mistake,' said he, 'but it's home to plenty of your people, isn't it?'

No attempt at repartee; he was just following the impulses of his big innocent Fulham Broadway head.

NOT EXPENSIVE

But it wasn't a bad retort, for all that. I became a little bit more disgruntled, and began to see his case in a different light. Many of his countrymen had

I met, after the first few intoxicating nights around Pigalle and finding out that one night of the Gay Paree act would cost him the whole of his holiday money, and the forlorn search for cheap, English-speaking company, where they can all talk over their woes together.

An American tourist would have money, and the Irish, of the variety best known to me, would be happily absorbed in the problem of seeing who they could do next.

Paris is not an expensive city by London or Dublin standards. It is very much cheaper if the tourist gets it into his cliggin that the laws of have-it-yourself-or-be-without-it apply there just as they do in most other parts of this sinful world.

But I have seen English people, who would never dream of going to the Savoy Hotel or Claridge's[315] for a drink because they would know it was not for poor people, thinking they should be able to drink in the Crillon.[316]

It's a hangover from the days 'when a pound was a pound' and every man could wallop his own niggers.

DEAD DOG

Even the meanest Englishman felt that, abroad, he was 'somebody', with a retinue of natives following him even unto the rickshaw door and screaming out in their quaint and monotonous chant: '*Baksheesh, sahib!*'[317]

That dog is dead. It is fortunate for us, now, that we never had any niggers[318] to wallop, but were rather on the wrong end of the stick as far as walloping was concerned because at least, it saved us the pitfalls of the colonial attitude.

I have watched with admiration the almost occult efficiency with which a party of Irish pilgrim farmers could steer themselves to a back-street bistro, where they could enjoy the luxury of a good brandy at eightpence the nip. Talk about moving through the fair!

When the train pulled into Dieppe I opened the offside carriage door and cleared the barrier like Shaggy Lad, the liveliest day he ever saw, and into the nearest store.

This was formerly owned by a Limerickman, and any of Mac Lir's water-front clients that sailed on *Menapia* or *City of Antwerp* would have little difficulty in remembering it, for it is next door to the café of the redoubtable Mimi's.

Mimi's father had printed on his business cards: *Me, Old Contemptible; Beer freezing cold; tea as hot as hell, just as mother likes it. Café open 24 hours to 24 hours, shut for eating, Mondays. Up the IRA.*

This last was added at the behest of his clients of Cork, Ardglass, Clogher Head, Corporation Street, and the Faythe, Wexford.

DIABOLICAL

The boat was crowded for a cross-Channel boat, though to a survivor of the Holyhead run it seemed as deserted as the Fifteen Acres on a Monday morning, but a man and woman sitting beside a vacant seat invited me to sit down.

'You could easily get your typewriter damaged,' said the girl.

'And besides,' said the man, 'we could get worse than a writer sitting beside us.'

It was a diabolical journey. Most of the people were sick and I was not feeling too good myself.

We stopped a few miles out of Newhaven and had an opportunity of examining the chalk cliffs of England for some two hours as the ship waited to get over.

Several times she took a run at it, and stood up, almost perpendicular, till she crashed back again, and lay shuddering to collect her strength for another go.

OPTIMIST

A young priest from the West of Ireland discussed the matter in Irish.

'*Nior chuala mé trácht riamh ar raic ar bit ar an dtruip seo ach, is dócha,*' he finished cheerfully, '*gurub é sin an rud bhíodar á rá an* Princess Victoria.'[320]

'*Is dócha é,*' said I, at this stage of the game not caring whether we were wrecked or not.[319]

But we were not, and my two friends insisted on giving me a lift to London in their car, where we could have a drink with themselves and a cartoonist on a London paper who would also, they felt sure, enjoy hearing my views on their native land.

The Irish Press, 26 February 1955

61
'I'M BACK FROM THE CONTINONG'

Like many a one since 1950 I'm apt to say: 'I've just back from the Continong.' Well, I have and I can tell you one thing and that's not two, that the weather in most of France was every bit as bad as you had here. I arrived in Calais and stepped off the boat on to six inches of snow and more coming down.

Like the cute old sleveen[321] that I am, where anything connected with drinking and eating is concerned, I decided it would be better to buy a bottle of wine and some comestibles and eat it in the carriage, rather than trust to what the hawkers might present us with at the stops en route.

For on the third class from Calais at this time of the year they have no restaurant on the train.

On the Blue Train, of course, you could look in the windows of the Pullman and see the rich settling down for a banquet of some hundreds of miles, and I've no doubt you could order anything from a live trout to a young child if you fancied it, and had the money to pay for it, or the money to go first class.

But myself and my wife were only on that route because we missed the Newhaven boat train, which is cheaper and very comfortable.

DIEPPE TIP

I know Dieppe, Rouen and Dunkerque as well as I know Newry, Donaghadee or Drogheda, and Dieppe is a nice friendly place.

If you know how to do it, you can dodge out under the train at the Gare Maritime – it's out in the street – and snake over to a wine shop and get cheese and vin rouge, and get back on the train again before you could say Lennox Robinson.[322]

There used to be a wine shop owned by a Limerickman and called the BBC Wine Store.

They are very fond of third-class passengers in Dieppe, and at the height of the season the assmacrockery unloading the Rolls or the Daimler on the quay seem a little out of place, but Calais was not so well disposed towards the poor.

The town is so far from the quay that setting off to look for my supplies, my wife waved an almost tearful goodbye as I shuffled over the snowy wastes in my crêpe soles (thirty-two and six in Henry Street), looking like the late Rin Tin Tin[323] going to do something very faithful.

The town was too far away to get within an ass's bawl of a shop, so regretfully I trudged back after fifteen minutes in the blizzard.

'AMEYENS'

But what a heartfelt welcome greeted me at the carriage window of my Calais–Paris express (via Amiens and Ville-Cochon-sur-Mer with a couple of dozen stops at intervening points to let old ones on with goats).

With what a heartfelt sigh of relief my first wife breathed down at me through the snow. 'Brendan, I thought you'd never come back.'

'*Oh, go raibh maith agat go deo, a ghrá, mar gheall ar an bhfáilte lách sin.*'[324] I smiled, manlike. It may be that I owe that much that I have to go to Mass in a cab. What if I was unsuccessful in digging up some scoff for the trip?

Somebody anxious that I should come back. 'Your heart was in your mouth, thinking I'd be lost?'

'Well, you've got the tickets and the passports. I'd look well, I'm sure, left wandering round with no papers, looking for the price of a telephone call to the Irish embassy from somewhere between Ameyens and Paris.'

MONSTROUS TYRANNY

'Amm-ee-ah.'

'What's that?'

'Amm-ee-ah. The place between here and Paris.'

'It's Ameyens. A-m-i-e-n-s.'

'Yes, but it is pronounced "Amm-ee-ah".'

'Listen, if we ever get home and thaw ourselves out in the Gulf Stream well enough to walk, just try walking up to a Guard in Talbot Street and ask him to direct you to Amm-ee-ah Street Station?'

However, in the heel of the hunt we got to the railway station of Saint-Lazare.

'EIFFEL TOWER!'

In the course of the next few days I showed my wife the Opéra and the Louvre. She said when I said, 'See that, that's the Eiffel Tower,' that her sight, thanks be to God, was not so bad that she would be likely to miss the tallest object in Europe at a distance of ten yards.

In return, when we did get home and tottered off the B&I[325] and got three-quarters way up the North Wall, she brought me round the corner of Store Street and pointed. 'See that?' she asked.

I said I did.

'Well,' said she, 'that's Amm-ee-ah Street Station.'

The Irish Press, 12 March 1955

62

NORTHSIDERS, DON'T MISS
THIS BOOK

I have just finished reading the most exciting book I've read in twelve months. The book is *The Parish of Fairview: Including the present parishes of Corpus Christi, Glasnevin, Larkhill, Marino and Donnycarney*, by the Rev. John Kingston, CC, published by the Dundalgan Press (W. Tempest) Ltd, Dundalk, at six shillings.

Our parish was the adjoining one of St Agatha's, North William Street, but my family connections with the Church of the Visitation are long-founded. The Behans worked in it, with and for their revolutionary confederates the Gouldings, in the decoration of the church and some of our family, still living in the area, sent over the book to us exiles, out here in Kimmage.

WHIPPED

For any native of North Dublin, the book is one to beg, borrow, or steal, and for anyone that's not going round half-dead, and has an interest in any of a hundred notabilities from Swift[326] and James Joyce to Big Jim Coghlan, mine host of the Cat and Cage,[327] who was whipped round the place for sheltering highwaymen, not to mention:

'*Morrogh O'Monaghan stationed to beg. He brought from the wars his share of the plunder, a crack on the crown and the loss of a leg …*'

This book will prove fifty times as engaging as its title.

RECREATIONS

Father Kingston describes the Norman Conquest and the reconstruction of the Cathedral of the Holy Trinity by this 'very virile race' who 'granted the monks considerable land in County Dublin'.

He goes on to describe the happy life enjoyed by clerk and serf, with 'ample farm buildings and a church for the workers … who, in payment for a small rent, helped the monks at harvest time':

> 'Meat and bread was the staple diet of the people … Vegetables were not much used, but rabbits, hares and all kinds of game was plentiful. For drink there was ample home-brewed ale and milk. The monks ate well themselves, and saw to it that the men and their families did likewise. In those days men worked hard, from dawn to dusk, but they had complete rest on Sundays and holydays … they had their recreations: archery, running, horsemanship, swimming and dancing; they had special festivals and were content.'

EDIFICATIONS

This bit of Merrie England must have provided a scene of great edification to my aboriginal ancestors, who were chased off their land to make way for the Archers and the Ramsbottoms, any time they snaked down from the Three Rock Mountain after a hearty feed of nettles and frockins to come and have a look at the happy swains and dairymaids dancing round ye maypole under the kindly eye of ye old abbotte, and a right generous landlord was he, and aisy for him, with other people's ground:

> 'Their tenants were well treated and protected so far as humanly possible, in time of war. It may well be asked what the monasteries wanted with so much land … But chiefly we must remember that monasteries acted as hotels, almshouses and hospitals.'

Even the King, when he came to Ireland, often stayed in St Mary's, 'more nor civil of him, I'm sure …'

Moreover, the feeding of the poor was 'a conscious occupation' but no Irish need apply for. Father Kingston tells us: 'The Norman foundations were kept the preserve of the Ascendancy – no mere Irish could hope to enter them.'

You can imagine the scene in the refectory: 'Sorry, Paddy, nothing for you today. Come round in about five hundred years' time.'

'OLD' NAMES

Father Kingston also considers it a pity that the 'old names like Richmond and Goose Green should be allowed to disappear. I can only say that I was never asked by the Paddington Council, when a resident of that borough, whether my countrymen and myself would feel more at home if they changed the name of Praed Street to Bothar Bui, and as regards the 'illustrious churchman, Lord Rokeby, who became Protestant Bishop of Armagh' who improved the cathedral, built a fine primate's palace and a still more famous library and observatory, built a new Royal School and a gaol – I've an idea that if myself and his lordship had met, it's more likely that it would be in the last mentioned that accommodation would have been found for this Milesian.

Drumcondra Castle is now an asylum for the male blind, in the care of the Carmelites, and in the chapel attached to the original castle on a Sunday evening in 1591, Hugh O'Neill[328] was married to Mabel Bagenal. The wedding celebration lasted for five days, and then O'Neill took his bride home to Dungannon. We are told that marriages were performed by the Bishop of Meath before many Englishmen of good sort.

GLASNEVIN

Glasnevin in the early seventeenth century had a reputation, according to Dr King, the Protestant Archbishop, 'for dishonesty and immorality'. Swift satirised the extravagance of his friend Dr Delaney in the building of Delville:

> 'For you, forsooth, your all must squander,
> On that poor spot called Delville yonder ...'

When he was not engaged on the building site, 'he found time to write a number of unusually bad books on the most weird subjects such as the lawfulness of eating blood, the procreating of man after the Flood, and the advantage of a plurality of wives.'

The house built by the Coghills and now part of the ecclesiastical College of All Hallows, on the Clonliffe Road, was the scene of the marriage of Hester, who 'arranged that the marriage should take place at the Temple by the light of the moon, so that her bridegroom who was much younger, would not hesitate to take his marriage vows. Unfortunately, the Major died a few years later ...'

HOUSE REPAIR

The first Jewish community in Ireland, refugees from Tenerife and the Canary Islands, acquired an amount of land on Fairview strand to found the cemetery.

Father Kingston says that 'the attitude of the Irish Parliament after the Williamite Wars on both Catholics and Dissenters frightened the Jews and made them believe they were unsafe in the city. They moved north of the Tolka and founded the first Jewish settlement at Annadale in 1718.'

Neither Catholic nor Dissenter nor Episcopalian, it appears, had much scruple about using Jewish tombstones to repair houses and a 'Jew, paying a visit to a Christian friend in the vicinity of Ballybough Bridge, found him in the act of repairing his house. Examining the improvements, he perceived, near the fireplace, a stone with a Hebrew inscription, intimating to the astonished Israelite that the body of his father was buried in the chimney ...'

We Northsiders get over things like that. It was a Jewish boy from Jones Road, off Clonliffe, who wrote the hit song of the thirties: 'Did Your Mother Come from Ireland?'

To any Dubliner I can only say that I'm dazed from this extraordinary book. Protestant, Catholic, and Jew, it has something for us all, and I'm exhausted.

The Irish Press, 19 March 1955

63

WE FELL INTO THE
WAXIES' DARGLE

'I'm fed up, and brassed off,' said Crippen, 'with the Continong.'

'I thought the extent of your travels was to the point of the Wall,' said I. 'When were you on the Continent?'

'I'm gone blue melancholy from reading about it, looking at you in the paper. Why can't you write about something natural? Like the time we fell into the water at the Waxies' Dargle?'

'Or the time,' said Maria Concepta, 'the slaughterhouse went on fire.'

'Or, the Lord be good to us all,' said Mrs Brennan, 'the time the holy chap told us the end of the world was come to Dún Laoghaire and we were all going to meet a watery end at the butt end of the East Pier.'

'It's like the time,' said Maria Concepta, 'we seen the film about the King and all the people stood up.'

STERN

'I'd have stood up for no king,' said Crippen crossly.

'You would,' said Mrs Brennan, 'if you'd have seen this one.'

'He was masterful,' said Maria Concepta, 'like me first husband, who was only five foot nothing, but very stern.'

'Maria Concepta,' said Mrs Brennan, 'give us that little stave about the Waxies' Dargle.'

'Well,' said Maria Concepta, 'I'm not as good as I was the time I took first place and silver medal at the Fish Coyle.'

'Ah, poor ould Fish,' said Mrs Brennan, 'he wasn't bad when he had it.'

'Well,' said Crippen, 'give us the stave.'

STAVE

'I will so,' said Maria Concepta, making a noise like a cinder under a gate:

> *'Oh, says my ould one to your ould one,*
> *"Will you come to the Waxies' Dargle?"*
> *And says your ould one to my ould one*
> *"Sure I haven't got a farthing ..."'*

'God love your stomach,' said Crippen.

'Amen, oh Lord,' said Mrs Brennan, with feeling.

'Thank yous, dear faithful follyers,' murmured Maria Concepta. 'It may be the last time I'll be singing at yous.'

'Thank *you*,' said Crippen.

> *'But there's them that says the divil is dead.'*

MASSIVE

'Not half sooing enough,' said Mrs Brennan, 'to hell with him.'

> *'And there's more that says he's hearty,*
> *And some says that he's down below, eating sugary barley ...'*

Maria Concepta finished on a low and throbbing note.

'That was massive,' said Mrs Brennan.

'Not a diver in the Port and Docks could have got under that,' said Crippen.

'I would like, as you're the most melodious mezzo soprano that ever muffled the markets,' said Mrs Brennan, 'if you'd condescend to give us a verse of the Zozzoligcal Gardings.'

'Ah, the dear old days,' said Maria Concepta.

'Quite right,' said Mrs Brennan, explaining, 'we both met our husbands in the zoo.'

'Quite right, ma'am, and damn the lie,' said Maria Concepta. 'Myself and my poor fellow'– she choked from emotion – 'we met in the monkey house. And shared a bag of nuts with an orangutan.'

'Well, carry on the coffin, the corpse'll walk,' said Crippen, jovially, 'give us that bit of a bar.'

'I will so, and the divil thank the begrudgers,' said Maria Concepta, 'with no more ahdo,' and without further ado, she broke into a croak:

> *'Oh, I brought me mot up to the Zoo,*
> *To show her the lion and kangaroo,*
> *There was he-males and she-males,*
> *Of each shade and hue,*
> *All inside the Zoological Gardens ...'*

'My poor ould uncle Oney—'

'Owney?' I asked.

'Oney a marriage relayshing,' went on Mrs Brennan, 'he used to sing that. Till they buried him – after he died – in Kilbarrack. Out be Howth direction. They all said it was a very healthy graveyard, situated so near the sea. It was that healthy for dead people that if a live one had have went out there, they'd be there yet, and going on for all time, meeting themselves coming back.'

The Irish Press, 26 March 1955

64

THE FAMILY WAS IN THE RISING

O But we talked at large before
The sixteen men were shot,
But who can talk of give and take,
What should be and what not
While those dead men are loitering there
To stir the boiling pot?
      (W.B. Yeats, *Sixteen Dead Men*)[329]

'To take as a headquarters the most prominent target in the while city,' said a man in a middle-aged growl, 'what ridiculous strategy.'

Old George Roberts took the tumbler from his little full lips and stroked his beard, 'But what taste – what impeccable taste,' said he.

MEMORIES

Me life on you, said I: for I knew what he meant. Hadn't I stood in the Queen's Theatre with the frenzied Saturday-night crowd for the 'Transformation Scene: Burning G.P.O.' while the very amplifiers carrying Pearse's oration over the grave of Rossa were deafened in a mad roar of cheering that went on till the darkness came down and we had till the end of the next act to compose our features and look at our neighbours without embarrassment?

In my childhood I could remember the whole week a damn sight better than I can now, for I have learned enough arithmetic to know that I could not possibly have taken part in the Rising, which happened seven years before I was born.

IN THEM ALL

When I was nine years old or so, I could have given you a complete account of what happened from Mount Street Bridge out to the Battle of Ashbourne, where I was giving Tom Ashe[330] and Dick Mulcahy[331] a hand. I could have told you how Seán Russell and I stopped them at Fairview, and could have given you a fuller description of Easter 1916 than many an older man. You see, they were mostly confined to one garrison – I had fought at them all.

There was nothing remote about it. I grew up to be rather surprised by and condescending to any grown-up person who had not taken part in the Rising. I sorted out my uncles with garrisons: Uncle Michael, Uncle Peadar and my stepbrother's father, Jack Furlong, were in Jacob's, with Paddy Manning, a native speaker from Kerry, and father-in-law of the writer Valentin Iremonger.[332] Our bread man, who was called Georgie Mannin, and no relation to Paddy. Our Uncle Joe was in the Post Office and up in Nelson Street the whole family were feeding messengers and keeping a stopping place for despatch carriers, from my Aunt Maggie and my mother down to Lorcan and Rick Bourke and Jimmy Kearney, who were expected to dodge round and in under the feet of enemy cordons as quick as schoolboy impudence could carry them.

FIANNA

Jimmy Kearney is still in the communications business, but as a totally pacific telephone man below in Crown Alley.

I was in the Fianna with a boy from Mountjoy Street direction who was called Finbar Howard, and his brother was killed in the Rising. I knew Pa Fox from Dunshaughlin, whose son was killed in it, and the Healys of Phibsboro Road whose son Seán was the youngest republican casualty, shot dead at the age of fifteen.

I had heard of Tom Clarke's[333] gleeful remark, when the flag went down and they were marched to the Rotunda in defeat: 'God, it was great to see them run.' And I heard tell of how Charlie Goulding, an Old Invincible, pleaded with his sons, and their in-laws the Costellos, to bring him to the Rising, though he died in his bed before the week was out. And wasn't the loveliest song of this (or any other) Rising 'The Tri-Coloured Ribbon', written by my Uncle Peadar to my Aunt Eva?

MY PADDY

'They were all very busy getting everything right,
For the young and the old were both eager to fight,
Every man there, worked hard at his own barricade,
When the rifles rang out from the Dublin Brigade.'

So they were, and on Tuesday morning Hanna Mortis was down at the GPO looking for her husband.

Stepping over a dead lancer or so, amidst the flame and shuddering of the blazing street, between shell bursts, with machine guns tearing hell out of all round her, she shouts up at the shattered windows: 'Have yous got my Paddy in there?'

A horrified Volunteer shouts at her for God's sake to take herself out of that. A shell hits Laird's the chemist's, and when the smoke has cleared and the dust has settled he looks out again to see how many pieces Hanna is in.

She is still there, brushing the debris off herself, and shouts up, 'You needn't be so impiddent about it. I only wanted to know was he going to his work this morning.'

BALLAD

'I'll sing you a song of a row in the town,
When the green flag went up, and John Bull's came down.
'Twas the neatest and sweetest thing ever you saw,
And they played the best game played in Erin go Bragh.

Our brave de Valera was down at Ringsend,
The honour of Ireland to hold and defend,
He had no veteran soldiers but Volunteers raw,
Playing sweet Mauser music for Erin go Bragh.

A great British captain was raving that day,
Said he: "Give one hour and I'll blow them away;"
But a big Mauser bullet just stuck in his craw,
And he died from lead poisoning in Erin go Bragh.

Here's to Pearse and Connolly and Plunkett that died,
And Tom Clarke and MacDonagh, MacDermott, MacBride,
And here's to Seán Heuston, that gave one hurrah.
Then he faced the machine guns for Erin go Bragh.

Here's a health to the men of the brave rank and file,
And the lion-hearted women of Erin's green isle,
Let true men salute them, with wonder and awe,
For they played the best game played in Erin go Bragh.

All glory to Dublin, 'tis hers the renown,
Through the long generations her fame will go down.
And children will tell how their forefathers saw
The red blaze of freedom in Erin go Bragh.'

AT LEAST

They played it all right, and some of them, like 'Mac Ui' Comerford died above in the Union. Would it be too much to ask that those who survive are at least as well looked after as if they had fought for England?

The Irish Press, 11 April 1955

65

A GLORIOUS SPRING

'Oir, feúch, do chuaidh an geimhreadh thoruinn, ata ann fearthuinn thoruinn agus ar nimtheacht; Taisbeanuidh na blatha air an talamh; tháinig aimsir ceóil (na néun) agus do chlos guth na nfearáinn ionnar tirne; Cuiridh an crann fhigeadha úra amach, agus na fineamhna (maille) ris an caoir mbig ag tabhairt bholaidh (maith) uadha. Eirigh, a ghrádh, moa on breágha, agus táirr uait ...'[334]

(Cáintic Sholamh, 2: 11, 12, 13)[335]

'For, look, the winter's over,' and about time and all. The Irish is from the Bible in the grand prose of '*an TSEÁN TIOMNA ar na dtarruing ón teanguidh úghdarach go Gaidhlig tré Churam agus Saóthar, an Dochtúir Uilliam Bhedel*' and is the gem of that body of Protestant literature upon which many a wistfully envious Papist and Gaelic eye has been cast during the last three or four centuries.

An article of Roddy the Rover's,[336] the sod rest lightly on him, in this newspaper sent me looking to read Bedell,[337] O'Donnell[338] and Carswell,[339] whose works are still in Sunday use in the Scots Gaeltacht.

FRANCISCANS

I had read Tomás O Cleirigh's book about the Franciscans and the modern language (*Na Pronsianaigh agus an Nua-Ghaeilge*), and gloried in the exiled friars gathering their habits about them, to give Gustavus Adolphus 'who began it' in faraway Prague when the threatening armies of the Reformation came from the Lutheran north.

Still, I had to believe that Bedell, Ussher,[340] Carswell, O'Donnell, for all that their work was done in quieter places and with government encouragement, were inspired by a careful, torturous love for the Irish language that has left all Irishmen forever in their debt, whether Queen Elizabeth paid them or not.

RAFTERY

It was the spring that put *The Song of Solomon* in my head. Raftery had a good bit about it too:

> *'Anois, tigheacht an Earraigh béidh an lá dul chun sineadh,*
> *Is tréis Féile Brighde, árdóchad mo sheol …'*

which I translated:

> *'Now, in the spring time the days getting longer,*
> *On the feast of St Bridget, up my sail will go,*
> *Now my mind is made up, and my step will get stronger,*
> *Till I stand once again, in the plains of Mayo.'*

IREMONGER[341]

I could not manage anything to knock you on the head with such an unexpected belt as Valentin Iremonger's:

> *'Spring stops me suddenly like ground*
> *Glass under a door, squeaking and gibbering,*
> *I put my hand to my cheek and the tips*
> *Of my fingers feel blood pulsing and quivering.*

> *'… And from the window of a farther tree I hear,*
> *A chirp and a twitter; I blink.*
> *A tow-headed vamp of a finch on a branch*
> *Cocks a roving eye, tips me the wink*
> *And instantly, the whole great hot-lipped ensemble*
> *Of buds and birds, of clay and glass doors,*

Reels in with its ragtime chorus, staggering
The theme of the time, a jam-session's rattle and roar ...
With drums of summer pattering in the background
Dully, and deeper down, and more human, the sobbing
Oboes of autumn falling across the track of the tune,
Winter's furtive bassoon like a sea-lion, snorting and bobbing ...

'... So up in the garden I go with spring
Promising sacks and robes to rig my years
And a young girl to gladden my heart in a tartan
Scarf and freedom from my facile fears ...'

RODGERS

And to console you against the springtime pounces of the tax-gatherers, there's the last verse of W.R. Rodgers's[342] *Spring*:

'Old lonely men lean back in limousines,
Miser-fingers locked on their bellies' purse,
Looking fixedly ahead as they slide
Silently on like shadows across screens
Past the Easter crowds bunked up on pavements.
Waiting for a wedding, mobbing a bride ...'

Though I remember a spring Sunday, outside the Wren's Nest in the ever-beautiful Strawberry Beds, and an old man singing exultant in the warm sun:

'Sure, if he spent it on mountainy dew,
I'd sooner he drank it nor gave it to you,
And met on the street and left you black and blue.
Says the Wife of the Bould Tenant Farmer ...'

The Irish Press, 16 April 1955

66

DUBLIN IS GRAND IN THE SUN

Given any sort of fine weather at all, it's hard to beat this city. In London you'd die in a desert of little streets, and in Paris, the Luxembourg would be a few tired trees set in a patch of dry dust.

But go through the Green these days, and the richness of the cool grass and the riot of flowers at lunch hour would put work out of your head for the rest of the day. Not to mention the girl students and the typists, shaped, as the poet says, like tulips.

Not that you'd want to be minding them poet fellows, a dangerous clique, be the best of times. Nor, for that matter of that, I hear a voice say over my shoulder, that it would take much to put *you* (meaning *me*) off *your* work.

BAY BREEZE

And in Dublin, you never get dehydrated, as you do in places further from the sea. On the hottest day there is a breeze from the Bay there, and the mountains to look at, and people lift their eyes to the hills and work on through the heat and burthen of the day in better heart.

The mountains, they say, kept the faith, 'our loyal allies, the hills.'

A voice from over my shoulder again puts in its prate to say that there is sorrow fear of certain parties going unlubricated in any kind of weather.

Like the hot day my respected father was mopping his brow while he watched, with great satisfaction, the froth settle on top of a pint: and an elderly T.T. merchant,[343] standing beside him remarked: 'You know, porter does not really quench your thirst, my good man.'

His good man looked at him with upraised tumbler, preparatory to the first long, deep draught: 'No,' says he, 'I'll tell you what does, though ... a good mug of sawdust!'

Since our own people took over, they've gone through the slums, like the wrath of God.

NEW HOUSES

I've seen the new flats at Dolphin's Barn there by the canal, and they are a credit to the housing authority. The new houses at St Anne's Estate in Clontarf made me feel so proud that when a foreign newspaperman asked me what he should see I wanted to bring him there. (He wasn't having any; it wasn't what he came for.)

But it will be a year or two yet and the childhood of many a child from off Pearse Street to up round Power's Court gone past, before they are taken off the streets.

The Irish Press, 23 April 1955

67

ON ROAD TO KILKENNY

With Brendan Behan.

Did you ever see a stuffed Derby winner? 'If ever you go to Kilkenny, look out for the Hole in the Wall; you'll get eggs there a dozen a penny, and butter for nothing at all.'

'Thanks be to God,' said Crippen, 'it's not the one way we all go mad.'

Or did you ever see a fighter aircraft on the side of the Naas Road?

'Well, it must have been an awful thing for your poor mother to be looking at you, when she came to the reeleysayshing that you were gone round the bend,' said Mrs Brennan.

'Tell us,' said Crippen, 'is it long since you went mad?'

Were you ever in a village with ne'er a pub?

'Now, here,' said Crippen, 'don't be giving us that – stuffed Derby winners, aeroplanes on the side of the Naas Road. What will you think of next, and tell us you saw it?'

Well John Devoy's little cottage just outside of Kill. And the huge motor assembly plant just outside the city, and the Irish-American drainpipes plant further on.

All this I saw on the road to Kilkenny, ye faire citie, the other day.

IN ALIEN HANDS

I'd say the motor assembly people should be as welcome as the flowers of May; they bring Continental technique and a width of ideas as wide as Europe to our shores.

As we proved in the cases of aviation and electrical engineering, our people are not bad at the catching-on business, but it was sad to see the best and biggest fields in the hands of the foreigner.

I would not be the instigator of animosity toward anyone, no matter what their class or nationality, but it's easier for the foreigner to buy an acre of Ireland than a foot of France.

If the people take advantage of that, and the lower taxation, I don't see how they can be blamed; but you have political parties and armies and leagues, all claiming that their particular brand of patriotic craw-thumping is best designed to undo the conquest, and here is the very heart of Ireland in alien hands.

I saw, on the way through Carlow, bigger fields than I knew existed in this country, all in the hands of big people from another land.

WEARY FACES

I thought of the patient toil of the Aran people to make a little bit of ground with sand, seaweed and sweat, and remembered the weary faces set to the Liverpool boat, and thought of an old song of my grandmother's:

> 'Yes, yes, 'tis a dear little pot of it,
> Yes, yes, 'tis a dear little isle ...

> 'Now, come on and rise, every man of you,
> Now is the time for a stir to be made,
> Ah, Paddy, who made such a lamb of you ...'

And as regards four-fifths of the country, there is no need for guns or pikes to adjust the situation.

You could look for miles and not see anything but the roof of the next big house, and nothing except animals on the broad acres in between, and there I thought of the little houses set nearly back to back round Carraroe.

NOT RESPECTABLE

I walked under the trees that shaded Rinuccini[344] in the city of Kilkenny and sampled the ale. I stood on a bridge under the Castle and looked in the fat and sluggish river.

The man I was with described it well when he said that Kilkenny City is a place unto itself.

We were standing in the hotel, nourishing ourselves, and this prosperous-looking individual, on being introduced to me, asked me what I was.

I said I was a writer, but later on got the telling of it from the man I was with.

'What do you mean,' says he, 'saying you're a writer? I've to do business with that old fellow, and let on to be a bit respectable. I told him you were an unemployed painter.'

I was only a minute in Castlecomer, but the next chance I get I'll stop longer. It's a darling, sturdy, sizeable town, and plenty of jizz about it. The coalmines are not far away and Wolfhill only the bawl of an ass from it.

I liked the looks of the people, and, for the short while I was there, relished their chat.

THE BOXER

A miner who was waiting on his wife to finish her shopping pointed down to an elderly, very correct-looking man wearing a black suit and a butterfly collar and savouring a drop of gin for himself.

'That's the Boxer down there,' said the miner.

'The boxer,' said I, wondering at the vagaries of the fight business, and Nel Tarleton[345] from Liverpool winning a British Empire title with only one lung, and after being rejected as unfit for service with the British Navy.

This old chap looked like the hard collar was holding him up, and had a pair of shoulders like a naggin bottle.

Well, said I to myself, the wind bloweth where it listeth.

'The boxer,' said I.

'That's right,' said the miner, 'that's what he known as in ___,' mentioning the place. 'When that fellow puts you down, you stop down.'

'Goodness gracious,' or words to that effect, said I, 'you don't mean he's still at it?'

'Bedad he is,' said the miner. 'He's left a couple in the cemetery this very morning – he's the undertaker in them parts. That's why they call him the Boxer.'

The Irish Press, 30 April 1955

68

MAIR A CHAPAILL AGUS GHEOBHAIR FÉAR

'Dear Sir – Having read Saturday's *Irish Press*, "Brendan Behan", I presume the Derby winner is in that column. Will you please send me the winner? I enclose stamped addressed envelope for a reply. I will not tell anyone you sent the winner to me. If you cannot enter into correspondence with me, please let me know by return. And oblige, yours faithfully.'

If the Derby winner is in this column, mine faithfully, Miss Mary ___, he'll be well acquainted with that old saying you see up above, which being translated, means: 'Live horse and you'll get grass.'

I may tell you, here, between you and me and Lennox Robinson that, at the risk of having the sporting correspondents of this newspaper gunning for me, the information you seek shall be yours, and that before the next call-over.

As soon as I can get to my friends who are knowledgeable in these affairs, I'll ask Andy Magee to have a word with the stewards on the matter so that whatever our tip is, it'll have to be first past the post.

SHOVEL

It's like a story of the day a horse belonging to the lady whose head adorns the quite useless stamp you sent me won a race in England and it was announced on the amplifiers at the Curragh meeting.

A fellow I know who had backed something else, and had a good cut at it, in the bitterness of his disappointment, said: 'Sure, her horse had to win the race. The other jocks had to let your man go past them. Otherwise they'd finish up the shovel for high treason.' ('Shovel' is short for 'shovel and pick', or 'nick', a term used by low persons to denote prison and from where a good deal of them should never have been released.)

A good, horse-faced old noblewoman, for such her tweeds and red neck proclaimed her to be, got up off her shooting stick so quickly that she nearly fell off it.

'How dare you, you monster, you neutral assassin, you leavings of the moving of the first reading of a Bill, to ban blood sports, you Continental horse exporter, you Compulsory Irishman, you death duty, you ___.'

DISASTER

Incidentally, at the Irish Two Thousand,[346] a day of disaster for Gall and Gael, when Tale of Two Cities did not come from behind quick enough, and the groans of the punters rose like the cry of an anguished heart over the multitude, I noticed a remarkable thing.

I am not related to Michael O'Hehir,[347] and my relations with Raidió Éireann have ever been of the hit and run variety, but it was surely a compliment to both of them that experienced racing people moved round him on the stand as he spoke into the mike on his chest to hear his broadcast as they came the first bit of distance from the off.

FICTIONAL

I am a little perturbed at this business around my name. I am grateful for the trust Miss Mary ___ reposes in me, but do not yet want to be made into a semi-fictional figure, as Parnell said of Tom Kettle,[348] 'one whose name is a household word', to be listed prematurely with Conn of the 100 Battles, Niall of the Nine Hostages, Peg Woffington, Thomas Conneff, John McDaid, the Village Blacksmith, the Mother of the Maccabees, the Last of the Mohicans, the First of the Few, the Man for Galway, the Man that

Broke the Bank at Monte Carlo, the Man in the Gap, John L. Sullivan, Sir Alfred Munnings, Spike McCormack, Peter the Hermit, Peter the Packer, the Bold Soldier Boy, Group Captain Townsend, Arrah na Pogue,[349] Waddler Healy, Dolly Mount, Sydney Parade, the Lily of Killarney, Myles na Gopaleen and Dante Alighieri.

When all is said and done, I didn't call you 'Miss Mary _____,' did I?

The Irish Press, 7 May 1955

69

FROM TOLSTOY TO CHRISTY MAHON

Liam Ó Rinn[350] wrote a book in Irish about his friend Stiofán Mac Enna, about whom the most interesting thing is that his father was a captain in the Kinnegad Slashers.

There are more interesting things in the book.

Where Mac Enna is correcting Liam's French accent:

'*Le 'na Gaedhilge atá agat. Ní mar sin adéarfadh Francach é. Is cuimhin liom go maith nuair a bhí Landru, an dunmharathóis, ar a thrial, mar a bhíos i láthair ag éisteacht gach aon uair a tugtai puinte anuas ina choinnibh deareadh se, "prouvez-le; prouvez-le".*'

'You have the '*le*' of Irish. That is not the way a Frenchman would say it. I remember well when Landru, the murderer, was on his trial, because I was there listening – every time they brought down points against him, he used say, "*prouvez-le, prouvez-le*".'

SIMPLE LIFE

He was on a visit to Tolstoy with someone called Micheal Mac Daibhid.[351] Whether this is the Land Leaguer, father of Cahir and Bob Davitt, of our own time, I do not know. Tolstoy was preaching that everyone should live the simple life of hard work and less grub than encouragement like the

Russian peasant apparently unaware of the fact that millions of people, from Kiev to Connemara, were doing that very thing because they had no chance of doing anything else.

Tolstoy put it round among the lovers of the poor that he was living like any other peasant on his estate in Tula, and getting very high marks for himself from the Lady Aberdeens of Europe, but when Mac Daibhid and Mac Enna came on his land at Tula they saw the sage, in an elegant Savile Row suit, like any other gent, walking in the garden, till they were announced, when he ran in and through the library window they saw him assisted by the butler, struggling into his big boots and peasant blouse.

WAR AND PEACE

You can imagine the scene, 'Quick, Ivan, my yorks, my rake, and my muck. Oh devil take you for an idiot. I won't half give you the knout[352] when my fellow humanitarians are gone off. My muck ...'

'Yes, little father, in a moment, I shall run out and get it and throw some muck on you – in a moment, barin.'

Still and all, a few *geáitsí*[353] like that are neither here nor there, from the author of *War and Peace*, to which incidentally I was introduced by Seán Kavanagh,[354] Ó Rinn's friend and my own, whose copy reclines on a shelf in front of me and which, conscience stricken, I here and now promise to return.

Ó Rinn is at great pains to tell us that his Mac Enna is not Stephen MacKenna, the novelist, which he needn't have, since most of the people reading his book had never heard of either one of them before. I do not care whether Stephen MacKenna was Stephen MacKenna or vice versa. Ó Rinn's book grows on you, for the sake of Ó Rinn. It is another story of Stiofán that brings me to my point.

FINE, HARD IRISH

Mac Enna and J.M. Synge were in Paris together and it seems that it was said, by the people whose business it is to say these things, that Mac Enna lived on what he tapped from Synge, and Synge on what he touched from Mac Enna.

Mac Enna having read Tomás O Máille's[355] book *An Ghaoth Aniar*, makes the comment that 'the West Wind' was, he feared, a dry wind.

He needn't have feared. Though it's a collection of articles and verse from *Stoc*, where Ó Máille had a 'spot' from 1917 to 1919, and much of it is about the problems of the period, like conscription and Redmondism, which is dead as Lord Norbury – except in Monaghan – there are very good things in it. It is in the fine, hard Irish of Ó Cadhain and O'Flaherty, whose broadcast of his own short story, 'An Beo', is guaranteed to bring tears to a brick.

I don't think, anyway, that Mac Enna could have read the book properly. He didn't understand Irish well enough. I shall be called a cad for saying this, which in some places is as bad as calling a card-playing gent a cheat in a West End club.

One of the most interesting articles in *An Ghaoth Aniar* concerns the real-life hero of Synge's *The Playboy of the Western World*.

The Playboy was a young man, born some say in Erris Mhor, and more say that he was born in the Calath between there and Cloch na Rón, two places that are not far from one another. He was the son of a farm labourer, reared with the hardship of the world.

But even at that, the people said that you would not get in a day's walk a better or a finer specimen of a young man. Good-humoured, well read and a noted athlete. More people described him as 'a lively sturdy man, without being too tall'.

Now, I can tell you that I knew relatives of the Playboy and presided at the obsequies of a horse belonging to one of them at Kilmurvey strand in Aran, where he lies to this day, and I delivered a fine funeral oration over the beast in the Irish language.

The Irish Press, 21 May 1955

70

'O, TELL ME ALL ABOUT
THE ... RIOTS'

It was my privilege, at the age of ten years, to march behind the coffin of the veteran Fenian James Stritch,[356] who, I was told afterwards, gave the signal for the boys to attack the van in the famous Manchester Rescue. I saw the late Joe McGarrity[357] once, and damn near plucked up the courage to ask him what he meant by helping to organise the riots against the *Playboy* on the famous Abbey tour of forty odd years ago. For it is his name that appears on the list of bail bondsmen for the Clan na Gael drama critics who went in to wreck the show in Philadelphia.

Joe might have told me to go and chase myself, or might have said that they weren't going to have the country made a jeer of.

If he had, I'd have quoted Padraic Pearse's remarks on censorship to him, for Pearse was not of the same mind as Joe McGarrity on the matter, which goes to show that a mutual interest in Irish independence does not always mean a common taste in literature.

CENSURED CENSORS

Pearse lifted the censors out of it in a passage, quoted by me in the original Irish, in an article in this newspaper on St Patrick's Day last. I shouldn't think in this dear land that everyone would have agreed with it.

It must be that the censors don't read Irish, or maybe the ones that do don't read *The Irish Press*. Of course they shouted to Cyril Cusack that they didn't understand Irish when he was making his curtain speech in the Gaiety, the first night of O'Casey's play.

Be that as it may, I'd have let a few shouts at the *Playboy* myself, on the first night, only for (i) I wasn't present and (ii) the play is a good gas.

For the carry-on of the people on the stage and their old chat is so phoney that no corner boy, in the days of my childhood, felt that his repertoire was complete, barring he could take off the *Playboy*. 'Oh man of the roads, with your long arm and your strong arm, be after pulling me a pint of porther,' and all to that effect.

NO ARCHERS THEY

The speech is not the speech of native speakers trying to speak English, for that is usually done in an American accent, and the idiom of the lower orders of the United States is even prevalent in the Irish itself. I have heard a little girl go into a shop and ask for a *'paicéad cáise agus punt* crackers' and another child asked me did I fancy 'cereal *is bainne'* for my breakfast.

REAL PLAYBOY

Andrew Marvell[358] in his Horatian Ode congratulating Cromwell on his 'Return from Ireland' says:

> *'And now the Irish are ashamed,*
> *To see themselves in one year tamed,*
> *So much one man can do,*
> *That does both act and know.'*

It is not so much that, but being conquered by such a dull lot of cawbogues that couldn't even cook or make good drinks. Now if it had been Napoleon I'd nearly have been in the 'B' Specials ...

The real Playboy, an O'Malley from Erris, as I wrote last week, was described by Tomás Ó Máille as a 'sturdy, lively young man, without being too tall'. If he had been alive in 1919 he'd have been eighty years of age, which means he was born sometime round 1840. His father was a man that had a strong weakness for drink, God forgive him, and your man had to leave home and go to sea at an early age.

The Playboy, as we'll call him, sent home money to the father to buy a bit of land, which would go to him when he came home from the sea because he was the only son, and anyway it was bought with his money.

He came home in due course, got married and everything passed off very civil, as the man said, till the mother died, when lo and behold the old fellow decides to have another puck off his hurl and get married again himself.

INA THORAIDHE

'Niorbh ail leis greim ar bith, a thabhairt don mhac. Níor réidhtigh an bheirt le cheile go maith (Ni nach ioghnadh – B.O.B.) B'ain leis an fear óg gardha beag fatai a chur dhó fhéin. Ní ligfheadh an tathair dhó é, agus chuaidh sé dá bhachadh ... Rug sé ar an laighe go mbaineadh sé dhe é. San eadarscain a bhi eatorru fuair an Seán fhear iarraidh agus thuith sé min marbh. Nior cailleadh amach 's amach é. Thug na mná isteach un a tighe é, agus dubhairt stad leis an mac dul ar a theicheadh mar nach raibh aon tsúil leis an Seán-fhear. Bhi an beirt aca fábhrach dhó in abhaidh an athar, mar bhi seiSeán in a shúighteóir chomh mór agus ina bhaichin cómh crodhanta sin is nach raibh meas ag aon-duine air. D'imthigh an mac annsin ar a theicheadh agus chaith sé ráithe ar fuaidheadh fá Chonamara agus na poilios sa tóir air, agus ni hé an ait a ncodlu-igheadh sé an oidhche a mbiodh sé le fághail ann ar maidin ach a' sior imtheacht ina thóiridhe ...'[359]

BELT OF LOY

The old fellow wouldn't even let our poor Playboy have a little potato garden, and one day he comes out to seed a few spuds for himself and the care, the old fellow goes out to beat him out of it, and starts struggling with him for the 'loy' (laighe) till in the course of combat the Playboy hits him a belt and the old fellow falls to the ground, looking very dead.

Howsomever, he is not altogether gone for his tea, and the women bring him into the house and tell the Playboy not to stall, but get himself away as quick as he can. They're not that gone on the old fellow either.

The Playboy goes on the run and spends some time hiding in Connemara – three months if we are to take Tomás Ó Máille literally – 'and it wasn't the place he slept the night he'd be found in the morning but forever on the move as a fugitive – a tory –'.

He went through many adventures the time he was in Connemara hopping over bogs and mountains, night and day, and often he had to swim a lake to bring his skin with him in one piece. When he was nearly done for he made his way to the island of Garumna, where he got a boat to take him over to Aran.

OFF TO CORK

He has relations there, in Kilronan; a girl of the O'Malleys was married into the Hernons. (I was a chief mourner at the obsequies of a horse belonging to one of them.) He stayed with them for a while. When the word came that the police were after him there, she had him brought to Inis Meadhon by boatmen of the MacNeela Clan – a decent people to this very day, as I well know.

He spent a time on Inis Meadhon till the others got the word that he was there and they came over and surrounded the house in the middle of the night. The man of the house told the Playboy to get offside and he would give himself up and pretend he was the man they wanted, and when the police came to the door asking for O'Malley, the Playboy opened it for them and said, 'He's inside – take him with you.'

The Playboy shook hands to the man of the house when they brought him off, and by the time the police had found their mistake he was away and off down to Cork via a potato boat taking a cargo from Aran to Kerry.

He sailed into Galway Harbour years afterwards as a captain of an American steamship, unknown to anyone except a few people that had helped him. He treated them well in their turn, and that was the last known of the Playboy – and that Synge and him and the rioters and actors may get space above to argue it out – a bed in heaven to them all – even the critics.

The Irish Press, 28 May 1955

71

IT'S TORCA HILL FOR BEAUTY

And forget Victoria.

As I think I told you before, one of my teachers was a young lady who was very refined.

This refined young lady teacher of mine came in one Monday morning and told us that she had spent the Sunday at Killiney.

'But,' said she, in tones of mournful refinement, 'it's ruined now with trippers. The place is full of them.'

Not knowing what she was talking about, but anxious to get in a bit of tee-hee before she'd ask me for an exercise that I hadn't done, I shot forward with fluent sleeveenery into the conversation.

'Ah, sure, teacher,' said I, 'isn't Dollymount the same, full of trippers. I was there yesterday with me da and me ma and Rory and Seán and Seamus and Brian and Dominic and Carmel in the pram, and it was rotten with trippers.'

'But Dollymount,' said my refined teacher, 'Dollymount is *for* trippers.'

I have never gone to Killiney since without thinking of her.

TORCA

Sunday and Monday, I was out there. Looking out from the railway bridge at White Rock, along that curving beach and the wooded hills behind, it bears comparison with any part of the Côte d'Azur. Bernard Shaw said that the view from Torca Hill was so magnificent that no man that ever looked out on it was the same again. But the beach is not so good as Portmarnock, or even at the strangely neglected seaside of Baldoyle.

Situated between Howth and Kilbarrack is the beach with the sea running up to the edge of the racecourse, and very convenient, Billy Carroll the bookie says, for despairing fav. fanciers when the good thing drops dead a length from home.

DAN HEAD

Kilbarrack, my father always maintained, was the healthiest graveyard in the country with the sea air. Last St Patrick's Day on the way to the races I looked out for the tricolour that used to wave over the grave of Volunteer Dan Head,[360] killed at the Custom House. Never a funeral went out from the Northside to Kilbarrack but the people would go over, after their own dead were buried, to gather round the flag and say a prayer for Dan Head. The ordinary people, without prompting from any organisation.

And before I go back the other side of the bay to Killiney, I may tell you that in Howth they have a paper of their own, in which is reported the wedding of a girl from the Hill. The affair was carried out with function and capernosity by all accounts, but my colleague from the *Howth Review* is not going to accept anything on hearsay. He says: 'The honeymoon is being spent in Minorca' (understood to be an island in the Mediterranean).

I hope it was there when the happy couple got to it.

IMPERTINENCE

Now, to get back to Killiney. At the top of the hill, in a park maintained by the ratepayers, there is a peculiar-looking relic of the days when an eccentric and charitable landlord could indulge his dull fancies cheaply by getting the people to build follies and wonderful barns, and get a good name for himself as a philanthropist at the same time.

This object has a marble inscription at the top which says: *LAST year being hard with the poor, the WALLS about these hills, and the &TC, erected by JOHN MAPAS, Esq., June 1742.*

JOHN MAPAS and his *&TC* are bad enough but could be left there as a curiosity and to remind the people of what our ancestors had to put up, but another notice is a standing piece of impertinence on behalf of the late Herrenvolk. It says: *Victoria Hill*:

Acquired by the Queen's Jubilee Association Dublin, the 21st June, 1887, the day appointed for the celebration of the reign of Queen Victoria, 30th June, by his Royal Highness Prince Albert Victor of Wales.

Well, we may deplore *JOHN MAPAS*'s taste in *TC*s but at least the building of it might have saved some poor creature from the Famine. Queen Victoria's good deed for the day, during her more famous famine, was the presentation of five pounds to the relief fund. It was said she gave another five to Battersea Cats and Dogs Home the same day to prevent jealousy.

The Irish Press, 4 June 1955

72

UP THE BALLAD SINGERS

"An' sure, if he spent it on mountainy dew,
I'd sooner he drank it, nor gev it to you,
You lavins of bailiffs should be hung from a yew –
Tree," says the wife of the bould Tenant Farmer.'

I heard this good song from an old County Dublin man in the Wran's
Nest,[361] out in the Strawberry Beds, last summer, and it goes to the air of
Fágaimid Siúd mar atá Sé.

I write 'an' instead of 'and' and 'gev' and 'lavins' instead of 'gave' and
'leavings' because that was how the man pronounced it. I write 'Wran's Nest',
instead of 'Wren's Nest' for the same reason; in case you think I don't know
any better.

According to some nationally minded citizens, it would be as much as
your life is worth to even hint that the English-speaking Gael hasn't got the
same way of speaking as the BBC or Oxford University. The same nationally minded citizens practically killed the old ballads of Dublin forty years
ago with the rise of the Gaelic League.

ASHAMED

My mother could sing '*Casadh an tSugáin*' and a lovely song it is, but her generation were made ashamed of the old tunes that kept up the hearts of the people for years, and it was only because I was curious, and still am, to find out what they used to sing in the times before herself and other good people picked up a bit of Irish, and because I made a point of listening to the old songs from the unregenerate pre-Gaelic League people, that I know them.

I often heard it regretted that most of the people in the country parts lost the language in one generation removed from the older people of now, but surely it was some loss that the people of the period of 'sixteen and after were told that the old songs of the Northside and the Liberty were 'stage-Irish', 'coarse', 'made a show of the country' and were made ashamed of the old songs to such an extent that even the sad and lovely 'Kevin Barry',[362] known and sung the two sides of the Irish Sea and the Atlantic, has been, all its life, an outlaw from any Dublin hooley.

INVINCIBLES

Even poor old Tom Moore's songs were only remembered because they could not forget them. I am prepared to admit that the words of 'The Last Rose of Summer' are not as good as those of 'Jimmy, *mo mhile stór*' to the original Gaelic air, but the music is, even in its dolled-up drawing-room style, a bit above the level of the air they put to Mangan's 'Dark Rosaleen' and the song was considered by Flotow good enough for insertion into the opera *Martha*.[363]

The most ardent pikemen songsters felt a little squeamish about the so-called Park Murders, and it is to the ballad-makers of the hidden Ireland of the slums that we are indebted for songs about the Invincibles. They never got into the books.

JOE BRADY

One of the best of them came from the Falls Road and it was from a man of the Pound Loanie that I heard it, to the air of the *Crúiscin Lán*:

> '"Get up," says Skin-the-Goat, "and I'll drive you to the boat,"'

and

> *James Casey with his son, to the Castle they did run,*
> *But Number One was gone, boys done …'*

Alas, that's all I remember of it.

But the best one can be heard nearly any morning round the markets from the old ones with a bit or a drop of prompting:

> 'I am a bold, undauntitude, and Joe Brady is my name,
> From the chapel of North Anne Street, but
> All on Sunday, as I came,
> To my surprise, who should I spy,
> But Moreno and Cockade,
> And says one unto the other, boys,
> Here comes the Fenian Blade.'

… to an air that Raftery wouldn't have scorned to use.

IN CAGES

Though they weren't above looting a tune or so from the London musical shows, when it suited their own suave and savage humour, in the Tan time:

> 'Oh, never marry a soldier, a sailor or a Marine,
> If you can get a rebel in his uniform of green,
> How right you are …
> The Boers put them in khaki, the Germans bet them black and blue,
> But the boys put them in cages, like the monkeys in the zoo.
> How right you are, how right you are …'

I was told by Mrs Dolan, a rebel and the mother of rebels, from Percy Street, Ton Street or Durham Street, off the Falls Road – I can never remember which – that in the pogroms the people used to warn each other of the approach of the murder gang from street to street by rattling the tops of the dustbins, which would drum an ever-increasing din that could be heard all over Belfast and gave rise to the song:

> 'Come out and rattle your bin, tiddy-fol-loll, tiddy-fol-lay.'

MORE TURF

In the Boyne Tavern, in the Shankill, I was called upon for song myself, and as cute as a Christian, what do you think I sang? 'Put More Turf on the Fire, Mary Anne'. Discretion was the better part of valour. Though the company were decent Protestant workers, you never know what half fool is lying in the background wanting to make a name for himself by crowning the stranger with a porter bottle – you get them everywhere.

For the matter of that, it was a Protestant navvy who wrote one of the master anti-recruitment songs of the 1914–18 war:

> '"Come on, you land of saints and bards," says the Grand Ould Dame Britannia,
> "Will you come and join the Irish Guards?" says the Grand Ould Dame Britannia.'

To the first reader to write and tell me his name I will give a ticket for two seats at a play I'm finishing for the first night and the riot.

The Irish Press, 11 June 1955

73

INVINCIBLES WERE PART OF THE FENIANS

Jim Hurley of UCC writes an interesting letter, and after a civil and well-deserved bow in the direction of 'Carbery' of the Annuals, asks me for the words of the song I quoted last week – the one about Joe Brady, the Invincible.

'I am a great admirer of poor Joe Brady' – good on you, Jim boy, as the Corkies say – 'and heard that ballad you referred to on the wireless a few years ago. As you say the air it went to was certainly haunting, and I have found myself since humming the line ... "He died a Fenian blade." If you have the words, perhaps you would let me have them at your convenience, some time.'

This is my convenience, Jim, and you shall have them in a minute; but first again to use Cork language, which I learned from Jim MacDonald, a house-painter and a rebel from Blarney Street, I must 'get stuck in you' over the next paragraph in which you say:

'The instinct of the balladmaker in endeavouring to make Fenians of the Invincibles was a worthy one. Our friend Dan Breen courageously wrote somewhere once that the only difference he saw between Joe Brady and Co. and his own comrades was that Joe and Co. were unsuccessful in the attack.'

THEY WERE

So far as I always heard from people who should be in a good way of knowing what they were talking about, the Invincibles *were* Fenians.

They were a dissident branch of the organisation and had headquarters in Denzille Street, were known as Denzille Street Fenians and the street was renamed Fenian Street in their honour by the Dublin Corporation which, whatever its faults, in many ways reflected the feelings of the people it represented at a time when the majority of native Dublin-born and Irish people had to take the other side of the road if they saw one of the Ascendency looking for the rent.

Dublin Corporation can always boast that they had the widow of one of the greatest of the Fenians for a Lord Mayor – Mrs Tom Clarke.

INVINCIBLE BLOOD

Peadar Kearney, who wrote the most popular of Fenian songs, and was himself a member of the Supreme Council of the IRB, told me that the Invincibles were members of the main Fenian organisation; and an aunt of my own father's, Julia O'Connor (*née* Behan) who lived in Ardee House in Talbot Street and knew some of the Invincibles personally, claimed that they were in receipt of funds from, and had a working arrangement with, the Irish Parliamentary Party.

Frank O'Connor's very moving play[364] was a noble tribute to their memory, and I, ever proud to know that I had Invincible blood in me, am happy to state that it was myself that scripted the programme on Raidió Éireann in which Jim Hurley heard the song, and that it was sung, if my memory, which for a variety of reasons is a bit hazy about that day – serves me fair, by none other than his fellow Corkonian, Joe Lynch.

OUT ON GUR

I got the song from a woman neighbour of ours in the old days on the Northside, before they put the people out on gur in Kimmage and Cabra, the widow of a relation and namesake of Joe Brady's, and here it is for you, Jim:

'I am a bold undauntitude, and Joe Brady is my name,
All from the chapel of North Anne Street, boys, one Sunday as I came,
To my surprise who should I spy, but Moreno and Cockade,
And says one unto the other, boys, here comes the Fenian Blade.

I did not know the reason why they ordered me to stand,
And I did not know the reason why they gave me such a command,
But when I saw James Carey there, I knew I was betrayed.
But I'll face death before dishonour like a true-born Fenian Blade.

They marched me up North Anne Street without the least delay,
The people stood up on the path, it filled them with dismay,
My sister said, "I'll see you, Joe, if Mallon gives me lave,
And keep up your heart for Ireland, boy, like a true-born Fenian Blade."

It happened in the Phoenix Park, all in the month of May,
Lord Cavendish and Burke came out, for to see the polo play,
James Carey gave the signal, and his handkerchief he waved,
But he gave full information all about the Fenian Blades.

It was in Kilmainham Prison the Invincibles were hung,
Mrs Kelly, she was there, all in mourning for her son,
She threw back her shawl and she said to all, "Though he falls to a limepit
*   grave,*
My son was no informer, boys, and he died a Fenian Blade.'"

The Irish Press, 18 June 1955

74

ON THE ROAD TO KINCORA

Near Limerick we had lunch, roast and boiled such as you'd dream about in Paris, and good meat such as you get nowhere outside Ireland, but old potatoes.

They were old and watery; and in the poorest home in Dublin, where a woman would be trying to manage on one man's wages to stuff seven or eight bread-snappers I don't believe they would have served them up, except chipped or in potato cakes.

The coffee was as good as you'd get in Grafton Street; and, as I say, the meat was good and plentiful. The girl serving us admitted as much but said the new spuds were very dear. Joe said that anything is dear when the people can't use it.

UP THE WALL

A gentleman at the next table, who seemed to be on a diet of poached eggs on toast accompanied by a glass of brandy with a ginger ale, looked up from his repast and muttered in sympathy with us.

'What would a foreign visitor think of us?' he wanted to know.

That is an attitude that drives me up the wall. Most of the people eating in restaurants in this country are Irish people, and it's as bad to give an Irishman bad potatoes as it is to give them to anybody else.

I was often a foreigner in other people's countries, and with a certain geographical exception, which does not include the Continental mainland, was very well treated; but nowhere did I ever see this attitude of what would the foreigner think of us serving bad old spuds in the third week of June.

It's a state of mind as rotten as the potatoes.

ADARE

We did not go short of anything in sweet Adare where we pulled up and went in and had a chat with a fellow Leinsterman by the name of Doyle.

And, talking about Leinstermen, going through Tipperary we noticed a sign reading: 'To the grave of the Leinstermen.'

Could anyone tell me more about it? I thought it might relate to the men who came down south and made a stand after the defeats in Wexford during '98.

'Mo ghreidhn iad ... na Laighnigh a d'aidhn an teine beo ...'
'My life on the Leinstermen, 'twas them that sparked the flame ...'

Though there's a better translation of that song by Máire Mhac an tSaoi and, of course, the Tipperary ballad of '*Sliabh na mBan*' is one of the loveliest of '98 songs.

I have happy memories of being paid twenty thousand francs at two in the morning for singing it on Radiodiffusion Française by the man that worked the oracle, Morris Sinclair, a decent man and the son of a decent man of this city.

NAMESAKE

I'm back to the ballads and I'd a pile to tell about Killalee and the house-painter who painted 'Up Clare!' the morning of the big match on a bridge which is Tipperary property from the middle of the Shannon.

The painter nearly had a swim for his trouble. Mrs Ryan and her son gave me a postcard to send to Joe Tomelty and, not having a copy left in the shop, sent up to a customer for a loan of an *Irish Press* for me to get the name of the hospital in England out of a news item about him.

I never heard of the Behans getting into the learned professions; but, things are looking up since our own took over, as Jowls Molyneux said when they made him a warble-fly inspector. For the apothecary beside the post office in Killaloe is a Mr Behan.

The view from the 'look-out' along the Shannon near Ballymackey and Port Ruadh is everything you said it was, Chris MacGrath; and the soft clear light just fading from the Clare side, over Lough Derg, with its Holy Island, and Aughinish, would be remembered by the people that go from the little white houses alongside, in the sadness of an exiled evening in New York and Boston, and even by us in Grafton Street or along the North Wall which, in a way, are as far from Kincora.

NOTE – Matt Noonan, of Surbiton, Surrey, who reads and occasionally writes in this paper, was the first to write and tell me that the author of 'The Grand Ould Dame Britannia', the best Great War's anti-recruiting song, was Seán O'Casey. He is accordingly awarded two seats for the first night of my new play and a place in the bulletproof car for the getaway.

The Irish Press, 25 June 1955

75

'YOU AND YOUR LEINSTERMEN'

Says Michael Ward to Brendan Behan.

A shut mouth catches no flies. Sometimes people seeking information are not so pleased with it when they get it. In answer to my question about a notice directing one 'to the graves of the Leinstermen' off a road in Tipperary, I discover that the Leinstermen in question were not United Men fighting a rearguard from Wexford in '98, but ... I'll quote the letter from our friend, Michael Ward, of Limerick:

'The graves are situated on the Ballina side of the Shannon, just about Derry Castle near Coolbawn. On this spot a great battle was fought just after Clontarf.

'History says that when the Dalgais, Brian's favourite troops, were returning from Clontarf to Kincora, they were intercepted at this place by Fitzpatrick, Prince of Ossory.' (And a right hole-and-taw prince in the light of what follows – B.B.)

STAKES

'They were travelling slowly, as they had a big lot of wounded. The wounded asked to be allowed to fight. "Let stakes," they said, "be driven in the ground, and suffer each of us to be tied to, and supported by one of these stakes, and be placed in his rank by the side of a sound man."

'Between seven and eight hundred men, pale and emaciated, in this manner appeared mixed with the foremost of the troops.

'Never,' says Michael, 'was such another sight seen in history.' Moore refers to the incident in his poem:

> '*Forget not our wounded companions who stood,*
> *In the day of distress, by our side,*
> *While the moss of the valley grew red with their blood,*
> *They stirred not, but conquered, and died …*'

'You and your Leinstermen,' I can hear a mutter from the Lizard, as that noted Dalcassian,[365] Paddy Moloney of Scariff ponders these matters.

CLARE

Let me hasten to add that I always thought highly of the Banner County.[366] I'm not trying to make up for Prince Fitzpatrick and my fellow provincials from Ossory, when I say that. I was reared to it: hadn't we a song about the Claremen:

> '*My home was where the Moher's heights*
> *Rise sheer above the wave,*
> *And Nature's scenes and Nature's sights*
> *Forbid man live a slave.*
> *Every wave that broke against the rocks*
> *Still thundered Liberty,*
> *And thus there grew, through weal and rue,*
> *This rebel heart in me …*
> *From rebel blood my life I drew,*
> *In rebel arms I lay,*
> *From rebel lips the lessons knew,*
> *That led me day by day,*
> *And rocked to rest, on a rebel breast,*
> *And nursed on a rebel knee,*
> *Awoke and grew through weal and rue,*
> *This rebel heart in me …*'

We honour the Banner County for its resounding answer to Maxwell's murderers,[367] when they went out, under the threat of his guns, to vote

Sinn Féin in the 1917 by-election; and, by the same token, Brian Boru's brave Dalcassians could hardly outdo the spirit of the old men and women that came gallantly and gayly hobbling down the mountains to show their loyalty to the men of Easter Week.

I need hardly say that Brian Boru is not the only Brian we honour Clare for.

> 'Ní dhéanfaimid dearmad go deó
> Ar Bhrian Mac Ghiolla Mheidhreach,
> Ar an "Chuirt," is a binneas beó,
> Gaelach, greannmhor, glormhar, gaibhdeach.'[368]

MERRIMAN

Brian Merriman and *The Midnight Court*. I believe his translators hold their general meetings in the Phoenix Park.

You might as well be out of the world as out of the fashion, and I had a puck off it myself. I lost the copy in the reconstruction of the church at the bottom of York Street, which I was working on as a painter, when it was being turned into a hostel for the Salvation Army.

I lent the ms to another painter to take home with him, and, when he finished reading it, he brought it back and I left it on top of a cubicle I was working in.

I often wondered what they thought of it down there.

I remember the front part, the bit we learned at school:

> 'Ba ghnáth me ag siúl, ar chúimhais na habhainn,
> Is an bhainscach úr is an drúcht go trom …
> On my usual walk by the banks of the stream,
> And the meadows fresh with dew's wet gleam,
> Beside the woods, in the high hill's shade,
> No shadow or doubt, on the lightsome day,
> It would gladden the heart, in a broken man,
> Spent, without profit, vigour or plan.
> Let hopeless eyes, long stuped in gall,
> View the treetops over all …
> The hunt with the horn loud sounding o'er them
> Strong running dogs and the fox before them …'

FORTY ACRES

I remember too, the puckered grin of the tough old republican veteran from West Clare who was asked whether his fight for Ireland had benefitted him personally.

'What did you get, now, for it all?' said a Job's comforter of an artist that I am quite sure had never spent an hour out of his bed for anyone.

'I got,' and his hardy old face twisted in a grin, 'forty acres, off this country. Forty acres – when the tide is out.'

The Irish Press, 9 July 1955

76

DANCE FOR LIBERTY

'Ye sons o' France away to glory!
Hark! Hark! What myriads bid you rise.
Your children, wives, and grandsires hoary –
Behold their tears and hear their sighs.
And shall we busily view the ruin,
While lawless force with guilty strides
Spreads desolation far and wide,
With crime and blood his hands embruing.
To arms! To arms, ye brave!
The patriot sword unsheathe,
March on! March on! All hearts resolved,
To Liberty or Death!'[369]

Did the Orangemen on the Twelfth remember how their ancestors marched for Ireland and for freedom when 'Antrim had been captured by the insurgents who, in fine order and under strict discipline, marched into it on June 7th, singing the Marseillaise'? David Hogan in the *Sunday Press* was writing about Henry Joy McCracken a fortnight ago and he mentioned this.

If there is a spark of affection for liberty, civil, religious or any sort, left in an Orangeman, he will admit that it is a bit of a fall in human dignity from the gallant tramp into Antrim town that fine June day in '98 to the circus procession of tame Tory workingmen that marched through the streets of Belfast the other day.

I prefer to move my memory from Royal Avenue on the Twelfth, to the Place de la Nation on the Fourteenth. Though I once attended a Twelfth of July celebration on the little island in the Seine, just opposite the rue de Seine, which ends where the river bounds the Latin Quarter.

It was a party given by some Northern Trinity students.

FOR LIBERTY

They will be dancing all over France today. In little stone Roman villages, high in the Alpes-Maritimes, like Montmichel, between Grasse and Cannes, which have its quota of Irish children of families settled there, to dance in the sun for liberty.

In the village there will be long tables laid out, with M le Curé and M le Maire to see that a proper respect is paid to the cloth and the tricolour sash.

Man-sized glasses of pastis will be left out to give the proceedings a send-off in good republican order, and, after lunch, the sports will begin with a seriousness about the young men taking part in them that easily finish up in a digging match, if it wasn't the day that was in it.

In Port Royal in south Paris in Belleville, on the other bank where the hard chaws come from, the old ladies of the quarter will come out to keep an eye to the capers in the street.

There will be dancing in Montmartre, and in Montparnasse, and in the boulevard Saint-Germain, where they were always very handy at throwing up a barricade, at which the legend has it, a young student from the Irish College fought in '48.

LATIN QUARTER

But the spirit of the dancing amongst the crowds in the streets and the market places of France will be as far removed from that of the expensive night spots as Puck Fair from Grafton Street.

You might say the Latin Quarter was bounded by the rue du Bac on the north-west by the river and the Irish College on the south-east of the rue des Irlandais, up behind the Pantheon, where Tone[370] plotted to free a people and destroy an empire on one hundred guineas and a hard neck, to where the students waved their black shovel hats and cheered John Mitchel[371] and the old republican Ulsterman son of a Unitarian minister wiped his eyes from the warmth of a Papist welcome.

BASTILLE

'Always Ireland with your people,' said an American to me, in Paris. 'You think of everything in regard to yourselves.'

Even the French Revolution, and who is more entitled? It was an Irishman led the people in the attack on the Bastille. He was a Wexfordman, and a cobbler, by the name of Kavanagh.[372]

The Irish Press, 16 July 1955

77

ADVICE FROM AN EMIGRANT

My favourite brand of civil servants are diplomats. From Lyon to Lewes I have found them a help and protection to the wandering Irish taxpayer, and altogether very good value.

Therefore a communication from a woman in the London embassy receives pride of place, not from reasons of protocol, but because of my affection for the Department of External Affairs, heretofore mentioned. I am beginning to write like a civil servant, myself; and, God knows, there is enough of them at the writing business.

The above-mentioned woman sent me a couple of numbers of the *Irish Leader*, a new weekly organ of the Irish in England. It is printed on very good paper; you can make out the faces on the photographs. The GAA news is fully reported. There is the usual complaint in letters from the girls saying the boys won't dance with them until after the pubs are shut. There is an excellent children's serial by Pat Mulloy,[373] who has written a children's novel, *Andy Tinpockets*, and an adults' novel, *Jackets Green*.

ADVICE

There is news of the county associations with Ena Morley as hon. sec. to the Donegal Association. I can tell you where she was educated. It was in a convent school within waving distance of the windows of St Eunan's College, so who has better right to be hon. sec. to the Donegalmen?

And last, but not least, there is the usual bit of advice from the exile as to how fix up the old place at home:

'British transport bosses are to spend a first small instalment on the improvement of canals in Britain … Irishmen in Britain will remember that there are also transport problems in Ireland, where … the excellent waterways, the Grand and Royal Canals, are gradually falling into disuse. It might be better to spend money on projects like this, with cheaper and possibly quicker transport, than on the several wildcat schemes, whose object is only to create work.'

NO PROFITS

Now, first and foremost, let me tell you this. Neither canal has, from the first day it opened, made money.

The Picture of Dublin for 1812 said:

> 'The Royal Canal, like the Grand Canal, extends from the city to the River Shannon and, like that, has been injured from the same cause, a too expensive establishment and jobbing. In consequence of the insolvency of the company, an Act was passed which now promises to be of considerable benefit to the creditors and the country.' (You'll be pleased to notice that the creditors come first.) 'The canal is now vested in the Director-General of Inland Navigation.'

The canal was not a very healthy proposition, even in its early days. Not that I have anything against it.

HEIRLOOM

My ancestors were reared on it, so to speak. My grandmother's great-grand-father (pick the bones out of that) got a house and a job at the Fifth Lock on the Royal when it was opened first, nearly two hundred years ago; and four generations of them lived, played, grew up and died on its banks.

I learned to swim at Jones's Road Bridge and went to school under Sister Monica and her efficient young successor Sister Ita, down at North William Street on the canal bank further down.

My grand-aunt, who died in a state of acute indignation brought on by the mistaken kindness of someone letting her hear Churchill's speech at the end of the war, had such a proprietary interest in the canal that she used to give us permission to swim in it.

She was born at the lock house and never moved far from it. She recalled her grandfather and his hospitable nature.

'I just live up there be the canal,' he'd say. 'Drop in, any time you're passing.'

DOGS PAID

By the same token, it was in Charleville Mall Library that I heard a lecture by Mrs John Brennan about the fly boats that used go between the Broadstone and Mullingar, and it must have been a lovely thing to set out on a fine summer's morning for the trip to Kilcock, 'three and twopence first class, two and a penny, second, to servants in livery admitted to the first cabin, and dogs to be paid for as passengers', pull up there and round to Billy Byrne's for the porter, how bad you'd be.

But the fact remains: the canals did not make money. And I don't know what my colleague on the *Irish Leader* means by 'wildcat schemes, whose only object is to create work'.

He surely does not mean the ESB, a great undertaking that has brought foreigners to study it from many countries, including England itself. Nor Bord na Móna,[374] nor the reclaiming of bog by Comhlucht Siúcre Éireann: and if there are roads into bogs, they are well used by giant machinery.

NOT WILDCAT

There is plenty to complain about in this country, and in every other country, but I know of no State or municipal undertaking that deserves the title of 'wildcat scheme'. The days of levelling the up hills to leave the down hills the way they are went out with John Bull.

But a great many people leave Ireland without really knowing very much about it. More shame to Ireland they have to leave it at all; but, it is true that many exiles gain their ideas of all Ireland outside of their own parishes from English and American sources.

Like the time Andy Magee was sitting in the Malt House, during Galway race week, and a well-meaning Yank with a big flowing tie came over to him, and said: 'It's a wonder you guys don't do something about digging out those docks down there.'

'I only got in on the Diesel an hour ago,' says Andy. 'But, if I've any time after the last race, I'll see what I can do.'

The Irish Press, 23 July 1955

78

THE TALE OF GENOCKEY'S
MOTOR CAR

'It's not every day in the week I get invited to an eviction,' said I.

'It's not an eviction,' said Dion. 'Only a seizure of the goods, as heretofore mentioned. One Chrysler motor car, on which there are twelve instalments owing to the Farmers and Merchants Heart and Hand United Mutual Assistance Company (Incorporated in Great Britain).

'I'm owed nothing. My commission came out of the first advance from the Farmers and Merchants, God bless them,' he added, cheerfully. 'I'm only there to identify the goods. We're meeting Mr Claythorpe of the Farmers and Merchants at the premises of Mr Genockey, the purchaser of the Chrysler car, aforesaid. Mr Carr here – very appropriate name – is going to seize the car. Or what's left of it, and give it over to Mr Claythorpe.

'I'm there to identify the goods, and renew acquaintance with Mr Genockey, who has, in the transaction, benefitted me to the extent of some scores of pounds, and is, in my opinion, one of the most remarkable men of our time. If you ask my opinion, he's a credit to his country, and the sort of man that Ireland wants. Mr Carr, as a Sheriff's man of some antiquity—'

WASHING MACHINE

'Fifty year, and only suspended once over me little trouble.' Mr Carr is a small man, wearing a black suit with little lapels and drainpipe trousers, like a Teddy Boy gone backwards, and with an old pair of eyes, God bless the mark, that look as if he's got them in a forced sale. 'And though I won't go as far as to agree with Dionysius about Mr Genockey, the defaulter in the present case, as to say that he is a credit to his country, I will say he keeps us Sheriff's men going. It's only a year or so since the case of the washing machine.'

'This Mr Genockey,' said Dion, driving North, from Lower Mount Street, 'hires a washing machine, pays one down payment, but no more, and after hiring it out to every old one in the neighbourhood at three bob an hour, and pay for the juice, for two years, they finally get round to seizing it. You were there, Mr Carr?'

FAIR GO

'Yes, Dionysius, it was one of my cases. He got it as a birthday present for his wife. Wrote his name in Irish on the order form. That's how they didn't twig him.

'They asked him how his name in Irish was spelt differently before, and he said there was different kinds of Irish, and he believed in giving them all a go, a fair field and no favour, "Up Down" and every man for his own county.

'The hire purchase man cried when he saw the state of the washing machine, but Mr Genockey told him to cheer him up, so to speak, that it was only where he'd lent it to a man to mix concrete in, a neighbour was putting down a bit of a path in the garden.'

We pulled up at the premises aforesaid, beside an expensive-looking black Humber. An expensive-looking gentleman with a moustache got out of it and stood with us on the pavement.

'Good afternoon, Mr Claythorpe,' said Dion.

'Effanoon, m',' said Mr Claythorpe, from between his cool white teeth, and nodding to Mr Carr, 'Effanoon, cur.'

'Good afternoon, sir,' moaned Mr Carr respectfully.

Mr Claythorpe looked at me. 'You a bailiff's man?'

'He's a newsboy,' said Mr Carr. 'He's only here with Dion, sir.'

'Well, I suppose we had better go in, cur,' said Mr Claythorpe.

We were met by a smiling big woman with a Munster accent.

FRIENDS MEET

'Yeer the man that's coming to see Mr Genockey about the ould car? Come in and rest yourselves a minute. Is that yourself, Mr Carr? Friends meet though the hills and the mountains doesn't. I didn't see you now, Mr Carr, not since the washing machine and God help you, it must have been an awful trouble to you carrying it down the stairs, and you sit down, sir,' she said to Mr Claythorpe, 'you're another friend of Mr Genockey's.'

'May neem is Claythorpe,' said Mr Claythorpe through clenched teeth.

'Ah sure himself'd murder me if I let you out of the house before he comes back. It's often he does be talking about you. He won't be long. He's only gone in the ould car to Athlone to bring back a few pigs. He brought down a load of coal in it, to oblige the man he's buying the pigs off. He said he'd be back at three o'clock to the dot, though the ould car might have broken down, it's only a heap of scrap, now, but sure nothing lasts only for a time, ourselves included,' – she put her hand to her ear – 'now here he is.'

Mr Genockey came into the room, kissed his wife and shook hands with Mr Carr and Dion. 'How's every bit of yous.' He looked at me and smiled. 'You the Sheriff? I'm a like a big kid I am. I'd love to meet the Sheriff. Have you your star? And your six-gun?'

Mr Claythorpe spoke from behind him, his face pale and his knuckles showing white where he gripped the back of the chair. He struggled to get out the hoarse words. 'Genockey! I'm Claythorpe!'

PEN PALS

Mr Genockey turned. 'Well, I'm more nor pleased to meet you in the flesh,' he smiled affectionately, 'though we're a kind of pen pals, we still only know each other by correspondence. Acushla, did you make Mr Claythorpe a cup of tea?'

Mr Claythorpe looks as if he could do with it.

'The old car is outside, and you can have it with a heart and a half as soon as I get the few pigs out of it.'

Later I asked Dion, what was Mr Carr's little trouble that got him suspended from his office?

'He discovered a law that said that all pawnbrokers that hadn't attended divine service the previous Sabbath had to pay a fine of seven and sixpence, and he went round collecting it and charging an extra half a crown for lip when they were slow to pay up.'

The Irish Press, 20 August 1955

79

THE TINKERS DO NOT
SPEAK IRISH

Round the corner there, on the more literary page of this newspaper, it would be a reserved sin to pass any manner of a disrespectful remark about tinkers.

There's great tinker-fanciers in them parts, as the poem says:

> 'Alanna machree, now listen to me,
> Me darlint go to res',
> You're safe from harm, all snug and warm,
> Wrapped up in your Irish Press.'

That's from the 'Tinker Ma to Her Wee Warbler' by Brian MacDonagh MacSigger, translated by machinery from the original Irish of 'An Sleeven Lobharach'.

MANY'S THE GOOD STORY

No, if me life is to be taken, and I'm to go in the midst of me sins for saying it. If I'm forever more to be denied the company of sonneteering civil servants, carolling customs men, brogueish brehons, I have to put all balladeering biromen right about this: *The tinkers do not speak Irish.*

For the matter of that, it's little enough any of them speak English.

The many's the good story you'll hear of them, mister honey, when the port is being passed round at dinner after the Petty Sessions, but though the company there, brilliant and gay, may have the lives and souls of the Munster Circuit on it they will hardly have the principal qualification for knowing the tinkers or anyone else. They haven't lived with them.

I have. In a house twenty-five or thirty years ago, when the McGowans came up for the Tailteann Games.[375]

SEED FACTORY SITE

They couldn't pitch a wagon nearer Croke Park than 13 Russell Street, which was my granny's house, and was situated on the site of the present Rowan's Seed Factory, with the DWD at the rear and Mountjoy Brewery on our right flank as you look down from the North Circular Road.

My grandfather was a moderate man who believed in having a pint and a half one every ten minutes, but not making a beast of yourself, and worked hard as a painting contractor, and had Number Thirteen well kept up with a shut hall door, grocer's porters calling with the message shout down the area and do not beat the knocker off, a beautiful double-breasted hat stand in the hall, which was also adorned with a reproduction of Turner's famous picture of a naval engagement being fought in a hayfield[376] ... at least, I thought it was hay, though an eminent English art cricketer has since told me it's the Atlantic Ocean ... faced by a picture of Smith, the Brides in the Bath murderer, whose likeness taken from the *News of the World* had been framed and hung by my grand-aunt Maggie Jack under the mistaken impression that it was the picture of a Fenian.

ALL ROUND CROKER

My grandfather was down the country painting a cathedral in county Wexford, leaving his own beautiful two-pair apartment vacant.

My grandmother looked out sadly at the milling crowds of people all round Croker and they willing to pay anything to be near the Games. Sadly she turned them away from her door when Mrs MacGowan, a Queen Tinker, came up and tempted her with a free fortune-telling in which she was to marry for the third time, a paisley shawl and five pounds for accommodation for all hands, jennets[377] and Christians.

That passed off very civil, though it was a bit disturbing when they got the jennet up to bed. He slept under it, and though he didn't make any more noise in his sleep than my granny, once he got there it was the rooly-booly[378] getting him there that was a bit noisy.

'Get up there, can't you, come on now you cross-born this that and the other, and whack!' he'd get a belt where it wouldn't blind him, till at last he was settled down and we could rest in peace.

HOME TO THE RODEO

Till my grandfather came home all of a sudden. He said he couldn't miss the rodeo, if you please. The rest of the Tailteann Games he didn't mind, nor he wasn't over-partial to seeing John Devoy, the Lord have mercy on them all, but the rodeo he would not miss.

Luckily he was late coming in and not noticing much what was going on, having spent a deal of time nourishing himself, eating and drinking at Lacey's of Gorey and points north, but in the morning he woke up and went out on the landing.

The jennet was standing the length of the stairs with his forepaws stretched in front of him, looking up at Angelica Kauffman's[379] ceiling. Then he lowered his eyes and looked into my grandfather's and my grandfather looked into his, like Garbo[380] looking into Robert Taylor's.

'May God protect us,' said my grandfather, in terror not unmixed with amazement, but mixed with it. 'Stephen Francis,' he pleaded.

My own father came out and asked my grandfather what was up.

'I don't know,' said my grandfather, 'what is it, you?'

'A jennet,' says my father.

'That he may be praised – now and for evermore,' says my grandfather, 'I thought I was in the rats.'

'In the jennets,' laughed my father with lovable repartee.

Later on I heard my grandfather and the MacGowans speaking together, and it was not Irish they were speaking, nor English.

The Irish Press, 27 August 1955

80

NUTS FROM THE CRIMEAN WAR

Round our way there were many candidates for the Brain garage. They were victims of the Great War,[381] as it used to be called; the Black and Tan War, the Civil War and the Economic War, when we were all a bit hatcha from eating free beef.

Mrs Ledbetter could have been nuts from the Crimean War[382] – she was old enough – but like many another, she was mad in her own right.

Her sister Mrs Moneypenny never recovered from a trip she'd made to Howth in the late summer of 1912, when she came back believing she had been turned into a lobster and was ever after apprehensive of the death she would suffer if the people decided to eat her.

GROUNDS OF COMPASSION

The sight of a pot of water, hot or cold, was enough to send her screeching from the kitchen. When she was finally brought back she would appeal to all and sundry not to put her in the pot.

Her first appeals were on the grounds of compassion, but she varied it by pointing out to the people that they wouldn't get much off her anyway.

In Summerhill there was a German fishmonger called Frankenstein for short, and he used to run in the back of the shop when he saw her coming and leave the messenger boy to face her.

Sorrowfully, she'd look down at the bright red bodies and claws on the slab, getting her emotions under control to give her screech in at fugitive fishmonger: 'Murderer! Torturer! Who murdered my poor brothers! And sisters!' And with a look in the direction of the dressed crab, 'and cousins!'

SOME SEVENTY SUMMERS

Then there was Mr Aloysius Giltrap, who used clap in the chapel and provoke Sergeant Cloonoe, who used to get his wife out of the floor at half two in the morning doing foot-drill and bayonet practice with the sweeping brush. But personally I always thought that the Macanaspies, of the back kitchen, Number Eleven, beat them all over the distance.

Mrs Macanaspie was an old lady of some seventy summers which, counting the winters, would leave her at the time of which I speak about a hundred and forty, which is what she looked, and not a day more.

Her son Paddins was a sort of neo-Old IRA man and dressed for the part. He wore a cap, a sports coat with leather buttons and split up the middle and knee breeches. He resembled very much a picture of a fearsome character depicted on the Cumann na nGaedheal[383] election posters of the time, which read *Vote for us and keep the shadow of the gunman from your home.*

AND THE FIRE BRIGADE

Very little chisellers like myself thought it was Paddins Macanaspie on the poster and gave him great respect, but the big fellows used to greet him on the corner with salutes and standing to attention and making him reports from the First Brigade, the Second Brigade, the Boys' Brigade and the Fire Brigade.

Poor Paddins would take it all for in the real, whereas it was only in the cod, and on Bodenstown Sunday he was a sight to free Ireland. With only a look at him, the British would have given back the Six Counties and thrown the Isle of Man in for good measure.

He wore his cap, but turned back to the front with the peak down the back of his neck to show that he was ready for active service, and a pair of leggings he'd borrowed off L.S.D. Regan, the dairyman from Santry also known as the heroic milkman, but known on a less national scale as Long Skinny Dominic, whence the initials.

He also had a bandolier, grimly bulging with rolled pieces of paper, and a water bottle over the sportscoat.

NO CURIOS FOR ME

At one of the street battles in Cathal Brugha Street that helped to pass the depression for the people, Paddins shouted up to a well-known public figure who was trying to address a meeting: 'You have the best of men in your jails, and I dare you to take me now.'

I may not, nor no one belonging to me, have agreed with his opinions, but the aforesaid figure was a Dubliner and seldom short of an answer. He leaned down from the platform to answer Paddins. 'I am not,' he said, 'a collector of curios.'

But with a fine disregard for the late Civil War the chaps on the corner didn't mind getting it up for Joshua Carroll, who was a part-time soldier in the government army.

JOIN THE MILITIA

Joshua was called up for training a number of times a year and had to go away to a camp. During the winter he stood in the evening time on the corner dressed in his green uniform, which for some reason had blue epaulettes. The big fellows had us chisellers trained to sing at him:

> *'If you're fed up with life,*
> *And you don't want a wife,*
> *Do what Joshua did.*
> *Join the Militia ....'*

Myself and my brothers joined in this with function and capernosity, as true little republicans, – apart from the excitement of annoying someone that was doing us no particular harm, an occupation indulged in, with less excuse, by many of us in later life – and were somewhat taken aback when Paddins Macanaspie chased us, and went to give our Rory a clout.

We expressed our indignation at such treachery but Paddins said: 'I respect Joshua, as one soldier to another,' returned to the corner and saluted Joshua, who returned the salute, when both forces reconoythered the position to see if they could make up between them the price of two pints.

The Irish Press, 3 September 1955

81

TIPPERARY SO FAR AWAY

'May God preserve us,' said an aunt of mine, 'from poets and playwrights.'

And why her, you might ask, any more than anyone else?

The family is rotten with them. And it's all over Tipperary. All because of Tipperary, as you'd say in better English.

'PHIL: He is probably havin' his supper. Remind me tomorrow about Barney Broderick's breeches.

'HONOR: I will. Mrs Kearney was sayin' Barney hadn't a stitch of decency for Sunday.'

We wrote that. At least, if one of the Behans didn't do it, it was one of the Bourkes. It's from *Phil Lahy* by my cousin Séamus de Búrca.

THE GLEN OF AHERLOW

And I'm not surprised. All belonging to us were reared, practically speaking, in the belief that there was a real Gaelic Ireland outside Dublin's borders that existed in Tipp.

Tipperary we loved ... out and out we loved the Glen of Aherlow, we never saw. We were reared on *Knocknagow* and wept for poor blind Sheehan.

We were brought up to know that our people knew Dan Breen and Phil Shanahan, for whose election to the First Dáil all our people worked very hard. He defeated Alfie Byrne in that election, and held the North Dock for Ireland and Sinn Féin.

DOWN IN THE VILLAGE

And we had the song about him that our uncle Peadar Kearney wrote:

> 'Oh, sad is the Muse and the theme of my story,
> Dark are the hours that are hovering o'er me,
> Far am I now from the snug and its glory,
> … far from the village we tarried so long …
> Hey, ho, slan the revelry,
> Shoutin' and dancin' and drinkin' so merrily,
> Red nights that we never again shall see,
> Down in the village we tarried so long …'

And Dan Breen and the brave Seán Treacy are in the song, but sure I'm only in from Tipperary just now, and I never saw it before, and better get on with the job of describing what I saw there before we've ne'er a bit of space at all.

A PAIR OF SOCKS

We were in Callan, a lovely little town, and it is a strange thing to think that this was the heart of the Gaeltacht less than a hundred years ago. Here Amhlaoibh Ó Suilleabháin[384] wrote his famous *Cinn-Lae*, renowned the world over for his descriptions of plants and flowers as they were in the 1830s.

We stopped there for a minute till I bought a pair of socks (to be honest with you) that I wanted and went on from Callan towards 'our loyal allies, the hills …'

On the beautiful road towards Clonmel, amongst the wooded ridge, where the road goes off towards Mullinahone.

That's where the magical Tipperary, and the tragical Tipperary, myself and Séamus de Búrca were reared up to comes in, the Zion we never saw but loved for poor old Kickham's[385] sake; as my mother often told when Kickham said, beginning his penal servitude: 'I can't knit socks.' 'You've plenty of time to learn,' says the screw.

THE MAGIC MOUNTAIN

And I saw the magic mountain, Slievenamon, and I sang a bit of a stave to myself in Irish and English:

> *'Is oth liom féinig, do bhuail an lae úd,*
> *Do dhul ar Ghaeil bochta, in ana chéadtai slad,*
> *Mar atá na méirligh ag déanamh game dinn,*
> *"a rá nach éinnindh leo pike na sleagha",*
> *Nior tháinig ar Major, ar dtus an lae chughainn,*
> *Ni raibheamar fhein ann i gcóir na gceart,*
> *Acht mar a sheolfai treada, de bha gan aodhaoire,*
> *O thaob na ghreine ... do Shliabh na mBan. '*[386]

ONCE MORE TO BATTLE

And the other verse translated by Richard Hayward:

> *'But the French are gaining and their fleets are sailing,*
> *And their masts are reigning, across the wave,*
> *And 'tis said, their faring*
> *Is bent for Éirinn, to fit the Gael for the fight again,*
> *But if I knew that tale was true,*
> *My heart would leap like the thrush upon the thorn*
> *To hear the bugle, assemble the true men,*
> *Once more to battle ... on Sliabh na mBan. '*

Like they wrote up in Hollyford, under the slogan, 'We Stands by the Treaty'... I hates bad grammar.

The Irish Press, 10 September 1955

82
THE TIME OF THE FIRST TALKIE

John Gilbert's daughter Lee Hart[387] was a friend of mine in the days just after the war when, on a stretch of high jinks extending from Grafton Street to the far ends of Kerry, we were members of a sodality that made anything you've ever heard of the Latin Quarter or New York's Greenwich Village seem like the Mission to Distressed Former Gentlefolk.

Lee now lives in Nevada, USA, where she is married to Walter Van Tilburg Clark,[388] author of *The Ox-bow Incident* and her mother is in Rome (Italy), consoling herself in the fading summer for the hot times of the twenties, when Hollywood was where-you-know, and sound hadn't brought to cacophonous triumph what Mrs Gilbert, eloquently indignant, described as 'a lot of noisy hams'.

For John Gilbert, her late husband, terrific in love, as his head moved over the vastness of the silver screen tensed for the clinch, did not sound as torrid as he looked. His vocal chords just did not produce the manly rumble you'd expect from the conqueror of Garbo.

As his widow put it, sadly admitting it, 'John squoke.'

Al Jolson[389] roared and sobbed him off the screen, and many more with him, when the first talkie, *The Jazz Singer*, came to the Capitol.

FUNNY THINGS

It's nearly thirty years ago, though I remember it better than I do last week or the one before.

I believe there were sounds made in the cinema before but on synchronised records. Huge wide plates of celluloid. We got old ones from the Queen's, and used to make stink bombs with them down our lane.

It was all they were fit for, because though the idea was that you played the dialogue, music and effects in time with the action on the screen, it didn't always work out that way.

The squeaking of great stars of the silent days was not the only hazard of the early sound movie. If the synchronisation got out of order all sorts of funny things were liable to happen.

I've seen a man being flung into a cauldron of boiling steel and murmur as he went down, 'Oh, how happy this makes me ... how I've longed for this moment ...'

And a mother, in the tender embrace of her soldier boy, roar at him, in the voice of a navy ganger, 'You dirty rat, I'm gonna take your right arm from out of the socket and beat your brains out with it.'

SIXTEEN STONE

Later on the crowds packed out the picture houses for the newsreels of the Emancipation celebrations. Even the old women dragged themselves out of the snug and away from the hob to go to the Plaza and the Blacquiere.

Some of them, from force of habit, and piety, knelt down at certain parts of ceremonies as they came on the screen, which was all fine and large, only the poor old creatures couldn't manage the tip-up seats to get back up again, and the manager had to come out and ask them to restrain their devotion, till the Granny Nulty who weighed, God bless her, sixteen stone at the time, was prized out with a crowbar.

As I was saying, I remember the time they showed *The Jazz Singer* or maybe it was *The Singing Fool*[390] on the Capitol.

This beautiful house, then known as La Scala,[391] was the scene of the famous Battling Siki–Mick McTigue[392] fight in 1922.

TWO LEOPARDS

Siki, a coloured gentleman of great ferocity, who usually travelled with two leopards on a leash, came into his corner and growled across the ring at McTigue, who shivered in anticipation, and even the punters on the ring-side seats looked away nervously from Siki as he snarled restlessly round him. Till a landmine went off in Prince's Street, and poor Siki passed out with the shock and had to be revived with sal volatile,[393] with his trainer stroking his hand, before the fight could begin.

That, however, was a bit before my time.

The first talkie was the talk of the city. You couldn't get in for love nor money, with crowds shoving one another the length of O'Connell Street to get to the pay-boxes of the Capitol, but my father knew someone that could get tickets for himself and my mother, if he had a stamp, to wit twenty shillings sterling, not an easy thing to come by on a Tuesday evening in the winter of 1927.

However, the stroke was worked some way or another, and after he came in from work my father and mother went off.

They had made provision for the entertainment of their several offspring, and next morning I paid my usual visit to granny next door in the top of the next house to tell her all about it.

CYCLONE BILLY

'You can hear doors shutting, me da says, and me ma says that there's a black man like Cyclone Billy Warren[394] singin' and me da gave Rory five shillin's to get sweets, cakes and Vimto for us to have a party and me ma gave three shillin's to ould Jane Boyd next door to come in and mind us and get a Baby Power, the quarter ounce of white snuff,[395] the three glasses in the jug and me da says you can hear motor cars' horns and me ma says you can hear every word of him singin'.'

'All out of the pound I lent her for the rent,' muttered my granny grimly from the bed.

Later on, my mother said I'd hang a parish, and my father said he didn't know where he'd got me.

I didn't know, either. There I was, and already a Low Infant at North William Street, with more to worry me.

AT NAAS

NOTE: Some of my Short Grazing friends may like to know that tomorrow, Sunday 18 September, is the occasion of the Kildare Senior Championship Football Final between Kilcock and Sarsfields at Naas.

The Kilcock bus leaves the Square at 1.30, the fare is five shillings, and amongst the players are three who have worn the Lilywhite jersey: David Dalton, Larry MacCormack's son and young Gibbons. If Kilcock wins it, it will be the first time since 1917, and I might even get down there myself if I could get a few makes in the pawn on what a Continental friend of mine describes as 'de old tripewriter'.

The Irish Press, 17 September 1955

83

OUR STREET TOOK A DIM VIEW ...

In our street, general indignation was stirred by the case of Jack versus Saorstát Éireann, consequent upon Jack being put off the labour by a hatch clerk who had seen him march on the Gaiety stage as an Austro-Hungarian infantryman in the second act of *The Student Prince*.

The hatch clerk, having seen him sign on that morning as an unemployed person, made a report and Jack's dole was stopped.

'I told him,' said Jack, 'that I was only appearing for the sake of art and the chance of lifting a white silk shirt, which as an Imperial Blaggard I wore as part of me get-up; but it was no use, he said it was employment within the meaning of the act and me dole is stopped, and I'm being had up in Number Two Court in the case of me versus Saorstát Éireann.'

'Sayers Todd Hernon,' muttered Lime Looney, grimly, 'that's buff – in the law racket now, is he? There's a result. I knew him when he had nothing.'

'Was it,' he stood up on his tippy-toes and rose his voice, 'was it for a scruff hound, and I can call him no less, like Sayers Todd Hernon, to be swearing away the life of Jack.'

POOR OULD WINNIE THE WITCH

'See the Releeving Ovvicer, Jack,' said the Granny Nulty from a corner of the snug. 'I softened his cough,' she smiled reminiscently, or rearranged her wrinkles; the nearest thing to a smile you ever saw.

'The time they tried to stop a day's money on poor ould Winnie the Witch because she missed a day's signing due to the ruffins in the room overhead hanging a sack over her window so that she stopped in bed forty-eight hours not knowing night from day. That's who I'd see. Tell him,' she simpered, 'tell him I sent you.'

Now, many right-minded people are of the opinion that to walk on in *The Student Prince* for fifteen shillings a week, while getting nine shillings a week for signing on as an unemployed man and thus making a total of one pound four shillings for a weekly income, is a great crime.

Most right-minded people, even in 1930, had an income many times one pound four shillings a week, but there weren't many of them around our way.

We differed in opinion over some things to an extent of extreme spikery round about Armistice Day, when a riot was caused in Jimmy-the-Sports by an ex-Dublin Fusilier telling a relative of mine that he had often seen a bigger row over beer in the canteen of a Saturday night than a certain Tan War ambush in which this relative of mine had taken part.

My relative informed him that if, he, the Fusilier, had killed any Germans, they were harmless ones to be killed be the likes of him that couldn't beat his way out of a paper bag.

IN THE MATTER OF JACK

But in the matter of Jack Rivers getting a few makes for walking on the stage in *The Student Prince* and not losing two weeks' dole money by telling the labour about the one week's work, we hadn't enough readies to enable us to meet a just and moral conclusion – we were all for Jack.

All his fourteen children, even Lollie that was not much liked since she clapped Chuckles Cleary on the back when he was blowing out a mouthful of paraffin oil on a lighted match. They all became great heroes, and when we saw the rozzers march down the road we ran down the lane with them, to hide them on Sayers Todd Hernon who, I personally thought, was a well-dressed gentleman of exceptional ferocity with apartments in Fitzgibbon Street Barracks, and dined off children whose fathers weren't working.

Sometimes when they had marched on in the direction of Croke Park we'd let a shout after them:

> 'Harvey Duff don't catch me,
> Catch the fellow behind the tree.'

And roared 'Up the Republic.' I wasn't sure why we roared 'Up the Republic,' only to annoy the rozzers. I was sure that the Republic had not much time for Sayers Todd Hernon.

CHASED UP THE NORTH CIRCULAR

But before Jack's case came off there was an election and TDs and would-be TDs of all and every political persuasion being chased up the North Circular, till they promised to 'look into the case'.

They did, and better than that, Jack got a job digging the Circular Road at the Big Tree at Dorset Street between Summerhill and the 'Joy (*If you've ever heard of that place*) and arrived there with his pick and singing as good as the next man.

At half past ten the foreman came up, looked at his watch and nodded, at which the assembled Gaels bowed their heads low and united their voices in:

> 'Happy Birthday to you, happy birthday to you,
> Happy Birthday, happy birthday, happy birthday to you.'

Jack asked the more experienced Gael beside him whether it was the ganger's birthday.

'No,' says your man, 'but it's the second anniversary of the hole.'

The Irish Press, 24 September 1955

84

WE DIDN'T TAKE IT BADLY

My first wife is from Donnybrook so my entire household is one hundred per cent Dublin. We were not able to get into Croke Park so we went home to listen to Michael O'Hehir on the radio.

I saw the two replays of the Leinster football final, Dublin versus Louth in 1934, and the very exciting matches of Dublin versus Galway in the football that year, and Dublin versus Limerick in the hurling final. We won, if you can remember that far back, neither.

THICK SHOWER

The next year Kilkenny and Limerick played a play and a replay in the hurling, amidst a shower of rain as thick as the boots we wore those times. I was sitting beside a priest on the sideline and when the people were going off he absent-mindedly gave me an Afton cigarette and remarked that some people were made of sugar. I thought that I must have a kind of dispensation against catching cold and stopped there in the showers of rain till the finish.

In such a downpour I arrived home in our street, which you may call Croke Park Street, just over the bridge past the Mountjoy Brewery, and I was home. I could have changed my clothes and got into bed only half

Ireland seemed to have got themselves into our street, looking for shelter, and if they weren't afraid to hide them from the Black and Tans on Bloody Sunday, fourteen years earlier all but two months, neither would the people of Russell Street put the crowd back out into the elements that day of deluge that many of you must remember.

HAD HOOLEY

In our house we had a hooley, and the measure of our accommodation was not such that we could have a hooley and get into bed at the same time.

My father played the fiddle, amiable as always, anything from 'The Blackbird' to 'The Lady in Red' and we danced and sang the night away, and in very short order I got pneumonia and found myself in Temple Street Children's Hospital.

Ned McCann and Charlie McMahon were the heroes of Dublin kids those times as Kevin Heffernan and Norman Allen are now, but we won neither hurling or football and had to put up with it.

We didn't take it too badly last Sunday, but speaking for my own household aforesaid we were looking forward to winning. There were great Dublin footballers like Cocker Daly of the North Wall and the MacDonnells in hurling and football comparatively recently.

But mostly we were accustomed as Dubliners to the cry, in case we won, that we were fielding the pick of Ireland. If we lost it just showed that Dubliners were not good at hurling or Gaelic football.

I saw a plea in an Irish-language paper to take the finals from Croke Park because they were helping the business of people that were not Irish Irelanders, and only became interested in Croke Park when there was money to be made out of the people that went there.

A LONG WAY

I remember Jimmy Gill from Longford, *go ndeanaidh Dia trocaire aire*, whose family carry on the pub on the corner of Russell Street and the North Circular Road. You'd have gone a long way to meet a better Irishman, or a more Gaelic one.

I remember a real 'pukka' Englishman, Sergeant-Major House, whose bristling moustaches covered his face in the front parlour window as you went down, and who hid Seán Treacy from the Tans.

I remember Michael Carr, son of a Jewish family from St Patrick's Terrace, those little red brick houses opposite the brewery, who wrote 'Did Your Mother Come from Ireland?'

We were delighted naturally that a native Dublin team were in the final, and we expected them to win, and so they will, another time, but nobody I met begrudged it to Kerry.

The Kingdom, as the newspapers call it, is very popular in Dublin. We begrudge nothing to the Murphys, Larry Martin, Jack, Bill, or Tom, to Jim Daly, nephew of Charlie, shot with Enright and Larkin, to John Joe Sheehy that I'm proud to call my friend, to Seán O'Brian (*as Bhaile an Fhirtearaigh*), to John O'Connor of Kilcock, or to Johnny O'Connor of Farmer's Bridge, to the O'Connells of Caherdaniel, for the matter of that to Tom Lynch, Dinny O'Leary on the battleship, to Dickeen Eager of Tralee, or Seán Ryan, the Myleses or Mick Fleming the chemist and the Flemings of Tir nab Poll … ah, to hell with it, wasn't it the next thing to winning it ourselves.

DRY MY TEARS

I'll dry my tears and sing a song about it:

> *'It was Kerry here and Kerry there,*
> *The cry was on the summer air,*
> *The cry was Kerry everywhere,*
> *The shout went, forward Kerry,*
> *Kerry weak or Kerry strong,*
> *Or Kerry short or Kerry long,*
> *Or Kerry right or Kerry wrong,*
> *The cry went on, "Up Kerry!"'*

John Ferris from Lawlor's Cross, I forgot about you, and the Landers element and the Conways of Tralee … Up the Republic, anyway! … and wait till next year!

The Irish Press, 1 October 1955

85

I'M A BRITISH OBJECT, SAID
THE BELFAST MAN

'I'm a British object,' said this elderly Belfast man to me, one Twelfth of July, a long time ago. We were in the little village of Millisle near Donaghadee in the County Down. We had gone out there to pass the beautiful day of high summer like true Irishmen, locked in the dark snug of a public house.

The Belfast man was an inebriate of some standing, whose politics were purely alcoholic. He was what they call in the north-east a wine victim, and carried his affection for things British to drinking port from the vineyards of Hoxton and sherry from Tooting Bec at five shillings the ten-glass bottle. He had come down for the day from the city and scandalised the assembled Orangemen by his reluctance to drink porter.

OLD MAN FROM MILLISLE

That lovely summer's day I'll remember too for the singing of an old man from Millisle. 'The Bright Silvery Light of the Moon'[396] and 'The Yellow Rose of Texas'[397] he sang, and disappointed me because he didn't sing something more Orange. The nearest he got to 'party politics' was a song about the Crimean War that went to the air of 'The Rakes of Mallow':

> 'All drawn up, Britannia's sons,
> Faced the Russian tyrant's guns,
> And bravely dared his shells and bumbs,
> On the Bonny Heights of Alma.'

We had a great day of singing and drinking and eating, and though I did feel a bit shamed by the bright sunshine when we came out blinking into it at closing time, it wasn't long before we got indoors again.

Next morning I didn't feel so good, but in the summertime nothing lasts long, and I was swimming around the harbour like a two-year-old and was shortly joined by a young man from the Shankill who confided in me that he could always 'tell a Fenian'.

'And how,' said I, lying on the sea, *bolg anairde*, and looking up at the sun, 'do you manage that?'

'Ah know them be their wee button noses.'

I felt my own snitcher, and reflected that it would make a peculiar, surrealistic sort of wee button. Have a look at it up there on the top of the article and see what you think.

The British object was not so politically unaware as I'd thought. He too appeared, ready for the waves, dressed in a high-necked black costume that bore some resemblance to a habit, and emblazoned with an enormous orange crest with the inscription *True to you* and surmounted not, as you might expect, by a ten-glass bottle of Liverpool champagne but by a head of the late King Edward the Seventh.[398]

He dived in and thrashed about like a man in the jigs, and I confidently expected the sea to become wine-coloured after him, like 'the wine coloured ocean' of Homer.[399]

I went fishing in Belfast Lough with the Fosters and the Neilsons and went ashore at Bangor, which none of us liked much.

I'd not have believed a person if they'd told me that summer would ever end, or I'd have believed them as one believes a mathematical proposition from the mind out only.

PAVEMENTS LIKE TOP OF AN OVEN

It seems years ago since the summer when we were crowded jam tight from Merrion to Seapoint and half-doped from the sun when the pavements of

Grafton Street were like the top of an oven and you had to dodge into Mac's and get yourself on the high stool for the safety of the soles of your feet.

Is it only a few weeks ago that I stood at ten o'clock of an evening in the little town of Callan and went over to read the inscription over the house of Humphrey O'Sullivan[400] the Gaelic diarist and poet now most appropriately a fish-and-chip shop?

Poets are great one-and-one[401] men. I don't know about diarists.

I'll sample the chips another time, with a bit of ray,[402] but that evening I had eaten at Mrs Coady's, and after her huge rounds of prime beef and fresh vegetables you wouldn't be in humour of anything for a good while.

I come out from her place trying to remember the name and getting mixed up, muttering in a daze of good living like an incantation, charm or spell, the words, 'Mrs Callan of Coady,' I mean, 'Mrs Coady of Callan ...'

AFTER-HOURS RAID

And the Guard I met, that told me of raiding a pub after hours and finding three men in it. And the publican starts 'ah-sure-ing' him that they're only friends that he wants to give a farewell drink to because they're off to Lourdes the following day.

The Guard says all right, and not be too long and, going out, meets three others on their way to the hall door.

Regretting his previous mildness, he enquires sarcastically, 'And I suppose you three are going to Lourdes too?'

'Musha, no, Sergeant, a mhic, we're going to Knock.'[403]

The Irish Press, 8 October 1955

86

ELEGY ON THE DEATH OF
MOBY DICK

A well-known and industrious novelist nodded his head accusingly in my direction. 'You,' said he, 'are living on your future.'

I looked sadly out at the dying autumn day, and drew the mantle of Lear tighter round my poor old shoulders.

I'm still caoining[404] the lost summer. Yesterday was such a day that, if I hadn't been standing round Grafton Street, listening to the intellectuals abusing one another (or what's left of them, emigration having taken as heavy a toll of them as of the farm workers), I'd nearly have gone out to the Forty Foot for a swim. You'd not have thought at two in the afternoon that it was the middle of October.

MOBY DICK DEAD

But at five o'clock the light had gone pale and wintry and the crowds hurrying home from work came into a northern European city that's already counting shopping days to Christmas.

The summer I knew was gone beyond reprieve when I found the dead body of Moby Dick on the bottom sash of my kitchen window.

Since last May he had evaded me, through that heat wave when we were driven mad from flies.

I conducted a mighty campaign against them, armed with a DDT[405] gun. One fellow eluded me – a big black-looking baste of a bluebottle. I chased him all over the pitch, but to no avail.

CALL HIM RASPUTIN

He disappeared in clouds of DDT buzzing heartily and reappeared again, as large as life, coughing sometimes through the barrage, but otherwise undamaged or even uncomfortable.

Such was his resistance to showers of DDT that would have killed a division of ordinary flies that I thought of renaming him Rasputin.[406] Curses were showered on him, which I learned for the special purpose. I swore to get him:

> 'From east to west, from north to south,
> I hunted that bluebottle out,
> From the dresser to the crate of stout
> (Empties) he did evade me.
> With DDT in showers I sprayed
> But he buzzed on there undismayed,
> And lived to make another raid
> On jam and ham to plague me …'

Corkmen may recognise the metre of the entire work, but that bit of iambics, 'jam' and 'ham' is picked up from close and intensive study of the works of Lawn Tennyson,[407] the gentleman poet.

DEAD AS A DOORNAIL

Still and all, *ni fhanann aon rud ach seal*[408] and the other morning I found him, as dead as a doornail, between the upper and the nether window sash, with the draughts blowing him this way and that, like an Independent on the Corporation.

My beaten foe, it wasn't I that killed you in the heels of the hunt, but time, the enemy of us all, and I pitied you lying there for the reason that I pity myself and everything that was born and must die:

> 'I'd not begrudge you a slide in the gravy,
> A swim in the milk, or a jig in the jam.

I'm sorry I cursed you, ah, why did you leave me?
A word between friends doesn't matter a damn.
You could have all your friends to a ball in the butter,
A ride to the rasher, an 'At home' in the tea.
'Tis a welcome you'd get not a moan or a mutter,
Me gallant bluebottle, if you came back to me.
A Mhoby, mo chroí, and no DDT.'

We'd be in a bad way without our enemies. How would we know we were in it at all if it wasn't for them?

'I saw you first, when May was so shyly
Warming the spring with a promise of heat,
Rambling, gambolling, fleetly and flyly,
Climbing the side of a lump of pig meat.
Sweet rest to you, Moby, and know one thing surely,
If I had you back, you I'd appreciate
But alas! You're gone off on the waves of the sewer,
The sad words I must utter,
"Farewell, it's too late."'

My notes from the kitchen are completed with the remark of Parnell introducing a young nationalist candidate to the people of North Dublin: 'and his name is Kettle,[409] a household word in the constituency'.

A FAMILY ALBUM

Which by easy stages brings me to a play of Séamus de Búrca called *Family Album*, in part of which the Tans raiding a house come across a picture of the Chief:

'HICKEY: Gentlemen, I appeal to you. Be careful, it's only a painting.

TAN: It's a picture of an old gurrier with a beard.

HICKEY: (alarmed) Gentlemen, it's invaluable to me.'

The Tan puts his foot through Parnell's portrait, but Hickey is somewhat consoled by the loud noise of a landmine that meets them shortly after wrecking his house.

The Irish Press, 15 October 1955

87

RED JAM ROLL THE DANCER

'Bombardier Billy Wells,'[410] said *The News of the World*, 'is the finest type of British gentleman – a natural aristocrat.'

Georges Carpentier,[411] who knew Wells's face from having it looking up at him off the canvas better than he knew his own, remarked, 'He is most certainly the finest type of British horizontal gentleman, and a natural aristocrat, with a title – "The Count of Ten".'

I am reminded of these matters by an encounter I had this day with a former opponent of mine, pugilistically speaking. I do not mean that our encounter this day was a pugilistic one, but it was pugilistically speaking we last spoke. And that at the lane running alongside the railway end of Croke Park.

Our street was a tough street, and the last outpost of toughness you'd meet as you left North Dublin for the red-brick respectability of Jones's Road, Fitzroy Avenue, Clonliffe Road and Drumcondra generally.

DANCING!

Kids from those parts we despised, hated and resented. For the following sins: they lived in houses one to a family, which we thought greedy, unnatural and unsocial, they wore suits all the one colour, both jackets and pants, where we wore a jersey and shorts, they carried leather schoolbags where we either had a strap round our books or had a cheap check cloth bag.

Furthermore, it was suspected that some of them took piano lessons and dancing lessons, while we of the North Circular Road took anything we could lay our hands on which was not nailed down.

We brought him to our corner and bade him continue his performance, and thereafter any time we caught him he was brought in bondage to the corner of Russell Street and invited to give a performance of the dance: hornpipe, jig, reel, or slip jig.

This young gent in addition to being caught red-footed was by colouring of hair red-headed, and I've often heard since that they are an exceedingly bad-tempered class of person, which, signs on it, he was no exception, for having escaped from his exercises by reason of an approaching Civic Guard, by name Dirty Lug, he ran down to the canal bridge, which was the border of our territory, and used language the like of which was shocking to anyone from Russell Street and guaranteed to turn thousands grey if they hailed from some other part.

However, our vengeance was not an empty one, for the insults heaped upon us by this red-headed hornpiper that thought so bad of giving the people an old step on the corner of the street.

One day, not alone did we catch him but he had a jam roll under his oxter – steaming hot, crisp and sweet from the bakery, and the shortest way from Summerhill to where he lived was through our street. He was tired, no doubt, with wearing suits and living in a house with only his own family and carrying that heavy leather schoolbag, not to mind the dancing lessons: no doubt he thought he had a right to be tired, and he took the shortest way home with the cake for his ma.

He could see none of our gang but the fact that he didn't see us didn't mean we were not there. We were as a matter of fact playing 'the make in' on Brennan's Hill down by the Mountjoy Brewery when his approach was signalled by a scout, and in short order the 'make in' was postponed while we held up the red fellow and investigated his parcel.

We grabbed the booty and were so intent on devouring the jam roll that we let the prisoner go over the bridge and home to plot his vengeance.

SURROUNDED

He was a hidden villain all right. Long weeks after, myself and Scoil (or Skull, have it any way you fancy) Kane were moseying round Croker, not minding anything in particular. Kerry was playing Cavan in hurling, or Derry was playing Tyrone in anything, but it wasn't a match of any great import to any save relations and friends, and a dilatory class of a Sunday afternoon was being had by all when the Scoil (Skull) and myself were surrounded by a gang, if you please, from Jones's Road, and who but the red-headed dancing master at the head of them.

But we didn't take them seriously.

'Sound man, Jam Roll,' said I, not knowing what else to call him.

'I'll give you jam roll in a minute,' said Jam Roll.

'You're a dacent boy,' said I, 'and will you wet the tea as you're at it?'

'Will you stand out?' said Jam Roll.

'I will,' said I.

'In the cod or in the real?'

'The real,' said I, 'd'you take me for a hornpiper?'

BOWERY BELL

He said no more, but gave me a belt so that I thought the Hogan Stand had fallen on me. One off the ground. The real Bowery Belt.

'Now,' says he, when I came to, 'you won't call me Jam Roll again.'

You were wrong there, Jam Roll.

The Irish Press, 22 October 1955

88

A WORD FOR THE BRAVE CONDUCTOR

There is some connection between Donnybrook and the zoo.

Old and respected resident: 'What do you mean, you cur?'

The Number Nine and Number Ten bus. I saw the time you could go from John Reddin's to the very gate of the Phoenix Park and have change out of a pound.

For the next few days we will be thinking of the increases in the bus fares and will continue to feel a twinge every time we part with the extra few coppers a day till something else goes up and we've got used to the new bus fares because we're too busy moaning about the rise in the price of something else. And quite justifiably so. But not at the conductors, I hope.

A BARKING LADY

I do not set up as a paragon of good civic behaviour, but I was very annoyed a few days ago to hear a most respectably got-up lady giving out dog's abuse to a bus conductor because she had gone past her stop.

She may have made the genuine mistake of thinking she had told him where to let her off – as a matter of fact she had said nothing to him beyond grunting when he gave her ticket and change – but even so her manner was that of an ill-trained dog suffering from a bad dose of hydrophobia.

She went off in the direction of the canal, still barking and yapping, but to herself.

I'm sorry to say that all of us are inclined to be unreasonable with public servants who are, after all, not paid to be public doormats.

We come late for an appointment and expect the bus should just be there as we go to the stop. We wait a bit, and one of these querulous individuals that goes in for such sport because it's cheaper than talking in public houses opens the betting with a remark that it's always when you want a bus that there's never one there, and getting well into it now, that them fellows don't care if the people froze to death along the route while they were lounging there at the terminus smoking and chatting.

AT RUSH HOURS

Then an acid-toned mezzo-soprano joins in: she doesn't know what these people are coming to these days, but when the public are willing to put up with it etc. till the bus comes and the unfortunate conductor, before he has a chance to even ask for the fare, is glared at by such a double line of Draculas and Frankensteins that you'd nearly be demanding horror money for having to look at them at all.

At rush hours in the city it's hell open to sinners on a wet night if a conductor dares to regulate the stampede from the queue.

True, it's no nice thing to go home in damp clothes, but it's not the conductor's fault if the bus only holds a certain number of people. As I heard one remark to a man trying to force his way on a well-loaded bus, 'Hey, mac, it's not made of rubber.'

Dustmen, too, are a breed of citizens that well earned their six and a half quid.

People putting the most shocking kind of debris into their bins are a hazard, but the Irish people, whatever their faults, have great natural cleanliness and self-respect, and that is not the worst source of extra annoyance to the fellows in the cleansing department.

They tell me themselves that they mostly fear makeshift bins with jagged edges. It doesn't take much imagination to picture the chances of getting a savagely infected cut across the palms in their business.

THE DUBALIN MAN

Then, of course, I must not leave out the most pestilential of my own nearest and dearest and next of kin – the professional 'Dubalin' man.

Your gills that can't go on a bus, into a post office or stand in front of a bar, but he's looking for 'bogmen' like Cromwell snuffling for Papists. His ear detects an accent from beyond the Pale, and then woe betide the young man or woman that fumbles with a stamp or pulls a flat pint. How many a tear was cried in a lonely digs during the first week up after a few nasal jibes about 'the counterryman' from this snuffling catarrh player?

(NOTE: – To the writer: This is what you could easily turn into yourself. Noted – B.B.)

His good woman, 'th' oul' mot' Madame Catarrh is not far behind him in her seeking out of the native strain of people. Though her standards of 'Dubalinism' are severer, going back Nordic fashion to the immediate ancestors.

AND THE GOLDEN GLOVES

Like the old lady I heard discussing the return of a friend of mine from the golden-gloves boxing tournament in Chicago where he had won a title:

'Deh hung ous a banner for him, so deh did, the bewzivul banner we had over from the Congress with St Patrick with green whiskers riding on a bewzivul snake, the faz of a bullig eh was, like he was a saint or sumpthin, and sed '*kayed meela vawicha*', a hundred touzand welcomes and yer a credit to deh cizzy and sure hees not a cizzy fella at all, hees mudher was a Monster—'

'A what?'

'A Monster woman – from Monster down in Cork iz iz – like Ulzter – oney diz iz Monster, have you me? The counterry iz iz – dere y'are now, sez I, all dat come motion over a counterryman, an now err one deezan Urrishmen going round an noz a word aboudem.'

The Irish Press, 29 October 1955

89

OUR BUDDING GENIUS HERE

'I'm suspended that much I don't know whether I'm coming or going,' said Mrs Brennan. 'If we oney knew what she was going to do, one way or another, but she'll have to make up her mind about him, I can't stand being suspended any more; can you, Mr Cripping, sir?'

> 'If we only knew,
> What she was going to do,
> Did she but reach a decision,
> And end our surmission.'
>   quoted Crippen,

adding, 'Them lines is be Yeets.' He turned to me. 'I suppose our budding genius here—'

'That's what he is, Mr Cripping. A pudding cheenis. I knew his poor granny, God be good to her, and she was another, and never used any but white snuff, so she didn't, isn't that right, Maria Concepta?'

'Trew, trew, trew, Mrs Brenning, ma'm,' croaked Maria Concepta, 'but go on, Mr Cripping, with the pottery. Carry on with the coffing, the corpse will walk.'

YOU'LL BE BONA FIDE

'I was going to ask Behan here, this honorary journalist, whether he was familiar with that poem be Yeats that begins, "Oh, to have a little house …"'[412]

'The Scotch House,' muttered Maria Concepta. 'He has you there. Been here, onrey churnalist, and pudding cheenyus, you've the shape of wan anyway, what matter.'

'Maria Concepta, you're rambling that far, you'll be bona fide[413] in a minute,' said Mrs Brennan. 'Get a grip of yourself be the two hands and pull yourself together.'

'I can't help it, Mrs Brenning, ma'm, I'm in suspenders over this other one. Will she, or won't she?'

'We're all the one way,' said Mrs Brennan, 'I ahpreeshy ate your pree dick ah meant, as the gentleming said and him trying to get the hot sassidge outa the coddle, but that's not to say, be the same toking of regard that we're all to drop down dead of the drewth while she makes up her mind. This is the hour of decishing—'

A SUP OF PEPPERMINT

'Maria Concepta, you're wandering again, what are you having? – that'll bring her to.'

'I'll have a drain of the other, Mrs Brenning, ma'am. Me nerves is gone from straying.'

'It's a straying on all of us. Michael, will you have the deezensy to stop picking your nose there and do what you're supposed to do be the powers of your special exemptjing – to wit, supply persons lawfully attending said fair and market with a gargle?'

'All right, all right,' said Michael, 'and no word about him and her yet?'

'Not a word,' said Crippen. 'She's gone away to the country for a few days, I heard.'

'Ah, now, when all is said and done, a little sup of peppermint in that, Michael, ee you pleeze, it's hard on her. I feel it as if it was me daughter,' said Mrs Brennan. 'Wimming feels for wimming, isn't that right, Maria Concepta?'

'You could sing it, Mrs Brenning, and play it on a mellowjing if you had an air to it. Wimming feels for wimming – and, of course, when all is said and done, it's for love. I remember my poor fellow, I often told yous, Cripping and Being, no need to tell Mrs Brenning there, she knew him well—'

'Is it poor Gobbles, Maria Concepta? Didn't I separate him and me own poor deer deeparted, the night they came out of the hot meat shop in Thomas Court Bawn and went to fight a jewel with a backbone each?'

THE SOMALI VILLAGE

'I met him, the Lord have mercy on him, and he coming out of the Somali village, the year of the exhibishing. I sees this pig me, as black as your boot, and pouring sweat though it wasn't for all he was wearing, after doing the war dance of the Mosambongas, and he runs after me with the spear. I screeched meela murder and ran like the hammers of hell, with him after me till he got me in a corner, and I near went in a weakness. I thought of offering him me glass beads from off me neck, but they were a pair I borried off me sister, Teasy, and I was more afraid of her, but I looked into his black face, and his eyes rolling in his head, and I moaned and said, "You Zulu," and I was going to say "Me too," God forgive me, when he caught me pashing at lee to his heaving boozem, and whispered, "Would you ever go down as far as Searson's for three glasses of porter in a jug?"'

'Ah, yes, the course of trew love is ever up a hill,' sighed Mrs Brennan. 'Mr Cripping, sir, you have sorceresses of informayshing, do you think she will or she won't?'

'I don't know,' said Crippen, 'I heard the clergy say she shouldn't, and some of the people says she should, and I don't like this going off to the country for a few days—'

But there was a commotion in the street outside and Mrs Brennan dashed out in the middle of his sentence, closely followed by Maria Concepta. Crippen and I were making hurried efforts to finish our pints when they burst back in the door, just as quick.

'It's all over,' said Mrs Brennan, 'she's not going to do it. I'm nearly weak, so I am.'

'So am I,' muttered Maria Concepta, reaching her hand out on the counter for a tumbler to grip.

'I'll stand,' said Michael. 'What are yous for?'

Maria Concepta struggled to the door again. 'They're coming down here – her and him linking her. Here they are.' In great excitement she held open the door and in came a woman with a black eye, followed by a man.

'I couldn't do it, in the finish,' said the black-eyed lady. 'Not when I saw that ould Bridewell.[414] I couldn't charge him; not if he gave me a black eye in every part of me body – and out in the country, in the sister's place in East Finglas, I missed him.'

'And I missed her,' muttered your man.

'Maybe she won't miss you, the next time, with a pot,' said Mrs Brenning severely.

'I suppose,' said Crippen, 'it's better to be fighting than to be lonely.'

The Irish Press, 5 November 1955

90

MUSIC BY SUFFERING DUCKS

'What is your occupation?' the judge asked the Hop Connell.

'I'm a Suffering Duck, your warship,' said the Hop.

So he was, too. He played the oboe in it. The Unemployed Band was its official name, and they were in court due to a suspected incitement to a breach of the peace.

When during the 1913 strike[415] they serenaded the Royal Irish inhabitants of Fitzgibbon Street Barracks with the endearing strains of 'The Peeler and the Goat' and followed a marching column of police with the lively tune 'Here's the Robbers Passing By' in step with these stalwarts of the force proceeding on their majestic, imperial way to O'Connell Street.

'You call it a band of musicians,' said the magistrate. 'I call it a band of hooligans.'

OFF WITH A CAUTION

But there was such a roar from the thousands of other hooligans round the court that he decided that the pax Britannica was best served by letting them off with a caution, when the band marched off triumphantly playing the loyal air 'The British Grenadiers'[416] to the special lyrics of their supporters, who roared the chorus all the way back up through Parnell Street and Summerhill:

> *'The Boers they were marching and the British wanted fight,*
> *The Boers fired their rifles and blew them out of sight,*
> *Sound the bugle, sound the drum,*
> *Three cheers for ould Paul Kruger …'*[417]

The Hop led the parade to the North Circular Road where the proceedings were adjourned to the corner shop, for there's not many a musician but likes having his whistle moistened or his bow rosined.

THE BARD OF BRAY

The only notable exception was James Whiteside,[418] the 'Bard of Bray', who played the harp, the pipes and the fiddle and composed the following song:

> *'Sobriety is making way in the Ireland of to-day,*
> *Fill the bumper fair, every drop is poison,*
> *Will you walk into my parlour, said the spider to the fly,*
> *'Tis the prettiest little drunkery, that every you did spy,*
> *Oh, join the abstainers and you'll be the gainers …'*

James, like Bach, another notable musician, is no longer composing but decomposing this many a long year. I am bound to state, however, that this is no discredit to his teetotal habits as he was born in 1844 and no engine, no matter how well oiled, can be expected to go on forever.

The aforementioned Hop was one of a number of republican musicians I knew in my childhood. They were friends of my father's and of my uncle's, both of whom were good fiddlers.

IN RATHMINES FOR PENNIES

Vivian Mercier,[419] former editor of *The Church of Ireland Gazette*, once wrote feelingly in *The Bell* of the 'unhappy Republicans of the 'Twenties'.

I heard of two fine musicians in the years immediately after the Civil War kept out of their jobs by the oath of allegiance, and playing the violin in Rathmines for pennies. Unfortunately, through embarrassment they kept to the back streets and didn't get much. They often told me about it since over a 'bumper fair' in a comfortable lounge, I'm glad to say. We live through the winter and the divil would not kill us in summer.

The Hop and bands and musicians came into my head last Saturday night when myself and my first wife, wandering through my native parts after coming down from the Film Society show in Phibsboro, met two friends who were saddened by the news that the Fintan Lalor Pipers have to leave their premises in the Butcher's Hall in Gardiner Street.

THE SCREECHING PIPES

The evacuation is unavoidable, it seems, but a band needs a central position if it is to keep its members together, and it would be a great loss to the cause if the Fintan Lalors, with their great Citizen Army tradition, had to go homeless in the city of Dublin in 1955.

Someone said of the bagpipes that the best thing about them was the fact that they didn't smell too, but what foot could keep easy when the pipes were screeching 'Allistrum's March', 'O'Neill's' or 'The Brian Boru'.[420]

I heard the East Belfast come down the Shankill on the Twelfth, playing 'Rosc Catha na Mumhan' disguised as 'The Boyne Water'[421] and be damn but I nearly fell in behind them and their King Billy banner.

It would make the dead walk even to hear the names of the tunes the uilleann pipers played – 'Give Me Your Hand', 'The Unfortunate Cup of Tea', 'Young Roger Was a Ploughboy' (I knew the *words* of that too), 'Upstairs in a Tent', 'Larry Grogan', 'The Cronan Gabhair' and where do you leave the flower of Irish music, 'The Coulin'? As recalled in the 'London Letter', it was the tune Commandant Reggie Dunne[422] played on the fiddle the night before he was hanged in Pentonville with his comrade Volunteer Joe O'Sullivan, and it is part of the London-Irish tradition for Frank Lee to play it on the organ in Maiden Lane after their annual Mass.

CRIPPLES, NOT CONSCRIPTS

I often heard it told how the Hop Connell got a hold of a tin whistle somewhere on the way to Frongoch and struck up 'O'Donnell Abu' and lifted the tired feet of his comrades into a defiant tramp to captivity. Not that he was much in the marching line himself.

'I see,' said a British officer, looking down at the musician, 'they have cripples in their army.'

The Hop removed the tin whistle from his mouth: 'We have,' said he, 'but no conscripts.'

NOTE: My friends in Augher, Omagh, I'm doing 'Shimmering Way', each and every way, and hope you're still my friends at four o'clock today.

The Irish Press, 12 November 1955

91
FOR CAVAN, TURN RIGHT AT NAVAN

'I wish I could sing a tune out of this letter to you', says a reader from Leeds. 'The article about the old musicians reminded me of great tunes I heard played, when they'd have a bit of an evening, that usually went on all night, when I was a gassin in New Inns, County Cavan, fifty years ago. I suppose you wouldn't know those parts?'

You supposed wrong, decent man, I know it well, and have friends in it, and I know Ballyjamesduff, and if I don't know Lappanduff Mountain I know the song about it and heard it sung first on the Falls Road, in the Centre Half Bar at that time owned by Mickey Hamill (*go ndeanaidh Dia trocaire air*):

> 'on *Cavan's mountain, Lappanduff, one fought with brav-er-y,*
> *Until the English soldiers shot brave Seán McCartney ...*'

Cavan of the little hills. For Cavan, the man said, you turn right at Navan. This happens to be true. I've done it.

THE SWINEGATE

And if it goes to that, I know Leeds too, and as I'm often accused of running England down I'll say that it's not what you'd expect at all (this is getting into a back-handed class of a compliment) but a clean, bright, and pleasant city, of which I remember the Swinegate, bluntly named as befits a street in the capital of Yorkshire, with an old bridge over the little river at the end of it, Albert Cowling's Wine Lodge, which I heartily recommend for a good sup and a bite, and Cross Flatts Park, which is in a suburb somewhere on the tramline past Armley Prison.

I remember it (the park, not the shovel-and-pick)[423] because there was a kiosk in the middle, which in the cold weather I was there, had a blazing coal fire and tables for games and chairs where old men and women sat round and talked, or played shove ha'penny, and where to lighten up the February evenings a gentleman like Wilfred Pickles[424] led choruses of old songs with an accordion.

I stood with the people outside looking in, for there was a notice which read 'No admittance, except by special invitation, to anyone under sixty-five years old.'

BOOLABOSS

I got a special invitation – voice from Crumlin: 'Leave it to you, no show without Punch' – because myself and the Wilfred Pickles chap had met the previous night, in a premises not far distant, and he knew that I fancied myself as a singer.

Nothing loth, as the man said, first removing a jockey of Tullamore tobacco from his jaw, I went in and got up and sang an Irish song, to wit, 'In Glendalough Lived an Ould Saint' and received much boolaboss.[425] Amidst the Yorkshire talk, 'Good lad, Paddy,' and so forth, I heard one aged gurrier distinctly use the words: *'Maith an bhuachaill thú.'*

God bless my soul, said I, or words to that effect, looking around for the source of this salutation. I saw an old man smiling beside me and he said: 'Kane kee will too, Paddy?'

'Táimse go maith, go raibh maith agat,' said I in some wonder.

'That's as far as I can, lad,' said he, and told me a bit about himself. He was from Leeds, had been born and raised there and except for the First World War had never been outside of it.

HUDDERSFIELD

But his parents were from the Joyce country, and he said 'Fifty year ago round York Road, with all the old people, on Saturday nights and Sunday mornings, when they met together, it was always Irish they used. The young ones couldn't help picking up a bit here and there listening to them.'

For the matter of that, the great Irish preacher and missioner of the Gaeltacht, an tAthair O Conghaile, whose father, brothers, relatives and in-laws are old friends of my own, I'm proud to say, conducts a retreat in Irish in Huddersfield every year for the Connemara workers there.

But my present Leeds correspondent wants to hear more about musicians and has the cheek and impudence to say he 'never heard of many Dublin musicians'.

Take me home and bury me decent, I wish I could sing a tune out of this article at you, my fine feathered friend, that would soften your cough.

THE NAUL

What about Mrs Kenny, the Queen of Irish fiddlers? And Flanagan the piper, her son-in-law. Still with us is Séamus Mac Aonghusa, Pride of the Naul, alias James Ennis, with whom myself and my father smoked cigars and indulged in cordial refreshment together in honour of his son Séamus Ennis, who is now in the BBC and rearing another generation of uilleann pipers.

And my mother and aunts danced under the master of the day, Dinny Cuffe, with Tommy King, father and uncle of Tommy and Paddy King, who are playing now with some dance bands in town.

Talking of dance bands, Johnny Devlin, that suave rector of ball rooms, in private life a traditional musician of demonic intensity, is a first cousin of Rory O'Connor the step dancer. And there is Gus Murphy, another noted floor tapper.

And, of course, there is Leo Rowsome, whose great ancestors before him were pipers of distinction, the time of the Markeys, whose descendants descended to house-painting.

HEMPSON

Like myself and Joe Fagan, the step-dancer, Nicholas Markey was a spoiled house-painter, and forty years ago at the back of St Joseph's school this pupil of the celebrated Willie Taylor of Drogheda and Philadelphia gave tuition in the Irish uilleann bagpipes.

I'm sorry I can't claim for Dublin the famous harpist Denis Hempson, who played for Bonnie Prince Charlie in Edinburgh in 1745, and for a better man, Theobald Wolfe Tone, at Belfast in 1792.

'He'd been in O'Carolan's company in his youth, but never took pleasure in playing his compositions preferring such ancient strains as "The Coolin", "The Dawning of the Day", etc.' (O'Neill).

He married at the age of eighty-six at Magilligan in his native county of Derry, and of his wife remarked, 'I can't tell if it was the devil himself buckled us together, she being lame and I being blind.'

The devil could have done worse on him. He lived to be a hundred and twelve on it.

The Irish Press, 26 November 1955

92

THE SCHOOL BY THE CANAL

Kate O'Brien[426] says that the bread in Ravenna tastes like grey serge. I was never in Ravenna to know what the bread tastes like, nor for the matter of that, have I ever tasted grey serge.

My mother was, and is, one of the best bread-makers in Ireland, and within her own range, from potato cakes to currant cake, I'd back her against any baker from here to Ravenna.

Miss O'Brien didn't mention bread in her talk a few nights ago on the wireless. The bread remark was made in *The Bell* once upon a time. On the wireless she was talking about nuns and the time she was at school and had a part in a play and had to describe from the stage '*aisling a bhi aici aréir*'[427] for the benefit of a nun whose feast day it was and who wasn't anything the better of the proceedings, by reason of the fact that she was an English Tory and didn't understand one word of the Irish language.

A WHOLE ORCHARD

Kate O'Brien described this lady as a 'gentle English Tory', which to me is like talking about a tame cobra, dry water, a poor publican, or a tall duck, but then everyone will talk well about their own nuns, no matter how they were brought up or what vagaries of politics they may have been reared to.

They say that the nun is the apple of God's eye, and if so, in North William Street, He has a whole orchard.

It is not the sort of place you'd go looking for orchards, being well into what we may call the Seán O'Casey country.

If you stood at the canal side of the school, you'd see looking one way the docks and cranes and gantries rising the far side of the North Strand, out past the barren space where shops and houses stood till one night the quiet of the late spring sky was rent by the crashing bombs.[428]

If you turned the other way you'd see the Cusack Stand,[429] and from the bridge beside it you'd have seen me diving if you'd have been there any summer day twenty years ago, and had your eyes open.

THE SOLDIER'S SONG

The big red-bricked buildings with their castor-oil plants in the window don't look the height of good architecture to me, now that I've set up in the intellectual line, but I can still remember the fun we had round this time of the year, with parties and diversion and Sister Monica beaming on all and sundry and calling them by their father's names, for she'd been there since the nineties, which she and her order made a bit gayer for generations of boys round that quarter.

There was Sister Columba putting me on a desk to sing three verses of 'The Soldier's Song' for the benefit of a nun next door, I discovered afterwards, wasn't our way of thinking at all.

There was long Sister Magdalene who kept us sternly in order and never looked for human affection, though when she died she couldn't stop the mothers of big families carrying one and dragging two down to St Agatha's to pray for her, and breaking down crying for their friend, one worse than another, and the babies joining in with their mas, so that there was such a noise of grief that it would go through you even to think of it, so we won't, but get on to something more seasonable.

SHE WAS A LADY

I mention by name no living teacher, nun or civilian, as old Sergeant-Major House called them, but there was one young lay teacher I remember playing a mouth organ at her Christmas party while her class danced round her and only stopped for long enough to cram more sweets or cake into their gobs to go on jigging and chewing as if they were mobile digestors and there to give a demonstration.

I had a lay teacher the time the nun stopped me on the stairs and I coming in late. She asked me which nun was my teacher. This was not Christmas-time nor Easter, nor any other time of bacchanalian indulgence but a stern, frosty morning, when late-comers stood in line for punishment. She repeated her question, and at last I gave my answer:

'Please, Sister, my teacher is not a nun – she's a lady.'

She relaxed her arm on the bannisters and laughed so much I thought it was most extraordinary. Another nun was coming down from the head nun's room, and she looked in some concern at the nun on the stairs, who called her over and repeated my remark to her so that the two of them laughed helpless on the stairs and could only tell me to go on.

GIDDY AND GIGGLY

At the other side of the block was the girls' school, presided over by, to the best of my recollection, Sister Philomena.

Here our female contemporaries went to school with the girls of St Vincent's Orphanage, who range from plump little girls of next door to no age, to demure 'demoiselles in their teens.

To us boys they seemed the very moral of mysterious and ladylike decorum as they filed in, in their neat school outfits, to sing a hymn or so at the children's Mass, but according to the girls from our street who went to school with them they were as giddy and giggly as the next in the classroom.

And one time my father had exercised his decorative art on a wolf's head for their annual pantomime; I had to deliver it to the convent where, I'm sure, white man or black had never before set foot.

There were big girls, haughty or condescending; there were little girls being swung round by medium-sized girls; there were blondes, brunettes and redheads, and only a nun I knew rescued me and gave me tea and rich cake, I'd have died of embarrassment.

They don't make the poor mouth, but you'll agree that it would be a fine thing to participate in the good work of helping the nuns to make a happy Christmas and New Year for their flock, from baby girls to young ladies.

The address is: Sister Superior, St Vincent's Orphanage, North William Street, Dublin.

Got you!

The Irish Press, 10 December 1955

93

THE FUN OF THE PANTO

'Fun with vulgarity' was the motto of our pantomime. It opened on St Stephen's Night, feast of St Stephen, and I never heard it called Boxing Day.

For long weeks before the whole of the North Circular, from one side to the other, was a seething mass of intrigue and allying and counter-allying, crossing and double-crossing that would have done credit to the United Nations, if such a thing had been going at the time.

At first it was the city side against the Croke Park side. Not all of these people knew each other and indeed there were sore hearts in one street, which was highly respectable, and in flats, rather than rooms, at the thoughts of having to get up on the same stage as people from our street, but we had the good singers, and also, if we were not adequately represented, we would not come except to make trouble, and whatever our shortcomings in the matter of shut hall doors or prams and bikes in the hall, it was generally recognised that we were good at making trouble.

A BABE IN THE WOOD

But by the time the rehearsals had started, the quarrels and jealousies had reached an intensity that had ceased to regard any considerations of class or social position.

Many a lifelong enmity was firmly founded on the question of whose little girl was to play a babe in the wood, or whose big girl was to be a principal boy.

By the time the curtain was ready to go up the hall was grimly seething in a mood far too serious for anything so frivolous as fun, let alone vulgarity.

The stewards were the subject of intense, whispered discussion, frequently libellous.

'Did you see who they had taking in the money in the one and sixpennies – ould Baldy Conscience.'

'That's right. The same fellow used to go be the name of Sawdust Pocket when he was on the chapel door.'

'And sure, if he's bad, the fellow's with him is worse. They put the Boy Scouts on the door of the chapel while they were on holidays and they got that much extra they never let them pair back.'

'It's up there on the stage they ought to be, giving a conjuring turn, now you see it, now you don't.'

'Sh-sh, the curtain's going up.'

The band played its opening bars, and the girls went into their line number singing one of many songs, all of which were like this:

> 'Oh, happy, happy day, and we hope you may,
> Enjoy our little show tonight,
> That it may your heart delight,
> And make you merry and bright,
> Too-o-o-o-ni-ght.'

There was applause then from such of the audience as were personal supporters of members of the chorus. The rest waited for their own nominations to come out and contented themselves with a thin bringing together of the palms of the hands, but discreetly so as not to make noise. There was usually comment on the chorus ladies.

A DIAMOND JUBILEE

'I see that one of the Hegartys is out again. That blondy one there.'

The speaker's eldest daughter had been kept out of the chorus and a scalded heart will say many's the thing. 'I'd be long sorry to see any girl of mine got up in that get-up.'

'All the same, it's wonderful how she's able to get round the stage for a woman of her years. She's deserving of a diamond jubilee presentation, I don't care what anyone says – forty years she's getting up on them boards. Oh, yous can laugh and sneer, jibe and jeer, but which of us would be that active at her age?'

Later in the show the court scene was in full swing:

Judge: 'How would you like your poor mother to be here and see you in the dock?'

Prisoner: 'Ah sure the bit of a outin' of the 'Joy would do her good.'

I LIKE BANANAS

In the audience, herself is putting himself through it for laughing, in burning vitriolic whispers, till he squirms in the seat.

'You cur to go laughing at the red-nosed ruffian and his low jokes about the 'Joy. Of course, you and him could shake hands on knowing more about the place than most people – and you hadn't as much as a grin on you when your daughter, your own child, was up there singing "I wish I had a little cat". But wait.'

'Miss Eyelash Nick Gabbin – Nick I mean – she's a pain—'

A fierce jab of a programme in the ear attracts the attention of the speaker. 'Who are you to call my daughter, Éilis Nic Gabhann, a pain?'

'I was only saying she was a pianist. That's what they have her down here as. And I was only saying "Nick" is a funny name for a girl.'

'You're only showing your ignorance of your own language – that's her name in Irish, *gan teanga, gan tir*, you perisher.'

A few nights later we'd be all out to get the paper and read about it:

'To introduce the various items, there was the popular Dublin master of ceremonies Paddy (Whacker) Whelan. The accompanists were Johnny Nola (piano) and Bill Gannon (drums).

'The popular song "I Like Bananas, Because They Have No Bones" was a big hit, as was the song-scene with the sunflowers.'

The Irish Press, 17 December 1955

94
A TURN FOR A NEIGHBOUR

In Cloghran.

One Christmas Eve, though not this one nor the one before, there was a man coming in from Cloghran, CD, on a horse and cart to do his Christmas business, selling and buying.

When he got as far as Santry, CD, he remembered that there was an old neighbour dead in a house, so he went in to pay his respects and after saying that he was sorry for their trouble and all to that effect, he enquired whether he could offer any assistance of a practical nature.

'Well, if it's a thing you wouldn't mind, collecting the coffin, it's ready measured and made and all. It would be a great help to us.'

'I do not indeed mind carrying the coffin back for you, though I won't be home till a bit late, having to do her shopping. I've a list as long as your arm of sweets for childer, snuff for her old one, rich cake, a jar of malt, two bottles of port wine, snuff for my old one, a collar for the dog, a big red candle to put in the window, a jockey of tobacco for myself, a firkin of porter, two dolls that'll say "Ma-ma", one railway train, a jack-in-the-box and a monkey-on-a-stick, two holy pictures, rashers and black and white pudding and various other combustibles too numerous to mention.

'But I'll stick the coffin up amongst the rest of them and take the height of good care of it, and it'll be me Christmas box and hansel for me poor old neighbour, and a good turn for myself because I'll have luck with it.'

So off he went at a jog trot into the city down from Santry, CD, past Ellenfield and Larkhill through the big high trees and the sun just beginning on a feeble attempt to come out, and then having a look at the weather was in it, losing heart and going back in again, till your man came to Whitehall tram terminus, where they were just getting ready to take the seven o'clock into town.

'Morra Mick,' shouts a tram fellow with his mouth full of steam, 'and how's the form?'

'If it was any better,' shouts Mick off the cart, 'I couldn't stick it.'

'More of that to you,' shouts the tram fellow, 'and a happy Christmas, what's more.'

'You too, and many more along with that,' shouts Mick, and along with him down the Drumcondra Road.

So away he goes into the City, over Binn's Bridge and into the markets. Before dinnertime he had his selling done, and was on to the buying.

He had a good few places to visit, meeting this one and that, but with an odd adjournment he had everything bought and the coffin collected and on the back of the cart with the rest of the stuff by evening time. It was dark and cold and the snow was starting to come down the back of his neck, but he tightened the collar well round him and having plenty of the right stuff inside him began a bar of a song for himself, to the tune of 'Haste to the Wedding':

> *"Twas beyond at Mick Reddin's at Owen Doyle's weddin',*
> *The lads got the pair of us out for a reel.*
> *Says I, "Boys, excuse us," says they, "Don't refuse us,"*
> *"I'll play nice and aisy," said Larry O'Neill.*
> *Then up we got leppin' it, kickin' and steppin' it*
> *Herself and myself on the back of the door,*
> *Till Molly, God bless her, fell into the dresser,*
> *And I tumbled over a child on the floor.*
>
> *Says herself to myself, "You're as good as the rest,"*
> *Says myself to herself, "Sure you're better nor gold,"*
> *Says herself to myself, "We're as good as the best of them,"*
> *"Girl," says I, "sure we're time enough old."'*

So with a bit of a song and a mutter of encouragement to the old horse, Mick shortened the way for himself, through snow and dark till he came to Santry, CD, once again.

There was light and smoke and the sound of glasses and some fellow singing 'The Bold Tenant Farmer' and Mick, being only human, decided to make one last call and pay his respects to the publican.

But getting in was a bit easier than getting out, with drinks coming up from a crowd that was over from the other side of the county, all Doyles from the hill of Kilmashogue, the Drummer Doyle, the Dandy Doyle, Jowls Doyle, Woodener Doyle, the Dancer Doyle, Elbow Doyle, Altar-Boy Doyle, the Hatchet Doyle, Coddle Doyle, the Rebel Doyle, Uncle Doyle, the Shepherd Doyle, Hurrah Doyle and Porter-Nose Doyle.

There was singing and wound-opening and citizens dying for their country on all sides and who shot the nigger on the Naas Road and I'm the first man that struck a monkey in a dustbin and came out without a scratch, and there's a man there will prove it, that the lie may choke me, and me country's up and me blood is in me knuckles, 'I don't care a curse now for you, or your queen, but I'll stand by my colour, the harp and the green.'

Till, by the time he got on the road again, Mick was *Maith-go-leor*, as the man said, but everything went well till he was getting near Cloghran, and he had a look round, and there he noticed – the coffin was gone! Gone like Lord Norbury with the divil, as the man said.

Ah, what could he do at all, at all. He sat on the cart for a minute and wondered how he'd face your man if he had to go and tell him that he'd let him down not doing the turn for a family with enough trouble this Christmas Eve.

Still, looking at it never fattened the pig, so he got off and went back along the road in the direction of the city, and was moseying round in the snow when an RIC man came up from Santry Barracks.

'Come on now, and what are you doing walking round this hour of the night?'

'I'm after losing a coffin, constable,' says Mick.

'They sells desperate bad stuff this time of the year,' sighs the policeman, taking Mick by the arm. 'Come on, my good man, you'll have to come down the road with me now till we investigate into your moves.'

Poor Mick was too disheartened even to resist him and, sad and sober, trudged through the snow till they came to the barracks. They went into the dayroom and the constable said to the sergeant, 'I've a fellow here wandering abroad, and says he's after losing a coffin.'

'He may well have,' says the sergeant, 'because we're after finding one. There it is, standing up behind the door.'

They looked round and Mick's face lit up with joy and relief. 'Praise Him,' said he, running over and throwing his arms round it, 'there it is, me lovely coffin.'

He explained all about it, and they let him go off carrying it back to the cart.

'Take better care of it, now,' says the constable and the sergeant from the door.

'I wouldn't have minded,' says Mick, 'only the coffin is not my own. Goodnight, and a happy Christmas to you and to everyone.'

Which is the wish of this column – *Nollaig shona dhibh uilig.*

The Irish Press, 24 December 1955

95
NOT ANOTHER WORD
ABOUT TURKEY

I don't feel much better than yourself, if it's any ease to you.

I spent Christmas Eve with the Anglo-Irish nobility. Better people I hope never to spend it with, though they all strike me as being very tall. But they were the real old stock, though they appeared very tall to me, who am as broad as I'm long.

We had a lovely girl on the staff to dance us 'The Blackbird' while I played a chromatic mouth organ. We followed her into the kitchen for that and a right performance she gave us.

One of the Boys of Wexford drove us down in a Rolls-Royce and an Ulster Presbyterian drove us back in a station wagon, so you'll see that all classes and creeds were catered for.

WHERE WE WAKE UP

I went up then with my mother to see the eldest fellow of us, and we drank *poitín* and my first wife said it was very nice, which it is if you get it right.

But now, glory be, I'm coming to the part where we wake up and start counting on our ten fingers, or whatever few we have left, the cost of it all.

What, in the name of our sacred and dearest old creditors, are we going to do for readies? It seems, between hopping and trotting, lepping and dancing, we got all through some readies.

I thought to myself Monday morning that I was feeling like a corpse that didn't get a Christmas burial, but after I backed Brenair II and Roddy Owen at Leopardstown, on expert advice, I seemed to rally, and back I came to relish a bit of turkey.

Now, if I may digress for a minute, and it's a thing Dean Swift was very fond of doing, never again let me hear a word about turkey.

There is a kind of a class of a fashion, about saying it's not worth this and that, and such a thing is as good.

CREDITORS AND BILLS

Now, it's not from mixing with the quality I'm speaking. I spent lovely Christmases and we had a sight less turkey but youth at our side to make as merry a Christmas as ever you saw, because for one thing we were noisy teetotallers, not wanting much else but the excuse to be gay – but when all is said and done, with advancing years, a bit of turkey is very light, highly nutritious and altogether delectable and acceptable of a Christmas time.

I was on the subject of creditors and bills and not feeling so good at all, at all, when I did my rallying trick. All the other citizens sympathising with one another was an assistance. They all said they hoped it would be as long again till it came around next year, and all to that effect, and at the last time of calling were making feeble efforts to wish one another a happy New Year.

But one young man I remember had an electric light inside his bow tie, which went on and off to the terror of his slightly nervous elders, and I'd say that's a thing to remember, wouldn't you? That's a thing to keep up. No house in the land should be without one.

ANGELIC SMILE

Fancy walking up to a young fellow and saying, 'Well, my little man, you're a good deal higher than when I saw you last,' and his angelic smile looking up at you till you looked down and swooned at his bow tie, winking luridly at you, as much as to say, 'And, my big man, you're a sight wider than when I saw you last.'

After turkeying and coming out on the street again and meeting people, all of whom were moaning and groaning and wondering how they'd get through January after asking one another how they'd got over the Christmas, I felt great.

If the boat's big enough, and we're all sick together, we'll get over anything.

Like the poor fellow I listened to that was trying to keep it up.

A HAPPY EASTER

He was delayed two days getting in from sea, and he wondered why the rest of us gazed at him listlessly as he raised his voice in celebration:

> 'I saw from the beach a poor exile from Erin,
> And the skin on his ears as tight as a drum.
> He looked at the spuds, at where they were boiling,
> Cried he, "Holy Farmer, will they never be done?"'

He looked around at us and reproached us for our silence.

We wiped our heads, shook them, and wished him a happy Easter.

We are a Renaissance people, and enough is enough for the time being.

Cáisg fe mhaise dhibh uilig,[430] and let the New Year do for the frostbitten heathen.

The Irish Press, 31 December 1955

96

OVERHEARD IN A BOOKSHOP

'Could I have a Dineen?' asked this respectable-looking party in the bookshop.

'No, sir, we wouldn't have such a thing,' answered the lady assistant. 'I don't know would you get one in Dublin at all. Ectu-ahly,' she finished, 'It's a kind of Cork hoarse doovray, isn't it?'

Your man went off in some puzzlement, and the lady assistant remarked to her young man elegantly, 'Coming up here and the mark of the stirabout spoon still in their mouth and looking for them things in a bookshop. You could easy see it was not a pork butcher's. But maybe he thinks it's like the shops back home in the bog where they sell you *Old Moore's Almanac*[431] and a pound of black and white pudding off the one counter.'

Her young man murmured something appropriate and continued to gaze into her eyes, long and pleadingly. She returned to their own conversation and shook her head for the fourth or fifth time.

'Ignayzeous, I'm really very, very sorry, but I deffiny could not make it. Genuine I couldn't,' she signed, 'not but what I'd loved to.'

An old gentleman came up to ask for a New Testament.

'Desperate sorry I am, sir,' said Ida Lufftoo, 'but I am afraid it's not out yet. We have the old one, of course, but I suppose you've read that.'

The old gent looked at her in some dismay and retreated towards the door.

A NORTHERN

'Cheek and imperance of them old fellows when you go to give them a peas of information. Another fellow comes to me yesterday, a Northern by the sound of him, and he asks for a book about gorilla dazes[432] in Ireland. I told him I'd never seen gorillas dazed, or any other way, in Ireland. Maybe they have them in Ulster, but if so I said that was the place to keep them. Then another pair comes in, Yanks they were be the sound of them, and ask me did I know Joyce is useless. I told them I didn't care whether he was or not, not knowing the man, T.G. One fellow has the common gall to laugh up into my face and tell me that was the sharpest crack he'd heard from a European.

'Go way, you dirty low cur,' said I, 'to insult a lady. I'm no European, but an Irish girl bred, born and reared in Donnelly's Orchard.'

Her young man muttered something fierce, but she waved her hand deprecatingly.

'That's all right, Ignayzeous, what you'd a done, if you'd been here, but you're like the Garda Seo Caughtyeh, never where you're wanted. Then another fellow comes in and asks me for a new green, and I directed him to the top of Grafton Street, and said he might do the best he could with the old one because it was the only one I'd heard of in these parts, unless they'd have a new green in Ballyfermot or Donnycarney, out at the new houses, but I'd not know much about them places. Ours is a purchase house, fifty pound down and you own it in 2006, if God spares us.

'Then there was an old chap in a Teddy Boy suit, velvet collar and all, drainpipes, and I don't know who he thought he was fooling. Going round in that get-up like a fellow of eighteen and I declare he was seventy if he was an hour, and he tries to get off his mark if you please asking me if I liked kippilling.

'How would I know?' I asks, 'when I never kippilled, and if I did it would be with some one more me equals than you.'

COOK SHOP

'And that put him in his place I can tell you. He wasn't long clearing off. And all those dead and alive old books, you'd be lost for a bit of a read only I do bring me *True Romances* with me. I'll be out of this place after the Christmas rush anyway. I went back to the fellow in the labour and he says to me, "I thought you liked working in a bookshop? You said you worked in one for three years."

"'A bookshop?" says I, "I told you I worked in the cook shop, in the biscuit factory, where they fill cakes and biscuits with jam and suchlike when they come out of the bakehouse."

"'Oh, is that so?" says he, "my mistake, well keep your mouth shut till the first week in January, and let on you can read and write."

"'You're desperate funny, you are," says I, "you're that sharp, you'll cut yourself. I can read as good as you," and I read him a real high-class bit out of a book I borrowed here – the real classical it is, all knowledge, and I read him a bit that stuck him to the ground:

'Ah, my precious little girl, for God's sake cast occasionally a word or look of encouragement from your velvety lips or saddened eyes! Don't my treasured hope, don't allow the slightest frown ever formed by the merest movement of nature to dwell on your sinless brow, else I die. Yes, by Venus; ere I'd yield to have you torn from my arms of life-long companionship. I'd resign my rights of existence to a region of undying flame.'

She put down her book, and smiled gently at Ignayzeous's praises.

NO FREE READS

A tall lady of foreign, almost diplomatic appearance approached, and with an apologetic smile asked Ida if the Everyman edition of *Anna Karenina* was in stock.

Ida smiled back interrogatively, 'Urm? Annakarra urm?'

'Tolstoy's *Anna Karenina*,' said the lady.

Ida nodded mysteriously and smiled her inscrutable smile. *'An bhfuil cead agam dul amach?'* she asked.

The lady looked at her and at Ignayzeous, and said, 'Quite, er, thank you.'

Ida's gaze followed her up the shop. 'It doesn't do to let yourself down before these foreigners. When they speak to me in their language, I believe in answering them in mine.'

Then her eye took me in. 'Just a minute, Ignayzeous.' To me: 'Did you want to buy something?'

'Well, I was just having a look around,' said I, 'I was just—'

She gently but firmly removed the volume from my lifeless fingers, and smiled but shook her head. 'Sorry, but no free reads.'

I nodded desperately and turned in the direction of the door, her voice trailing after me. 'I may only be here for a week, Ignayzeous, but I don't want the shop robbed barefaced!'

The Irish Press, 7 January 1956

97
THE HOT MALT MAN AND
THE BORES

'Wipe your bayonet, Kinsella, you killed enough.'

'Go on,' says I.

'That's genuine,' said Kinsella, 'that's what Lord Roberts says to me in Blamevontame[433] in 'o1. I knew him before of course, from the time we were in Egg Wiped.[434] 'Shifty Cush!' says Bobs, when he seen me on parade, 'is that you, Kinsella?'

'It is,' says I, coming smartly to attention, 'who were you expecting?'

'You've killed enough of bores,' says Bobs.

There was a sharp-featured gentleman sitting beside us having a drop of malt, hot. A great odour of cloves and old Irish rose from him as he turned round. He glared at Kinsella in a nationalistic fashion. 'That did you great credit, I'm sure. The bores never done this little country any harm for you to be killing them. Are you an Irishman?'

'I am,' said Kinsella. 'Are you a bore?'

'*Ná bac leis* whether I am or not,' says Hot Malt. 'The bores was always good friends of this little country, and I don't see what call you had to go killing them.'

The Bottle of Stout man glanced nervously up from his bus guide and spoke querulously at us, 'Sure, what's the good of arguing over that now. Wouldn't they all be dead of old age, be this time, anyway?'

'I don't see what they should be,' said Hot Malt. 'This mercenary foe of theirs is alive yet.'

'Look at here,' says Kinsella, 'I'm no Mendecency[435] foe of anyone. Maybe you know more about the Mendecency Institution than anyone else in this lounging bar.'

The Bottle of Stout man glanced again at his bus guide and called the assistant. 'How much is your clock fast?'

'The usual ten minutes, Mister O.'

'I see, I see, bring us another bottle.' Then he fell to anxious calculations. 'It'd leave the Parkgate at eight forty and to the Pillar at eight forty-eight, say, and ...' He glanced round again and we saw the front of a bus come past the window. The Bottle of Stout man fell to the floor like a trained guerrilla fighter and cowered below the level of the window.

The bus drew alongside the stop outside the pub, and its top floor was on a dead level with the lounge in which we sat. The narrowness of the street made ourselves and the passengers intimate spectators of each other.

Only one of them took advantage of the proximity this afforded; a stoutly built lady who swept the features of each of us with a searching sharpness and then not altogether satisfied with what she'd seen, nodded grimly and almost threateningly as the bus bore her off.

'Eh,' says Kinsella, 'that was a dangerous-looking ould one that looked in at us off the bus – the one with the face of a DMP man.'

The Bottle of Stout man rose to his feet, and after a look out the window, turned to Kinsella who nodded and said, 'You didn't miss much there, she's a right hatchet, whoever she is.'

A TRAINED MIND

'Excuse yourself,' said the Bottle of Stout man, 'she is my wife and I'll thank you to keep a civil tongue in your head.' He spoke round at the company: 'You can't expect a man to put up with remarks like that about the woman he loves.'

Heads were nodded approvingly, and Kinsella was in some confusion.

'How was I to know she was your wife? And how did you know yourself it was her I was talking about? You were sitting on the floor and you didn't see her.'

'I recognised her from your description,' said the Bottle of Stout man, with the quiet dignity of a trained mind.

An elderly lady in the corner shook her head and murmured enigmatically into her port: 'As the ole oopera says, "What the eye doesn't see the heart won't grieve for." I love you because you love her. Love's young dream, as I always said about my poor spowce: "Better the divil you know than the one you don't."'

'But, anyway,' says Kinsella, resuming his conversation with me, 'the first man I sees at zero hour one two, this was in the next war, was Jowls Loughrey of the Dirty Shirts.'

SPEAK NO GERMAN

'"Halt," says he, "who goes there?"

"It's me, Jowls," says I, "Whacker Kinsella from Messer Street – down beside the hospital."

"Don't be so familiar with your Jowls," says Jowls, "How do I know you're not a German?"

"I can't speak a word of German," says I, "I'm from Messer Street."

"That doesn't prove anything," says Jowls, "I'm from Francis Street and I can't speak a word of French – how some ever I'll take your word for it. The attack is off. We can't go over the top kicking the football in front of us tonight."

"Why not?" says I, "the men in my spittoon was looking forward to the bit of exercise."

"They're after losing the ball," says Jowls.'

Just at that moment the Bottle of Stout man after a hurried look at his bus guide and at the clock fell to the ground, swift as before.

'Like one of them Syrup Pots,' said Kinsella admiringly.

But he was not swift enough.

The lady shouted in from the top of the bus.

'I saw you,' she screeched, 'dodging down there, hiding on the floor. Making a jeer of your poor wife with your drunken bowsies of companions.' We all visibly blenched and cowered down, not on the floor altogether with the Bottle of Stout man, but with our faces not far off it. 'I know yous, yous low lot, tell him to get up the floor now, the bus is moving.'

It moved and we rose again.

'Don't mind me asking you,' asked the Hot Malt of the Bottle of Stout man, 'why is it you don't go in another pub where she can't see you.'

The Bottle of Stout man sighed. 'You must forgive a sentimental old fool.'

'Certainly, certainly, so,' muttered Kinsella, 'as an old solder, I con, cur.'

The Bottle of Stout man wiped his eyes. 'This is how we met. She looked in at me off the top of a tram. I'll never forget it.'

Said the Hot Malt, 'Neither will we.'

The Irish Press, 14 January 1956

98
MY GREAT RED RACING BIKE

This wintry weather reminds me of Dún Laoghaire.

Not that, I hasten to add, there's anything more wintry about the Dún than any place else this time of the year. The sea may lash up and over the East Pier, but then with my own two eyes I've seen the blue-clad Corporation employees of a famous Riviera town collecting newly fallen snow and throwing it into the Mediterranean. And a tourist nearly going in after it for trying to take a snapshot.

But when I was a young house-painting fellow of eight stone or so, and that's not today nor yesterday, taking one thing with another, weight for age, I was the possessor of a red racing bicycle called, if I remember rightly, a Phoenix, and inherited by me from my brother. His house-painting activity had taken him by train and car round the province of Connacht, from Boyle Cathedral to the Irish College in Tourmakeady, County Mayo.

MILD AND GENTLE
He fell a total of more than a hundred feet in those two places, so his perambulations had something of the quality of a circus tour.

Of the bicycle I was very proud, and a very skilful cyclist in traffic, I could get from the city to Dún Laoghaire while you'd be saying Lennox Robinson.

So when my employer wanted some stuff to be brought out to a job in the Borough, I took the tram fare, but used the bicycle to get out there.

Which is how I came to have a shilling on a Tuesday.

It was the month of January and fairly cold in the morning, but nothing exceptional about it, when I was starting off, but going through Ballsbridge it began spitting snow-water, and by the time I was at Blackrock the real genuine, undiluted stuff was coming down, in soft flakes, mild and gentle like a talk about Partition on the Third Programme. And by the time I got into Dún Laoghaire I was pushing through a blizzard.

The door of the house we were doing up was opened for me by an elderly painter, who was doing the job on his own. He was a native of the Channel Islands and went by the name of Janey.

'YOU POOR PEEG'

I am not inventing this name. Poor Janey is no longer at this end of the plank, but I often wondered afterwards who did invent it. Maybe it was a corruption of his name in French.

'Come in, come in, young man, you are welcome,' said Janey, 'it's cold, isn't it?'

I shook myself like a whippet and admitted that it sure was, that you could play a melodeon to that.

'You 'ave terrible journey out to thees place,' said Janey. He always kept up a sort of French fur-trapper's accent. The boss said the old ones in the good class trade liked it. I shook myself and nodded. 'You poor peeg,' said Janey.

Then after a minute or two, he asked me, 'W'y you no come out in the, er, what you call, tram care?'

I told him I did not come out in the what-you-call tram care because I had a bike and wanted the shilling for myself. He nodded vigorously at this.

After we had a drop of tea and a bit of bread and brawn, Janey said it was no good my going back to the shop in that class of weather. I could get into stripping a room.

I went up to one of the upper rooms with stock brush and scraper and set to work, but first I had to take up some linoleum.

AN ANXIOUS MOO

This was a hazardous business for me. I never could resist reading old newspapers, and for me to raise a piece of old linoleum was like opening the door of a library.

I promised myself that I would only read a little bit, that I would just glance at the papers before I threw them into the snow outside, but when I raised the linoleum and saw the headline *Viceroy's visit to Grangegorman. Vicereine waves green linen handkerchief, scenes of mad enthusiasm*, I was lost and read it inch by inch, through the serial *Pretty Kitty*.

For new readers: Lord Mauleverer has fallen in love with pretty Kitty Hackett, daughter of Honest Tom Hackett, a country butcher. She helps her father in the slaughterhouse and one day she is busily gutting when an anxious moo is heard.

Till at last Janey came into the room, and caught me there. The old English drop-pattern paper unscarred by hand of mine as I bent over the morning paper for Tuesday, 12 June 1901.

FIVE SHILLINGS BACK

'So,' he moaned in his saddest Quebec accent. 'You 'ave down nowthing, no?'

'No,' said I shamefaced.

'So,' said Janey, 'You are ere 'alf day and you 'ave down nowthing. You come 'ere at 'alf nine. That is right. On bicycle.' At this point his face increased. 'You 'ave mawnay.'

'That's right,' says I, 'I've a shilling.'

It seems Janey could do with the loan of a shilling: no sooner said than done. He went down the stairs with my shilling, and I went back on my floor to my papers.

But I misjudged him, even though it was a deal from my point of view.

At half past two he came back and gave me five shillings. He was all smiles but said, 'Now we do some graft, yes, no?' I agreed yes, no, it wouldn't kill us one in a way.

When we quit that night Janey told me he'd backed Pappegeno II, which won at a hundred to six – in a blizzard.

'In the boogies I did it. They 'ave boogies 'ere too,' said Janey. 'Jus' like 'ome in Daublin.'

The Irish Press, 21 January 1956

99

DIALOGUE ON LITERATURE
AND THE HACK

A voice (hoarse, relentless) 'Where were you in 'sixteen?'

'I wasn't born till twenty-three.'

A.V.: 'Excuses … always excuses.'

('You borrowed that from *Living with Lynch*.'[436] 'I stole it, sir. An artist never borrows.')

A mirthless laugh rang through the snug at the far end of the shop. A shudder ran through me and I ventured to the side door to have a look in the mirror and a better view of the source of that awful sound (the mirthless laugh, I mean).

I only knew the voice too well, and the face and all. It was the face of the Rasher Cambel, the Dolphin's Barn genius.

'Well,' he looked around at me, 'hack.'

'I was a hack,' says I, 'before you came up.'

I gazed down at my vis-à-vis, as the man said; he could not deny it. (At fifty, George Moore[437] learned the comfort of semi-colons; us national schoolboys pick it up a bit earlier.)

HARDCOVER BOOK

'My friend, Ma Loney, ah dear heavens,' says the Rasher, in the one breath and looking very hard at the two fellows out of the Artists' Fellowship. These were two youths out of the Corporation, and looked hard at me when he said these words, 'was a liar.'

'Shut up your big mouth now,' says Mister Moo, as he is called for short. 'I do not allow that kind of abuse of my customers, even if they have monthly pensions itself.' He nodded round, and we nodded. It was the best of our play ... as the man said.

'Mister Moo,' said I, that being short for his name, 'sure I never wrote a book with a hard cover? You're the man that knows that.'

'Bedad and you never did, barring you did between the hours of half two and half three.'⁴³⁸

'Oh indeed and he did not,' said Maria Concepta from the corner, 'indeed and he did not, ever go in for anthin' so forren as writin' books. Sure that boy, he can't reed never mind right.'

THE MAN IS A HACK

'I don't know whether he did or not,' says the Rasher. 'He attacked in print a friend of mine. One who is not in the common run of ... ah ... ah ... Ha ...'

'Now, now, ha-ha yourself,' said Maria Concepta, 'I'll give you ha-ha.'

'He attacked in print,' said the Rasher impressively, 'a friend of mine who is not in the common run of ha-ha ...'

'Ha-ha is not proper abuse, sir,' said Maria Concepta.

'Ha-hackery,' said the Rasher, 'the man is a hack.'

I shivered my nostrils and whinnied.

'Well, now,' said Crippen, 'he has a look of the quinine spee shes', and added with elegance, 'when you see under the gate.'

'My friend,' said the Rasher, 'the liar.'

'Ah no, that's enough,' said the Rasher with dignity.

'I'm sorry, descent man,' said Mister Moo, 'you meant a lawyer; sure no one would have an hour's luck attacking the likes of them fellows; no man of education would attack the like, and I can see you're an Eaton man like meself.'

'Aye,' muttered Crippen, 'and a drinkin' man if you went into it.'

'That's not ayther here nor there, now,' said Mister Moo, 'I'm not waiting on the likes of you to tell the likes of me that.'

'But all the same,' said the Rasher, who had been in Soho for some time, 'actually – that person.'

'Oh, indeed now,' said Maria Concepta, 'there's no need for language the like of that. Going round calling people persons. And they not doing a ha'porth on you.'

'The lady's right,' said Mister Moo to the Rasher, 'there's no persons here.'

'No, indeed,' said Maria Concepta, 'we served and seen every class of people here, but no persons.'

'Never the less,' screeched the Rasher.

'Oh, never the less,' said Maria Concepta, reasonably.

'But very much the more,' said Crippen, sincerely.

SLIM SHEAF OF VERSE

'That hack,' said the Rasher looking straight at me, 'attacked a friend of mine. A friend of humanity's. A real writer – not ...' he shouted, defiantly, 'one whose name will be found on the flyleaf of thick volumes, but whose more delicate moods ...'

'The same again, men?' asked Mister Moo.

He was waved away.

'But whose happiest sentiments may be found ...'

'In the slim sheaf of verse,' murmured Crippen.

The Rasher nodded. 'How did you know, red ...'

'Redolent of the faintest faerylike feeling,' muttered Crippen.

'Genius,' said the Rasher respectfully, 'how did you know?'

'Never mind poor Brending Being,' said Crippen. 'He doesn't know what he writes.'

'How so?' asked the Rasher.

'Sad case,' said Crippen, looking at me with commiseration, 'only went to school half the time, when they were teaching the writing – can't read.'

The Irish Press, 28 January 1956

100

EMANCIPATION PARSON:
SYDNEY SMITH

'The moment the very name of Ireland is mentioned the English seem to bid adieu to common feeling, common prudence and common sense, and to act with the barbarity of tyrants and the fatuity of idiots.'

These were the words of an ordained clergyman of the Church of England – a canon of St Paul's, no less.

A canon very much out of the ordinary, of whom George the Fourth[439] said: 'A more profligate parson I never met.'

Many a one, in that day and age, would have agreed that George the Fourth should have been a good judge of a profligate, but his friend Dan O'Connell described Sydney Smith[440] as 'the ancient and amusing defender of our faith'. Thomas Moore[441] was his friend, and his wife referred to him as 'my noble-hearted husband'.

Still, the opinion of a wife is no certificate of worthiness, less than a parent's, for the wife does more than love the wayward child, she takes over the matured and finished sinner. Which is why they are not compelled by law to testify in court against their husbands.

BURNT-OUT WRECK

But Queen Victoria, who practically owned respectability, 'used to go into fits of laughter at the sayings of Smith, which were repeated to her by Lord Houghton.'

And Dickens,[442] a more important witness said, '... old Lady Holland, whom I see again crying about dear Sydney Smith, behind that green screen as we last saw her together ...'

I stood one night at the gate in Holland Park Road in that part of London that lies between Kensington and Hammersmith and gazed up the drive through the trees and thought of Sydney Smith, 'ancient and amusing defender of our faith', and was sad because the old Holland House is a burnt-out wreck. Not that it matters very much. The old liberal spirit was dead as a doornail long before Lloyd George made liberalism into a thing taken on a tank to weaker people.

But I was sorry for Holland House, surrounded as its ruins are now by the dwellings of what Gilbert Harding[443] describes as 'chinless nonentities', when I thought of how the Holland family had entertained the most relentless minds in Europe.

HEART OF HERRICK

What wit in what heads must have been carried up that drive from a road whose present claim to fame is that it contains the headquarters of a firm of caterers, giving employment on a daily basis to thousands of pearl-divers – dish-washers.

As sorry as I am for Luggala in County Wicklow, burned recently, where anyone could say anything they liked if they did not take too long over it, and had wit.

It was not that he was so religious, even for a clergyman, for as Chesterton[444] said, 'he was not only a Puritan, but he was not a submerged or secret Puritan. In his red blood was no such vinegar at all; for whatever we call the blood feeding such a brain, Christian, Pagan, or Anglican, it had flowed through the heart of Herrick ...'

Sydney was born at Woodford in Essex, right in the centre of Churchill's constituency, on the third of June 1771. His father was the son of a merchant and had been in his day something of a traveller.

A TOUGH WORLD

He was sent to Winchester, and did not fancy the public schools system a lot:

'At a public school every boy is alternately tyrant and slave ... This system we cannot help considering an evil – because it inflicts on boys, for two or three years of their lives, many painful hardships and much unpleasant servitude. These sufferings might be of some use in a military school but to give to a boy the habit of enduring privations which he will never again feel ... is surely not a very useful and valuable severity in education. It is not the life in miniature which he is to lead hereafter, nor does it bear any relation to it ...'

I am not an ex-public-school boy, but I'd damned near say amen to that. The world is sometimes a tough place, but you were never in a worse position to meet its cruelty than as a schoolboy.

Sydney went on to Oxford and became a clergyman. He wrote for the *Edinburgh Review* and talked up for Catholic Emancipation. Not because he was attracted to the Faith, it must be admitted, but because, as Chesterton said, 'Sydney Smith was truly and exactly a Liberal-loving freedom, he felt himself free ...'

NO MORE WAR

He was also more blessed than most Englishmen with what they imagine to be an English thing, common sense, and at a time when Napoleon could easily have turned to Ireland rather than to Egypt, he wrote about Catholic Emancipation: 'To deny the Irish this justice now, in the present state of Europe, and in the summer months, just as the season for destroying kingdoms is coming on, is a little short of insanity.'

He made jokes about the Scots, though he had happy times in Edinburgh and remembered them to the end of his life. 'Palmerston,' said Sydney, 'when speaking is like a man washing his hands; the Scotch members don't know what he is doing.'

But there is little enough harm in that, any more than in my own father's story of the raffle in which the first prize was a week in Belfast and the second prize a fortnight.

On the subject of war he was, as the man said, fumigating with sense. He wrote to Lady Grey:[445] 'For God's sake do not drag me into another war! I am worn down with protecting and crusading and defending Europe and mankind. I am sorry for the Spaniards – I am sorry for the Greeks – I deplore the fate of the Jews; the people of the Sandwich Islands groan under the most detestable tyranny; Bagdad is oppressed, I do not like the present state of the Delta – Tibet is not comfortable.'

But – 'am I to fight for all these people? No war, Dear Lady Grey! No eloquence; but apathy, selfishness, common sense, arithmetic!'

He died on a Saturday evening in February 1845 and as Hesketh Pearson writes, 'shook Lord John Russell, silenced Macauley, caused Lady Holland to forget her ailments, stopped the pen of Dickens, reddened the eyes of Thomas Moore and upset Luttrell's dining arrangements.'

Sydney Smith for Irishmen is the Smith of Smiths, not forgetting of course our native and Olympic defender, Ernie Smith.

The Irish Press, 4 February 1956

IOI
REFLECTIONS ON 'VITTLES'

A rising young painter (he gets up at half eleven every morning) accused my democratic self of having eaten and drunk with the nobility and with film directors.

He had not been asked to either hooley, but I could not resist the soft impeachment. I went, and enjoyed myself, and being well used to company from my childhood up, was in no way the most modest of the parties or the most retiring of those present.

I am fond of a bit of diversion, as the man said, and will even down a glass with the nobility, if asked politely.

I am reminded in this connection of a story about the late Bishop Duggan of Clonfert,[446] the Land League Bishop, as friends and enemies called him.

He was seated at some do or other, and the waiter poured him a glass of champagne. This old voitin was sitting beside him and she said, in shocked tones, 'I thought Your Grace was a teetotaller.'

'I am,' replied His Grace, 'a porter teetotaller. I never said I was a champagne teetotaller.'

IN THE PARLOUR

Which also brings to mind a story attributed to an tAthair Peadar about Maynooth.

It appears (but not in *Mo Scéal Fhéin*) that the scoff in that institution was not by any manner of means too lavish. The students, mostly big strong young men from the country and used to a decent bit, did not have half enough as they could have managed in the line of dinner.

Also, they had the idea, as everyone has, that their elders did a bit better than they did, and that the stuff in the parlour, where the professors ate, was a bit better than their own.

This young sub-deacon was being examined in theology and was asked: 'Could you, if there was no water available, baptise a child with whiskey?'

'No, I don't think so,' said your man. 'The content would be mostly spirit and not water.'

'Could you baptise a child with tea?'

'I wouldn't be sure,' says your student.

'Well, could you baptise a child with soup?'

The lad pondered his answer lovingly for a while. 'You could,' said he, 'with the students' soup. I don't know about the parlour's.'

THE PRESSURE COOKER

One of the best hooleys I was at was in Kilmurvey on the big Aran island. Máire Conghaile had quests of half-a-dozen European nationalities there, and I take the liberty of having been real proud of her cooking.

German and French were united in praise of her art, delicate and lavish. As well they might; for I'm a fair judge, well used to the good grub and knacky manipulation of sauce and meat by my mother, who cooked at one time for Maud Gonne MacBride, and my wife, no mean performer on the pressure cooker.

(A Voice: Didn't know yous had one.

B.B.: Well, you know now.

A.V.: I knew yous when yous had nothing. It'd answer yous better to—

B.B.: Put that man out.)

BREAKFAST FOR FARMERS

I was listening to Jimmy O'Dea and Myles Heffernan[447] and they deciding that the Royal should be named the Republican.

I'm as rebel as the next, but that proposal would cause endless confusion.

'I'm going down to see the Republican.'

'I'd save the wear and tear on my legs, if I was you. It's only throwing good money after bad. That fellow owes that much he has to go to Mass in a cab.'

But that's not what I wanted to say.

Jimmy O'Dea, whose ancestors are from Kilkenny, once told me that his earliest memories were going down Bridge Street the morning of the market and smelling the farmers' breakfasts.

'Many's the time,' he said, 'I sat in the desk at school, still sniffing the memory of them, till the teacher would come down and ask me in a threatening manner if I found anything obnoxious (pron: ob-knock-say-us) about his school.'

NINEPENNY PIG'S CHEEK

Incidentally, if I may get back to literature for a minute, there's a reference in James Joyce's *Finnegans Wake* to an old Dublin music-hall song about a cake:

'There was pul-ums and pur-ewns and cherries,
Oranges, lemons and cinnamon too,
There was pee-ell and cree-em and berries,
And the cur-ust, it was nailed on with gal-ue,
There was caraway seeds in a bun dance,
To give you a fine headache,
It would kill a man twice,
To be atin a slice of Miss Holligan's Christmas Cake!'[448]

Like the time my mother was sent by my granny for ninepenny pig's cheek. Such a thing at the price was not easily come by, even twenty-five years ago.

But anyway, in the heels of the reels, Mr Hug Melinn of Dorset Street, as then was, finally dug up a cheek which he was willing to part with at the price mentioned. The poor cheek had been squeezed up against the side of the barrel, which twisted his jaw and gave his one eye a most alarming squint.

My mother looked at it for a moment and ventured to say to the shop-man: 'Mr Hug, that's a very peculiar–looking cheek.'

'And what,' asks Hug, 'do you expect for ninepence – Me Hall Mock Lallamore?'[449]

NOTE: It's as well for a fellow not be getting any way big in himself.

The Irish Press, 11 February 1956

102
A SEAT ON THE THRONE

I knew a man from Nicholas Street that sat on the Throne of England.

He was working for a painting contractor at the time, and must have occupied the royal seat six times a week at least.

'At every tea break in the morning,' said the Drummer, 'at lunchtime, of course, we went out for beer.'

They were doing up Buckingham Palace at the time, and the tea was made in the usual way, in a billycan stuck over a blow lamp.

The Drummer sat up on the throne because it was the handiest way of looking out into the yard and keeping an eye out for an approaching foreman.

The Family were not in residence at the time, though this did not present unscrupulous persons, a plasterer's helper and a decadent scaffolder, from selling to elderly females in the pub nearby what purported to be bottles of Their Bathwater.

'Some of them just kept it in a bottle and looked at it,' said the Drummer, 'then there was a gentleman that bought the full of a bird bath off them for three pints of bitter an' a pork pie. He wanted to give his budgie a dip in it for a birthday treat.'

THE THREE GREETINGS

But his finest hour was yet to come when They were returned from Their Holidays. The Drummer was painting the flats and risers of a stairs leading to Their Apartments when it happened.

Her Majesty came noiselessly down the stairs and was beside him, ere he knew it.

He was still bent over his work in a kneeling position and his head bowed devotedly as he coated the current riser.

Then a small and beautifully encased shoe nudged him in the ribs, in the region of the paper-brush pocket.

In surprise he glanced up and tried to rise, in great confusion. 'Your Majesty, I'm so sorry, I ...'

But she only smiled graciously and in soothing tones remarked: 'Don't stir, Drummer. I'll step over you.'

'And when we left,' said Drummer, 'every man got a hundred box of three-greetings cigarettes.'

'There were three greetings on them?'

'There was three wrappings. Like this way. The company that made them would issue them for Christmas, and they'd have holly and ivy and Santy Clauses and log fires and a *Happy Christmas* on the label. But then say Christmas passed, and they weren't got rid of, well, the people giving them could tear off the first label and underneath was another one, with little yellow chickens and a *Happy Easter* on it, and if you didn't get rid of them, then you'd tear off that label and underneath was a notice saying, *They're getting stale, you'd better smoke them yourself.*'

THE MUSIC MULE

A small man drinking a fill-up for himself nodded in agreement, 'They gave us them too, in the Palace.'

'Were you there too?'

''Deed and I was,' said little fill-up, 'at sympathy concerts.'

'You were playing at these concerts?' I asked him.

'I don't know whether he was or not,' muttered the Drummer.

'I didn't say yet whether I was or not,' said little fill-up, 'I only said I was at the sympathy concerts. If yous want to know, I was in charge of the music mule, attached to the sympathy orchestra for carrying the instruments, in particular a most unhuman big drum.'

'You weren't playing?'

'No, I had me work cut out trying to soothe the mule, and he outside nearly going mad from the noise of Beethoven's *Fifth*. Just as well, if it had have been last, I often thought and me struggling to keep Grace Darling, that was the mule's name, on account of her being so vicious, a joke, if yous folly me, from going wild round the Palace grounds and we waiting to carry the instruments back. Then there was Mozart, there's a fellow come on a lot since.'

SHEIK OF ARABEE

'Them was nice goings-on,' said a snarly-looking customer, 'smoking cigarettes and drinking tea on the Royal Throne of England, and playing music, and the dead dying in dozens for Ireland every minute of the day. Them was nice things; oh, Mother Éire, you're rearing them yet.'

He strangled his utterance on a sob and bowed his shoulders on the counter.

'Ah, don't take it too much to heart,' said little fill-up, 'I told you, I only guided the mule.'

'Well,' said the Drummer, 'it was all aiqual to me whose ceiling I whitened. I'd wash a stretch for the Sheik of Arabee once he paid the rate.'

The Irish Press, 18 February 1956

103
SNOW THROUGH THE WINDOW

I sat down this morning after a kipper, some mushrooms, cheese, black coffee with bread and marmalade and butter and looked out of the window, thinking of the poor.

While the turf was blazing itself into a white heat of fragrant, caressing warmth, I digested my breakfast and reflected on the excellence of my condition.

'The wicked,' I thought happily, 'prosper in a wicked world.'

But alas, not the worst of us is free from the improving influence of a good woman. My first wife came in and said, 'I thought you were doing that bit of an article today.'

I looked out the window again and shuddered.

'You're not expecting a man to work in that kind of weather?' said I, with a look at the blizzard.

But she was adamant, and pointed to this masheen, as the man called it, and I only got out of the house by a mutter about a telephone call to be made from Peter's. I reflected during my hundred-yard battle through the snow that if the Corporation would not build a tunnel from our house to Peter's I'd have to get my overcoat out of the pawn.

OUR IGLOO

I may say that the height of good humour prevailed in this igloo of ours.

There were elderly ladies of a loyalist nature from Ballsbridge, and pensioners from the Indian army. There were former ladies of the Sweep, two Mayo chaps off a building job on wet time, a deported American, a couple of African medical students, a man that sold pigs the day before yesterday, a well-known builder and a publican equally well known in his own shop, myself and Packy from Scariff. There were some English people over for a holiday in Peter's and a man who used to stop greyhounds for a living.

Now it is not to be thought that we were not thinking of those less fortunate than ourselves that were stuck out in it. Nor is it to be implied that we thought lightly of the sufferings of any worker in bad weather, from the docker trying to graft over the freezing waters to the man chasing a ewe up the sides of Tóin le Gaoith[450] in the County Wicklow. But it was the way we were looking out the window and counting our blessings, for ourselves.

And, as is the case in times of general dislocation, there was, as I said, the height of good humour, like what Raftery described at Galway Races:

> 'Bhí sluagh mor daoine ann,
> From every airt and part,
> Siad deas macánta, croidhiúl ann,
> And singing with good heart,
> Ag rinnce is ag órdú dighe,
> Ag gabháil an 'Cruiscin Lán',
> The day we spent in Paul's house,
> Maidin a sneachta báin.'[451]

That's not what Raftery wrote, but it's as well as I can remember, and go and write one of your own if you think you can do better.

I heard it told there, as the first of a series of lectures that should be entitled 'We'll neither work nor want' the story of a man that had a slight accident in a very great industrial concern. Your man has this accident and is laid off for a week or so and then he comes back to be examined by the company doctor.

'But there's only one little thing,' said the doctor, 'just a teeny-weeny bit of bone. A splinter, and no more only it's aimed straight at your heart. We'll have it out in no time.'

'You will,' says your man, 'in my eye.'

'Ridiculous,' says the doctor, 'it'll only be a very slight operation, a matter of a couple of days in bed to extract this bit of bone – but,' and he calls for two minutes' silence, as these fellows will when they're out to put someone through it, 'if you leave this little bit of bone in you, it's going straight for your heart like a torpedo.'

'That little bit of bone,' says your gills, 'I make me own arrangements about, and you're not operating on me.'

The doctor sighed, and the next week your man was out on full pension, which they gave him cheerfully enough as he wouldn't live more than a week or two to draw it with that little bit of bone in him.

The week he got the pension he went into hospital and had the bone taken out, and last week threw snowballs at the passers-by as he waited to draw the one-thousand-and-eighty-sixth weekly instalment of his pension.

Something like the boneman's stroke would suit me down to the ground and keep me in out of the elements these cold days.

I was reared a pet, God love me.

The Irish Press, 25 February 1956

104
POLAND IS THE PLACE
FOR FUR COATS

I am putting this at the top of the article, for a riddle to literary punters for the Spring Double: 'It was the best of times, it was the worst of times, you could only describe them as quare times.' Now, pick the bones out of that.

Thanks be to God, we are back to our own kind of weather. There was a sign of rain on the sky this morning and maybe we will have it before the day is out, but what call have we to be complaining? Didn't six hundred die in the continent of Europe and a few score in England?

TWO FUR COATS
I know a Polish girl is married to a Dublin man and she told me that in her childhood, which is not long before the last war, a person facing the winter in Poland had to have a couple of fur coats.

'I suppose,' said I, 'they were dead cheap.'

'They were not,' said she, 'but about fifty pounds in your money.'

'Well, what happened if you didn't have fifty pounds?'

'You died of the cold, and you weren't troubled by the cold thereafter.'

'I see,' says I, 'a neat arrangement for them that had fur coats.'

'Yes,' says she, 'we had great winter sports.'

'If you'd have happened to have been born a bear,' says I, 'you were in – on the first count.'

This lady told me that when she saw Ireland on her geography book, it looked so small that she thought everyone aboard went around carrying an umbrella any time they walked round the island.

DECENT LADY

'Of course,' she said, 'I know now that you are quite civilised.'

'That's shockin' decent of you,' I replied, with the true courtesy of the Gael.

I was thinking along these remarks, waiting on a bus at Westland Row last Saturday after the Scotland–Ireland match.

There were Northern cars, with their different tax badges and their differing number plates, and ruddy, innocent young Irish faces stuck out of the windows shouting 'Up Ireland.'

Podgy Dubliners like myself waved Sinn Féin umbrellas and like true rebels croaked, 'You too.'

It was not that we were any more lacking in enthusiasm than our Ulster brothers for the 'combination of chemical elements called Ireland', but we were thinking of the rent, the ESB, the CIE and anyway, we live here all the time.

For all that, and secretly, it would be a mean heart never rejoiced by the greetings of these Ulster boys, for all I make jokes and sneers at the North now and again.

Sure, when all is said and done, don't I let them make jokes about me?

Doesn't the whole of Ireland do it about the jackeens?

I was thinking, too, that there must be one unit of thirty-two counties, because I certainly could not imagine these voices raised in shouts of 'Come on Great Britain' or 'Up the United Kingdom' or 'Lurry them up, the Commonwealth.'

SONGFEST

I thought back to another international match when I spent the night in Trinity, singing all manner of rebel songs, and to a Twelfth of July I spent at a party on an island in the River Seine, singing Orange songs while the Paris river firemen played the searchlights of their boats on us under the impression that our was a rather premature celebration of the Quatorze Juillet.

Everyone only the poor Irish is allowed to have a difference between North and South.

Damn it, we can't open our mouths here but the stranger has it made into the basis for a thesis on racial relations.

In France the miner from Pas-de-Calais and the Norman farmer, even, refer to their countrymen of the south as '*les nègres*' and all combine to heap the foulest abuse on Paris and its people. In Italy the Milanese and the Calabrian speak what are nearly two different languages and in England itself, the Geordie from Newcastle-on-Tyne speaks a dialect incomprehensible to the Cockney, who incidentally despises him as a 'Suede-basher'.

But nobody set up a Boundary Commission to separate Cannes from Caen, nor has it been suggested that there should be frontier posts from the Severn to the Wash with a border in Birmingham cutting the Bull Ring in half, with the Mitre one side and the Rose and Crown the other.

And if we can't do anything more about it, the least we can do is knock Nelson off his perch.[452]

The Irish Press, 3 March 1956

105

UP AND DOWN SPION KOP

'When I was young, I used to be,
As fine a man as e'er you'd see,
And the Prince of Wales, he says to me,
"Come join the British army."

'Toora loora loora loo,
They're looking for monkeys in the zoo,
And if I had a face like you,
I'd join the British army.

'Sarah Curley baked the cake,
'Twas all for poor Kate Condon's sake,
I threw myself into the lake,
Pretending I was barmy.

'Toora loora loora loo,
'Twas the only thing that I could do,
To work me ticket home to you,
And leave the British army.'

On Wednesdays, and I a child, there were great gatherings of British army pensioners and pensionesses up on the corner of the North Circular in Jimmy the Sports.[453]

When the singing got well under way, there'd be old fellows climbing up and down Spion Kop[454] till further orders, and other men getting fished out of the Battle of Jutland,[455] and while one old fellow would be telling of how the Munsters kicked the football across the German lines at the Battle of the Somme,[456] there'd be a keening of chorused mourners crying from their black shawls over poor Jemser or poor Mickser that was lost at the Dardanelles.[457]

Jimmy the Sports Bar did not at all relish the British army or anything to do with it, but a publican is a kind above politics.

My family would be shocked out of their boots at any of us listening to such 'loyalist' carrying-on, but I ... oh, woe to me in the times of republican wrath ... I lusted after false gods, and snaked in among the widows and orphans, and sat at the feet of the veterans to sell my country for a glass of Indian ale and a packet of biscuits, and as Jembo Joyce would say, 'putting up me two hands to thank heaven that I had a country to sell'.

APPEARED LIKE PORTER

Indian ale is a thing like the Ballybough tram – gone out. It was sold out of a barrel in pubs and grocers' shops as well, because it was a TT drink.

Us children were ardent TTs because we thought it had something to do with Stanley Woods[458] and the Isle of Man races, and with Doctor Pat O'Callaghan, Colonel Fitzmaurice, R.N. Tisdall, John Joe Sheehy, Larry Cervi and Bertie Donnelly.

This Indian ale was like porter in appearance, and it might happen at these pension days in Jimmy the Sports' that glasses would get mixed up and you wouldn't know what you were getting, sitting down there on the floor out of sight and snapping biscuits from one another.

Besides, the older ladies believed in a sup of porter for children of pre-Confirmation age[459] and even said, 'Let them have a taste of it now, and they'll never bother with it when they're grown up.'

Sometimes, *mo bhron*,[460] these theories have little or no scientific basis.

A DANGEROUS CLAN

When the Imperial bounty of a grateful monarch had gone a good way in the process of liquidation, one lady was sure to stand up and sing a song about her late husband who was a machine-gunner and met some quicker machine-gunner on the cousin's side.

My father always called it that, and said the dead or wounded of the Great War were an example to people not to be getting mixed up in family quarrels. And the Guelphs, Saxe-Gotha, Windsors,[461] or whatever they call themselves, he regarded as the most dangerous clan in the whole of the world.

FROM SHOPS AROUND

Besides, I knew the lady, and she was kind to all children, her own and any other ones, and she had a good voice, which is a thing I admire in a citizen, being no mean performer on the gargle trap myself.

Then Chuckles would stand up to give a bar. Chuckles, as far as I know, had not taken part in the European disturbances of 1914–18, nor had he played anything more than the part of a social worker in the wars of 1919–23 round NCR.

In time of siege he fed the civilian population with hams and sides of beef augmented by flour and canned foods, which he collected from the shops around. He described his collecting as 'armed begging' and only once did he meet with anything like a refusal.

At a big branch of an English combine the manager's wife came down to say that her husband was phoning up head office in Liverpool to see what he could spare, that it was clearly contrary to the laws of God and man that people should benefit by war to the extent of eating things like ham that they never tasted in peace.

'I hope,' said Chuckles, with a pious glance at his Colt 45, 'your husband is in a state of grace.'

'Oh,' said the manager's wife when she saw the skit, 'I didn't know you were a millingterry man. That's different. Will you give a receipt, sir, with your name and rank?'

'Right,' said Chuckles, calling up his supporters.

When they'd filled the handcart he gave his official receipt signed, *Me, Chuckles, O/C Looters*, saluted and went off.

P.S. Don't miss next week's gripping instalment of *My Struggle*, 'How I saw my father killed at the Dardanelles.'

The Irish Press, 10 March 1956

106
SHAKE HANDS WITH AN ALSATIAN

I wish you all a happy St Patrick's Day and that you may not go entirely short of provisions is the sincere wish of me and mine to you and yours. (You can be fairly certain that I won't – not if I have to shake paws with half the Alsatians in the country.)

Talking about Alsatians – you can knock off those brackets '( )' – I don't know what I put them up there for, only to be literary – they are not my favourite animal. I was related to an Alsatian by marriage. Wolf was his name, and he barked his head off any time I put my head in my first wife's family's door.

They always reassured me that he meant well, and that his bark was worse than his bite, but that could easy mean that his bite could be bad enough.

In any event, if he got away with a good lump of me, it would not be much good running after him to get it back. He was at least a 30.50 dog.

IN LATTING CLASS

I like little dogs like Pomeramans and Petingeeses. Nobody could imagine one of them at one end of a strap and a policeman at the other, but my favourite animal is Anna Kelly's famous cat, Groucho.

He has the longest whiskers in Catland, and I think should be more properly called Salvador Dalí,[462] after the painter, who maintains that his extra-long whiskers are the wireless aerials of his soul.

I'm not sure that my favourite animal taken one way or another is not Mr M. Cash's Umindme b.g. by Umidhhan, which did me a great oblige-ment at Two-Mile-House Point to Point on Tuesday, but anyway, poor old Wolf, my Alsatian-in-law is now croaked and *demortuis nil nisi bom bom*, as they used teach us in the Latting class in my old school.

The happiest animal I have seen is Spanish Battleship, and I must say that he even seemed to put his connections into good humour, but when all is said and done.

My grandmother had an enormous cat that went by the name of Beeshams. I can only describe it by saying that his father's name was Lynchehaun, and it looked every inch a son of its father.

SNIFFED THE SNUFF

It was a rather outstanding animal, by reason of the fact that it seemed to enjoy white snuff. Be damn but, that's a thing you don't often meet with in a cat, but it was the truth about Beeshams.

My granny had it rest upon her bosom, with his two front paws round her neck and his fat old head wagging from side to side with every intona-tion of her voice, as if he knew what she was saying.

His two eyes fixed on hers, as if she was Sir Anthony Eden[463] and he was a licensed grocer from Bangor, Co. Down, hoping to be mentioned in the New Year's Honours List.

White snuff fell generously about her person but Beeshams did not mind. He even sniffed the snuff, and wrinkled his chops as if he liked it.

WHAT'S A BRUTEEN?

'Me poor *lanna walla*,' my granny would say, under the impression that she was speaking to the beast in the Irish language.

Her ideas of that tongue were of the sketchiest, but her heart was good, and she usually addressed Beeshams in Irish for a go-off as she maintained that only he understood her dialect.

'Me poor *lanna walla*,' she'd croon, and the old cat would wag his head slowly, 'sure it's the queer *drisheen* I'd be after begrudging you,' upon which she would produce a piece of Herr Youkstetter's good old Irish black pudding, and this happened regularly, though Beeshams was restricted to Sundays and Patrick's Day in Lent.

'Beeshams bucked,' she would moan, 'I might as well be boss of Erin if it wasn't for you, me good old *bruteen*.'

'What's a *bruteen*?' I asked her.

'A *bruteen* is a little cat.'

'It's no such thing,' said I, being in Fifth Class and knowing all about Algebair and *Teageasc Críostaí agus an Sheeva Mor an Atlantaigh Thuaidh agus an Tuiseal Geineamhnach Uimhir Iolraidh*.

'You're an impudent cur to downface your own granny.'

'A little cat is *cat beag*.'

'You caught no bug in this house, barring you brought it in with you,' and she spoke into Beeshams's old face, 'oh *culla culla*, no luck'. Then she turned to me and said, 'I suppose you have the brass imperence to tell me that "no luck" does not mean "no mice".' And Beeshams would give a deep purr and she'd answer, 'Ah-ha, *colleen bawn*.'

'And if it goes to that, it should be *buachaill ban*, Beeshams is a he-cat,' I said.

'You mind your own business, me little man cut short,' she said. 'Beeshams is not asking you what he is,' and she directed her gaze into the cat's face, 'Ah, bah, *carrageen*?'

The Irish Press, 17 March 1956

107
MY FATHER DIED IN WAR

An indignant reader from South Armagh wishes to know when I'm going to give, as promised, my eyewitness account of my father's death in action at the Dardanelles.

As I was saying a week or two ago, I was a great attender at the celebrations of British army pensioners and pensionesses on Wednesday on our corner of the North Circular Road.

So this day they are all talking about a film that's on in the Old Royal.[464]

It was called *Tell England* when it was made, but they thought it more tactful to call it *Gallipoli* when it was shown here.

'Iz a mazziv pit-chewer,' said the Granny Carmody in Grenville Street language. 'Yes zee all the poo-war japs and the' coming offa the Brizidge battle chips and been mone dow-in in the wawdher.'

'What Japs, granny?' I whispered up at her. 'Who were they up for in the war?'

'All the japs, the japs in the Dubal-ins – in the View-shalleers. Poor Bogo Brennan, hees ozziver was shot offa hees horse. A vunny plaze to brin a horse, but the old quality couldn't be sebaraze-ed from their beastises. The'd even try and brin them to bed widhem. Bogo said he lived three days on jockalate. Some said eh waz az much az ever he got at home, but all the japs waz livin on jockalate, at the Dardanelles.'

VIRTUOUS COMPANY

Us chisellers on the floor discussed the matter and agreed that the Dardanelles would not be a bad place to be if you got chocolate all the time as a principal article of diet, but we gathered from the conversation of the men that there were people living there called the terrible Turks, and what they did with you if they got their hands on you was a matter to be whispered.

(I see by the same token that since they're in military alliance with Great Britain their manners have improved five hundred per cent. It just shows you the improving effect of virtuous company.)

Tell England alias *Gallipoli* was a silent picture, technically speaking.

A great deal of its attraction lay in rumour, assiduously circulated no doubt by the publicity men, then as ever on.

'Yes, you'll see the boys won't let them away with that,' said my father. 'There will be a land-mine exploded down there that'll give them "Tell England, and tell any other place,"' and he hurried out with his money, Granny Carmody and all, though she had seen nothing of the screen since the lantern slides of Parnell's funeral.

The picture got off to a good start, with the fellow in the orchestral stalls knocking hell out of his drum during the bombardment of the shore batteries.

The next thing we saw was what we were waiting for – the soldiers charging down the gangplanks of the landing craft.

From every part of the gods the screeches went up, 'Oh, there's our Mickser.' Other old ones screeched, 'Oh, take me out, I can't stick it, there's me husband in the water.'

Granny Carmody was not be bested, and let a roar out of her that you'd hear in Gallipoli: 'Oh, me own sweet onion, there he is, me poor first husband's brother.'

As the face that appeared close up that moment was that of a bearded Indian, I was very much impressed by the Granny's relations.

'Oh, there's me da,' I let a roar for the good reason that you might as well be out of the world as out of the fashion.

'Ah, God help the poor child,' some old one screamed from behind, 'hee's gone in a wakeness.' I wasn't, until she put the idea in my head, and then I did, and moaned, 'Da, da, da.'

The old one behind called for a nurse who was in attendance, and I was brought to the manager's office and given tea and cake, while I told how I'd seen my daddy killed by one of them Turks. To tell the truth, I thought the Turks was a family, and that Turk was their name like Behan was mine.

'Don't mind the dirty little liar. Hee's faddher was in the IRAh,' said the Granny Carmody. The next thing there was a loud crash from outside and windows smashed and plaster fell off the wall. 'That drum player again,' said the Granny, 'he should be more careful.'

The Irish Press, 24 March 1956

108

THAT WEEK OF RENOWN

'Who fears to speak of Easter Week,
That week of famed renown,
When the boys in green went out to fight
The forces of the Crown?'

Twenty-six Nelson Street is as well entitled to a bronze plaque as more public buildings.

Presided over and directed by the late P.J. Bourke, it was a dressing station, a canteen and an intelligence centre for the whole First Battalion area during the Rising.

Lorcan Bourke is now a grandfather, but a very young one.

In 1916, however, he was a chubby boy of eleven, running through shot and shell, in and under the legs of the enemy anywhere he was sent and closely followed by his panting, pudgy younger brother Rick and Jimmy Kearney, who now presides over a few million telephone wires below in Crown Alley.

SONS OF THE SEA

These three little heroes were carrying a message for a high republican officer.

They came to the corner of Dorset Street, where the Tommies had the people held up and were searching them, and Lorcan, to the amazement of his two confederates, sang up a verse of 'Sons of the Sea, all British boys, sailing the ocean, where our flag still flies, they may build their ships by night, build their ships by day, but you can't beat the boys of the bulldog breed, who made old England's name ...'

The Tommies grinned to each other, patted Master Lorcan on the head and let him pass, followed by Rick and Jimmy, who looked at him reproachfully, and said, 'What are you singing that oul' British song for?'

Lorcan grinned, in his turn, when they were well past the Tommies, and replied, 'Stragedy, that's what that it, stragedy.'

Later on, it might have been called Lorcan Bourke enterprise.

THROUGH SHOT AND SHELL

> *'Then came ten thousand khaki coats,*
> *Our rebel boys to kill,*
> *Before they reached O'Connell Street,*
> *Of fight they got their fill.'*

There was this citizeness and her husband was in the GPO. So she goes down looking for him on the Wednesday, and weaving her way through shot and shell, till by a miracle, carrying a little baby, she is standing amid the ruins, and fire, and flame, shouting up at the windows and waiting for an answer.

'Eh, mister, is my Mick in there with yous?'

'Go way, go way,' screams the amazed Volunteer, 'you'll be killed.'

'Tell him to come to the window, anyway,' she says, and insists.

A shell lands on Lairds the chemists beside her and she spits out the dust and shouts up, 'I only wanted to know if he's going to work this morning.'

> *'They shot our leaders in a jail,*
> *Without a trial they say,*
> *They murdered women and children, too,*
> *Who in their cellars lay,*
> *They dug their grave with gun and spade,*
> *To hide them from our view,*
> *Because they could neither kill nor catch,*
> *The rebels so bold and true.'*

Outside the Atlas Furniture store in Henry Street a man played a piano for a crowd of revellers who kept him well supplied with drink.

RAGTIME COWBOY JOE

All during the week over the noises and heat of the battle, he kept it up.

The old Volunteer who told me the story had fought in that area with The O'Rahilly.[465]

He remarked, 'I very nearly died for Ireland to the inspiring strains of "Ragtime Cowboy Joe".'[466]

When the surrender was beginning and the republicans were making their way up to the Rotunda, your man had begun his recital for the day.

He stopped as the defeated Volunteers went past him to captivity. 'Ah, boys, are you bet?' he asked.

They nodded and went on and he struck up 'A Nation Once Again' as they went up to the street to the surrender.

> *'And we will love old Ireland,*
> *And shall while life remains,*
> *And we shall say, God speed the day,*
> *The rebels will rise again.*
> *Though Irish slaves and English knaves,*
> *May try us to deceive,*
> *Remember those who died for us,*
> *And Pearse and Connolly's grave.'*

The Irish Press, 14 April 1956

109

A WEEKEND IN THE FOREIGN LEGION

I walked from Italy to France in three minutes on a hot day in 1949. The Italian customs men showed no great wish to detain me and after bored glances at my papers the Frenchman on the other side waved me on.

He was at that time, he said, interested in people bringing in gold, and it seemed clear to him that I did not have any.

The border just there, at a little place called Valenciennes, some miles from Grenoble, is in a triangle between France, Italy and Switzerland, and like our own little border in Ireland, people think little of crossing into some area or another for a drink or a package of cigarettes.

FINE CITY

Nobody minded that, said this douanier, but they were very interested in anyone carrying gold around the place. I said that if I met anyone with any gold, I'd tell them. Having thanked me, and given me an American cigarette, he waved farewell and I trudged on towards Grenoble.

This is a fine city, with Alps all round it the same as you would see on a postcard, and a cable railway that runs from one alp to another. It's a little cab holding about a dozen people, and while we were being carried on the cable twelve hundred feet over the River Isère I took my mind off my revolving stomach by reading a notice on the door which said, in four languages: *In case of emergency push bar open.*

I had a glass or two of pastis when I got out, and went on in the general direction of these islands, north-west along the Lyon road.

MORE DRINKS

The pastis is the descendent of the old absinthe, reduced to forty-eight per cent pure alcohol. But it is still to me a soothing and reviving drink.

I got into Lyon and decided to do a skipper there for the night, to sleep under the southern moon on the banks of the Rhône.

I had by this time drunk several other pastis and had also acquired three used copies of the local journal (twelve pages and very thick) for the purpose of wrapping myself up.

Everyone should do a skipper a few times in his early youth. It will teach him for the rest of his life to appreciate his bed, even when he's dying in it. But nobody can sleep out after 3.30 am and no one should sleep out at all two nights in succession.

I had not the price of a bed when I lay down, and I had not the price of a bed when I woke up, and I was not likely to have the price of a bed by bedtime. There was only one thing for it – I must join the Legion.

It was Friday. In France any *clochard* on the toby and lucky enough to be in Metz, Paris, or Lyon joins the Legion for the weekend.

You don't chance it in Marseille because down there it's too near the boss, so to speak. You're liable to finish up in Sidi Bel Abbès instead of getting back on the road after your weekend visit.

IN TIME FOR DINNER

The *bureau d'engagement*, the recruiting office, shuts at 6.50 on Friday evening. To get the maximum benefit from your service with the French army you join up at 6.30 – well, 6.35 in case there's some conscientious recruiting officer doing a bit of overtime.

By then he has put his little stamps and wafers and seals and oaths of allegiance safely away for the weekend.

So you go in and join up just in time for dinner, and before he comes back and opens his office again on Monday morning you scarper and are safely on the road again.

I got up off the riverbank, folded my newspapers, and made my way to the markets where the first pubs are open.

In the course of my wanderings that day in the city of Lyon, I encountered an English lady who with her husband was enquiring the way to the silk-weaving factories. I was able to direct her because I'd seen hundreds of workers on overcrowded single-storey trams making their way there in the morning. To her it seemed as if I must know the place inside out. 'Well, I've been here since I was six years old, madam.'

'RIDICULOUS!'

'Of course, you speak French like a native.'

'Like a native of Ballaghaderreen, ma'am.'

'*Comment*, I beg your pardon?'

'The divil a word of it do I speak, ma'am. Not one word.'

'But that is ridiculous. Surely you must have gone to school here?'

'I never went to school much anywhere, ma'am,' which was true enough.

'But surely you must have picked it up, living in the place?'

'I couldn't pick it, ma'am, for I never heard a word of it. I'm stone deaf.'

'Well, if you're stone deaf, how on earth can you hear what I'm saying?'

'Because I lip-read, ma'am.'

'But why can't you lip-read French in the same way?'

'Because, ma'am, I went deaf in Ireland in an explosion and I'd already heard sounds of English. I've never heard the sounds of French, and therefore how can I lip-read it when I don't know what it sounds like?'

LOCAL 'ROWTON'

Her husband had joined us by this time and looked from one to the other of us in a daze. She nodded slowly and gulped, and he reached in his pocket, and handed me some change, including two hundred-franc notes.

They turned and smiled and she came back and bawled in my face, 'GOODBYE,' and he came back and smiled as well as he could and roared, 'Erin go bragh hagh hagh! What?'

I shouted 'TAGH-TAGH!' and waved my money in the air as they went down the street.

With all this cash I was tempted to rent a bed for the night in the Palais du Peuple, which is what they call the Rowton over there, but I was saved from temptation by various factors during the day, and 6.35 to the dot found me walking up the two sides of the avenue Garibaldi to the Casernes de la Part-Dieu (the barracks of God's borough), which is where Beau Behan was to join up.

I forgot anyway. I forgot everything except a young conscript with a Sten gun and a bootlace round his shoulder, when I followed him to the billet, indicated by the orange and green grenade of the Légion étrangère and the motto *'Legio Patria Nostra'*.

When I woke up I opened my eyes, and felt my head, and moaned 'Dear me' in some language.

Two black eyes gazed into mine, and a voice asked: 'You OK buddy? You ready for the doctor?'

'Yes, indeed,' said I, making a weak search for a flask of a substance known as Rhum Negrita. 'I've got the doctor here. Though maybe an undertaker would save time.' I sighed, and drew the cork. I had a good slug of the old Rh. Neg. and passed the bottle to him. 'Here, you have a go. It's good for what ails you.'

'NOT NOW'

He shook his head and said, politely: 'Not now, later, after the doctor. He's examining us for the Foreign Legion.'

'What? What Legion? I thought there was no enlistment on Saturdays.' The parcel of scabs, I thought bitterly.

'You are impatient to join, I know, but you can't be enlisted till Monday, really. But to have us all ready, the doctor examines us today, Saturday. But not till Monday can you join up, I'm sorry.'

'Forget it,' said I, and took another slug of Rh. and went off with him to the doctor's queue, and stood proudly there till my turn came and I went in, and sprang to attention in front of the doctor like I learned in Feltham Boys' Prison, Middlesex, a movement only spoiled by the Rh. splashing round in the bottle when I removed my shirt, which caused the doctor to squeeze my stomach very carefully and gaze at me very earnestly.

'You are from Ireland?'

I nodded and slapped my feet together again. 'Yes, doctor.'

TESTING THE LEGS

'But you speak English?'

'Yes, doctor.'

'You 'ave any eelness, any weakness?'

'I suffer from weakness of character, doctor.'

He nodded understandingly and smiled reassuringly. 'I know, but ees not serious. I notice your weak knees when you come in the surgery. The Légion will make them straighter.'

He was dead right. For the first ten kilometres out of Lyon on Monday morning, Ronnie Delaney wouldn't have caught me.

The Illustrated Chronicle, 17 February 1957

NOTES

Translations from the Irish by Ceithleann Ní Dhuibhir Ní Dhúlacháin

1 Behan published his short story 'After the Wake' in the Paris-based magazine *Points*, edited by Sindbad Vail, in the December 1950 issue. The magazine was reviewed in *The Hudson Review*, a literary magazine based in New York in the summer of 1951, by Thomas Barbour. Barbour in fact used the word 'syntactical' to describe another writer's work, and only 'sensuous' to describe Behan, but Behan alters the quotation to suit his comic needs.

2 If you worked as a painter or decorator, under labour laws in Ireland you were entitled to be paid a benefit for any periods in which you were supposed to be working, but could not work because of rain or bad weather. This was known as 'wet time'.

3 Irish counties often have nicknames, such as 'the Rebel County' (Cork) or 'the Wee County' (Louth). Wicklow is known as 'the Garden of Ireland'.

4 Landlord and patron of the poet Antoine Ó Raifteirí (Anthony Raftery), 1779–1835. Raftery was reputedly banished by Taaffe after he had accidentally maimed Taaffe's best horse.

5 'so far so good'.

6 The rivers Avonmore and Avonbeg meet just north of Avoca, and this is known as the 'Meeting of the Waters', made famous by Thomas Moore in his melody of the same name.

7 The Irish Transvaal Brigade was raised by republican leader John McBride, who was later executed for his role in the Easter Rising of 1916. The brigade

consisted mainly of Irish workers in South Africa who joined the Boers in their fight against the British in the Second Boer War of 1899–1902, and was strengthened by volunteers who travelled from Ireland and America in sympathy with the Boer cause.

8 Samuel Johnson (1709–84), English writer, who is renowned to have said, 'No man will be a sailor who has contrivance enough to get himself into a jail; for being in a ship is being in a jail, with the chance of being drowned,' and also to have added, 'A man in a jail has more room, better food and commonly better company.' As Behan had recently spent a great deal of time in jail, and some at sea, he had reason to remember this observation.

9 George Orwell's first book, published in 1933, which no doubt resonated with Behan as he had spent some time between 1948 and 1951 living in poverty in Paris. Behan is likely to have owned the 1940 Penguin paperback of Orwell's book.

10 Behan was imprisoned in Hollesley Bay, a borstal institution in Suffolk in 1940–1, and the River Orwell is about ten miles away.

11 Do you understand that? / Why wouldn't I, sure didn't I compose it? / Well done, begor, it's worth a drink as it's a long time since I spoke to a poet.'

12 The 1798 Rebellion, organized by the United Irishmen, was a major uprising against British rule and initially had considerable success in County Wexford until the rebel forces were defeated at the Battle of Vinegar Hill.

13 A 'Jackeen' is a gently derogatory word for a Dubliner used by people from outside Dublin.

14 A mainly Protestant and loyalist area of Belfast, adjacent to the railway station at Great Victoria Street, which was then the terminus for the train from Dublin.

15 Dublin Metropolitan Police, the police force in Dublin from 1836 to 1925, when it was absorbed into the newly created An Garda Síochána, the national Irish police force.

16 Local Security Force, the original name for the local volunteer force raised to defend Ireland from invasion in the aftermath of the fall of France in May 1940, under police command, which from 1941 onwards became the LDF, Local Defence Force, under army command.

17 'See the lights of the docks across a river from us, sharp, bright, cold. / Listen, call of the ships, in loneliness far from us, at the mouth of the harbour / The darkness of night is deep in the silence of the mountains, / May God and Mary bless you, / Waterford, the queen of the Decies.'

18 The Abbey Theatre was destroyed by fire on 18 July 1951 after a performance of Seán O'Casey's *The Plough and the Stars*.

19 A village in Wicklow situated on a land spit created by the flooding of the valley in the 1930s to create the Poulaphouca reservoir that serves Dublin city.

20 A members' club, mainly associated with the wealthy and aristocratic, and based between 1782 and 1977 in Kildare Street, Dublin.

21 Founded in 1893 by Douglas Hyde, a key figure in the Irish cultural revival, the Gaelic League sought to revive and promote the Irish language.

22 A popular radio programme on Raidió Éireann throughout the 1940s and 1950s, to which Behan contributed in the early 1950s. The programme was developed and presented by the writer Bryan MacMahon, who collected songs from around Ireland.

23 Playwright, novelist and story writer (1909–98) best known for the short-story collection *The Lion Tamer* (1942), and his translation of the Irish-language classic memoir, *Peig*.

24 Poet and playwright (1913–85), famous also as an author and collector of songs.

25 Killorglin is a small town in County Kerry that hosts an annual festival, the Puck Fair, at which a goat is crowned 'King'.

26 'What shall we do now without timber?', 'Loch Léinn' and 'Dear soldier of my heart, will you marry me?'

27 'Arise, o water, wash the land, / Poverty is drowned, in your depths, / Waves in power, constrained in cooperation, / Strength of Ireland in your race, o river.'

28 The correct words are 'I am a bold undaunted youth,' but Behan transcribes this phrase to mimic a Dubliner's pronunciation.

29 The steamboat which ran a regular service between Galway and the Aran Islands between 1912 and 1958, owned by the Galway Bay Steamboat Company, and bought originally with support from the Congested Districts Board.

30 'They're saying that something is wrong with her. Engine trouble, I think.'

31 Meaning 'The Twisting of the Rope', a traditional Irish love song from which Douglas Hyde drew inspiration for his one-act play of the same title and which Behan originally intended to make ironic reference to in his play *The Quare Fellow*, about a hanging, which was first entitled *Casadh an tSugáin Eile* (*The Twisting of Another Rope*).

32 Behan is describing a westward walk on the main island of the Aran islands, Inis Mór, from Kilmurvey out to the western tip at Bungowla.

33 A colloquial term for someone who disposes of dead animals, especially horses. In Ireland it is also an offensive term for the Traveller community.

34 Dublin slang for girlfriend, derived from the Irish *maith*, meaning good.

35 'God bless the work.'

36 'Do you know what sort of songs the English have here?'

37 'Did you do much work this morning?'

38 Townland in the western part of Inis Mór.

39 Inis Meáin.

40 Stage name of French actress and singer Jeanne Florentine Bourgeois, who debuted in 1885 and died, after a long career in entertainment, in 1956. Her legs were reputedly insured for 500,000 francs in 1919.

41 The word derives from the name for itinerant tinsmiths, who would travel from place to place to make small repairs for a living. It became associated with travelling peoples generally, and was used, often in derogatory ways, to refer to them in Ireland and elsewhere.

42 'God bless you' said I to Siobhán and Bartle, sitting either side of the fire, 'There is a tinker here, he's looking for work, and he doesn't speak a word of Irish.' 'Well, thank you, Brendan.'

43 'What do those letters mean, John,' asked the doctor. 'Well, read away, "Doctor",' said John.

44 Rawhide shoes traditionally worn on the Aran Islands.

45 Known as the wormhole, a naturally created rectangular-shaped hole at the base of the cliffs on Inis Mór.

46 A traditional Irish love song, addressed to Thaighg (Tadhg, or Tim).

47 Slang term for a lively party, particularly linked to sailors.

48 Scholarship.

49 Irish Republican Brotherhood, also known as the Fenian Brotherhood, was a secret revolutionary organization dedicated to rebellion in Ireland.

50 Slang for thrashing or whipping.

51 The chief officer of a Masonic or Orange Lodge, who presides over meetings.

52 A fictitious entertainer, although based on real examples of blackface performers who were popular in Ireland, Britain and the US in the early twentieth century.

53 Famous Irish republican rebel (1842–1928).

54 A fraternal organization of Irish Catholics, mainly based in America, established in 1836.

55 An area just south of the American Ambassador's residence in the Phoenix Park, Dublin, which was used in the eighteenth century for drill practice by garrison troops and became known as the Fifteen Acres. The reference to Merville and Bendigo has not been identified.

56 The official authority for lighthouses in England and Wales.

57 'Good on them, the Leinstermen / Who ignited the flame ...'

58 A blackface minstrel song written by Stephen Foster in 1860.

59 Behan is parodying the speech patterns used by blackface minstrel performers to figure the speech of African Americans.

60 'the golden way of moderation'.

61 A sentimental song of longing for the town of Warrenpoint in County Down.

62 Manannán Mac Lir was the Celtic sea-god of the otherworld.

63 *Royal Iris* was famous as the ferry that crossed the Mersey in Liverpool. Larssen has not been found in ship registers of the period.

64 The original name for Dublin International Airport.

65 Cockney rhyming slang for 'mate', or friend – 'china plate = mate'.

66 The Saltee islands are off the coast of South Wexford.

67 Roman Catholics.

68 A temperance movement established in Leeds in 1847 and dedicated to teaching children the virtues of sobriety.

69 During the Second World War the *Al Rawdah* was used as a prison ship for interning Irish republican prisoners. It was moored off Killyleagh in Strangford Lough.

70 Famous Irish ballad written by Irish nationalist Thomas Davis.

71 Moore Street in Dublin is famous for its fruit-sellers.

72 The London, Midland and Scottish Railway company, which owned the Northern Counties Committee railway in Northern Ireland and operated services from Belfast to the north and west of the city.

73 Joseph Tomelty was an Irish novelist, actor and playwright (1911–95). His latest novel would have been *The Apprentice* (1953).

74 Beasts, or cattle.

75 Belfast-born poet and a notable left-wing activist (1907–87).

76 Behan is gently mocking the reputation of Baggot Street and Pembroke Road in Dublin as literary haunts. They are associated particularly with the poet Patrick Kavanagh.

77 William Carleton, Irish novelist and story-writer (1794–1869).

78 Northern Irish playwright, novelist and biographer (1883–1971), who was once the manager of the Abbey Theatre but left the post after the 1916 Rising and was henceforth hostile to the Irish Republic. He became chiefly known for his biographies of Carson, Craigavon, Oscar Wilde and George Bernard Shaw.

79 James Joyce (1882–1941), Irish writer and renowned author of *Dubliners* (1914), *A Portrait of the Artist as a Young Man* (1916), *Ulysses* (1922) and *Finnegans Wake* (1939).

80 Northern Irish novelist (1875–1947), known particularly for his stories of boyhood.

81 John Millington Synge (1871–1909), Irish writer most famous for his play *The Playboy of the Western World* (1907) and his book *The Aran Islands* (1901).

82 William Butler Yeats (1865–1939), Irish poet and playwright and one of the most influential figures in Irish literature of the twentieth century.

83 W.H. Auden, English poet (1907–73).

84 English novelist (1879–1970) most famous for *A Room with a View* (1908) and *Howards End* (1910). Forster was a friend of Forrest Reid and also, as Behan mentions, wrote the introduction to the English translation of Muiris Ó Súileabháin's *Fiche Blian ag Fás* (Maurice O'Sullivan's *Twenty Years A-Growing*).

85 Irish writer, editor and intellectual (1900–91) who founded *The Bell* literary magazine and published Behan's first short story, 'I Become a Borstal Boy', in 1942. Ó Faoláin was one of the most influential figures in Irish literary culture of the twentieth century and a prolific author of short stories, biographies and novels.

86 Salvador de Madariaga, Spanish diplomat and writer (1886–1978) who campaigned for a united and peaceful Europe and wrote books about Columbus, Cortés and Spanish history.

87 Latin for 'Who Knows?' This was not the motto on the 'waterfront' or masthead of the newspaper, of course, which reads instead 'The Truth in the News'.

88 Irish poet (c. 1747–1805), chiefly known for his 1000-line comic poem *Cúirt an Mheán Oíche* (*The Midnight Court*).

89 The Irish language became a compulsory subject of national education at primary school level in the Irish Free State in 1922.

90 'Behan is translating from the opening lines of *Cúirt an Mheán Oíche*.

91 The 31st International Eucharistic Congress was held in Dublin in 1932 and included celebrations attended by a quarter of the Irish population. The Congress demonstrated the close relationship between the Catholic Church and the new Irish State.

92 Laurence O'Toole (1128–80) was Archbishop of Dublin at the time of the Norman Conquest of Ireland. As a result of his endeavours to negotiate peace and to avert the slaughter of civilians, he gained a reputation as the protector of the city.

93 North Circular Road, Dublin.

94 Le Mabillon is located in the Saint-Germain-des-Prés district of Paris, which Behan frequented in the late forties and early fifties.

95 Prominent sea-bathing places for Dubliners. The Bull Wall is in the north of Dublin Bay, and was completed in 1825 to form a sea wall to deepen and protect the entrance to Dublin Port. The Forty Foot is a rocky promontory at Sandycove in the south of Dublin Bay, and has long been a site popular for sea-swimming.

96 There have been floating swimming pools on the Seine since 1796, conventionally on barges, and popular during the summer.
97 Grangegorman in north Dublin was the site of the main psychiatric hospital in the city.
98 M.W.J. Fry (1863–1943), Professor of Natural Philosophy in Trinity College Dublin, who served as Junior Dean and Senior Proctor, in which roles he would have had responsibilities to maintain student discipline.
99 A luxury French car.
100 Nelson's Pillar was a granite column, 134 feet tall, which stood in the centre of Sackville Street (now O'Connell Street), the main thoroughfare street in Dublin's city centre. Built in 1809 to commemorate Admiral Nelson's victory and death at the Battle of Trafalgar, it dominated the city centre skyline until it was destroyed by an IRA bomb in 1966.
101 British athlete (1929–2018) famous for having broken the record for running a mile in under four minutes (3:59.4) in May 1954.
102 A suburb of Dublin associated with affluence.
103 A splinter group of the Irish Republican Brotherhood, or Fenians, who were responsible for the assassination of two prominent members of British rule in Ireland, Chief Secretary Frederick Cavendish and Permanent Under-Secretary Thomas Burke, in the infamous Phoenix Park murders in 1882.
104 The BBC radio station which, between 1946 and 1967, was associated particularly with arts programming. The other BBC radio stations were the Home Service, which was mainly news and talks, and the Light Programme, which was light entertainment and music.
105 Michael Dwyer was a republican rebel (1772–1825) from the Glen of Imaal in Wicklow, who led the United Irishmen in a guerrilla campaign against British forces in Wicklow and Wexford.
106 An Tóstal (the Gathering) was a festival of Irish culture inaugurated in 1953 to take place around Easter, which was intended to encourage tourists to visit Ireland.
107 A British slang term for girl or woman.
108 General Post Office, located on O'Connell Street, Dublin, and the focal point of the Irish Rebellion in Easter 1916.
109 *Dick Barton – Special Agent* was a BBC Light Programme radio show that ran from 1946 to 1951 and featured the eponymous hero solving crimes and saving Britain from terror and disaster. Three films were also made based on Dick Barton's adventures by the Hammer film company, between 1948 and 1950.
110 Prominent English writer and critic (1903–74) who edited *Horizon* magazine from 1939 to 1950. Connolly's mother was Anglo-Irish and he spent part

of his childhood in Clontarf Castle in Dublin. Behan became friendly with Connolly through mutual friends in Dublin.

111 Daniel O'Connell (1775–1847), known as the Liberator, was the Irish politician and lawyer who advocated for equal rights for Catholics, which he partly achieved through what became known as Catholic Emancipation in 1829, and who also advocated (though unsuccessfully) for the re-establishment of a separate parliament in Ireland.

112 'Water – yes?'

113 'Limerick thunder'.

114 A *feis* is an Irish festival of culture and music, which usually includes competitions for music, recitals, dancing, etc. Atha Cliath is the Irish name for Dublin.

115 American actor (1880–1961) who played the role of Pancho in films and the television series *The Cisco Kid*.

116 The names of cinemas in Dublin.

117 Seán O'Casey (1880–1964), Irish playwright, who came to prominence with his Dublin trilogy *The Shadow of a Gunman* (1923), *Juno and the Paycock* (1924) and *The Plough and the Stars* (1926).

118 Micheál Mac Liammóir (1899–1978), was born and raised in England as Alfred Willmore, before migrating to Ireland and re-inventing himself as an Irish actor and director. With his partner, Hilton Edwards, he established the Gate Theatre in Dublin, and was one of the most influential figures in Irish theatre in the twentieth century.

119 'Listen, my love. The waves will sing our wedding song to us tonight …'

120 'Water, Fionn, bring me a drink of water …'

121 'Look into my eyes, Gráinne.'

122 Another soldier.

123 'Par bleu, what matter if there is an odd mistake, here and there.'

124 Man and Superman, also the title of a George Bernard Shaw play (1903).

125 George Bernard Shaw (1856–1950), Irish playwright and critic who became renowned for his plays that conveyed serious political and social ideas.

126 English writer (1915–48) known in particular for his fictionalised autobiography *Maiden Voyage* (1943), from which this tailpiece is quoted.

127 William Maxwell Aitken (1879–1964), Lord Beaverbrook, Canadian-English publisher and politician who owned and ran several newspapers including most notably the *Daily Express*, known for its jingoistic, right-wing politics.

128 Mrs Brenning is referring here to the Irish International Exhibition held in Ballsbridge, Dublin, in May 1907. It featured a wide range of exhibits including 'The Shooting Jungle' that had animal models, and a Somali village containing a family making traditional craft items.

129 A famous Irish ballad about the United Irishmen and the 1798 Rebellion.

130 English writer (1903–66) particularly known for his novels *Brideshead Revisited* (1945) and the *Sword of Honour* trilogy (1952–61). Behan frequently uses the same comic misunderstanding of Waugh's gender, widely shared as Waugh was briefly married to Evelyn Gardner, whereupon the couple became known as 'He-Evelyn' and 'She-Evelyn'.

131 'Don't bother.'

132 See later in the volume, 'The Hot Malt Man', where the same phrase is used.

133 Robert Burns (1759–96), known as the national poet of Scotland and as a precursor of the Romantic movement in poetry.

134 These are in fact two separate institutions. Trinity College Dublin is officially the University of Dublin, whereas the National University (since 1908) was the federal body that linked constituent colleges (University College Dublin, University College Cork and University College Galway).

135 A trade war between Ireland and the United Kingdom in the 1930s, prompted by the Irish government's refusal to pay land annuities on land purchased by Irish farmers under British rule.

136 'Londonderry, smallpox to you, / Like the shadow laden with powder, / And the many supple long blonde-haired warriors, / Unsheltered from the wind, nor the clay of their powers, / *Alas! Woe is me ...*'

137 The traditional day of celebration of William of Orange's victory at the Battle of the Boyne in 1690, still commemorated by Unionists in Northern Ireland with bonfires and marches.

138 Irish commander of Jacobite forces during the Williamite Wars of 1688–91.

139 'On Bonapartes who betrayed us, / May our friends appear in the midst of our enemy, / That we destroy the Gauls ...'

140 'Welcome to the French women and a hundred thousand to follow.'

141 'Seán O'Dwyer of the Glen' is a renowned Irish folk song that recalls the eponymous rebel who fought against Cromwell's New Model Army in the 1640s and 1650s.

142 A prison built to house military prisoners and a site famous in Irish republican lore as the burial place of fourteen of the leaders of the Easter 1916 Rising.

143 Irish writer (1906–70) best known for his modernist novel *Cré na Cille* (published in Irish in 1949), who claims to have recruited Behan into the Fianna (IRA Youth Wing) in the 1930s, and who spent time with Behan in jail in the 1940s as a republican prisoner.

144 Patrice de MacMahon (1808–93) was president of the French Republic between 1875 and 1879 and descended from a wealthy Irish family who had been forced into exile after the Cromwellian and Williamite Wars in Ireland.

145 Gustave Paul Cluseret (1823–1900) was a French soldier who fought in Algeria and Crimea before leaving the army and taking up various causes around the world, including fighting for Italian unification, for the Union Army in the American Civil War, and with the Fenian insurgency of 1866–7. He returned to France to become embroiled in communard revolution, and took up the position of Delegate of War, commanding the Commune's military efforts.

146 Louis-Lazare Hoche (1768–97) was a French General in the Revolutionary Army who was given command of the attempted invasion of Ireland in 1796, designed to prompt and support an insurrection of the United Irishmen.

147 Prolific Irish writer (1902–90) who published widely in both Irish and English and whose first major work was his biography of Parnell, published in 1937.

148 Member of the Irish Republican Brotherhood who had a key role in orchestrating the Phoenix Park assassinations in 1882, but who betrayed his accomplices to the police when he was arrested the following year. On his information, five of his accomplices were hanged for murder.

149 The French Revolution of 1848, which established the Second Republic.

150 Success to her.

151 P.J. Bourke (1883–1932), actor-manager of the Queen's Theatre, Dublin. He was married to Margaret Kearney, sister of Kathleen, Brendan Behan's mother.

152 A traditional Irish jig, dated back to the eighteenth century, which is also found in English and Scottish music traditions.

153 Jimmy O'Dea (James Augustine O'Dea, 1899–1965) was an Irish actor and comedian celebrated for comic character sketches and his pantomime appearances.

154 Irish actor and comedian (1925–2004) who began her career as a child actor working in pantomimes and comic routines with Jimmy O'Dea.

155 One of the main theatres in Dublin since its foundation in 1871, associated in particular with musical and light operatic theatre, including pantomime.

156 English writer (1894–1963) most famous for his novel *Brave New World* (1932). *Music at Night* is a collection of essays by Huxley published in 1931 and reissued as a Penguin paperback in 1950.

157 Hilaire Belloc (1870–1953) was an Anglo-French writer, historian and politician.

158 Irish republican activist and leader (1893–1939) who fought in the Easter Rising of 1916, orchestrated IRA activities against the Irish government in the 1920s and rose to become leader of the IRA in the 1930s. Controversial for his attempt to secure Nazi Germany's support for the Irish republican cause, he died on a German U-boat on his way back to Ireland.

159 Probably best described as pidgin Irish, these terms are corruptions of Irish words for an expression of surprise (*musha*), my child (*allanna*), my love (*astore*), and do you understand? (*tiggin too?*).

160 Pablo Picasso (1881–1973), world-renowned Spanish artist and sculptor.

161 Ernest Hemingway (1899–1961), American novelist and short-story writer best known for his novels *For Whom the Bell Tolls* (1940) and *The Old Man and the Sea* (1952).

162 F. Scott Fitzgerald (1896–1940), American novelist celebrated for *The Great Gatsby* (1925).

163 French novelist and philosopher (1905–1980) whose work became synonymous with existentialism.

164 Les Deux Magots and the Café de Flore, on the boulevard Saint-Germain-des-Prés, are two cafes associated in the 1940s and 1950s with literary clientele.

165 French writer and playwright (1910–86) imprisoned in the late 1920s for various acts of petty crime and who famously turned his criminal and prison experiences into art, a lesson not lost on Behan.

166 Christopher Marlowe (1564–93), English playwright and contemporary of Shakespeare, whose life seems to have been more eventful than his plays.

167 Irish playwright, poet and novelist (1854–1900) more famous for his imprisonment for homosexuality than for his literary works.

168 American dancer and philosopher (1874–1966) who ran the Akademia in Paris, a school devoted to the arts, attendees of which dressed in an approximation of classical Greek clothing.

169 A musical band associated with the Irish Citizen Army, founded in 1913. Their costumes, which consisted of kilts, shawls, brooches, and balmoral caps, were reputedly designed by Seán O'Casey.

170 The École des Beaux-Arts is the national school for teaching painting, drawing and other fine arts, founded in Paris in 1671.

171 The Irish national association of youth hostels.

172 Maud Gonne MacBride (1866–1953) was an English actress who became an Irish revolutionary. Most famous as the subject of W.B. Yeats's infatuations, Maud Gonne married Major John MacBride, who had led the Irish Brigade in the Second Boer War. Behan's mother, Kathleen, worked as a housekeeper in Maud Gonne's house after Kathleen's first husband, Jack Furlong, died from influenza in 1918.

173 A book about his time convalescing in the Swiss Alps by Gaelic League author Micheál Breathnach.

174 An inner-city suburb of Dublin, to the west of the city centre on the Southside.

175 A suburb on the outskirts of Paris and home of a famous château of the same name.

176 Legendary Irish king of the 5th century AD, who is reputed to have led an expedition across the channel and to the Alps, where he was killed by lightning and his body had to be transported back to his home in Connaught.

177 A suburban street in Dublin that runs through Kimmage and Crumlin.

178 A seaside resort in the French Riviera.

179 American boxer (1921–89) celebrated for both his legendary achievements as a boxer and his flamboyant lifestyle.

180 The strand of North Bull Island in Dublin Bay, a bathing and leisure place for Dubliners.

181 American actor (1912–96), known for his singing and dancing performances in films such as *An American in Paris* (1951) and *Singin' in the Rain* (1952).

182 'It is a good thing to be young.'

183 'For the glory of God and the honour of Ireland.'

184 Historic sites of worship in the early Christian church in Ireland.

185 A small square of Georgian housing around St George's Church Dublin, officially named George's Place, but known colloquially as George's Pocket.

186 Known as 'Skin-the-Goat', Fitzharris (1833–1910) was a Fenian and member of the Invincibles, the gang who conducted the Phoenix Park assassinations in 1882.

187 A Chevrolet, a US-made car, which in 1950s Ireland would have been an indication of affluence and style.

188 Celebrated French restaurant in Dublin, 1901–67.

189 Irish rebel (1888–1916) who fought in the Easter 1916 Rising and was executed as one of its leaders.

190 Irish nationalist politician and father of the Easter 1916 rebel leader Joseph Plunkett, George Noble Plunkett (1851–1948) made several diplomatic expeditions on behalf of the nationalist cause and was made a count by order of the Pope.

191 Maternity hospital in Dublin, in existence in the same location since 1757. The building complex includes a 'round room' used as a cinema between 1897 and 1999. In 1953 the building underwent renovations, hence Behan's question, 'what are they at with the Rotunda?' It re-emerged as the Ambassador Cinema in late 1954.

192 Irish poet (1803–49) whose early work focused mostly on translating poetry from other languages but who became one of the most influential nationalist poets of the nineteenth century.

193 'Oro, my boat is swimming to the harbour.'

194 An aniseed-flavoured alcoholic drink traditionally served as an aperitif, popular in Marseille and the surrounding area.

195 A formerly common name for followers of Islam, or Muslims.

196 A theological schism in the Catholic Church in the seventeenth century, which had many prominent followers based in the abbey at Port Royal-des-Champs.

197 The term 'Apache' refers to a group of native American tribes mainly in the south-west of what is now the United States of America, but as a result of US expansionist wars in the nineteenth century it became synonymous with fierce warriors and was used colloquially to refer to any violent gangs.

198 From the late nineteenth century onwards, the 'Gorbals' was a densely populated slum area of Glasgow.

199 On the edge of the Liberties, historically a slum district in south-west Dublin.

200 French singer and actor (1906–94) who became an international star on radio, film and through his popular music records.

201 A small section of New York, near Broadway, which became associated with music publishers and thus with the global influence of American popular music.

202 Charles Boyer (1899–1978), was a French-American actor who became famous in Hollywood films in the 1930s, especially romances such as *Algiers* (1938) and *Love Affair* (1939).

203 Distinguished scholar of the Irish language (1915–81) who became Professor of Irish at Trinity College Dublin in 1953. He would later publish an influential study, *The Irish Language*, in 1966. Behan would have known Greene as a fellow writer for the Irish-language journal *Comhar*.

204 James Macpherson (1736–96), Scottish poet, who published *Fingal* (1761) and *Temora* (1763), collectively known as *The Poems of Ossian*, which were hugely influential on the Romantic era of poets in English literature, and again on the Celtic Revival of the late nineteenth and early twentieth centuries. Macpherson claimed to have collected the poetry from ancient Scottish sources, but the provenance and authenticity of the poetry has been debated ever since publication, most famously by Samuel Johnson, who called them forgeries.

205 Poem written by Earl Gerald Fitzgerald (1338–98), translated by Thomas Kinsella as 'woe to him who slanders women'.

206 An offensive term for low-paid labourers, usually from Asia and specifically China.

207 Irish writer (1882–1928), mainly of short stories. Ó Conaire lived in London from 1900 to 1915.

208 Nationalist leader and IRB revolutionary (1890–1922) who led the IRB and IRA intelligence activities during the War of Independence, and became Commander-in-Chief of the Irish army until his death in an ambush in August 1922. He lived in London from 1905 to 1916.

209 IRB revolutionary (1877–1927) who initiated Michael Collins into the IRB and directed revolutionary activities in London during the War of Independence. He lived in London from 1897 until 1923.

210 IRB revolutionary (1844–1940), who organized Fenian activities throughout the late nineteenth century. He moved to London and established a medical practice there in 1882, leaving it to return to Ireland in 1924.

211 Seán McGrath, or John Joseph McGrath (1882–1950), IRA organizer and intelligence officer, mainly operating in London.

212 'May God have mercy on him.'

213 The short name used to refer to Patrick Dineen's *Foclóir Gaedhilge Agus Béarla: An Irish-English Dictionary*, published by the Irish Texts Society in 1904.

214 The Poor Law Amendment Act of 1834 was devised to reform how poverty was relieved in Britain, and introduced the workhouse system whereby poor citizens would be housed and fed in the workhouse in return for labour. It was largely despised as a kind of punishment for poverty. Wellington was not in fact responsible for the Poor Law, which was enacted by the Whig government.

215 The name given to the coastal port of Dún Laoghaire between 1821 and 1920. The name was adopted after King George IV's visit to see the construction of the modern town in 1821, but was changed back to its Irish name as the establishment of the Irish Free State became imminent.

216 Unveiled in 1872, the monument in Kensington Gardens in London commemorates Prince Albert, Queen Victoria's husband and consort, who died of typhoid in 1861.

217 Built in 1689, the Royal Palace at Kensington was Queen Victoria's birthplace. Princess Louise, her daughter, commissioned the statue of Victoria in 1893.

218 The decisive battle in the Franco-Prussian war of 1870, in which the Prussian army surrounded and defeated the French, wounding their commander, Marshall MacMahon, and capturing the Emperor Napoleon III.

219 Maryborough prison, County Laois, now known as Portlaoise prison.

220 Dan Breen (1894–1969), IRA volunteer and politician from Tipperary, who published a memoir of his participation in the War of Independence, My *Fight for Irish Freedom* (1924).

221 IRA volunteer and leader (1897–1980) from Cork who published an account of his exploits with the 'flying columns' waging successful ambushes against the British army, *Guerrilla Days in Ireland* (1949).

222 British political and cultural magazine associated with the Fabian society and generally with centre-left and liberal political views.

223 London-based publishers of art books.

224 Ballybough cemetery in Fairview is the oldest Jewish cemetery in Ireland, and has the date '5618' from the Hebrew calendar inscribed over the door.

225 A popular song, performed most famously by Bing Crosby and written by Michael Carr, who was born Maurice Alfred Cohen (1905–68), a lyricist and composer brought up in Dublin.

226 A slang term for mental hospital.

227 The most famous cemetery in Ireland, which contains the graves of many notable leaders in Irish history including Daniel O'Connell, Charles Stewart Parnell, Michael Collins and Éamon de Valera. Brendan Behan is also buried here.

228 American modernist writer (1874–1946) who spent much of her life in Paris and associated with key figures in literary and artistic modernism.

229 Wimpey and McAlpine were the two most successful construction firms in Britain, founded in 1880 and 1869 respectively. Both firms were heavily involved in house-building, road construction and in major infrastructural projects. Both were also large-scale employers of cheap Irish labour. Brendan's brother Dominic wrote a ballad about such migrant labour, entitled 'McAlpine's Fusiliers'.

230 Irish actor (1888–1961), born William Joseph Shields, who appeared under his stage name in such films as *How Green Was my Valley* (1941) and *The Quiet Man* (1952).

231 Notorious serial killers of the 1940s and early 1950s. John Christie (1899–1953) is known to have killed eight women by strangulation in his flat in Notting Hill. Neville Heath (1917–46) was a captain in the South African Air Force, and murdered two women, the first in Notting Hill and the second in Bournemouth. John Haigh (1909–49) was known to have killed at least six people, either by beating or shooting them, and then disposing of the bodies with sulphuric acid. During this time he was living in Gloucester Road.

232 A popular chocolate bar in Ireland in the 1940s and 1950s, which had twelve squares of chocolate with nuts and raisins.

233 Annual final matches of the Gaelic Athletic Association competitions in men's football, women's football, hurling and camogie, usually held in September. Teams are organized by county.

234 Between 1905 and 1971, rule 27 of the Gaelic Athletic Association membership rules prohibited any member from participating in or encouraging 'any imported game', which included soccer, rugby and cricket.

235 Dalymount is the stadium of Dublin soccer team Bohemians. Shelbourne Park was the stadium of Dublin soccer team, Shelbourne Rovers, until the late 1940s.

236 The stadium of Everton Football Club in Liverpool.

237 Slang term for Croke Park, the national stadium of the Gaelic Athletic Association situated at the end of Russell Street, where Behan lived as a child.

238 'A traditional Irish song written by Michael Joseph McCann in 1843. McCann was a Fenian and the song, a war-cry calling the O'Donnell clan to victory, became a staple of romantic nationalist culture.

239 Goalkeeper for Celtic Football Club (1909–31) who died tragically during a match against rivals Rangers after an accidental clash with Rangers' player Sam English.

240 Irish writer (1919–2007) and former literary editor of *The Irish Press*.

241 Short for Glasnevin.

242 'Brendan Behan, on his way to death on Waterloo Bridge.'

243 Irish for value or respect.

244 From the Irish *Giolla*, meaning boy-attendant or servant, but with connotations of subservience.

245 A low mountain range in Eastern France, bordering with Germany.

246 Irish artist (1927–83) who met Behan and other writers and artists in McDaid's pub in Dublin.

247 British-born art dealer (1907–81) who established a successful gallery in Dublin in 1928. Waddington became a central figure in promoting Irish art, notably the work of Jack B. Yeats, Seán Keating, Colin Middleton and Patrick Swift.

248 The Dublin Grand Opera Society brought Debussy's opera to the Gaiety Theatre on 5 May 1948.

249 Irish writer and editor (1925–92), who founded and edited *Envoy* magazine in Dublin (1949–51) and wrote a memoir of the literary generation that included himself, Behan, Patrick Kavanagh and Flann O'Brien, *Remembering How We Stood* (1975).

250 Irish composer (1911–85), who was musical director at the Abbey Theatre (1936–48) and composed *Spring Nocturne* (1938), *Songs for Prison* (1941) and *Sunlight and Shadow* (1955).

251 Irish journalist (1888–1958), who spent most of his career in Dublin and London as a freelance journalist, and also authored several books of short stories and travel.

252 French artist (1882–1963), best known for his Fauvist and Cubist works of art. As Behan mentions, he began his working life as a painter-decorator.

253 English politician and prime minister (1874–1965). Well-regarded in the British art world for his paintings, he exhibited on many occasions. He was also a prolific author and was awarded the Nobel Prize for Literature in 1953.

254 English artist (1878–1959) best known for his paintings of horses.

255 Hugh Lane was an Irish art collector and dealer (1875–1915) who was killed when the *RMS Lusitania* was torpedoed and sank in 1915. His Municipal Gallery of Modern Art, opened in Dublin in 1908, was the first public gallery in the world devoted to modern art. On Lane's death the ownership of his collection of modern art was contested between Dublin and London, and arrangements for sharing the disputed works only settled in 1959.

256 Ulster Unionist politician and author (1907–89) perhaps best known for his campaigns to decriminalize homosexuality. In 1954 he advocated in parliament for the return of the Hugh Lane art works to Dublin.

257 Irish newspaper owner (1845–1919), advocated for Home Rule but became notorious for refusing the demands of striking workers in Dublin, which led to the lock-out of 1913.

258 IRB revolutionary and songwriter (1883–1942) noted for writing the Irish national anthem, 'A Soldier's Song'. He was the brother of Brendan Behan's mother, Kathleen.

259 Patrick Pearse (1879–1916), Irish revolutionary and poet, rose to prominence for his role as the founder and headmaster of St Enda's School in Dublin in 1908 and member of the Gaelic League. He led the Easter Rising in 1916 and was executed by the British authorities.

260 Jeremiah O'Donovan Rossa (1831–1915), IRB revolutionary who spent most of his life organizing revolutionary activities. Patrick Pearse gave the oration at O'Donovan Rossa's grave, contending that Ireland unfree would never be at peace and that the graves of the Fenian dead were a call to arms to Irish nationalists.

261 A distinguished list of historical Irish warriors and rebels.

262 Irish writer and theatre costumier (1912–2002), wrote a biography of his uncle Peadar Kearney entitled *A Soldier's Song*, published in 1957. He also wrote a short biography of his cousin Brendan Behan in 1971.

263 Irish politician (1874–1931), who took part in the Easter Rising of 1916 and became Sinn Féin MP for Dublin Harbour area in 1918.

264 IRB revolutionary (1895–1920), prominent in the War of Independence, shot in a firefight with British intelligence agents in 1920.

265 IRB revolutionary (1886–1963), rose to leadership of the Dublin Brigade of the IRA during the War of Independence and led the attack on the Custom House in 1921.

266 'Farewell to the years I am recalling; / Under the light of the moon I often saw, / The young men preparing to fight for freedom. / A hundred blessings from my heart to the Soldiers of the Fianna. / ... And in the Heavens they are seated at the right hand of our Lord. / A hundred blessings from my heart to the Soldiers of the Fianna.'

267 English race-horse jockey (1935–2022), who won the Epsom Derby in 1954. This was his only major win at the time when Behan was writing, although he went on to become one of the most successful horse-racing jockeys in the history of the sport.

268 Oliver Cromwell, English statesman (1599–1658), Head of State of the Republic and Commonwealth, notorious in Ireland for his brutal campaigns of repression and genocide.

269 William or Billy Nevett (1906–92), English race-horse jockey who won the Epsom Derby three times in the 1940s.

270 Slang term for the War of Independence, 1919–21, so called because the British 'Black and Tan' force was the most reviled enemy of the IRA.

271 The war between the Irish Free State and Irish republican rebels who were opposed to the Treaty with Britain, 1922–3.

272 British Broadcasting Corporation, the national and publicly funded television and radio broadcasting company of the UK since 1927.

273 Córas Iompair Éireann, the national transportation company of Ireland, responsible for railways and buses, formed as a private company in 1945 but nationalized since 1950.

274 A notorious day in the War of Independence, 21 November 1920, which began with the assassination by IRA gunmen of leading agents of British intelligence in Dublin, for which the British forces retaliated by firing indiscriminately into a crowd of Gaelic football spectators at Croke Park, killing fourteen and wounding sixty people.

275 British politician (1863–1945), prime minister during the War of Independence. Winston Churchill was his Secretary of State for War during this period.

276 Irish soccer player (1912–85), played with a number of Dublin teams in the League of Ireland before joining Glasgow Rangers in 1932 and Everton FC in 1939.

277 Irish boxer (1912–62), competed for Ireland in the Olympics of 1932 and was lightweight boxing champion of Ireland for much of the 1930s.

278 'If you are a Gael, you should know that Seán O Donnabhan, a comrade of Petrie and O Comhraidte, lived at 49 Bayview Avenue, North Strand for a long time. And by the way, do not forget what he himself says about the despicable charity: Poverty is not the worst for me, / Nor will it ever be, / But the contempt that follows it, / That won't cure the brave.'

279 In December 1954 gale-force winds and torrential rain resulted in a series of floods in Ireland, most seriously the flooding of the Shannon and Tolka rivers. The Tolka burst its banks in Northside Dublin and resulted in the evacuation of hundreds of residents from East Wall. The floods resulted in a large-scale rescue effort by emergency services.

280 'limited company'

281 Horse-racing venues close to Dublin.

282 Brian Boru was the high king of Ireland in the late tenth century, whose renown is associated principally with the Battle of Clontarf in 1014. Both Brian and his son Murchad were killed at the battle, although it is famed as the battle in which the Irish defeated the Vikings.

283 The Royal Dublin Fusiliers was a regiment of the British army, formed in 1881, and which recruited mainly from Dublin and the eastern counties of Ireland.

284 US film, radio and television series, enormously popular throughout the 1930s, '40s and '50s.

285 English actor and writer (1921–2004), renowned for his versatility as an actor.

286 A term for utopia or earthly paradise, from the fictional place depicted in James Hilton's novel *Lost Horizon* (1933).

287 Behan includes his own poem, elsewhere titled 'An Jackeen ag caoineadh na mBlascaod' or 'A Jackeen Laments for the Blaskets'.

288 'Do not laugh, child / There is no joy, / Do not listen to the fairy tales. / There are no fairies / Do not lift your head, / The heavens are not above, / Out of every cloud screams ___ / Death ...'

289 The correct title is *The Reminiscences of an Irish Land Agent: Being Those of S.M. Hussey by Samuel Murray Hussey*, compiled by Home Gordon (London: Duckworth, 1904).

290 A reference to King Lear as portrayed in Shakespeare's play, wrapped in clothing against the storm.

291 British short story writer, Hector Hugh Munro (1870–1916), who frequently published under the pseudonym 'Saki'. His father was Charles Augustus Munro, who was Governor General in Burma where H.H. Munro was born. Behan is referring here not to his father but to his brother, also called Charles Augustus Munro (1869–1952), who was governor of Mountjoy Prison.

292 Irish writer (1906–89), best known for his play *Waiting for Godot* (1954), which like many of his works was written originally in French. Behan befriended Beckett when in Paris in the late 1940s.

293 Irish poet (1887–1917) from Slane, Co. Meath, who was killed in the First World War.

294 Irish poet and theatre director (1896–1941) from Trim in Co. Meath.

295 Irish-language scholar (1863–99) from Athboy, Co. Meath, whose primer *Simple Lessons in Irish* (1894) sold thousands of copies in Ireland and became a household item.

296 A lapel badge denoting ability and willingness to speak the Irish language, either silver or gold depending on proficiency, introduced first in 1916.

297 IRB member (1866–1963) and the last Governor General of Ireland, appointed at the instigation of Éamon de Valera in 1932 as a ruse to diminish the role, supposed to represent the King in Ireland. Ó Buachalla refused to accept any invitations in the role, lived in a modest house and undermined the purpose of the office at every turn.

298 Eddie Chapman (1914–97), thief and safe-cracker in the 1930s, double-agent between Germany and England during the Second World War and smuggler

in its aftermath. During this time in the late 1940s Brendan Behan accompanied Chapman on numerous voyages around the ports of the Irish Sea and northern France.

299 Behan's mocking term for An Tuiseal Ginideach, the genitive case in Irish language grammar.

300 Leo Tolstoy (1828–1910), Russian novelist and short-story writer best known for *War and Peach* (1869) and *Anna Karenina* (1878). Towards the end of *War and Peace* Tolstoy writes of the relationship between chance and genius: 'To a herd of rams, the ram the herdsman drives each evening into a special enclosure to feed and that becomes twice as fat as the others must seem to be a genius.'

301 Carlow people are colloquially known as 'scallion eaters', a nickname which dates back to the time when Carlow was renowned for growing onions for the Dublin market.

302 British writer (1868–1952), best known for his novel *South Wind* (1917), based on his experiences in Capri.

303 Swedish doctor (1857–1949), who spent much of his life in Italy, especially in Capri where he restored a villa, about which he wrote in *The Story for San Michele* (1929).

304 A small street off Moore Street in Dublin, now demolished, which contained second-hand stalls.

305 Irish actor (1910–93), famous in theatre and film internationally in the 1930s and 1940s and renowned for his performances in the plays of Seán O'Casey.

306 One of the best-known novels by Fyodor Dostoyevsky (1821–81), published first in 1869.

307 The ambitious hydroelectrification scheme designed and built at Ardnacrusha on the River Shannon in the 1920s, which was the new Irish State's first and most elaborate infrastructure project.

308 Irish for airy or light-hearted.

309 The national airline of Ireland, founded as a state company in 1936.

309 The first Battle for the Somme in 1916, in which French and British troops launched an offensive against German lines, resulted in the heaviest casualties ever suffered by the British army. Irish units of the British army were heavily involved, and suffered among the highest death tolls.

311 The historical docklands area of Northside Dublin, located between the financial services centre to the west and the current port area to the east.

312 The region in Belgium and north-east France which saw some of the most intense fighting of the First World War, including the battles of Ypres and Passchendaele.

313 Offensive, racist terms for non-white, Asian and black people.

314 Anti-colonial insurgents in Kenya, where an uprising against British rule had been taking place since 1952.

315 Luxury hotels in central London.

316 Located at the foot of the Champs-Élysées, one of Paris's most luxurious hotels.

317 Terms used in Persian and Urdu to beg for money or a gift from a stranger.

318 An offensive, racist term meaning black people.

319 A ferry ship which sank in a severe storm off the coast of Northern Ireland in 1953 with the loss of 133 passengers and crew.

320 'I've never heard of any wreckage on this trip but, probably,' he finished cheerfully, 'what they were referring to was the *Princess Victoria*.' 'Probably,' said I, at this stage of the game, not caring whether we were wrecked or not.

321 From the Irish, *slíbhín*, meaning a sly or cunning person.

322 Irish playwright and director (1886–1958), who managed and directed at the Abbey Theatre between 1919 and 1958. He wrote a weekly column for *The Irish Press* published beside Behan's in the mid-1950s.

323 A German shepherd dog (1918–32) which became an international film star in the 1920s, often billed as the star actor.

324 'Oh, thank you forever, my love, for that warm welcome.'

325 Officially called the British and Irish steam packet company, but popularly known as the B&I, the company operated ferry and freight services between Britain and Ireland between 1836 and 1992. It was nationalized as an Irish state company in 1965 but privatized in 1992.

326 Jonathan Swift (1667–1745), Irish poet, novelist and satirist, famous for *Gulliver's Travels* (1726).

327 The Cat and Cage is a famous pub in Drumcondra, north Dublin, and has been in the same location since the early eighteenth century. It is said to have played a role in the Irish Rebellion of 1798, acting as a signal post, for which its owner was reportedly hanged.

328 Known as the Great O'Neill (1550–1616), the Earl of Tyrone, who led the rebellion against English rule in Ireland in the Nine Years' War of 1593–1603, ultimately leading to the decimation of the remaining Irish aristocracy. He married Mabel Bagenal, daughter of an English general who commanded forces in Ireland, in 1591, against her family's wishes.

329 Written in December 1917, the poem is a more direct expression of Yeats's growing radicalization about the impact of the Easter Rising of 1916 than his better-known poem, 'Easter 1916'.

330 IRB revolutionary (1885–17) who led the Fingal battalion of the Irish Volunteers during the Easter Rising, killing eleven policemen at the Ashbourne barracks. He died the following year when violently force-fed during a hunger strike.

331 IRB revolutionary (1906–71), fought with Tom Ashe in north County Dublin during the Easter Rising. He later became the IRA Chief of Staff and Commander-in-Chief of the Irish army after the assassination of Michael Collins, and went on to serve in various ministerial posts in the Irish government.

332 Irish poet (1918–91) who published few collections but was an influential editor of Irish poetry and short stories.

333 An IRB revolutionary (1858–1916), Clarke devoted his life to organizing Irish rebel activity and played a key role in advocating for and planning the Easter Rising of 1916, for his part in which he was executed by British authorities.

334 'For, lo, the winter is past, the rain is over and gone; The flowers appear on the earth; the time of the singing of birds is come, and the voice of the turtle is heard in our land; The fig tree putteth forth her green figs, and the vines with the tender grape give a good smell. Arise, my love, my fair one, and come away' (King James Version).

335 Irish for the Canticle of Canticles, or Solomon's Song, from the Bible.

336 A column in *The Irish Press* written by Aodh de Blácam (1891–1951). The column ran from 1931 to 1947 and featured the humorous exploits of Roddy rambling in the countryside.

337 Protestant clergyman (1571–1642) who became Provost of Trinity College Dublin in 1627, instituted services in Irish and translated parts of the Bible into Irish. He also published a catechism in parallel Irish and English text.

338 William O'Donnell (1570–1628), Church of Ireland Archbishop of Tuam who published the first full translation of the New Testament in Irish in 1603.

339 John Carswell, or Séon Carsuel (1522–72), Scottish clergyman who published the *Book of Common Order* in Scottish Gaelic in 1567.

340 James Ussher (1581–1656), Archbishop of Armagh in the Church of Ireland, who wrote much about the early Irish church based on Irish sources.

341 The poem quoted at length is Valentin Iremonger's *Spring Jag*, published in Iremonger's collection *Horan's Field and Other Reservations* (Dublin: Dolmen Press, 1972).

342 Belfast poet (1909–69) who published two collections of poetry, *W.R. Rodgers: Belfast poet (1909–69) who published two collections of poetry, Awake! And Other Wartime Poems* (1941) and *Europa and the Bull* (1952).

343 Meaning teetotaller, a person who abstains from alcohol.

344 Giovanni Battista Rinuccini (1592–1653), Italian Catholic Archbishop sent to Ireland in 1645 as Papal Nuncio to support and arm the Irish Confederacy, which was based in Kilkenny, against the English forces.

345 British featherweight boxer (1906–56) who won the British featherweight title three times.

346 An annual horse race held at the Curragh in May.

347 Irish sports journalist and broadcaster (1920–96) who became the voice of Gaelic games and horse racing on Irish radio.

348 Irish writer and politician (1880–1916), killed in the First World War serving as an officer in the British army. Parnell, who died in 1891, is mentioned here in error. Behan may have been thinking of Padraic Colum's remark that Kettle's name would be listed on a roll of great Irish patriots.

349 Anna of the Kiss, the title of Dion Boucicault's play of 1865.

350 Irish civil servant and translator (1886–1943) best known for translating Peadar Kearney's 'A Soldier's Song' into Irish.

351 Michael Davitt (1846–1906), Irish nationalist and Land League organizer who lived from his journalistic writings. He met Tolstoy in 1904 after he had written about anti-Semitism in Russia in *Within the Pale* (1903).

352 A heavy punishment whip with multiple thongs attached to a long handle.

353 Irish for airs and affectations.

354 Kavanagh (1897–1984) was governor of Mountjoy Jail for thirty-four years, including during the time when Behan was an inmate.

355 Irish-language scholar (1880–1938) whose book *An Ghaoth Aniar* (The West Wind) was published in 1920.

356 Fenian revolutionary (1855–1933), as a young boy is reputed to have taken part in the breakout of Fenian prisoners in Manchester in 1867.

357 Irish-American political organizer (1874–1940) who led Clan na Gael in America.

358 English poet (1621–78), mainly renowned for his satires.

359 'He didn't want to give his son a bite. They didn't get along well. (No wonder – B.O.B). The young man wanted to plant a little potato farm for himself. The father wouldn't allow him, and he went to prevent him. He grabbed the spade to take it off him. In the struggle between them the old man took a turn and dropped as still and insensible. He wasn't killed outright. The women took him into the house, and they told the son to flee as the old man was not expected to live. Both of them favoured him over his father, as he was such a sly and despicable man that no one respected him. The son then fled and he spent three months on the run in Connemara with the police in pursuit of him, and where he slept at night was not where he would be found in the morning but constantly fleeing ...'

360 IRA volunteer (1903–21) who was killed in the attack on the Custom House in 1921 when he was shot while throwing a grenade at a troop lorry.

361 The Wren's Nest is a pub located in the Strawberry Beds, west of Dublin along the River Liffey. The pub has been on the same site since 1588.

362 An Irish ballad commemorating the execution of a young IRA volunteer in 1920.

363 An opera in four acts composed by Friedrich von Flotow entitled *Martha oder: Der Mark zu Richmond* (1844). Moore's 'The Last Rose of Summer' is sung by Martha in Act Two.

364 Frank O'Connor was a prolific novelist, short-story writer, critic and playwright (1903–66), born in Cork as Michael O'Donovan. His play *The Invincibles* was first performed at the Abbey Theatre, Dublin, in October 1937.

365 The Dál gCais were a famous ancient Irish dynasty whose power base was located on the banks of the River Shannon in modern County Clare. Several High Kings of Ireland, including Brian Boru, hailed from the dynasty.

366 The nickname for County Clare, so-called because of its inhabitants' reputation for carrying banners to political meetings in the nineteenth century.

367 General Sir John Maxwell was British Military Governor of Ireland, appointed in the aftermath of the Easter Rising in April 1916 to impose martial law. Under his orders, fifteen leaders of the Rising were executed.

368 'We will never forget / Brian Mac Giolla Mheidhreach / On the 'Court' and his living sweetness, Irish, funny, glorious, strong.'

369 These lines approximate to the words of the French national anthem 'La Marseillaise' with some adaptations or errors. The first line, for example, should be 'Ye sons o' France awake to glory.'

370 Theobald Wolfe Tone (1763–98), founder of the United Irishmen, a revolutionary movement dedicated to rebellion against British rule in Ireland.

371 Irish nationalist (1815–75) who supported various campaigns for rebellion and civil disobedience in Ireland and was sentenced to penal deportation in 1848.

372 Joseph Kavanagh was a Wexford cobbler who became famous while working in Paris for leading the charge of the Parisian people against the Bastille.

373 Civil servant employed in the Irish embassy in London who founded the Irish Club, which provided a social venue for the Irish in London. He was also the author of several literary works, including a play, *Here We Dwell* (1951), a children's book, *Andy Tinpockets* (1950) and a novel of the revolutionary period, *Jackets Green* (1936).

374 Irish State-owned companies. The ESB was formed in 1927 as the Electricity Supply Board. Bord na Móna was originally formed in 1933 as the Turf Development Board, and became Bord na Móna in 1946 – it aimed to mechanize the extraction of turf as a source of fuel. Comhlucht Siucre Éireann was the state-owned company for producing sugar in Ireland, formed in 1933 by the nationalization of a private company based in Carlow.

375 Based on a festival of games, laws and funerary rites held in ancient Ireland, the Irish Free State revived the Tailteann Games in 1924, 1928 and 1932, partly modelled upon the timing of the Olympics.

376 J.M.W. Turner (1775–1851) painted a number of famous scenes of naval engagement, including *The Battle of Trafalgar*. Behan is likely referring here to a study of a sea battle in which the sea is indeed the colour of hay.

377 A small Spanish horse, or female donkey.

378 A corruption of the Irish '*ruaille buaille*', meaning commotion or ruction.

379 Swiss painter (1741–1807) known for her neo-classical and history paintings, and particularly for decorating the ceilings of notable buildings in London with such scenes.

380 Greta Garbo and Robert Taylor starred in the popular romantic film *Camille* (1936).

381 Widely used term in the 1920s and 1930s for what is now known as the First World War, 1914–18.

382 Fought between Russia on one side and Britain, France and the Ottoman Empire on the other, 1853–6, so called because the British, French and Ottoman forces countered Russian advances into Romania by landing on the Crimean Peninsula, which became the scene of the bloodiest battles at Balaclava, Inkerman and Sevastopol.

383 A political party that governed the Irish Free State from 1923 to 1932 and merged with other parties in 1933 to form the Fine Gael party.

384 Irish author and politician (1780–1838) whose *Cinn Lae* is a diary he kept from 1827–35, recording insights into daily social and political life, and into his natural surroundings.

385 Charles Kickham, Irish revolutionary and author (1826–82), most famous for his novel *Knocknagow* (1873).

386 'I regret myself, that that day struck, / On the poor Irishmen, in hundreds slain, / For the villains are making game of us, / Saying that a pike or a spear was nothing to them, / Our Major didn't come to us at dawn / We were not there ourselves rightly equipped, / But sent like cattle with no cowherd, / From the sunny side of Slievenamon.'

387 John Gilbert's daughter was Leatrice Gilbert (1924–2015), who became the first wife of Irish writer Ernest Gébler (1914–98), but who divorced him and left for the US with their son in 1952. Behan knew Gébler through mutual friendships with John Ryan and Desmond MacNamara. There is no mention of Leatrice Gilbert marrying Walter Van Tilburg Clark in biographical sources, so perhaps Behan is in error.

388 American novelist (1909–71) best known for *The Ox-Bow Incident* (1940) and *The Track of the Cat* (1949).

389 American singer and actor (1886–1950) who became famous in the 1920s, especially for his blackface performance in *The Jazz Singer* (1927). The movie was renowned as the first 'talkie', in which images and sound were synchronized.

390 A movie starring Al Jolson screened in 1928, which was even more successful than *The Jazz Singer*.

391 La Scala Theatre and Opera House was opened in 1920 on Prince's Street, off O'Connell Street. It was renamed the Capitol in 1927 when it was taken over as a cinema but continued to show theatre and opera shows.

392 A famous boxing match and contest for the World Light Heavyweight Championship title that took place in La Scala in Dublin on 17 March 1923. McTigue was an Irish fighter known as 'the Cyclonic Celt' who had become famous boxing in the USA. Battling Siki was the fighting name of Louis M'Barack Fall, a Senegalese fighter who took up boxing while enlisted in the French army and became World Champion in Paris in 1922 when he knocked out Georges Carpentier (the Battling Siki had reputedly been told to take a dive, but instead was angered by Carpentier's racist remarks). McTigue won the fight in Dublin on points after twenty rounds.

393 Smelling salts, a scented solution of ammonium carbonate used to revive someone who has fainted.

394 Billy Warren was a boxer who settled in Dublin in 1908–9 and became a local character, frequently seen in the GPO on O'Connell Street. He was occasionally interviewed by Irish newspapers about his life as a boxer, in which it was reported that he was the son of an African-American slave. Others claimed that he was Australian.

395 Snuff is a powdered form of tobacco, usually sniffed or inhaled up the nose. Common forms are brown, like tobacco. White snuff is a form of snuff cut with other substances either for a particular scent or to dilute the strength of the tobacco.

396 A traditional folk song dating back to the early nineteenth century, not to be confused with the popular song 'By the Light of the Silvery Moon' written by American songwriter Edward Madden. Given Behan's disappointment here, he may be referring to the folk song in error.

397 An American folk song that became a popular hit in the mid-1950s when arranged and recorded by Mitch Miller, but which first appeared as a Christy Minstrel song in the mid-nineteenth century.

398 Eldest son of Queen Victoria and King of England from 1901 to 1910.

399 Ancient Greek author of *The Iliad* and *The Odyssey*. 'Wine-dark sea' is the standard English translation of a phrase that Homer uses in both texts to refer to dark seas.

400 The English version of the name Amlaoibh O Suilebháin.

401 A Dublin phrase for fish and chips, apparently derived from an early Italian purveyor of fish and chips in Dublin who would ask customers if they wanted one of one and one of the other.

402 Ray was such a popular fish in Dublin that Ringsend was known as 'Raytown'. It likely became popular because it was a cheap by-catch of the Ringsend trawlers and was smoked and dried by the Ringsend fishing community.

403 Lourdes, a small town in the foothills of the Pyrenees in France, is a major site of pilgrimage for Catholics since the Catholic Church acknowledged it as the site where the Virgin Mary is supposed to have appeared in a cave to a young girl, now canonized as St Bernadette, in 1858. Knock in County Mayo is another site of pilgrimage, particularly for Irish Catholics, and is based on the account of the apparition of Mary, St Joseph and St John the Evangelist to a small number of inhabitants in 1879. Pilgrims believe that both are holy sites, and Lourdes in particular is attributed with powers to heal the sick.

404 Often spelled in English as keening, meaning a particular Irish tradition of lamenting for the dead.

405 Dichlorodiphenyltrichloroethane, a chemical insecticide developed in the late nineteenth century and used during the Second World War to stop the spread of malaria and typhoid. It became widely used on farms and in houses as a domestic insecticide until increased evidence and awareness of the dangers it posed to health and the environment. Rachel Carson's *Silent Spring* (1962) played a key role in the argument against its use.

406 Grigori Rasputin (1869–1916) became infamous in late Tsarist Russia as a self-styled monk and mystic who had considerable influence over the Russian royal family.

407 A pun on the name of Alfred, Lord Tennyson (1809–92), the most famous English poet of the Victorian era.

408 'Nothing lasts forever.'

409 Andrew Kettle (1833–1916), Irish nationalist politician close to Charles Stewart Parnell and father of Tom Kettle.

410 British heavyweight boxer (1889–1967) and British champion from 1911 to 1919.

411 French heavyweight and light heavyweight boxer (1894–1975), who defeated Bombardier Billy Wells twice in 1913 to win and retain the European Championship.

412 As Behan's readers will all likely have known, this is the first line of Padraic Colum's poem, 'The Old Woman of the Roads', a poem taught in primary schools in Ireland.

413 This refers to so-called bona fide pubs. Pubs in towns and cities were regulated in terms of their opening hours, but pubs beyond three miles of a town or five miles of Dublin which could prove that they served 'bona fide' or genuine travellers were permitted to ignore the restrictions. This loophole allowed Dubliners, for example, to travel to pubs beyond the geographical limit to get a drink during closing hours.

414 Common name for a prison or jail which derives from a prison in London based on the site of a holy well dedicated to St Bride.

415 The worst strike in Irish history, caused when a prominent employer, William Martin Murphy, dismissed workers for being members of a trade union. The union called a strike and involved other workers in Dublin in sympathetic strikes. The employers responded by locking out their striking workers and hiring other workers, and hence it is also known as the Dublin Lock-Out.

416 A traditional marching tune widely used by regiments of the British army, which dates back to the seventeenth century.

417 South African political leader (1825–1904) and president of the Republic of South Africa from 1884 to 1900. He was revered in Irish nationalist circles for leading the Boers in their war against the British Empire.

418 Prize-winning musician and songwriter, born in Monaghan in 1844, but who worked as a schoolteacher in Bray for forty years.

419 Vivian Mercier (1919–89), prominent Irish literary critic and scholar.

420 Three well-known traditional marches for the pipes, all commemorating battles.

421 The same tune is indeed known by both names, and there are other variants also. The original provenance of the tune is unclear.

422 Dunne and O'Sullivan were members of the London IRA who assassinated Field Marshal Henry Wilson in June 1922. Both had served with the British army during the First World War, and Dunne claimed that he joined the IRA to continue to fight for the same principle of defending small nations as he had done as a British soldier. Both men were hanged.

423 Cockney rhyming slang for 'nick', which is itself is a slang term for prison.

424 English actor and radio presenter (1904–78).

425 Anglicization of *bualadh bos*, meaning applause.

426 Irish writer (1897–1974) best known for her novels *Mary Lavelle* (1936), and *The Land of Spices* (1941).

427 'a dream she had last night'

428 On 31 May 1941 German bomber planes dropped bombs along the North Strand, Dublin, killing twenty-eight people, injuring hundreds and destroying hundreds of houses. It was the worst incident of a number of presumed errors by German bombers who were engaged in the 'blitz' campaign against Britain.

429 The Cusack Stand is on the east side of Croke Park, the national stadium for Gaelic games, and was built in 1938. A new stand with the same name was built in 2005.

430 'Happy Easter to you all.'

431 An annual Irish publication, which commenced in 1764 and contained a miscellany of topical information. It has been published continually since then and was particularly popular with farmers and merchants.

432 Tom Barry's *Guerrilla Days in Ireland* (1949).

433 Bloemfontein was the capital of the Orange Free State, a Boer Republic, in the Second Boer War (1899–1901), and was captured by the British in 1900.

434 A malapropism for Egypt, which Britain conquered in 1882.

435 A malapropism for Mendicity, referring to the Mendicity Institution in Dublin (founded in 1818), which sought to alleviate poverty.

436 The first Irish radio comedy series; it ran from 1954 to 1958 and starred the actor Joe Lynch.

437 Irish novelist and short-story writer (1852–1933), best known for his novels *A Drama in Muslin* (1886) and *Esther Waters* (1894).

438 Colloquially known as 'the holy hour', when pubs in Irish cities were closed.

439 King of England, 1820–30.

440 Anglican cleric (1771–1845) known for his preaching and wit. He was a powerful advocate for Catholic Emancipation.

441 Irish poet and writer (1779–1852), renowned for his ten-volume publication of songs and poems, *Irish Melodies* (1808–34).

442 Charles Dickens, English novelist (1812–70), best known for *Oliver Twist* (1838), *A Christmas Carol* (1843) and *Bleak House* (1853).

443 British journalist and broadcaster (1907–60).

444 G.K. Chesterton, English writer and theologian (1874–1936).

445 Mary Elizabeth Ponsonby (1776–1861), wife of the British prime minister, Lord Charles Grey.

446 Bishop Patrick Duggan (1813–96) was the Catholic Bishop of Clonfert, County Galway, from 1872 until 1896. He was known as the Land League Bishop because of his overt support for land and tenant rights.

447 IRA member (1907–68), who was interned in the Curragh at the same time as Behan.

448 There are several references to this song in Joyce's *Finnegans Wake*. Behan's younger brother, Dominic Behan, recorded the song as 'Mrs Hooligan's Christmas Cake' in 1958 on an EP, and wrote for the sleeve notes: 'This must have been one of the first songs I ever heard my mother sing. So far as I know, no-one else in Dublin sings it, though I have it on the authority of *Finnegans Wake* that it was definitely written by somebody. Tune: Dublin music hall. Tradition: street.'

449 Micheál Mac Liammóir (1899–1978), English-born actor who moved to Ireland as a young man, changed his name to sound Irish and became legendary as the founder and manager of the Gate Theatre in Dublin with his partner, Hilton Edwards.

450 One of the highest mountains in Wicklow, the name of which translates as 'backside to the wind'.

451 'There was a big crowd there, / From every direction / They were pretty honest, cheerful there, / And singing with good heart, / Dancing and ordering drink, / Signing an 'Cruiscin Lán',/ The day we spent in Paul's house, / The morning of the white snow'

452 A monument celebrating Nelson's victory at Trafalgar was erected in Dublin in 1809 on Sackville Street (later renamed and now known as O'Connell Street). Nelson's Pillar remained in place, as did many statues and monuments associated with British rule in Ireland, after Irish independence. Behan, among many other republicans, regularly called for its demolition. It was blown up by Irish republicans in March 1966 and its remnants destroyed.

453 James Gill's pub on the corner of Russell Street and North Circular Road was likely known as Jimmy the Sports as it was the closest pub to Croke Park.

454 One of the bloodiest battles of the Second Boer War, in which a disastrous British attack on a Boer position on top of a mountain led to over three hundred British dead and hundreds more wounded or taken prisoner. Most of the dead were from Lancashire regiments, but the Dublin Fusiliers also took part in the battle.

455 Naval battle fought between British and German fleets in the North Sea in 1916.

456 Legendary battle of the First World War fought between July and November 1916, with the British and French on one side and the Germans on the other. It is reputed as the bloodiest battle in history as approximately one million men were killed or wounded. There were twenty-three Irish battalions at the Somme, including those of the 36th Ulster Division, the Royal Irish Rifles and the Royal Irish Fusiliers, and indeed the Dublin Fusiliers.

457 A narrow strait in Turkey, strategically important for shipping, which became a key site of contest during the First World War. British and other Allied troops were landed at Gallipoli in 1915 to try to control the straits, but were forced to withdraw after eight months of desperate fighting as a result of heavy casualties.

458 A roll-call of Irish high achievers in sports and other feats – Stanley Woods (motorcycling), Pat O'Callaghan (athletics), Colonel Fitzmaurice (transatlantic flight), R.N. Tisdall (athletics), John Joe Sheehy (Gaelic football), Larry Cervi (soccer) and Bertie Donnelly (cycling).

459 At the Catholic ceremony of Confirmation (around age twelve), children were expected to take a pledge of abstinence from alcohol.

460 'My sadness', or 'alas'.

461 Queen Victoria was descended from a European Royal dynasty that traced its origins to House of Welf (or Guelph) in the tenth century; she married Prince Albert of Saxe-Gotha, and their son, King Edward VII, continued

that dynasty on the British throne. Edward's son and successor George V changed the name of the family dynasty to Windsor to avoid the association with Germany, as Britain was at war with Germany during his reign.

462 Noted modern artist (1904–89) from Catalonia, associated with surrealism.

463 British politician (1897–1977) who was prime minister (1955–7) at the time Behan wrote this.

464 The Theatre Royal, Hawkins Street, Dublin, which opened in 1935 as a cinema.

465 Michael Joseph O'Rahilly (1875–1916), was known as 'The O'Rahilly', meaning that he was chief of the O'Rahilly clan (seemingly self-styled). A founding member of the Irish Volunteers, he was killed in the Easter Rising of 1916 by British machine-gun fire.

466 A ragtime song popularized by the vaudeville singer Bob Roberts in 1912.

The Power of Practice

How Music and Yoga Transformed the
Life and Work of Yehudi Menuhin

KRISTIN WENDLAND

Cover image: Photograph of Yehudi Menuhin, Tel Aviv, February 27, 1951. © Benno Rothenberg, Meitar Collection, National Library of Israel/the Pritzker Family National Photography Collection. CC BY 4.0.

Published by State University of New York Press, Albany

This book is freely available in an open access edition thanks to TOME (Toward an Open Monograph Ecosystem)—a collaboration of the Association of American Universities, the Association of University Presses, and the Association of Research Libraries—and the generous support of Emory University and the Andrew W. Mellon Foundation. Learn more at the TOME website, available at: openmonographs.org. A manifold version of this title can be accessed here: https://manifold.ecds.emory.edu/projects/the-power-of-practice.

Photos 4.1a–d: Photos of Iyengar and Menuhin in various yoga poses taken by Jacques Naegeli, Gstaad Palace Hotel, 1954. Foyle Menuhin Archive reprints, used by permission from Naegeli Studio, © Jacques Naegeli Gscaad; Photo 4.4: Menuhin demonstrating "fiddler's prayer" in Life Class, © Malcolm Crowthers/ ArenaPAL (digital use limited to 10 years).

© 2024 Kristin Wendland

All rights reserved

Printed in the United States of America

No part of this book may be used or reproduced in any manner whatsoever without written permission. No part of this book may be stored in a retrieval system or transmitted in any form or by any means including electronic, electrostatic, magnetic tape, mechanical, photocopying, recording, or otherwise without the prior permission in writing of the publisher.

For information, contact State University of New York Press, Albany, NY
www.sunypress.edu

Library of Congress Cataloging-in-Publication Data

Name: Wendland, Kristin, author
Title: The power of practice : how music and yoga transformed the life
  and work of Yehudi Menuhin
Description: Albany : State University of New York Press, [2024] | Includes
  bibliographical references and index.
Identifiers: ISBN 9781438496030 (hardcover : alk. paper) | ISBN 9781438496054
  (ebook)
Further information is available at the Library of Congress.

10 9 8 7 6 5 4 3 2 1